Advocating Social Change through International Law

Advocating Social Change through International Law

Exploring the Choice between Hard and Soft International Law

Edited by

Daniel D. Bradlow
David B. Hunter

BRILL
NIJHOFF

LEIDEN | BOSTON

Library of Congress Cataloging-in-Publication Data

Names: Bradlow, Daniel D., editor. | Hunter, David B., editor.
Title: Advocating social change through international law : exploring the choice between hard and soft international law / edited by Daniel D. Bradlow, University of Pretoria and American University Washington College of Law, and David B. Hunter, American University Washington College of Law.
Description: Leiden ; Boston : Brill, 2020 | Includes bibliographical references and index. | Summary: "The range, scope, scale, and speed of cross- border activity has significantly increased over the past half century.* Today in addition to the linkages created by international trade, foreign investment, international diplomacy, and state- to- state relations, the world is connected through deep and dynamic technological, social, cultural, and environmental interactions. The result is a profound shift towards more international connectedness through migration, trade in goods and services, social media, tourism, education exchanges, cybercrime, communicable diseases, invasive species and environmental pollution.1 Despite the drag caused by persistent and occasionally resurgent nationalism, the intensity and diversity of these interactions is likely to continue growing"– Provided by publisher.
Identifiers: LCCN 2019037998 (print) | LCCN 2019037999 (ebook) | ISBN 9789004382480 (hardback) | ISBN 9789004417021 (ebook)
Subjects: LCSH: International law–Social aspects. | Soft law.
Classification: LCC KZ1249 .A38 2020 (print) | LCC KZ1249 (ebook) | DDC 341–dc23
LC record available at https://lccn.loc.gov/2019037998
LC ebook record available at https://lccn.loc.gov/2019037999

Typeface for the Latin, Greek, and Cyrillic scripts: "Brill". See and download: brill.com/brill-typeface.

ISBN 978-90-04-38248-0 (hardback)
ISBN 978-90-04-41702-1 (e-book)

This book is printed on acid-free paper and produced in a sustainable manner.

Printed by Printforce, the Netherlands

Contents

Acknowledgements VII
List of Abbreviations VIII
Notes on Contributors XI

1 Introduction: Exploring the Relationship between Hard and Soft International Law and Social Change 1
Daniel D. Bradlow and David B. Hunter

2 The Softening of Hard Law and the Hardening of Soft Law: an Extended Synopsis 16
Upendra Baxi

3 Promoting Social Change through Treaties and Customary International Law: the Experience of the Inter-American Human Rights System 33
Claudio Grossman

4 Children's Rights: Social Change through the Application of Hard and Soft International Law 55
Ann Skelton

5 The International Criminal Court and the Use of Hard Law in the Quest for Accountability for Core International Crimes 84
Angela Mudukuti

6 The Hard Choices in Promoting Environmental Access Rights 110
Natalia Gomez Peña and David B. Hunter

7 The Hard Choice for Soft Commitments in the Climate Change Regime 138
David B. Hunter

8 A Turning Point in a Slow Revolution: the WHO Framework Convention on Tobacco Control 169
Patricia Anne Lambert

9 Soft International Law and the Promotion of Financial Regulation and Responsibility 200
Daniel D. Bradlow

10 Levers for and Obstacles to Social Change: Bank Lending, the Law and the Equator Principles 228
Sheldon Leader and Luis Felipe Yanes

11 Non-Judicial Grievance Mechanisms: Hardening the Soft Law of Corporate Accountability? 250
Nikki Reisch

12 Hard and Soft International Law and Their Contribution to Social Change: the Lessons Learned 282
Daniel D. Bradlow and David B. Hunter

Index 305

Acknowledgements

An edited book is by definition a collaborative project. It is therefore important for us to acknowledge all those who contributed to this book.

First, we wish to thank all the participants in the workshop at which many of the authors presented the first drafts of their contributions to this book. That workshop would not have been possible without the able administrative support of Thandeka Rasetsoke and the financial support of the South African National Research Foundation. At the workshop, the authors benefitted not only from the feedback of their co-authors but also from an enthusiastic group of doctoral students, including Oluwatosin Igabayiloye, Francky Lukanda, and Nthope Mapefane.

Second, the editors wish to thank a wonderful group of research assistants whom, although they were spread across three continents and did not know each other, managed to collaborate and to work efficiently and effectively to ensure that all the contributions to this book were fully prepared for final consultation. They include Nthope Mapefane in South Africa, Mallika Sen in India, and Elena Gartner, Dimitar Georgiev, Alycia Kokos, Kate Morrow, Jenna Ruddock, Carly Steren, and Francis Waliczek in the United States.

We also wish to thank all our authors both for their first class contributions to this book and for their patience and flexibility in working with us to bring this project to conclusion. We thank Dean Camille Nelson of the American University Washington College of law for the financial and atmospheric support she has provided for this project.

Finally, we note that this is our second collaboration on an edited book that seeks to stimulate debate and research about important and complex topics in international law. In this case, we hope that the book will encourage international legal academics and practitioners to think creatively about how they can use international legal instruments to shape an international legal order that contributes to building a more equitable and socially and environmentally responsible international community.

Abbreviations

ACERWC	African Charter on the Rights and Welfare of the Child
ADB	Asian Development Bank
AfDB	African Development Bank
ADR	Alternate dispute resolution
ASEAN	Association of South East Asian Nations
BAT	British American Tobacco
BCBS	Basel Committee on Banking Supervision
BIT	Bilateral investment treaty
BP	British Petroleum
CEJIL	Center for Justice and International Law
CESCR	Committee on Economic Social and Cultural Rights
CERD	Committee on the Elimination of Racial Discrimination
CEDAW	Committee on the Elimination of Discrimination Against Women
CED	Committee on Enforced Disappearances
CESCR	Committee on Economic, Social and Cultural Rights (UN)
CHRB	Corporate Human Rights Benchmark
CO_2	Carbon Dioxide
CoP, COP	Conference of the Parties
COPIHN	Consejo Cívico de Organizaciones Populares e Indígenas de Honduras
CRC	Convention on the Rights of the Child (UN)
CRPD	Committee on the Rights of Persons with Disabilities
CRIN	Child's Rights International Network
CSO	Civil society organizations
DESA	Desarrollos Energéticos S.A
DRC	Democratic Republic of Congo
ECHR	European Convention of Human Rights
ECtHR	European Court of Human Rights
ECLAC	Economic Commission for Latin America and the Caribbean (UN)
ECOSOC	Economic and Social Affairs Council (UN)
EPs	Equator Principles
EU	European Union
FAO	Food and Agriculture Organization
FATF	Financial Action Task Force
FCA	Framework Convention Alliance
FCTC	Framework Convention on Tobacco Control (WHO)
FPIC	Free, prior informed consent
FSAP	Financial sector assessments

FSB	Financial Stability Board
GATT	General Agreement on Tariffs and Trade (WTO)
GC	General Comment
GHG	Greenhouse Gas
GRI	Global Reporting Initiative
HRC	Human Rights Council
IAADFS	International Association of Airport Duty Free Stores
IACHR	Inter-American Commission on Human Rights
IAIS	International Association of Insurance Supervisors
IBRD	International Bank for Reconstruction and Development (World Bank)
ICJ	International Court of Justice (World Court)
ICC	International Criminal Court
ICSID	International Centre for Settlement of Investment Disputes
IDA	International Development Association
IDB	Inter-American Development Bank
IFC	International Finance Corporation
IFRS	International Financial Regulatory Standards
IGO	Intergovernmental Organization
ILC	International Law Commission
ILO	International Labour Organization (UN)
IMF	International Monetary Fund
INB	Intergovernmental Negotiating Body
IOSCO	International Organization of Securities Commissions
IPCC	Intergovernmental Panel on Climate Change
IPR	Intellectual Property Right
ISO	International Standardization Organization
ITGA	International Tobacco Growers' Association
LAC	Rio Declaration on Environment and Development
MACR	minimum age of criminal responsibility
MADENSA	Maderas y Derivados de Nicaragua S.A.
MNE	Multinational enterprises
NATT	Network for Accountability of Tobacco Transnationals
NCP	National Contact Points
NJGM	Non-judicial grievance mechanism
NGO	Nongovernmental Organization
OAS	Organization of American States
OAU	Organization of African Unity
OECD	Organization for Economic Cooperation and Development
OTP	Office of the Prosecutor
PF	Project finance

PMI	Phillip Morris International
QUNO	Quaker United Nations Organization
RCAP	Regulatory Consistency Assessment Program
ROSC	Reports on Standards and Codes
SOLCARSA	Sol del Caribe, SA
SSB	standard setting body
TAI	The Access Initiative
TFI	Tobacco-Free Initiative
TFV	Trust Fund for Victims
TIRC	Tobacco Industry Research Committee
TRIPS	Trade-Related Intellectual Property Rights (WTO Agreement)
UK	United Kingdom
UN	United Nations
UNCAT	United Nations Committee Against Torture
UNCED	United Nations Conference on Environment and Development
UNCRC	United Nations Committee on the Rights of the Child
UNCROC	United Nations Convention on the Rights of the Child
UNCTAD	United Nations Conference on Trade and Development
UNDESA	United Nations Department of Economic and Social Affairs
UNEP	United Nations Environment Programme
UNESCO	United Nations Educational, Scientific and Cultural Organization
UNECE	United Nations Economic Commission for Europe
UNFCCC	United Nations Framework Convention on Climate Change
UNGP	United Nations Guiding Principles on Business and Human Rights
UNICEF	United Nations International Children's Emergency Fund
UNSC	United Nations Security Council
US, USA	United States of America
WCL	Washington College of Law
WCTOH	World Conference on Tobacco or Health
WHA	World Health Assembly
WHO	World Health Organization
WRI	World Resources Institute
VCLT	Vienna Convention on the Law of Treaties

Notes on Contributors

Editors

Daniel D. Bradlow
is SARCHI Professor of International Development Law and African Economic Relations at the University of Pretoria and Professor Emeritus, American University Washington College of Law. He was previously the first Head of the International Economic Relations and Policy Department at the South African Reserve Bank, and Director of the International Legal Studies Program at American University Washington College of Law in Washington, D.C. He has also served as the Chair of the Roster of Experts for the Independent Review Mechanism at the African Development Bank; a member of the African Commission on Human and People's Rights Working Group on Extractive Industries, the Environment and Human Rights; a member the International Law Association's Committee on Accountability of International Organizations; an Advisor to the Global Initiative on Fiscal Transparency; and a Senior Special Fellow in the Legal Aspects of Debt and Financial Management Programme of the United National Institute on Training and Research (UNITAR).

David B. Hunter
is Professor of Law at the American University Washington College of Law, where he researches and teaches international environmental and human rights law. Prof. Hunter was formerly Executive Director of the Center for International Environmental Law, Executive Director of WaterWatch of Oregon, an associate at the law firm of Skadden, Arps, Slate, Meagher & Flom, and Director of the International Legal Studies Program at American University Washington College of Law. He has consulted on the development of environmental and social standards and associated accountability mechanisms at several international organizations, including the United Nations Development Programme, United Nations Environment Programme, the Adaptation Fund, the Asian Development Bank, and the Overseas Private Investment Corporation. He is a Member Scholar of the Center for Progressive Reform, member of the OAS Expert Group on Environmental Law, and member of the International Finance Corporation's Compliance Advisor/Ombudsman's Strategic Advisors Group.

Contributing Authors

Upendra Baxi

is a Professor of Law at University of Warwick. He served as a Professor of Law at University of Delhi (1973–1996) and as its Vice Chancellor (1990–1994.) He also served as Vice Chancellor of University of South Gujarat, Surat (1982–1985) and Honorary Director (Research) of the Indian Law Institute (1985–1988). He was the President of the Indian Society of International Law (1992–1995). Professor Baxi has taught various courses in law and science, comparative constitutionalism and social theory of human rights at University of Sydney, Duke University, American University, the New York University Law School Global Law Program, and the University of Toronto.

Claudio Grossman

is Professor of Law, Dean Emeritus, and the Raymond Geraldson Scholar for International and Humanitarian Law at American University Washington College of Law (WCL). Professor Grossman served as WCL dean from 1995-July 2016. He was appointed Dean Emeritus by American University's (AU) Board of Trustees. Professor Grossman was elected to the United Nations International Law Commission in November 2016 for a five-year term, and previously served as member (2003–2015) and chairperson (4 terms, from 2008–2015) of the United Nations Committee against Torture and as chair of the UN Human Rights Treaty Bodies.

Patricia Anne Lambert

is the Director of the International Legal Consortium at The Campaign for Tobacco Free Kids, a Board member of Action on Smoking for Health, and a former president of International Women for Health. She was previously the Legal Advisor, Minister of Health, Government of South Africa in which capacity she represented South Africa in the negotiations of the Tobacco Treaty.

Sheldon Leader

is the Director of the Essex Business and Human Rights Project (EBHR) and a longstanding member of the Human Rights Centre at University of Essex. He is a member of the Advisory Committee to the Human Rights Committee of the Law Society of England and Wales. He teaches and lectures at the University of Essex, the University of Paris-Ouest and at a number of universities in the United States.

Angela Mudukuti
is a Zimbabwean lawyer currently with the Wayamo Foundation. She was previously with the International Criminal Court, the Southern Africa Litigation Centre, and Cherif Bassiouni at the Siracusa International Institute for Criminal Justice and Human Rights.

Natalia Gomez Peña
is the elected civil society representative in the negotiations of the regional agreement on access to information, participation and justice in environmental matters in Latin America and the Caribbean. Ms. Gomez was previously the Environmental Democracy Program Coordinator at Ambiente y Sociedad in Bogota, Colombia.

Nikki Reisch
is the Legal Director of the Center for Human Rights and Global Justice. Her work focuses on social and economic rights, with an emphasis on corporate accountability, economic inequality, and environmental justice. Prior to studying law, Nikki worked as an advocate with non-governmental organizations monitoring the effects of international financial and development institutions on communities in the Global South. She spent years conducting research and advocacy related to the human rights impacts of extractive industry and large-scale infrastructure projects, trade liberalization, and climate change, primarily in sub-Saharan Africa.

Ann Skelton
is a Professor at the University of Pretoria, and a member of the UN Committee on the Rights of the Child. She also holds the UNESCO Chair in Education Law in Africa.

Luis Felipe Yanes
is a Ph.D. Candidate, Human Rights Centre, School of Law, University of Essex; Core Member of the Essex Business and Human Rights Project; and formerly a Human Rights Specialist at the Inter-American Commission on Human Rights.

CHAPTER 1

Introduction: Exploring the Relationship between Hard and Soft International Law and Social Change

Daniel D. Bradlow and David B. Hunter***

1 Introduction

The range, scope, scale, and speed of cross-border activity has significantly increased over the past half century. Today in addition to the linkages created by international trade, foreign investment, international diplomacy, and state-to-state relations, the world is connected through deep and dynamic technological, social, cultural, and environmental interactions. The result is a profound shift towards more international connectedness through migration, trade in goods and services, social media, tourism, education exchanges, cyber-crime, communicable diseases, invasive species and environmental pollution.[1] Despite the drag caused by persistent and occasionally resurgent nationalism, the intensity and diversity of these interactions is likely to continue growing.

The speed and scale of these transnational activities risks overwhelming the capacity of every state, acting on its own, to manage the risks and rewards offered by these connections.[2] One challenge is that different aspects of these transactions often take place in different countries, placing at least some of their impacts beyond the reach of any one country's jurisdiction. For example, the producer of the defective part of the product that caused harm to a consumer in country A may be a sub-contractor that is incorporated in country B and is not subject to the jurisdiction of country A. Another challenge is that some of the impacts of an activity may be felt in a state other than the one

* SARCHI Professor of International Development Law and African Economic Relations at the University of Pretoria and Professor Emeritus, American University Washington College of Law.

** Professor of Law and Director of the Program on International and Comparative Environmental Law at the American University's Washington College of Law.

1 *See* RICHARD BALDWIN, THE GREAT CONVERGENCE: INFORMATION TECHNOLOGY AND THE NEW GLOBALIZATION (2016).

2 *See* DANI RODRIK, THE GLOBALIZATION PARADOX: DEMOCRACY AND THE FUTURE OF THE WORLD ECONOMY (2011).

DOI:10.1163/9789004417021_002

where the activity took place, making it hard for any one state to effectively regulate the activity and manage its impacts. For example, the operations of a farmer in country A may generate air pollution that has adverse effects on communities located in country B. A third challenge is that the intended targets of national regulation can relocate as much of their operations as necessary to another jurisdiction to avoid having to comply with the regulation. For example, individuals or corporations in country A, hearing a rumor that the government will raise taxes, can move their assets or relocate their income to country B before the government can pass the tax legislation.

One consequence of these developments is that an increasing number of non-state actors are actively engaged in transnational activities.[3] Consequently, international organizations, sub-national governments, communities, NGOs, corporations, and individuals all now have a direct and substantial interest in at least some cross-border discussions about norms and standards that apply to particular cross-border activities and some aspects of their countries' international relations.[4] In fact, in some cases, some of these non-state actors have taken the lead in developing international norms and standards applicable to the interactions that most interest them. These standards, even in the absence of active state participation, can become the *de facto* regulatory standard for the particular activity or sector. In other cases, non-state actors can push their states to lead or participate in the negotiating, drafting, agreeing, and ratifying of treaties or other international legal instruments. Working in conjunction with their own state or other interested states, these non-state actors may be able to use their expertise, resources, or connections to influence the negotiating and drafting process. Their participation may enhance the legitimacy of the resulting treaty or international legal instrument that could directly, and possibly adversely, impact many different stakeholders.[5] On the other hand, their exclusion from the international discussions can undermine the legitimacy or efficacy of the resulting international instruments. In short, globalization has deprived states of their exclusive control over their countries' international

3 *See generally* Cedric Ryngaert, *Non-State Actors: Carving out a Space in a State-Centered International Legal System,* 63 NETH. INT'L L. REV. 183 (2016).

4 *See* DAVID ARMSTRONG ET AL., CIVIL SOCIETY AND INTERNATIONAL GOVERNANCE: THE ROLE OF NON-STATE ACTORS IN THE EU, AFRICA, ASIA, AND THE MIDDLE EAST (2010); RICHARD A. HIGGOTT ET AL., NON-STATE ACTORS AND AUTHORITY IN THE GLOBAL SYSTEM (2000); Muhittin Ataman, *The Impact of Non-State Actors on World Politics: A Challenge to Nation-States,* 2:1 TURKISH JOURNAL OF INT'L RELATIONS 42 (2003).

5 *See, e.g.,* Patricia Anne Lambert, *infra* ch. 8 in this volume; Sheldon Leader & Luis Yanes, *infra* ch. 10 *see also* BALAKRISHNAN RAJAGOPAL, INTERNATIONAL LAW FROM BELOW: DEVELOPMENT, SOCIAL MOVEMENTS AND THIRD WORLD RESISTANCE (2009).

political and economic relations and over the transnational dialogue about the governance of global and transboundary activities.

In this context, both non-state and state actors understand that, sometimes working together and sometimes apart, they can use international forums and a variety of international instruments to drive social change. For example, some corporations and industry associations advocate for international standards to support a globalized market for their products or goods.[6] Transnational networks of national regulatory authorities collaborate to develop international standards for dealing with common problems that they cannot effectively regulate at a domestic level.[7] These standards harmonize their approach, fill gaps, or overcome perceived weaknesses in national regulatory frameworks. Similarly, advocacy groups may participate in international forums to promote their view of the appropriate standard applicable to, for example, public health, environmental protection, or the rights of workers, children, or people with disabilities.[8] These efforts can catalyze governments to adopt higher international standards, whether or not expressed in treaties; strengthen domestic regulations; identify minimum safeguards as a floor for activities; or take actions to demonstrate proof of concept for higher standards.

This reality challenges both state and non-state actors and their legal advisors to think strategically about how they can use international forums, their relations with other international actors including states, and either hard or soft international law most effectively to advance their interests or normative priorities, which may include reaching agreement to preserve the status quo. The purpose of this book is to help these actors and their legal advisers assess how they can use hard and soft international law to identify and pursue their priorities on the international stage.

Non-state actors have two advantages over states in this regard. First, they can afford to be both less flexible than states in any international negotiations relating to the issues that concern them and more pragmatic about the legal nature of the instruments that are the outcomes of these negotiations. In general, non-state actors are concerned about a narrower range of issues than states. This allows them to be more focused than states when they participate in international fora. States have to balance political relationships with many

---

6 *See, e.g.*, International Organization for Standardization (ISO), https://www.iso.org/standards.html.(last visited June 13, 2019).

7 *See generally* ANNE-MARIE SLAUGHTER, *A NEW WORLD ORDER*, (2005) and ch. 9 (by Daniel Bradlow).

8 *See, e.g.*, Claudio Grossman, *infra* ch. 3 in this volume; Ann Skelton, *infra* ch. 4 in this volume; Natalia Gomez Peña & David Hunter, *infra* ch. 6 in this volume.

different actors and across many different issues and fora, whereas non-state actors can concentrate on achieving their specific objectives in connection with their particular areas of concern.[9]

Second, non-state actors are relatively less concerned with whether or not they have succeeded in establishing a particular form of international standard or agreement than with changing the behavior of their state or non-state target. They are typically not concerned with whether their targets changed their conduct because of a perceived legal obligation or because of some other factor, like reputational risk, or changes in market dynamics.

The result is that non-state actors are more concerned with international law "in action" than with international law "on the books." In other words, the form of an international instrument—whether it is legally binding and enforceable or merely a voluntary and therefor avoidable promise—is only relevant to the extent it affects the instrument's impact on the target's behavior. The pragmatic approach of the non-state actors means that they are unlikely to be concerned with how their standards affect or reflect the development of international law.

Taken together, these developments present a challenge to the traditional formulations of the content of international law. Historically, international law has been state-centric so that, except for a small number of foundational principles, no state could be bound without its consent.[10] This view is embodied in Article 38 of the Statute of the International Court of Justice[11] which defines the primary sources of international law as being international treaties, customary international law principles, and general principles of law.[12] These instruments and principles create "hard international law" that consists of binding obligations for States.[13] In most cases, such instruments and standards do not impose obligations directly on non-state actors.[14] Instead, they require

---

9 *See e.g.*, Thomas Hale, *The Role of Sub-State and Non-State Actors in International Climate Processes* 4–5, CHATHAM HOUSE (2018).

10 ANDREW CLAPHAM, BRIERLY'S LAW OF NATIONS 47–53 (7th ed. 2012).

11 Statute of the International Court of Justice art. 38, Apr. 18, 1946, 33 U.N.T.S. 993.

12 *See id.* at art. 38(1)(a)—(c). Pursuant to Article 38(1)(d), these sources of "hard law" can be interpreted using case law and the writings of international law experts.

13 *See, e.g.*, Gregory C. Shaffer & Mark A. Pollack, *Hard vs. Soft Law: Alternatives, Complements, and Antagonists in International Governance*, 94 MINN. L. REV. 706, 712–17 (2010).

14 It should be noted that international organizations are the one group of non-state actors who would be bound by customary international law principles and could be signatories to treaties. Other non-state actors would only be obliged to comply with the terms of a treaty if the treaty was incorporated into the domestic law of the states to whose jurisdiction they are subject.

that states take actions to ensure that those non-state actors subject to their jurisdiction comply with the applicable international instruments and standards.[15] In principle, these obligations are enforceable against non-compliant states who are parties to the applicable treaties or are subject to the customary international law principles. They can be held internationally responsible if they fail to meet these international legal obligations.

By contrast, "soft international law" consists of those norms, standards, and instruments, which because they fail to qualify as one of the primary sources of international law set out in Article 38 are non-binding, but nonetheless exert some compliance pull on their relevant targets. Because only states can make hard international law, any norm, standard, or instrument made solely by non-state actors is necessarily soft, but so too are those made by states that do not comply with the applicable treaty-making requirements, which are set out in the Vienna Convention on the Law of Treaties.[16]

The exact legal status of soft international law is unclear. The claim that all international instruments and standards that do not come in the form of a treaty or custom are non-binding and unenforceable and so are not "international law" as envisaged by the drafters of Article 38 may be technically correct. However, it ignores the fact that sometimes these soft international law standards exert sufficient compliance pull to change the relevant conduct of their targeted actors.

If, as Phillip Allott contends, the essence of law is that it constrains unwanted behavior, then some soft law regimes are more "legal" than some hard international law regimes.[17] These soft international law instruments can also exhibit many of the characteristics of Abbott and Snidal's three components of legality: namely precision, obligation, and delegation.[18] Many of them are drafted with great precision and clearly stated requirements. Some are structured so that third parties can help *de facto* to enforce compliance with the standard. In this sense, they may have a greater compliance pull, and thus be more "legal," than hard international law instruments that are drafted in ambiguous language and without any identified mechanism for enforcement.

15 *See, e.g.*, General Comment 24 at ¶¶ 14–22, 30–35. *But see* Claire Methven O'Brien, *The Home State Duty to Regulate the Human Rights Impact of TNCs Abroad: A Rebuttal*, 3 BUS. & HUMAN RIGHTS J. 47 (2018).

16 Vienna Convention on Law of Treaties, May 23, 1969, 1155 U.N.T.S 331.

17 *See* PHILIP ALLOTT, EUNOMIA: NEW ORDER FOR A NEW WORLD (1991).

18 *See* Kenneth W. Abbott & Duncan Snidal, *Hard and Soft Law in International Governance*, 3 INT'L ORG. 421 (2000).

As indicated, both state and non-state actors in any international negotiations may have the choice whether to seek a hard or a soft international law instrument. Hard international law has a certain allure because it is formally binding and presumably enforceable. But the reality is more nuanced. For our purposes for an instrument that qualifies as a source of international law under Article 38, to be considered as truly hard international law—that is binding and enforceable—it must meet at least three criteria: (1) it must be in a form, such as a treaty, that is recognized as binding; (2) it must be drafted in mandatory language and with sufficient precision that the obligations are clear; and (3) it must provide a mechanism or procedures for enforcement and for sanctioning a non-compliant party. Without these latter two elements, even an instrument that is in the form of "hard" international law becomes *de facto* "softer." Similarly, international instruments that do not meet the formal requirements of hard international law under Article 38 may be "hardened" through the way in which they are drafted, how they are incorporated into, *inter alia*, national laws or private contracts, or through having some *de facto* enforcement mechanism.

Strict adherence to the formal Article 38 requirements for hard international law may understate the practical value and utility of soft international law instruments. Such instruments even when drafted in precatory or ambiguous language may exert effective compliance pull on the conduct of its signatories. In fact, depending on the instrument and the context, such treaties may be more influential in changing conduct than treaties drafted with more precise and enforceable language, but requiring lower levels of commitment from signatory states.[19]

Experience suggests that both states and non-state actors take a pragmatic approach to the choice of seeking a hard or soft international law instrument to promote social change. When they think it is useful and feasible to develop a hard international law instrument, state and/or non-state actors may choose to promote a treaty that mandates the desired changes in behavior.[20] Under this approach, a critical mass of states must be persuaded to support the proposed binding international legal instrument. These states will need to comply with all applicable treaty-making formalities and the diplomatic constraints that necessarily accompany the negotiating, drafting, and ratifying of international treaties.[21] In exchange for choosing the slower and more costly hard

19 DINAH L. SHELTON, COMMITMENT AND COMPLIANCE: THE ROLE OF NON-BINDING NORMS IN INTERNATIONAL LEGAL SYSTEM 10–13 (2000).

20 *See, e.g.*, Gomez & Hunter, *infra* ch. 6 in this volume; Angela Mudukuti, *infra* ch. 5 in this volume.

21 *See* UNITED NATIONS LEGISLATIVE SERIES, REVIEW OF THE MULTILATERAL TREATY-MAKING PROCESS 23–39, U.N. Doc. ST/LEG/SER.B/21 (1985).

international law approach, the negotiators are rewarded with an instrument that imposes binding obligations on its parties and may offer a robust enforcement mechanism, at least with respect to the behavior of states.[22]

On the other hand, both states and non-state actors may decide to forego a "hard" international law approach in favor of developing a non-binding "soft" international instrument, particularly if the price for making an instrument binding is viewed as too high. This "price" may be reflected in fewer states being willing to join the instrument or in a weakening of the substantive norms. How advocates strike the balance will depend on the context. For example, in some cases the most important regulatory target may not be states. Consequently, approaches other than formal treaties may be more effective if they are more directly applicable against these non-state targets.[23] Even where regulating states is the goal, soft law approaches may be tactically more feasible and quicker to complete. Non-state actors may also be able to participate more in negotiating and drafting a soft law instrument and may also play a greater role in its implementation. This can add to the instrument's legitimacy and enhance its compliance pull among a larger group of stakeholders. A soft law instrument may also be more flexible in adapting to changing circumstances or lessons learned. In addition, in some, but not all, cases, the soft law instrument may be viewed as a short-term compromise on the way toward a binding instrument.[24]

This book is intended to expand our understanding of the interplay between hard and soft international law by exploring how both state and non-state actors use hard and soft international law to promote social change. The book relies on case studies to explore the variety of factors that can influence the choice that advocates for social change make betweena hard or soft international law approaches, the perceived costs and benefits associated with both hard and soft international law, and the interplay over time between hard and soft international law in furthering a particular goal. The case studies explore these issues in light of the social change goals that drive the development or application of the norms.

The social change lens provides at least two advantages in exploring the distinction between hard and soft international law. First, non-state actors that

---

22 *See, e.g.*, Gregory C. Shaffer & Mark A. Pollack, *Hard Versus Soft Law in International Security*, 52 B.C. L. REV. 1147 (2011).

23 *See* Kevin Jackson, *Global Corporate Governance: Soft Law and Reputational Accountability*, 35 BROOK. J. INT'L L. 41 (2010).

24 *See, e.g.*, Hunter, *infra* ch. 7 in this volume; Sheldon Leader & Luis Felipe Yanes, *infra* ch. 10 in this volume; Bradlow, *infra* ch. 9 in this volume; Reisch, *infra* ch. 11 in this volume.

are driven by social change goals are not bound by the constraints of either the practical demands of international relations or the formalities of diplomatic relations. Unlike states, they have no interest in accepting a possible trade-off of their objective in negotiation A for an entirely unrelated substantive outcome in negotiation B. Moreover, these social change advocates view international law primarily as a tool to achieve their desired social change—and not as an end in itself. Consequently, they are more focused on the efficacy of a particular international norm, standard, or instrument rather than on its form or its status under international law. To further their objective, they will promote any instrument that they think can actually produce the desired change in their regulatory target, regardless of its legal form. The social change lens can thus help us understand the relative perceived effectiveness of soft and hard international law instruments in different contexts.

The second advantage is that, because the book is built around case studies of social change, it provides a consistent frame for tracking the evolution of the hard/soft international law relationship over time within one particular regime or issue area. In this way, we can potentially evaluate the effectiveness of using hard or soft international law for different strategies at different stages in pursuit of the same social change goal.

This approach, and the case studies presented in this book, allow us to explore a number of questions about the relationship between hard and soft international law. They are:

Is the choice between hard and soft international law binary? Public international lawyers tend to portray the choice between hard and soft law as a binary one.[25] This means that any instrument that qualifies as a treaty, international custom, or general principle under Article 38 of the ICJ Statute, is hard international law with the clear implication that it is binding, obligatory, and enforceable. On the other hand, any instrument that does not satisfy the requirements of a primary source of international law under Article 38, at most, is soft international law and is by implication non-binding, discretionary, and unenforceable. But from a practical results-oriented perspective, it may be more accurate and more strategic to think of the differences between hard and soft international law as points on a continuum.[26] This means, for example, that there can be formally hard international instruments that are not enforceable

25 *See, e.g.*, SHELTON, *supra* note 19; Andrew T. Guzman & Timothy L. Meyer, *International Soft Law*, 2 J. OF L. ANALYSIS 171, 174 (2010); Jan Klabbers, *The Redundancy of Soft Law*, 65 NORDIC J. INT'L L. 167, 168 (1996).

26 Gregory C. Shaffer & Mark A. Pollack, *Hard v. Soft Law: Alternatives, Complements, and Antagonists in International Governance*, 94 MINN. L. REV. 706, 715 (2010).

and soft international law instruments that are effectively enforceable, albeit not against states in the International Court of Justice. Where on the hard/soft continuum an instrument falls may depend on a variety of factors, including: the formal nature of the instrument; the language used in the text; the existence and accessibility of a formal or *de facto* enforcement mechanism; the existence of sanctions on non-compliant parties; the existence of a remedy for parties harmed by the actions of the non-compliant party; the willingness of state and non-state actors to promote compliance; the public's interest in, and awareness of, the issue; and market responses to non-compliance.[27]

What factors influence an actor's choice to seek either a hard or soft international law instrument? Actors can take several possible approaches in making this choice. One possibility is that the primary factor influencing the actors is their assessment of the most feasible way to achieving their objective. This would suggest that the advocates' first choice would always be to seek a hard international law instrument. However, if this does not seem an achievable objective or if the trade-off in participation or substance is too great, they may settle for soft international law alternatives as a second-best option. Alternatively, their choice could depend on an assessment of a wider variety of factors that can influence the prospects for achieving their desired social change.[28] In this case, it is conceivable that, after assessing all the relevant factors, both state and non-state actors might decide that their optimal outcome is a non-binding international norm or standard. The factors that might influence their choice would include the identity and nature of the targeted community, the ability of each state to deal effectively with the issue in its domestic law, the intensity of the controversy surrounding the issue, the technical nature of the issue, and the merits of including a wider range of non-state stakeholders in the development of the instrument.

Is there a linear progression from soft to hard international law, and what factors affect this progression? Soft and hard international law are often described as having a linear relationship in which soft international law instruments are primarily stepping stones to hard international law instruments.[29] In this view, the experience gained through the implementation and interpretation of soft international law instruments will lead to them being replaced by a hard international law instrument. This certainly describes the evolution of many regimes. But this linear progression does not always describe the complex interaction between hard and soft international law. In some cases, hard

27 *See* Daniel Bradlow, *infra* ch. 9 in this volume; Gomez & Hunter, *infra* ch. 6 in this volume.
28 *Id.*
29 Shaffer & Pollack, *supra* note 26, at 721.

and soft international law appear to interact dynamically with each playing different roles at different times during the process of creating, interpreting, applying, and enforcing a particular legal regime. For example, soft international law may influence the drafting of a treaty and then may subsequently be used to expand or contract its scope through interpretation.[30] This can be done, for example, through the use of soft international law instruments like general comments and declarations by supervisory bodies and treaty bodies, as well as reports by special rapporteurs. Alternatively, soft international law instruments can be hardened through being incorporated by national regulatory authorities into domestic regulatory regimes, or used by international and domestic courts and tribunals in their judgments and decisions, and included by corporations in their loan conditions or supply chain contracts.[31]

Are soft international law procedures more transparent and participatory than hard international law ones? One view is that soft international law processes are more transparent and accessible to multiple stakeholders than hard international law processes.[32] Greater transparency and broader participation arguably result in legal instruments and principles that are more democratic and legitimate, in the sense of being more representative of broader stakeholder concerns. But the relative transparency and accessibility of hard and soft international law-making processes to all stakeholders could be context-specific.

Hard international lawmaking, because it is based on respect for sovereignty and consensus decision making, is adopted through procedures whose formalities are designed to ensure that all states are able to participate and have input in the lawmaking process. On the other hand, the informality of soft international lawmaking processes may make them more vulnerable to manipulation by those state and non-state actors with power, influence, technical expertise, or resources than hard international lawmaking procedures.[33] In addition, the informality of soft international law making processes can lead to decentralization, in the sense that different groups of interested actors can develop competing instruments in a particular issue area. This in turn could increase the risk that the entities at whom these instruments are aimed can pick and choose the standards with which they want to comply and ignore approaches that they dislike with relative impunity.[34]

---

30 *See, e.g.,* Grossman, *infra* ch. 3 in this volume; Hunter, *infra* ch. 7 in this volume.

31 *See, e.g.,* Harold Hongju Koh, *Transnational Legal Process,* 75 NEB. L. REV. 181 (1996).

32 Shaffer & Pollack, *supra* note 26, at 719.

33 *See, e.g.,* Hunter, *infra* ch. 7 in this volume; Bradlow, *infra* ch. 9 in this volume.

34 *See, e.g.,* Leader & Yanes, *infra* ch. 10 in this volume; Nikki Reisch, *infra* ch. 11 in this volume.

Under what circumstances are hard international instruments more effective in achieving social change goals than soft international law instruments? The conventional wisdom is that, all things being equal, hard international law instruments are more effective at changing behavior than soft international law ones because signatory states are legally bound to comply with them and they can be enforced against non-compliant states. However, even hard international law instruments drafted in clear mandatory language may fail to change the conduct of their signatories. The actual impact of the instrument on state behavior appears to depend, at least in part, on the context in which it must operate. For example, hard international law may be effective in changing the conduct of states when the instrument establishes a clear legal standard and the other parties to the instrument are willing to use the available forums and mechanisms to enforce the standard. However, hard international law instruments may be less effective, regardless of how they are drafted, if the signatories lack the will to enforce the standard. In the latter case, soft international law instruments that rely on *de facto* means of incentivizing compliance, such as market forces, public pressure, or naming and shaming, may be more likely to produce the desired outcome.

How does the existence of a de jure *or* de facto *enforcement mechanism change the strategic choice between a hard and soft international law instrument?* An important factor in assessing the effectiveness of both hard and soft international law instruments is the existence of an accessible and definitive mechanism or process through which stakeholders can seek to hold the targets of the international instrument accountable for their failure to comply with the applicable standards. The robustness and efficacy of these "enforcement" mechanisms is likely to depend on such factors as the legal nature of the mechanism and of the applicable instrument, the accessibility of the mechanism to any interested stakeholder seeking to raise a claim against a non-compliant party, the extent to which the mechanism's decision-maker treats the instrument as applicable to and determinative of the claim, and the readiness of the losing party to accept the mechanism's decision and both abide by it and change its behavior accordingly.

As suggested above, the availability of an "enforcement" mechanism may also be too narrow a question for evaluating the relative effectiveness of an instrument in achieving the desired social change goal. There are many ways to incentivize compliance other than the threat of sanctions through enforcement.

Should less emphasis be placed on Article 38's definition of the primary sources of hard international law? The current era is characterized by a growing diversity of actors with influence in the formulation, adoption, and implementation of international standards and instruments, and with the ability to both create and utilize "enforcement" mechanisms in the international arena. To be sure, the primary sources of international law stipulated in Article 38 remain relevant to formal state-to-state relations and will continue to occupy a preeminent place in international law in this regard. But its focus on the role of states in international law-making perpetuates a formalistic view of the hard/soft international law distinction that may be outdated. When the actual intended target of regulation is a corporation or another non-state actor, the concept of international law may benefit from a more functional than formal approach. Such a functional definition would put greater focus on the clarity of the standards, the use of mandatory language, and the availability of enforcement mechanisms. It would also broaden the binding applicability of norms to states in cases where states have incorporated mandatory language into declarations that are neither a treaty nor reflective of custom.[35]

II Overview of the Book

Both state and non-state actors are willing to use hard and soft international law to achieve their objectives. This makes it useful to develop a better understanding of how they use both categories of instruments and what factors influence their choices. The ensuing chapters in this book explore these issues. Collectively, they provide useful information regarding the role of hard and soft international law in promoting social change. They also suggest that, at least in some cases, the traditional definition of the sources of international law is not adequate. It does not capture the fact that some formally non-binding international instruments are, because of either the way in which they are drafted or because of their impact on the state and non-state actors to whom they apply, at least as effective as formally binding international law in constraining conduct and producing change.

The book consists of ten chapters in addition to the introductory and concluding chapters. The first chapter discusses some theoretical issues raised by the distinction between hard and soft law. The remaining nine chapters present case studies, three of which relate to human rights and humanitarian law, three to the environment and public health, two to the financial sector, and one to enforcement mechanisms. The chapters are described below.

In chapter 2, Upendra Baxi offers an overview of the historical roots of the distinction between hard and soft international law. He describes two types of

35 *See* Daniel Bodansky, *Customary (And Not So Customary) International Environmental Law*, 3 IND. J. OF GLOBAL LEGAL STUDIES 105 (1995).

soft international law. The first type was formulated during the post war era of decolonization, self-determination, and super-power Cold War rivalry. Its function was to create new international values for a world recovering from the horrors of the Second World War and having to deal with the Cold War. The second type seeks to address the challenges arising from globalization and the advent of the Anthropocene.[36] Baxi argues that the benefit of soft international law is precisely that it lacks at least some aspects of the three characteristics of hard law identified in the mainstream literature, namely obligation (binding form), precision (clear mandatory norms), and delegation (an enforcement mechanism). As a result, it facilitates international legal and social experimentation and a counter-reaction to hegemonic power. He further proposes that, because the Anthropocene is posing new challenges that lie beyond the capability of individual states, our focus should be on the capacity of international legal instruments to respond effectively to the challenges that the international community faces rather than on the legal nature of the instruments. In this sense, the key concern is the potential for soft international law to become more easily enforceable and for hard international law to become more flexible and resilient.

In chapter 3, Claudio Grossman explores how legal advocates used impact litigation in the Inter-American human rights system to challenge extra-judicial killings, promote the rights of indigenous communities, block amnesty laws, and promote freedom of expression. Grossman argues that despite the hard international law character of the regional human rights system, it has relied on non-state actors—civil society and advocates—both to enforce international law and to ensure that states actually comply with the judgments against them. This chapter, among other things, shows how a hard regional legal regime is actively enforced can influence legal developments at the national, regional, and global level.

The fourth chapter is by Ann Skelton and focuses on three cases in which soft international law instruments have been used to help enforce both global and regional treaties dealing with the rights of children. The cases deal with the treatment of children of imprisoned parents, the minimum age of criminal

36 Generally, the "Anthropocene" refers to the time of human development in which humans' activity has become an "Earth-shaping force" having a "lasting change in the Earth system." Jorge E. Vinuales, *Law and Anthropocene,* C-EENRG WORKING PAPER (2016), available at https://papers.ssrn.com/sol3/papers.cfm?abstract_id=2842546; *see generally* Paul J. Crutzen, *Geology of Mankind,* 415 NATURE 23 (2002); *see also* CLIVE HAMILTON, ED., THE ANTHROPOCENE AND THE GLOBAL ENVIRONMENTAL CRISIS: RETHINKING MODERNITY IN A NEW EPOCH (2015).

responsibility, and the application of the death penalty and the sentence of life imprisonment without parole to children. In these cases, the advocates used soft international law instruments like the General Comments on the UN Convention on the Rights of the Child to build their cases. Skelton also notes that these examples highlight the risks of informal processes leading to the exclusion of some voices from the development of the law.

In chapter 5, Angela Mudukuti discusses the creation of the International Criminal Court.[37] Mudukuti discusses why both state and non-state actors viewed an international treaty as necessary to create the Court. Mudukuti also explains, through a discussion of the Court's case law, the challenges to states' continued commitment to the Court and participation in it that can arise in the course of implementing a hard international law instrument.

Chapter 6, by Natalia Gomez and David Hunter, analyzes the evolution of three environmental governance norms known collectively as environmental access rights: (1) the right to access environmental information; (2) the right to participate in environmental decisions that affect your life and livelihood; and (3) the right of access to justice in environmental disputes. The chapter describes how these norms have evolved from their debut in a global soft international law instrument to being the subject of two binding regional treaties, and explores the choices that proponents made along the way. .

In the seventh chapter, David Hunter discusses how negotiators of commitments to mitigate (i.e. reduce) greenhouse gases under the global climate regime have struggled with whether these so-called mitigation commitments must be binding. Although in theory all stakeholders favored binding mitigation commitments, such bindingness would likely come at the cost of lower participation (e.g., whether the United States or China would remain) and the substantive strength of the commitments. The recent adoption of nationally-determined (voluntary) commitments in the binding 2015 Paris Agreement[38] resolved the hard/soft trade-offs with an interesting hybrid of interlocking soft substantive mitigation commitments nestled in a hard law regime of reporting and verification.

Patricia Lambert in chapter 8 discusses the planning, drafting, and negotiating of the Framework Convention on Tobacco Control[39] and the role that

37 The International Criminal Court was created by the Rome Statute, which entered into force in 2002. *See* Rome Statute of the International Criminal Court, Jul. 17, 1998, 2187 U.N.T.S. 3.

38 Paris Agreement to the United Nations Framework Convention on Climate Change, Dec. 12, 2015, T.I.A.S. No. 16–1104.

39 World Health Organization Framework Convention on Tobacco Control, May 21, 2003, 2302 U.N.T.S 166.

states and non-state actors played in these processes. She also discusses how both science and soft international law instruments were used both to build the case for a treaty and to interpret the treaty once it had entered into force.

In chapter 9, Daniel Bradlow focuses on international soft law standards applicable to the financial sector. He maintains that two sets of standards are applicable to the financial sector with different efficacy profiles. One group consists of international financial regulatory standards that have been developed by national regulatory authorities in international forums to help them each meet their domestic regulatory responsibilities. The other group is international financial responsibility standards that have been developed by both official actors and civil society organizations and financial institutions to address the social, human rights, and environmental responsibilities of financial institutions. The chapter discusses these two sets of standards, the differences in their impacts, and the lessons that can be drawn from them about the efficacy of soft international standards.

The tenth chapter by Sheldon Leader and Luis Felipe Yanes focuses on the Equator Principles, which have been developed by the banking sector to address environmental and social issues in project financing. They suggest that one reason that these Principles have been less than optimally effective is that they give the banks great discretion in their interpretation and implementation and that they do not offer parties that may have been adversely affected by their implementation direct recourse to a remedy or a grievance mechanism.

In chapter 11, Nikki Reisch explores the use of non-judicial grievance mechanisms in business-related human rights cases. She discusses the challenges created by the fact that both the corporation's responsibility to create such mechanisms and to abide by their outcomes is voluntary and non-binding. She explains that this results in these corporations interpreting for themselves the applicable soft international law standards through how they operate day-to-day and how they resolve disputes that may be brought to the non-judicial grievance mechanisms. Finally, she considers the implications of this reality for the development of both hard and soft international human rights law.

The lessons that can be learned from these case studies, including with respect to the questions that are posed in this chapter, are addressed in chapter 12, the concluding chapter.

CHAPTER 2

The Softening of Hard Law and the Hardening of Soft Law: an Extended Synopsis

*Upendra Baxi**

1 Introduction

I have not studied the genealogy of the term 'hard' and 'soft' law in the domain of international law,[1] but it makes sense to say that vicious patriarchy preceded and co-existed with the invention of public international law by Jeremy Bentham in the seventeenth century. In domestic or municipal law, legal positivism marked a new beginning by searching the roots of distinction between law and non-law. As legal theorist John Austin said, a long while ago, one has to draw a distinction between "law properly so called" and "law improperly so-called," or non-law.[2] The latter was typically declared non-enforceable, creating no obligations of conduct made enforceable by courts in particular. It was called by various names—custom, "law in the making," "aspirational" morality (as distinct from the morality of duty), convention, etc. But if we were to subtract the notion of sanctions and yet retain the idea of law as intelligible (as H.L.A. Hart sought to do in his classic *The Concept of Law* it remains possible to make sense of law without sanctions or enforcement.

* Professor of Law at University of Warwick. Professor Baxi served as a Professor of Law at University of Delhi from 1973 to 1996, while serving as its Vice Chancellor from 1990 to 1994.

1 A word of apologies is, at the outset, called for placing in single quotes 'hard' and 'soft' distinction throughout this chapter. I know the ubiquity of these terms, yet as a practising feminist I object to these terms as they carry with them a testosterone-ridden suggestion that while male is 'hard' the female is 'soft.' Equally crucial, the expressions suggest the difference that goes deeper: hard reason and rationality is considered male, while women and girls practice 'soft' sentimental reason. This distinction is without foundation for at least two reasons: one, it is violently patriarchal in its denial to women of having 'reason,' and second, it demotes to a lowly status emotional intelligence and reasoning as an autonomous and equal realm.

2 JOHN AUSTIN, THE PROVINCE OF JURISPRUDENCE DETERMINED 133 (1954) ("[L]aws properly so called are a species of commands ... and hence it inevitably follows, that the law obtaining between nations is not positive law: for every positive law is set by a given sovereign to a person or persons in a state of subjection to its author.").

 | DOI:10.1163/9789004417021_003

How far international lawpersons replicated this search is another story, but if the quest was to identify difference in the "structure of coercion" (as a founder of social theory Max Weber said) as a source of legal obligation, difficult attempts to isolate effectiveness of international law by explicit state consent is reflected in the treaties as a source of law. The earlier set of precepts of authoritative natural law was replaced by versions of the *pacta sunt servanda* principle. We surely know all this as well as how the realm of debate between international law naturalists and legal positivists was conducted. But, as far as I know, and this is a subject of historical research, the 'soft'/'hard' law notions were unknown to the protagonists and opponents in international law and appeared only in very recent Cold War times with international relations theorists, who found a counterpart for 'soft power' in 'soft' law—the law in waiting, anticipations of a future law in the antechamber of international law, as it were.

As students of international law in the early sixties of the last century, we learnt to keep apart *lex lata* (law as it is) from *de lege feranda* (the law as it ought to be). But it was not always easy to sharply distinguish the two; in the long formative periods of international law, *de lege feranda* preceded, and accompanied, the slow and uncertain emergence of *lex lata*.

With the jusnaturalism that founded international law, the morality of aspiration grounded the morality of duty (to use expressions popularised by Lon Fuller).[3] It is only with ultra-legal positivism, when international law acquired the Westphalian edge and existence, that it became identified with what the states regarded as binding and authoritative. It is in this exclusionary era that it became the "law of civilised nations" and signified the savage reality of long periods of colonization and poignant realities of colonial dispossession, logics of primitive accumulation, racial discrimination, slavery, and apartheid.

My initial conclusions about the early histories of international law are that (i) at its diverse points of origin (including the contributions of non-European others), international law as a "gentler civilizers of states"[4] was preponderantly always 'soft' being jusnaturalist; (ii) it 'hardened' into a doctrine of positivistic international law, especially in the eighteenth and nineteenth centuries, into a "law of civilised nations" with all its regressive Eurocentrism; and (iii) the short

---

3 LON FULLER, THE MORALITY OF LAW (rev. ed. 1969); *see also* KRISTEN RUNDLE, FORMS LIBERATE: RECLAIMING THE JURISPRUDENCE OF LON L FULLER (2012); Jonathan Crowe, *Between Morality and Efficacy: Reclaiming the Natural Law Theory of Lon Fuller*, 5 JURIS. 109 (2014).

4 MARTTI KOSKENNIEMI, THE GENTLE CIVILIZER OF NATIONS: THE RISE AND FALL OF INTERNATIONAL LAW 1870–1960 (2004).

era of the League of Nations and the long epoch of the United Nations restored a kind of equality of esteem, and in some cases even status at least of evidence of state practice, to 'soft' law.

The 'soft' law in the early history of the United Nations particularly took the shape of 'manifesto' human rights including those enumerated in the Universal Declaration of Human Rights and the European Charter on Social and Economic Rights, which provided various itineraries for that law to become, in some respects at least, a 'hard' law.[5] On the other hand, the invasions, and incursions (notably, though in various ways, Kosovo, Iraq, and Libya), have 'softened' the 'hard' international law of war and peace, with the 'war on terror' accelerating the pace.

Theorization, as we know, helps us variously to study phenomenon at hand, provided the dangers of the 'theorrhoea' are fully recognized and avoided.[6] Although change occurs, at times profoundly, the shifts in the frame of understanding and problematizing of models and means of making the world are strangely familiar (we all are made aware of this with and since Thomas Kuhn's notions of 'paradigm shifts').[7] The main questions we pursue are: (i) whether the 'soft/hard' distinction has been theorized at all, (ii) if so, whether this has undergone any paradigm shifts, and (iii) whether this all applies to the Anthropocene era marking anthropogenic harm to the planet Earth (mainly through climate change). But as a prefatory concern we also explore the notion of soft power and its further development into 'soft' law.

II Soft Power

Although studies in critical etymology have yet to be fully undertaken, it seems safe to say that the term "soft power" was invented by political theorist Joseph Nye.[8] He concedes that a near cousin of that term prevailed earlier when 'goals of possession' were distinguished from 'milieu goals'—such as human rights, democracy free markets, and rule of law, or their socialist equivalents.[9]

---

5 *See* Universal Declaration of Human Rights, G.A. Res. 217A (III), U.N. Doc. A/810 at 71 (1948); European Social Charter, *opened for signature* Oct. 18, 1961, 529 U.N.T.S. 89, E.T.S. 35.

6 *See* RAYMOND TALLIS, THEORRHOEA AND AFTER (1999).

7 THOMAS KUHN, THE STRUCTURE OF SCIENTIFIC REVOLUTIONS (4th ed. 2012).

8 JOSEPH S. NYE, JR., SOFT POWER: THE MEANS TO SUCCESS IN WORLD POLITICS (2004).

9 *Id.* at 16–17 (citing the distinction made in the late nineteenth century by Arnold Wafers). The difference suggested here is between specific goals of possession and the more

Johannes Plagemann has recently introduced the related notion of "soft sovereignty."[10]

Nye maintains that soft power primarily is the cultural power of foreign policy and is often an alternative, when not supplemental, to hard power (threat or use of military force). He defines soft power as "the ability to get what you want through attraction rather than coercion or payments." It "arises from the attractiveness of a country's culture, political ideals, and policies." And it is enhanced when "our policies are legitimate in the eyes of others .... "[11]

It is then essentially a relational concept (as we learnt some time ago with Max Weber that all power is): problems arise when we have resentment or revenge in the place of attraction. Nye does not analyse the concept of "attraction"; he deploys it in the sense of "seduction" and "admiration" of American ideals by other states and peoples. He explicitly states that seduction is highly, even "more effective than coercion" and "many values like democracy, human rights, and individual opportunities are deeply seductive."[12] We develop a sense of what Nye means by attraction in his critique of commercial, rather than cultural, attraction. Referring to his earlier work,[13] Nye is later explicit that commercial attraction is not what he means. 'Soft power' is one of the three dimensions of American policy, the political and economic being the other two. However, some have "misunderstood it, misused, and trivialized it as merely the influence of Coca-Cola, Hollywood, blue jeans, and money." More "frustrating has been to watch some policy makers ignore the importance of our soft

---

general goal "like shaping environment conducive to democracy." Incidentally, Nye does not fully refer to socialist equivalents of the first three concepts he invokes, and I think that he equates human rights with the rule of law.

10 JOHANNES PLAGEMANN, COSMOPOLITANISM IN A MULTIPOLAR WORLD: SOFT SOVEREIGNTY IN DEMOCRATIC REGIONAL POWERS 4 (2015). ("[C]ontrary to democratic regional powers' foreign policy rhetoric as well as the (Western) public's imaginary, democratic regional powers' praxis of sovereignty neither stands for a neo-Westphalian world order nor does it serve as an empirical argument against (intermediate) cosmopolitan notions of political order beyond the nation-state. Instead, empirical findings on all three levels from Brazil, India, and South Africa suggest a process is occurring wherein the praxis of national sovereignty is softening. Soft sovereignty allows for subnational autonomy, the inclusion of non-state actors, and the embracing of transnational interdependence rather than autonomy by nation-states. . . . [S]oft sovereignty as an empirical assumption provides a more adequate starting point for theorizing a just political order beyond (and below) the level of the nation-state.").

11 NYE, *supra* note 7, at IX.

12 *Id.* at X.

13 JOSEPH S. NYE, JR., BOUND TO LEAD: THE CHANGING NATURE OF AMERICAN POWER (1990).

power and make us all pay the price by unnecessarily squandering it."[14] Nye seems then to exclude the commercial from political and economic attraction.

Attraction itself, after all, turns out to be an unattractive concept! It requires a certain quotient of transhuman capability to love a lawless state and an unconstitutional leader or a regime. It is difficult, outside collective frenzy, to practice statolatry (and have fidelity and faith) when victimized in the killing fields of imperialism, colonialism, the various phases of the Cold War, apartheid, global patriarchy, sex trafficking, and now in the accents and practices of a new genre of neoliberalism.

At the level of state and governments, it remains unlikely in the extreme that the conduct of diplomacy would in any sense be guided by "attraction." As to "peoples" being attracted, the difficult questions relate to the very conception of peoples, who constitutes them, and for which purpose, how may we explain their heterogeneity and differences ("masses" and "elites"), and whether attraction only extends to some people and not others (those without purchasing power at all are unlikely to travel—or even to read and write—and be attracted by commercial or political propaganda). In any case, for "people" who do so, the important question is what mechanisms they adopt in the face of disappointment of their expectations about a "Western" lifestyle. Nye could have used more complex conceptions such as Antonio Gramsci's notion of hegemony,[15] which would also extend to popular culture. The centrality of law (which more fully emerges with soft law, which we discuss later) is easier to foreground by the recourse to the conceptions of hegemony than "attraction." In fact, when Nye says that soft power and hard power occur in a continuum or "spectrum" that forms "smart" political power[16] and characterizes soft power—the "ability to shape the preferences of the other"[17]—the classical notion of hegemony stands installed and foregrounded. It does so, further, when Nye says that not just the state, but civil society, contributes to the formation of soft power. Hegemony arises because of its "co-optive" nature, that is the "ability to shape what others want"[18]; dwelling primarily in culture, political values,

---

14 NYE, *supra* note 7, at XI.

15 ANTONIO GRAMSCI, SELECTIONS FROM THE PRISON NOTEBOOKS OF ANTONIO GRAMSCI (Quintin Hoare & Geoffrey Nowell Smith trans., 1971); *see also* PETER D. THOMAS, THE GRAMSCIAN MOMENT: PHILOSOPHY, HEGEMONY AND MARXISM (2009); Richard W. Cox, *Gramsci, Hegemony and International Relations: An Essay in Method,* 12 MILLENNIUM, J. INT'L STUD. 162 (1983); STEPHEN GILL, POWER AND RESISTANCE IN THE NEW WORLD ORDER (2003).

16 NYE, *supra* note 7, at XIII ("[S]mart power is neither hard nor soft. It is both.").

17 NYE, *supra* note 7, at 5.

18 NYE, *supra* note 7, at 7.

and foreign policies.[19] Soft power is also dilemmatic: "winning peace" is more difficult than winning war.[20]

A *The Phases of 'soft' Law Regimes*

What then is the relation between the regimes (or the fact-law normative complexes) of 'soft power' and 'soft law'? Is the conception of 'soft' law developed from the notions of 'soft' power? Are the two equivalent or to be equated? Does 'hard' power go with the practices of 'soft' law? These, and allied, concerns are important as they further elucidate the function of 'soft' law and we make a few remarks on these in this Chapter.

The expression 'soft law' is attributed to Lord McNair who coined it in the early 1970s.[21] It may be seen that both expressions—soft power and soft law—arose in each other's vicinity in time and both were Cold War and post-Westphalia conceptions. What may distinguish uses of 'soft law' in the Cold War from its latter day uses are a fascinating facet of modern history that need to be further explored. But certainly, one may distinguish between two varieties of context: the SL1 ('soft' law regime of the cold war hegemonies) and SL2 (contemporary soft law regime).

SL1 coincides on a contradictory register marking on the one hand the rise of self-determination, the birth of 'new' nations, the incipient rise of a global civil society, and human rights discourse (theory, movement, and event), and on the other hand, a fierce rivalry of two superpowers and turning post-colonial societies into killing fields. SL1 arises at a time in the world where the Eurocentric world was recast by 'new' postcolonial nation-states and the short-lived era of global humanism tinged foreign policies—and was thriving at the United Nations[22]—giving rise to some exemplary developments in the normative enunciation of human rights. The function of SL1 was to install new

19 NYE, *supra* note 7, at 11 (recognizing popular cultures and commercial diplomacy play apart but reserves the soft power in culture and politics as far as these foster the pursuit of "universal values" that provide legitimacy).

20 NYE, *supra* note 7, at XII.

21 *See* René Jean Dupuy, *Declaratory Law and Programmatory Law: From Revolutionary Custom to 'Soft Law,' in* DECLARATIONS ON PRINCIPLES: A QUEST FOR UNIVERSAL PEACE (Robert J. Akkerman, Peter J. Van Krieken, Charles O. Pannenborg eds., 1977); COMMITMENT AND COMPLIANCE: THE ROLE OF NON-BINDING NORMS IN THE INTERNATIONAL LEGAL SYSTEM (Dinah Shelton ed., 2000); Wolfgang Reinicke & Jan Martin Witte, *Interdependence, Globalization, and Sovereignty: The Role of Non-Binding International Legal Accords,* in Alderman, et al., *supra* note 20, at 75, 76. Francis Snyder, *Soft Law and International Practice in the European Community, in* THE CONSTRUCTION OF EUROPE: ESSAYS IN HONOUR OF EMILE NOËL 197, 198 (Stephen Martin ed., 1994).

22 MARIN ALBROW, THE GLOBAL AGE: STATE AND SOCIETY BEYOND MODERNITY (1994).

international values in a world riven by the horrors of the Holocaust, Hiroshima and Nagasaki, and the cruelties of the unleashing of the various phases of the Cold War. This was then the foundational period of modern soft law. The formative histories of SL1 have still to be fully understood in their complexity, contradiction, and change.

SL2 formations, which remain conspicuous by the steady disappearance of the socialist empire, the rise of authoritarian statism[23] (the contradiction between substantive democracy for all and Neoliberalization), deadly ethnic riots,[24] the wars of and on terror,[25] the fragmentation of international law regimes, humanitarian intervention and naked aggression, and the advent of the apocalyptic Anthropocene.[26] If context gives meaning to sovereign power, the contexts provided in modern history by the various phases of the Cold War and the making of the post-Cold War worlds remain crucial. Much the same may be said about the distinctive contexts now provided with the rising Anthropocene.

'Soft' law denialism takes diverse forms but finally thrives on an analytic separation concerning law and morality based on positivistic conceptions of law and international law. As such, it operates a binary between law and not-law (legislatively, though not necessarily logically). Denialism maintains that which was not binding created no obligations of behaviour and conduct is simply not law. For example, it is argued that there cannot be a half-way house—the very notion of 'soft law' is logically faulty: law cannot be binding in the long run, either it is instantly binding or not.[27]

---

23 *See* MICHAEL HARDT & ANTONIO NEGRI, MULTITUDE: WAR AND DEMOCRACY IN THE AGE OF EMPIRE (2004); BOB JESSOP, NICOS POULANTZAS: MARXIST THEORY AND POLITICAL STRATEGY (1985); BOB JESSOP, STATE THEORY: PUTTING THE CAPITALIST STATE IN ITS PLACE (1990); BOB JESSOP, THE FUTURE OF THE CAPITALIST STATE (1990); Bob Jessop, *Poulantzas's State, Power, Socialism as a Modern Classic, in* READING POULANTZAS (A. Gallas, L. Bretthauer, J. Kannankulam, and I. Stutzle, eds., 2011); Christos Boukala, *No Exceptions: Authoritarian Statism. Agamben, Poulantzas and Homeland Security, in* 7 CRITICAL TERRORISM STUD. 112 (2014).

24 *See* DONALD L. HOROWITZ, THE DEADLY ETHNIC RIOT (2003); AMY CHUA, WORLD ON FIRE: HOW EXPORTING FREE MARKET DEMOCRACY BREEDS ETHNIC HATRED AND GLOBAL INSTABILITY (2004); Upendra Baxi, *Random Reflections on the Hugo Grotius Lecture*, 98 PROC. AM. SOC'Y INT'L L. ANN. MEETING 7 (2004).

25 UPENDRA BAXI, HUMAN RIGHTS IN A POSTHUMAN WORLD: CRITICAL ESSAYS 156–196 (2007).

26 Simon Dalby, *Anthropocene Geopolitics: Globalisation, Empire, Environment and Critique*, 1 GEOGRAPHY COMPASS 103 (2007); *see also* Hillel Elver, *Climate Change and Human Security in the Developing World, in* EXPLORING GLOBAL THRESHOLDS: TOWARDS 2030 104 (Richard Falk, Manorajan Mohanty, Victors Faessel eds., 2017).

27 Jan Klabbers, *The Redundancy of Soft Law*, 65 NORDIC J. INT'L L. 167, 168 (1996).

Nor, is 'soft' law something "out there."[28] It must be constructed as the meaning of the act of will (as Hans Kelsen always defined a norm). But law, whether 'soft' or not, is always constructed! However, the shift of emphasis to the hard law definition by Kenneth W. Abbott, Robert O. Keohane, Andrew Moravcsik, Anne-Marie Slaughter, and Duncan Snidal provides an alternative influential analysis.[29] They enunciate three criteria of 'hard law': namely, obligation, precision, and delegation. The learned authors specify as follows:

> *Obligation* means that states or other actors are bound by a rule or commitment or by a set of rules or commitments. Specifically, it means that they are legally bound by a rule or commitment in the sense that their behaviour thereunder is subject to scrutiny under the general rules, procedures, and discourse of international law, and often of domestic law as well. *Precision* means that rules unambiguously define the conduct they require, authorize, or proscribe. *Delegation* means that third parties have been granted authority to implement, interpret, and apply the rules; to resolve disputes; and (possibly) to make further rules.[30]

The domain of 'soft' law is constituted by relative absence of these three components. We do not dwell here on the potentially over-demanding nature of these criteria, especially the third requirement which involves the ceding of sovereign powers of interpretation to a third party and on to a supra-state level. Nor is "precision" related to context: what may count as "precision" in a framework treaty is differently present in a law-making treaty or treatise, which impose specific obligations here and now. We all know now also about the 'battle of brackets' that occurs in the context of some UN sponsored treaties.[31]

But the learned authors also acknowledge that "even nonbinding declarations can shape the practices of states and other actors and their expectations

28 *Id.*

29 Kenneth W. Abbott et al., *The Concept of Legalization*, 54 INT'L ORG. 401, 401–03 (2000).

30 *Id.* at 401.

31 The rampant (or sparse depending on the contestation around a particular treaty) use of square brackets betokens many things. First, it betrays some uncertainty and tentativeness. Second, these identify a phrase copied out from some source but drafting uncertainties surround as to their precision and aptness. Third, brackets are deployed to identify phrases or passages copied from other sources but whose consistency with other passages have yet to be verified. Fourth, some brackets indicate insertions proposed by NGO s with which some negotiating parties may be in agreement but would be resolved in a final text. In sum, brackets help to move to a next step in an ongoing negotiation and must be now considered an important aspect of the study of *travaux preparatories*.

of appropriate conduct, leading to the emergence of customary law or the adoption of harder agreements," and these may also "implicate the legal principle of good faith compliance, weakening objections to subsequent developments."[32] They say that as "acts of international governance, then, soft normative instruments have a finely wrought ambiguity." It is with this ambiguity that the resilience of 'soft' law dwells. I endorse their overall conclusion, (accentuating the view that inspires emphasis on international governance):

> Between these extremes, where most international legalization lies, actors combine and invoke varying degrees of obligation, precision, and delegation to create subtle blends of politics and law. In all these settings, to paraphrase Clausewitz, "law is a continuation of political intercourse, with the addition of other means."[33]

Is all 'soft' law politics by other means? The continuum approach calls attention to "varying degrees of obligation, precision, and delegation."[34] Some 'soft' law enunciations are dead on arrival (such as the New International Order or the New Information Order, although their normative debris have a long discursive shelf-life). While these attributes vary in all international 'soft' law, UNFCCC acquires, for example, considerable edge of obligation and enunciative precision. It is also true that these instruments prescribe goals and values to be followed by further diplomatic labours (the most recent being the UN Paris Framework). Some other 'soft' law instruments set very distant obligations (such as democracy, participation, the right of peoples to pursue development). Others (like the codes of conduct which affirm human rights obligations of multinational corporations and allied entities) are rejected at the threshold because traditional theory maintains that international law applies only to states (and not to non-state actors), but in the long march, it acquires traction. Already, in the contexts of the war on terror, some non-state actors, particularly members of armed opposition groups, are considered subjects of international law.[35] In short, international 'soft' law has many domains in

32 Abbot et al., *supra* note 29, at 412.

33 *Id.* at 419.

34 *Id.*

35 Noah Birkhäuser, *Sanctions of the Security Council Against Individuals—Some Human Rights Problems*, paper for ESIL Research Forum on International Law: Contemporary Problems (2005), www.statewatch.org/terrorlists/docs/Birkhauser.PDF; *see generally* Simone Gorski, "Individuals in International Law," MAX PLANCK ENCYCLOPEDIA OF PUBLIC INTERNATIONAL LAW (MPEPIL) (2017).

international law. Time is surely at hand to go beyond a mere inventory of types of international 'soft' law to the contexts of international law relations' varying general and specific obligations.[36]

An allied criticism is that to call something non-binding as law is misleading because this gives "the politicians the possibility to be released from their responsibility to take necessary measures to achieve a given effect."[37] Anthony D'Amato naming 'soft' law as a "naked norm" (bereft of any binding-ness, or, to put in languages of pop culture, all-dressed-up-but-nowhere to-go) maintains the view that the breach of 'soft' law proves cost-effective: reputational loss, thus somewhat entailed, is outweighed by the benefits that accrue from non-compliance with, or even repudiation of, the norm.[38] Worse still, it is said to legitimate an escapade from hard choices that result into binding obligations.

A difficulty with this sort of criticism is that it causally links validity of norms with their effectiveness in practice. Efficacy is of course important, but all state conduct fails, in some degree or another, to comport with the norms of international law. What quotient of effectiveness should be related to a measure of the validity of a norm is a difficult question; imperfect obligations do not cease to be obligations at all, and there happen to be available many means of enforcement, including the nudging function which is now fully conceptualized.[39] And the wider question of the relations between morals and law as being contingent or necessary remains deeply contested.

Those who would deny 'soft' law any attribute of "binding-ness" distinguish sharply between law and non-law and between a legally valid law and moral law. The category of non-binding law emerges as self-contradictory and no question of violation should ever arise simply because it is not a legal norm in the first place. Moral laws can be spoken of in the languages of violation but whether all so-called 'soft law' even may be said to approximate a moral law is

---

36 *See also* Klabbers, *supra* note 27.

37 *Id.* at 383.

38 Anthony D'Amato, *Softness in International Law: A Self-Serving Quest for New Legal Materials: A Reply to Jean d'Aspremont*, 20 EUR. J. INT'L L. 902 (2009).

39 Pelle Guldborg Hansen, *The Definition of Nudge and Libertarian Paternalism: Does the Hand Fit the Glove?* 7 EUR. J. OF RISK AND REG. 1 (2016); Péter Cserne, *Is Nudging Really Extra-Legal?* 37 THE TOCQUEVILLE REV./LA REVUE TOCQUEVILLE 159 (2016); *see also* RICHARD H. THALER & CASS R. SUNSTEIN, NUDGE: IMPROVING DECISIONS ABOUT HEALTH, WEALTH, AND HAPPINESS (2008); CASS R. SUNSTEIN, WHY NUDGE? THE POLITICS OF LIBERTARIAN PATERNALISM (2014); NUDGE AND THE LAW: A EUROPEAN PERSPECTIVE (Alberto Alemanno & Anne-Lise Sibony eds., 2015); Alberto Alemanno & Alessando Spina, *Nudging Legally: On the Checks and Balances of Behavioural Regulation*, 12 INT'L J. CONST. L. 429 (2014).

open to doubt and contention, at least if a function of such moral law is obligation (howsoever inchoate) rather than mere expressionism.

Further, it is not at all clear why an alternate approach of continuum rather than a binary standard is favored. 'Soft' law standards of yesteryear may become 'hardened' obligations of tomorrow and *vice versa*. "While naturally vulnerable to the growth of formal legal norms," as Richard Rawlings puts it, "soft law techniques are also apt to be stimulated by it, in part by way of supplement and/or experiment, in part by way of counter-reaction."[40] In a sense then 'soft' law means three things: an experiment, a supplement, and a counter-reaction to hegemonic power. Contextual analysis gains in saliency when 'soft' law is perceived by actors as counter-hegemonic to sovereign power.

Ilhami Alkan Olsson has painstakingly demonstrated categories of "Treaty Soft Law," "Non-binding Soft Law," and "Non-state Soft law."[41] This variant of continuum approach helps us to see clearly how 'soft' law standards also provide a law-in-the-making approach.

'Soft' law as law-in-the-making should always take full account of the reality of a state's bargaining power, which rarely is either a zero-sum game or a winner-take-it-all situation. The shifts in bargaining power, it has been recently argued, ought to be studied in the contexts of exit and renegotiation. In analysing 'soft' law, one must start with the premise that the "seeds of future actions are, however, sown in the soil of contemporary behaviour" and "one must integrate shifting power into one's theory of how states make law before one can fully comprehend how shifting power affects states' observance of law."[42] Analytically, for our purposes, this means that we segregate the making of 'soft' law from its 'observance' and grasp how states make tradeoffs that express their

---

40 *See* Richard Rawlings, *Soft Law Never Dies*, *in* THE CAMBRIDGE COMPANION TO PUBLIC LAW 215, 217 (Mark Elliot & David Fidleman eds., 2015) ("[T]he fallacy of forcing a contrast between law and practice at the point where the two ends meet.").

41 *See* Ilhami Alkan Olsson, *Four Competing Approaches to International Soft Law*, 58 SCANDINAVIAN STUD. L. 177 (2013) ("[S]oft law has ceased to be the 'substitute' (or 'second-best' solution) for hard law alternatives in inter-state relations and it has become the major 'legalisation form' of the norm-like activities of private and public-private crossbreed authorities . . . by implying the multiplicity of legal sources and subjects of international law and giving rise to a flexible and context-dependent norm-making process, informal soft law has been a central mechanism in privatising public power."); *see also*, Christine Chinkin, *Normative Development in the International Legal System*, *in* COMMITMENT AND COMPLIANCE, *supra* note 20, at 127 (speaking of 'soft international law').

42 Timothy Meyer, *Power, Exit Costs, and Renegotiation in International Law*, 51 HARV. INT'L L. J. 379, 381 (2010).

decisions and how much to take their future interactions "out of the realm of politics and put them into the realm of law."[43]

B *The Footfalls of Anthropocene*

Grasping the dynamics of this is important, perhaps even more as we hear a lot about the end of a human rights era and about the advent of a neo-Westphalian era diluting further concerns about global social change policy, especially the new impoverishment by the onset of the Anthropocene. This advent outpaces the glacial global change—in attitudes and dispositions—which occurred in the Holocene era (lasting for nearly 10000 -12000 years). In the very late Holocene occurred the great flowering of the ethical idea of human rights and international human rights law and jurisprudence. That period also witnessed the rise and the growth of environmental law and jurisprudence, which reflected a new vision of international law, relations, and organization. Immense challenges to human thought and action now stand posed by the Anthropocene.

To be sure, the Anthropocene is more than climate change, which is 'only the tip of the iceberg' (how cruel this saying now sounds); it also relates to the fact that,

> humans are (i) significantly altering several other biogeochemical, or element cycles, such as nitrogen, phosphorus and sulphur, that are fundamental to life on the Earth; (ii) strongly modifying the terrestrial water cycle by intercepting river flow from uplands to the sea and, through land-cover change, altering the water vapour flow from the land to the atmosphere; and (iii) likely driving the sixth major extinction event in Earth history ... Taken together, these trends are strong evidence that humankind, our own species, has become so large and active that it now rivals some of the great forces of Nature in its impact on the functioning of the Earth system.[44]

In this sense we are entering in the Anthropocene a "geological age of our own making."[45] Not merely are the humans themselves becoming a "force of

43 *Id.* at 425.

44 Will Steffen et al., *The Anthropocene: Conceptual and Historical Perspectives*, 369 PHIL. TRANSACTIONS ROYAL SOC'Y A 842, 843 (2011); see also P.J. Crutzen & J. Lelieveld, *Human Impacts on Atmospheric Chemistry*, 29 ANN. REV. EARTH & PLANETARY SCI. 17 (2001); R. J. Houghton, *Balancing the Global Carbon Budget*, 35 ANN. REV. EARTH & PLANETARY SCI. 313 (2007).

45 *See* Sandra C Chapman et al., *Limits to the Quantification of Local Climate Change*, 10 ENVTL. RES. LETTERS, Sept. 16, 2015, at 094018; ANTHROPOGENIC CLIMATE CHANGE

nature" in "the sixth major extinction event in Earth history,"[46] it may also be the time of our own unmaking if the urgency of human social action is not sufficiently realized. At the same time, anthropogenic climate change is not merely the cause of a series of catastrophes and crises: it marks a new opportunity to restructure our governance, social traditions, and global management of 'nature.' What is indicated thus is not thinking out of the box but smashing the box itself!

Doing this implies many things. One needs to listen carefully to those who warn of climate change catastrophes without succumbing to climate change conspiracy narratives. Also needed is the ability to differentiate 'dangerous' or 'catastrophic' scenarios of 'abrupt' climate change and global warming from the cumulative harms to the planet. The degree of policy and action urgency varies, though the kind of urgent attention and care must attach to all threats of human and nonhuman extinction. In this sense, for example, adaptation and mitigation of climate refugees appears now more urgent than the goals of achieving eventual post carbon economy.

While the theories about environmental and ecological law and justice that evolved in the last decades of the Holocene era provide valuable beginnings, these may not uncritically extend to climate change justice theory approaches. The circumstances and tasks of justice in the Anthropocene era make very different sorts of claims than cosmopolitan theories of environmental and global justice. Now is demanded a sort of planetary loyalty and multispecies solidarity, tasks which we never posed so insistently. One has also to find a new dynamic of anthropomorphism that embraces all living beings, and even unloved beings in Nature. Claire Colebrook is right in saying that:

> We are at once thrown into a situation of urgent interconnectedness, aware that the smallest events contribute to global mutations, at the same time as we come up against a complex multiplicity of diverging forces and timelines that exceed any manageable point of view.[47]

(Hans von Storch ed., 1999); Mathieu Richaud, ANTHROPOGENIC CLIMATE CHANGE (2015), http://www.oxfordbibliographies.com/view/document/obo-9780199874002/obo-9780199874002-0110.xml.

46 *See* Upendra Baxi, *Towards A Climate Change Justice Theory?*, 7 J. HUM. RTS. ENV'T 7 (2016).

47 *See* CLARE COLEBROOK, DEATH OF THE POSTHUMAN: ESSAYS ON EXTINCTION, VOL. I (2014); Audra Mitchell, *Beyond Biodiversity and Species: Problematizing Extinction*, 33 THEORY, CULTURE & SOC'Y 23 (2016) ("[Mitchell pluralizes] extinction [by providing categories] for several subjects of extinction [and]...ample grounds for revisiting the doctrines of species encoded in the images of 'biodiversity,' 'humanity,' 'unloved' subjects, and

Obviously, the continuum, rather than a binary, approach is called for by the problems of climate change and global warming. The importance of 'soft' law has escalated, through various United Nations Framework Conventions (from Rio to Kyoto and onwards to Paris 2015 and Agenda 2030). The notion of 'sustainability' in sustainable development has acquired more precision and obligations than in prior 'soft' law enunciations.[48] New norms have emerged—such as common but differentiated responsibility, special capacities, post-development—while the very late Holocene conceptions are appropriately updated, such as "sustainable development" and "disasters." Human rights norms and standards are in the process of fundamental readjustment with the imperatives of the Anthropocene. International 'soft' law in ferment characterizes the development of law as an instrument of perceiving the contours of the present-day climate change and global warming impacts; it also recasts the law and legal theory as a way of ecological resilience that may succeed partially in combatting atmospheric degradation. New standards and norms arise from, and guide, approaches towards Anthropocene justice theory.

That fully said, the question is: How does international 'soft' law meet the prospect of extinction? The end of humanity, and all forms of life on the planet, is a theme strongly associated with the growing understanding of the advancement of the Anthropocene. How may the call for "the consolidation of

---

'absent or non-relational subjects." She expounds and explores ingrained hierarchies and violence of the embedded exclusions and inequalities embedded in dominant discourses, and identifies possibilities for "plural ethico-political responses to mass extinction." She urges that we differentiate between ... the disappearance of the (meta) physical species [h]omo sapiens and the "figural" extinction ... of the normative figure of "humanity" produced by Western European humanism, modernity and capitalism."). *See also* TIMOTHY CLARK, ECOCRITICISM ON THE EDGE: THE ANTHROPOCENE AS A THRESHOLD CONCEPT (2015); JEREMY DAVIS, THE BIRTH OF THE ANTHROPOCENE (2016); H. R. MCNEILL & PETER ENGELIKE, THE GREAT ACCELERATION: AN ENVIRONMENTAL HISTORY OF THE ANTHROPOCENE SINCE 1945 (2016); ANTHROPOCENE OR CAPITALOCENE, NATURE, HISTORY, AND CRISIS OF CAPITALISM (Jason W. Moore, ed, 2015); JEDEDIAH PURDY, AFTER NATURE: A POLITICS FOR THE ANTHROPOCENE (2015).

48 Antto Vihma, *Friendly Neighbour or Trojan Horse? Assessing the Interaction of Soft Law Initiatives and the U.N. Climate Regime* 9 INT'L ENVTL. AGREEMENTS 239 (2009); Antto Vihma, *Analysing Soft Law and Hard Law in Climate Change, in* CLIMATE CHANGE AND THE LAW, IUS GENTIUM: COMPARATIVE PERSPECTIVES ON LAW AND JUSTICE 143 (E.J. Hollo et al. eds., 2013); *see also* JOHN S. DRYZEK, RICHARD B. NORGAARD, & DAVID SCHLOSBERG, CLIMATE CHANGE AND SOCIETY: APPROACHES AND RESPONSES IN THE OXFORD HANDBOOK OF CLIMATE CHANGE AND SOCIETY 9 (2011); THE OXFORD HANDBOOK OF INTERNATIONAL CLIMATE CHANGE LAW (Kevin R. Gray, Richard Tarasofsky, & Cinnamon Carlarne eds., 2016).

'humanity' and its 'possible demise'"[49] occur through 'soft' law? What role, if any, does the idea of human rights possess in the face of the ultimate extinction of the human species? Do the instrumental uses of the 'currency' of human rights enunciations frontally address the problem of mass extinction, or what may it mean to say 'human,' and 'having rights'?[50]

Climate change and global warming raises again, and urgently, the question of territoriality. How does international 'soft' law proceed to renovate the doctrine of sovereign equality of all states as the cornerstone of post-Westphalian international law, orderings, and organizations?[51] Indirect global governance is an exception to the norm of consent-based application of international law. It has been the grundnorm of all UN and many specialized agencies and activities. Despite manifest discontent with this, the late Holocene human rights and environmental law movements and norms have also been based on state consent. The Anthropocene, however, brings back the problematique of direct global governance at least in the sense that the extinction of human species, and other forms of dangerous climate change, lies beyond the capabilities of individual states. How then is one to blueprint a post post-Westphalian order of international law, relations, and organization in the early Anthropocene?

Closely related, of course, is the question of the communities of multinational corporations and direct foreign investors who claim immunity and impunity from domestic and global law as concerns the causation of mass disasters and social catastrophes. In effect, this continues to contribute to the privatization of governance, at all levels, from the local to the global. This privatization is made manifest by the three D's that mark the current form of globalization: Denationalization, Disinvestment, and Deregulation, in ways that make human rights more market-friendly and trade-related. How may 'soft' law standards be further sharpened to combat at least the dangerous climate change? And

---

49 Mitchell, *supra* note 47, at 5, 23–42, 28.

50 *See* Lavnya Rajmani, *The Increasing Currency and Relevance of Rights-Based Perspectives in the International Negotiations on Climate Change*, 22 J. ENVTL. L. 391 (2010); Sam Adelman, *Rethinking Human Rights: The Impact of Climate Change on the Dominant Discourse*, *in* HUMAN RIGHTS AND CLIMATE CHANGE 159 (Stephen Humphreys ed., 2010); Sam Adelman, *Climate Justice, Loss and Damage and Compensation for Small Island Developing States*, J. ENV'T. & HUM. RTS. (2016) (*available at* wrap.warwick.ac.uk/78600).

51 *See* Upendra Baxi, *Human Rights Responsibility of Multinational Corporations, Political Ecology of Injustice: Learning from Bhopal Thirty Plus?* 1 BUS. & HUM. RTS. J. 21, 40 (2016).

how may governance refashion to meet the tasks ahead—especially the post-carbon economy and the philosophy of 'de-growth'?[52]

III Towards a Conclusion

As we approach the end of the first quarter of the 21st century, the debate should not be about whether 'soft' law is law or not, but rather with the possibilities and potential of 'soft' law to 'harden' and 'hard' law to become 'soft.' In this dialectic, we need to ask uncomfortable questions as to the nature of old Holocene human rights. Clearly, we need to posit, as environmentalists of yore were wont to do, a collective human right of all peoples, species, and planet to survive endlessly in the future and a common global duty of peoples and states to develop planetary loyalty in the future. Such would be an all-encompassing collective human starting point of any exploration of rights and justice in the early Anthropocene. Human rights and justice would clearly be "less anthropocentric than the present [and] ... benefit society, not just individual victims ... enable litigants and NGOs to challenge environmentally destructive or unsustainable development on public interest grounds, ... [and] give the environmental concerns greater weight" in shaping and making a global social change framework.[53]

All this is valuable, but we also need to cultivate new ways of being, belonging, and reflecting on the intransigence of the Anthropocene. We certainly need to develop rapidly "a thorough notion of global environmental justice" that is "locally grounded, theoretically broad, and plural—encompassing issues of recognition, distribution, and participation."[54] Equally, there is a "vital need" to face "critically-informed, reflexive, epistemically humble and

---

52 TRANSITIONING TO A POST-CARBON SOCIETY: DEGROWTH, AUSTERITY, AND WELLBEING (Ernest Garcia, Mercedes Martinez-Iglesias, & Peadar Kirby eds., 2016); Joan Martínez-Alier, *Environmental Justice and Economic Degrowth: An Alliance between Two Movements*, 23 CAPITALISM, NATURE, SOCIALISM 51 (2012); Arturo Escobar, *Degrowth, Post-development, And Transitions: A Preliminary Conversation*, 10 SUSTAINABLE SCI. 451 (2015).

53 Anna Grear, *Human Rights—Human Bodies? Some Reflections on Corporate Human Rights Distortion, the Legal Subject, Embodiment and Human Rights Theory*, 17 L. & CRITIQUE 171 (2006); Anna Grear, *Deconstructing Anthropos: A Critical Legal Reflection on 'Anthropocentric' Law and Anthropocene 'Humanity,'* 26 L. & CRITIQUE 225 (2015) [hereinafter *Deconstructing Anthropos*].

54 David Schlosberg, *Reconceiving Environmental Justice: Global Movements and Political Theories*, 13 ENVTL. POL. 518 (2004).

renewing engagements with the question of who 'we' are in the Anthropocene age."[55] How may such a such a cluster of rights which is 'transformed' by the non-universal, non-essentialist notion of the 'human' and carries also the capacity for a "diverse entanglement with nature-culture" that might "co-inform a liberatory, restorative ontology, epistemology and ethics adequate to Anthropocene futures?" And, above all, how far 'soft' law standards and norms develop "an injustice-sensitive set of practices faithful to delivery of inclusion, compassion and resilience in a climate-threatened world?"[56]

---

55 *See Deconstructing Anthropos, supra* note 53, at 36.

56 *See id.*

CHAPTER 3

Promoting Social Change through Treaties and Customary International Law: the Experience of the Inter-American Human Rights System

*Claudio Grossman**

1 Introduction

This paper's purpose is to explore the possibilities and limitations of treaties and customary international law in promoting social change in the regional setting—in particular, human rights in the context of the Organization of American States (OAS). While the regional system was formally created by States that ratified the instruments constitutive of this system, non-state actors—victims, lawyers, judges, members of supervisory organs, non-governmental organizations (NGOs) that operate both at the national and international level—play a crucial role in shaping the implementation of the system. Both the role of non-state actors and the system's preferred method of implementing action are constantly evolving. During the time of authoritarianism and the reign of dictatorships in the region, the system dealt with mass and gross human rights violations mainly through non-binding country reports. As the region shifted toward democratization and a system of elected governments, opportunities for civil society expanded, and state policies of mass and gross violations of human rights generally declined.[1] Accordingly,

* Professor of Law, Dean Emeritus, and the Raymond Geraldson Scholar for International and Humanitarian Law at American University Washington College of Law (WCL). Professor Grossman served as WCL dean from 1995-July 2016. He is currently a member of the United Nations International Law Commission.

1 Claudio Grossman, El Fortalecimiento de la Democracia, 1 FOREIGN AFF. 115, 116–17 (2001); compare Petitions *Received*, INTERAMERICAN COMMISSION ON HUMAN RIGHTS, http://www.oas.org/en/iachr/multimedia/statistics/statistics.html (last visited Oct. 17, 2017), *with* Country Reports, INTER-AMERICAN COMMISSION ON HUMAN RIGHTS, http://www.oas.org/en/iachr/reports/country.asp (last visited Oct. 17, 2017). The first shows the gradual increase in petitions received by the system from 435 in 1997 to 2,567 last year and the second lists country reports through the years showing multiple reports almost every year between 1976–1997 and the gradual decrease in more recent years as the system's hard law nature grew stronger.

 | DOI:10.1163/9789004417021_004

the system evolved to the current technique, focused on hard law, with a larger role for civil society.

This paper will demonstrate how the system and more of the countries in the region have resorted to bringing cases—seeking to benefit from the hard law nature of the petition system to effect social change through impact litigation. The paper will also demonstrate the hurdles civil society and other actors overcame, their successes and failures within the system, and how these have developed the system to its contemporary status.

The human rights realm does not cover the whole topic of treaty and customary international law and their effects on social change. However, the manner in which international human rights norms are recognized and implemented might broaden, or even narrow, space for actions by societal actors who find in the human rights narrative a legitimate ground to present their claims. Therefore, the effectiveness of human rights has an impact in other areas of social action particularly because it relates directly to the legitimacy of participation and political action.

The regional experience, for the purposes of this paper, is limited to the Western Hemisphere, although it would be interesting to develop similar studies and analysis involving the other systems—the European, the African, and the ASEAN. The case for regionalism is well known and is based on geographic proximity and shared cultural tradition that binds people and nations together. It is therefore interesting to understand how this regional interconnectivity could create greater space for social change or, as was the case in the Western Hemisphere during the dictatorships of the 1970s, limit it. Further, this paper will briefly analyze the dynamics existing between the universal and the regional systems, which cannot be simply explained as the universal system acting solely in the case of regional failure. An analysis of the relationship shows a richer texture of mutual reinforcement, with both the regional and the universal systems contributing to the development of each other.

II The Inter-American System

A *Structure*

The Inter-American system is a combination of human rights norms and supervisory institutions within the Americas. The applicable norms consist primarily of the American Declaration on the Rights and Duties of Man[2] ("American

2 American Declaration of the Rights and Duties of Man, OEA/Ser. L./V.II. 23, doc. 21, rev. 6 (1948) [hereinafter American Declaration].

Declaration") and the American Convention on Human Rights[3] ("American Convention"). The institutions involved are the organs responsible for supervising compliance with the established norms: the Inter-American Commission on Human Rights[4] ("the Commission") and the Inter-American Court of Human Rights[5] ("the Court"). The system performs its supervisory functions through country reports adopted by the Commission, which describe the overall human rights situation in a country, and decisions in individual petitions alleging that internationally protected rights have been violated. Individuals have standing to file petitions only with the Commission, not with the Court. Only the Commission may decide to bring cases to the Court if a State, that has accepted the Court's compulsory jurisdiction,[6] fails to comply within three months with the Commission's recommendations in the underlying case.[7] The political organs of the OAS—the Permanent Council and the General Assembly—also share the responsibility of guaranteeing compliance with the American Declaration and Convention, as well as with the decisions of the Commission and the Court.[8]

---

3 American Convention on Human Rights, Nov. 22, 2969, 1144 U.N.T.S. 143 [hereinafter American Convention].

4 Inter-Am. Comm'n H.R., Annual Rep. 1998, ch. 6, OEA/ser. LJVJH. 102, doc. 6 rev. (1998).

5 Secretary General, *Annual Report of the Secretary General 1999–2000*, ch. III, OEA/Ser./L/V/II.111, doc. 6 rev. (2000).

6 For a review of the signatories to the American Convention, *see American Convention on Human Rights*, ORG. OF AM. STATES, http://www.oas.org/en/iachr/mandate/basics/conventionrat.asp (last visited Sept. 19, 2017). A total of twenty-two states have recognized the jurisdiction of the Inter-American Court.

7 For a description of the Inter-American system, *see* Claudio Grossman, *The Velasquez Rodriguez Case: The Development of the Inter-American Human Rights System, in* INTERNATIONAL LAW STORIES 81–84 (John E. Noyes, Laura A. Dickinson, & Mark W. Janis eds., 2007). The petition system has not always been the favored or the most efficient means to address human rights violations in the hemisphere. The Commission had resorted to country reports, some following visits *in loco* to the OAS member states, geared towards mobilizing public opinion, particularly in cases of massive and systematic violations. With the evolution of the political situation of the hemisphere and a dramatic decrease in violations of political rights, the petition system (cases) became the main vehicle for addressing human rights violations. States in the process of democratic transition generally participated in the proceedings. The petition system was adopted as the predominant means to enhance the protection of human rights and develop uniform and cohesive standards, while decreasing reliance on, but not entirely abandoning, the other mechanisms already in place.

8 Organization of American States, Charter of the Organization of American States, Apr. 30, 1948, 2 U.S.T. 2394, 19 U.N.T.S. 3.

B *Historical Developments*

The Inter-American system has progressed through several phases in its development. Three main phases can be identified, although they are not absolutely distinct or separate. During its early years, until roughly the 1980s, the system dealt with dictatorial regimes characterized by mass and gross violations of human rights. Examples of decisions adopted to confront those violations include the first three contested cases decided by the Inter-American Court dealing with forced disappearances in Honduras.[9]

A second phase is characterized by the rise of elected governments in the hemisphere, as well as attempts to analyze and review the legacies of dictatorial regimes. The Commission and the Court confronted issues including impunity, freedom of expression, and due process, and developed States' obligations under Articles 1.1 and 2 of the American Convention, such as duties to investigate and punish those allegedly responsible for human rights violations, and to conform States' domestic legislation to the American Convention. In addition, the adoption of the Inter—American Democratic Charter at the XXVIII Special Session of the OAS General Assembly on September 11, 2001, acknowledged and emphasized the hemisphere's new political reality. The Charter establishes the right to democracy and condemns member states that abandon this principle. It also strengthens the relationship between democracy and human rights, stating that respect for human rights is an essential element of democracy. This development contributed to the consolidation of the system's legitimacy as a promoter of democracy and fundamental rights and freedoms in the hemisphere. A paradigmatic decision of the Court, which illustrates the system's contributions to social change, involves the rejection of amnesty laws that were adopted for the purposes of avoiding accountability for human rights violations.

A third phase, the one in which we currently live, presents a new reality characterized by the need to address issues facing democratic societies, such as inequality and exclusion, poverty, participation, and corruption, among others. Although it may be difficult to summarily characterize this cluster of issues, it is helpful to visualize them as pathways to constantly expand democratic societies and democracy itself. In the political reality of the Western Hemisphere, these issues could be addressed in ways that can reinforce human

9 Fairén Garbi and Solís Corrales v. Honduras, Merits, Judgment, Inter-Am. Ct. H.R. (ser. C) No. 6 (Mar. 15, 1989); Godínez Cruz v. Honduras, Reparations and Costs, Judgment, Inter-Am. Ct. H.R. (ser. C) No. 5 (Jan. 20, 1989); Velásquez Rodríguez v. Honduras, Merits, Judgment, Inter-Am. Ct. H.R. (ser. C) No. 4 (July 29, 1988).

rights and democratic values and institutions. Or addressing the issues could provide a pretext for authoritarian regimes or charismatic personalities to present ideological alternatives to democracy and human rights as reflected in the Inter-American system.[10] During this third phase, some of the Court's notable decisions address structural issues that affect generally excluded groups, such as indigenous populations, and that ensure democratic values, such as freedom of expression.

Throughout these various phases, victims of human rights violations, lawyers, and NGOs found insurmountable obstacles to achieving their goals in the domestic legal systems. Norms that were left behind by authoritarian regimes, difficulties in legislating new laws, and limitations created by the judiciary—either caused by the existing normative framework or by the judiciary's composition and view of its own role—made absolutely necessary the ability of non-state actors, victims of human rights violations, and other such actors to resort to international law and international forums.

As a result of the serious limitations on victims seeking justice in a domestic setting, a "community of practice" emerged around the Inter-American system of human rights. There are numerous expressions of this community. For example, prior to the Commission's sessions, academics, non-governmental organizations, and others will meet to exchange experiences and best practices. Following those meetings, through social media and organizational networks, they continue to share information. The Center for Justice and International Law (CEJIL) has created a strong network with offices in Latin America and elsewhere, organizing meetings of NGOs around the Commission and monitoring the system's evolution and activities. Similarly, American University Washington College of Law in Washington, D.C. has created an Academy of Human Rights and Humanitarian Law, which, among other functions, conducts research and offers courses in English and Spanish on the Inter-American system. During three weeks in the summer at the Washington College of Law, NGOs, state representatives, academics, judges, and commissioners interact and work together to strengthen their community of practice.

10 For example, we have seen how the current government in Venezuela withdrew from the American Convention of Human Rights, presenting as an alternative an authoritarian model that allegedly is better suited to "fight inequality". *See Venezuela Denounces American Convention on Human Rights as IACHR Faces Reform*, INT'L JUST. RES. CTR. (Sept. 19, 2012), http://www.ijrcenter.org/2012/09/19/venezuela-denounces-american-convention-on-human-rights-as-iachr-faces-reform/.

III Illustrative Cases in the Inter-American System

This section describes and analyzes four cases that illustrate the three phases of the Inter-American system's development and its effect on social change, while providing a better understanding of the system and analyzing and evaluating its future as a valuable venue for non-state actors to pursue human rights claims. More specifically, this article examines the cases of Velásquez Rodríguez v. Honduras (1988),[11] analyzing mass and gross violations of human rights involving forced disappearances in the context of authoritarianism and dictatorships; and Barrios Altos v. Peru (2001),[12] addressing the legacy of dictatorships, particularly with regard to impunity, respectively covering the first two phases of the Inter-American Human Rights System. The current phase of the system will be illustrated by Mayagna (Sumo) Awas Tingni Community v. Nicaragua (2001),[13] examining the rights of indigenous peoples and, in a broader sense, the status of vulnerable groups and the need to expand and strengthen democracy through their inclusion; and General Usón-Ramirez v. Venezuela (2008),[14] examining liability for violations of freedom of expression, including criminal sanctions for "offensive" expression directed at public officials or against private individuals concerning matters relevant to society at large. The threat and imposition of penal sanctions for speech suffocates democracy and could support an authoritarian logic incompatible with a democratic society. Expression, by definition, creates civil societal space, so the way in which we treat it then becomes crucial for the expansion of social development.

A Velásquez Rodriguez v. Honduras (*1988*)

1 Brief Factual Overview

Angel Manfredo Velásquez Rodríguez disappeared on September 12, 1981, in downtown Tegucigalpa, Honduras. His friends and family never saw him again, the Honduran government denied any knowledge or involvement in his disappearance, and the Honduran courts would not hear the family's case.[15]

---

11 Velásquez Rodríguez v. Honduras, Case 7920, Inter-Am. Comm'n H.R., Report No. 22/86, OEA/Ser.L/V/II.61, doc. 44 (1986).

12 Barrios Altos v. Peru, Merits, Judgment, Inter-Am. Ct. H.R. (ser. C) No. 75 (Mar. 14, 2001).

13 The Mayagna (Sumo) Awas Tingni Community v. Nicaragua, Merits, Reparations and Costs, Judgment, Inter-Am. Ct. H.R. (ser. C) No. 79 (Aug. 31, 2001).

14 Usón Ramírez v. Venezuela, Case No. 12.554, Inter-Am. Comm'n H.R., n.14 (July 25, 2008).

15 For a more extensive analysis of the case, see Claudio Grossman, *The Velásquez Rodríguez Case: The Development of the Inter-American Human Rights System, in* INTERNATIONAL LAW STORIES ch. 3 (2007).

The petition in the *Velásquez Rodriguez* case was filed with the Commission in October 1981,[16] alleging that the Honduran government was responsible for Manfredo Velásquez's disappearance.[17] Disappearances constitute one of the most egregious violations of human rights because they are perpetrated by State authorities that later deny any knowledge or involvement in the situation. For Manfredo Velásquez's family, along with the families of many other victims, disappearances were a grim political and legal reality in Latin America during the 1970s and 1980s.

The Commission's report on the merits indicated that Manfredo Velásquez had been detained and most likely disappeared at the hands of state agents in Honduras, and that his disappearance violated the right to life (Article 4) and the right to personal liberty (Article 7) of the American Convention.[18] The Commission recommended investigating and punishing those guilty for his disappearance, as well as reparations. In 1985, after General Alvarez, the military strongman of Honduras, was ousted from power, the new government of Honduras requested additional time to conduct an internal investigation.[19] However, the investigation concluded with a four-sentence report stating that no evidence connected anyone in the military to the disappearance.[20] Favorably reacting to the claims presented by the victims and their attorneys, in April 1986, the Commission affirmed its earlier recommendation in its entirety and referred the case to the Court.[21]

The American Convention does not explicitly criminalize disappearances. Nonetheless, the Court ruled that forced disappearances constitute multiple

16 *See* Velásquez Rodríguez v. Honduras, Case 7920, Inter-Am. Comm'n H.R., Report No. 22/86, OEA/Ser. L./III.15, doc.13 (1986) (reporting that the Commission received the petition on October 7, 1981 and stating that the petition maintained that Manfredo Velásquez was in the First Battalion of Infantry in Tegucigalpa along with other missing political prisoners).

17 *See id.* ¶ 1 ("We assign responsibility for that action to Colonels Leonidas Torres Arias (G-2), Gustavo Alvarez (FUSEP), Juan Lopez Grijalba (National Investigation Department) and Hubbert Bodden (Commander, First Battalion of Infantry, Tegucigalpa).").

18 *See* Velásquez Rodríguez v. Honduras, Case 7920, Inter-Am. Comm'n H.R., Report No. 22/86, OEA/Ser.L/V/II.61, doc. 44 (1986).

19 *See id.* at ¶ 16 (relating that Honduras requested postponement of consideration of the case in its Cablegram of March 1, 1985 and that it stated that it had set up an Investigating Commission to examine the complaints and identify and punish those responsible).

20 *See* Claudio Grossman, *Disappearances in Honduras: The Need for Direct Victim Representation in Human Rights Litigation*, 15 HASTINGS INT'L & COMP. L. REV. 363, 368–69 (1992).

21 *See* Regs. of the Inter-Am. Comm'n H.R., art. 50, OEA/Ser.L.V/II.82 doc. 6 rev. ¶ 1 (1992); American Convention, *supra* note 3, art. 63(1).

and continuous violations of the rights enshrined in the Convention.[22] The Court concluded that the practice of disappearances violated four articles of the American Convention, specifically Articles 1 (duty to guarantee a legal order that prevents human rights violations[23]), 4 (right to life), 5 (right to personal integrity), and 7 (right to personal liberty): "The kidnapping of a person is an arbitrary deprivation of liberty, an infringement of a detainee's right to be taken without delay before a judge and to invoke the appropriate procedures to review the legality of the arrest, all in violation of Article 7 of the Convention which recognizes the right to personal liberty."[24] The Court interpreted Article 5's provisions regarding cruel, inhuman and degrading treatment and concluded that they prohibit incommunicado detention.[25] It also found that prolonged and isolated imprisonment harms the "psychological and moral integrity of the person."[26] Finally, the Court acknowledged that disappearances involving clandestine executions without trials and clandestine burials violated the right to life under Article 4.[27] The Court characterized the practice of disappearances as violating even more than the specific articles of the Convention, stating that "[t]he practice of disappearances ... shows a crass abandonment of the values which emanate from the concept of human dignity and of the most basic principles of the Inter-American system and the Convention."[28]

2 Impact on Social Change

The *Velásquez Rodríguez* decision, in the context of other domestic and international factors such as the end of the Cold War and the easing of tensions in the region, contributed to the end of the systemic state practice of forced disappearances as a political tool. The victims and their lawyers were successful in mobilizing the human rights movement and raising general awareness, both domestically and internationally, of this crime against humanity. *Velásquez*

22 Velásquez Rodríguez v. Honduras, Merits, Judgment, Inter-Am. Ct. H.R. (ser. C) No. 4 (July 29, 1988).

23 *See* American Convention, *supra* note 3, art. 1 (requiring States to develop a legal order that would prevent violations of human rights or if this is not achievable, investigate, punish, and fully compensate the victims).

24 Velásquez Rodríguez v. Honduras, Merits, Judgment, Inter-Am. Ct. H.R. (ser. C) No. 4 ¶ 155 (July 29, 1988).

25 *Id.* ¶ 156 ("[P]rolonged isolation and deprivation of communication are in themselves cruel and inhumane treatment, harmful to the psychological and moral integrity of the person.").

26 *Id.*; American Convention, *supra* note 3, art. 5.

27 Velásquez Rodríguez v. Honduras, Merits, Judgment, Inter-Am. Ct. H.R. (ser. C) No. 4 ¶ 157 (July 29, 1988).

28 *Id.* ¶ 158.

Rodríguez was the first contentious case decided by an international tribunal to declare the practice of forced disappearances illegal and to successfully challenge the pervasive culture of impunity and deniability in countries in the region. By exposing the State's responsibility for this inhumane practice and rejecting a status quo characterized by repression and authoritarianism, the case helped further the goals of human rights and democracy in the region.

Prior to the Court's decision in *Velásquez Rodríguez*, international and regional bodies responded to disappearances almost solely in general terms, including by issuing resolutions and country reports addressing the broader issue within that domestic framework.[29] Most human rights instruments created before the decision did not specifically identify and individualize all the circumstances of forced disappearances, as was the case in *Velásquez Rodríguez*.

This decision, the first one adopted by the Inter-American Court in a contested case, had a great impact. The decision influenced the identification and codification of the crime of disappearances, both regionally and internationally. The *Velásquez Rodríguez* decision was the impetus for drafting and passing the Inter-American Convention on the Forced Disappearance of Persons (which incorporates the definition of disappearances used in the *Velásquez Rodríguez* case and also encompasses the crimes of kidnapping, torture, and murder).[30] The Convention was passed in 1994 and entered into force in 1996. It also contributed to the inclusion of enforced disappearances in the Rome

---

29 *See* Velásquez Rodríguez v. Honduras, Merits, Judgment, Inter-Am. Ct. H.R. (ser. C) No. 4 ¶¶ 151–153 (July 29, 1988). *See also* Juan E. Mendez & Jose Miguel Vivanco, *Disappearances and the Inter-American Court: Reflections on a Litigation Experience*, 13 HAMLINE L. REV. 507, 514–15 (1990) (explaining that the United Nations General Assembly adopted resolutions condemning forced disappearances. The United Nations Commission on Human Rights created the Working Group on Enforced and Involuntary Disappearances to assist families in determining the fate of their relatives and to establish channels of communication between the families and the governments); Inter-Am. Comm'n H.R. Rep. on Argentina, ¶ 1, OEA/Ser.L/V./II/49, doc. 19, rev. (1980); Inter-Am. Comm'n H.R. Report on Chile, OEA/Ser.L/V/II.66, doc. 17 (1985) (proving that Inter-American Commission had previously condemned the practice and urged that it be investigated and stopped); OAS G.A. Res. 666 (XIII-0/83) (Nov. 18, 1983); OAS G.A. Res. 742 (XIV-0/84) (Nov. 17, 1984) (demonstrating that the OAS General Assembly characterized the crime of disappearances as "an affront to the consciousness of the hemisphere" and a crime against humanity).

30 *See* Inter-American Convention on Forced Disappearance of Persons, June 9, 1994, OAS/Ser. P AG/doc. 3114/94 rev. 1 (*entered into force* Mar. 28, 1996). Current state parties to the Convention are the following: Argentina, Bolivia, Brazil, Chile, Colombia, Costa Rica, Ecuador, Guatemala, Honduras, Mexico, Nicaragua, Panama, Paraguay, Peru, Uruguay, and Venezuela.

Statute of the International Criminal Court (ICC)[31] and the International Convention against Disappearances.[32] The Rome Statute defines forced disappearances as a crime against humanity that is subject to the jurisdiction of the International Criminal Court. [33] These developments at the regional and international level have made forced disappearances an international crime, further strengthening a normative framework that condemns and punishes this type of inhumane behavior.

Additionally, victims and their lawyers set other important precedents in this first contested case: (1) allowing for better representation of the victims in the system, (2) increasing possibilities of proving violations of human rights and (3) broadening the notion of victims. Procedurally, only the Commission could bring a case to the Court, and the American Convention was silent as to the role of the victims and lawyers. The victims' lawyers convinced the Commission to appoint them as its legal advisors, operating under its supervision. Their broad participation in the interrogations, cross examinations of witnesses, and other legal procedures, as well as the press conferences they regularly conducted, played a pivotal role in categorizing the acts of forced disappearances as a human rights crime. Also, faced with serious limits in proving disappearances, the attorneys articulated an evidentiary standard that was further developed by the Court, and that standard allowed for circumstantial evidence to link an individual violation to a practice of gross mass violations of human rights.

The lawyers also successfully argued that violations of human rights cannot simply be "repaired" by monetary compensation. In addition to economic damages, the victims must have access to measures of satisfaction and recognition that vindicate the honor of the victims and educate the society at large. Thus, the *Velázquez* decision was the starting point of some of the most important contributions to human rights law by the Inter-American system.

In summary, thanks to the relentless work of the victims themselves, as well as their lawyers who operated in the transnational framework of the

31 Rome Statute of the International Criminal Court, art. 7(2)(i), July 17, 1998, 2187 U.N.T.S. 90.

32 International Convention for the Protection of All Persons from Enforced Disappearance, December 20, 2006, 14 IHRR 582.

33 *See* Rome Statute of the International Criminal Court, art. 7(2)(i), July 17, 1998, 2187 U.N.T.S. 90. The crime is defined as "the arrest, detention or abduction of persons by, or with the authorization, support or acquiescence of, a State or a political organization, followed by a refusal to acknowledge that deprivation of freedom or to give information on the fate or whereabouts of those persons, with the intention of removing them from the protection of the law for a prolonged period of time." *Id.*

Inter-American system, the decision in the *Velásquez Rodríguez* case contributed to the evolution of human rights norms by exposing and delegitimizing the inhumane practice of disappearances. It demonstrated that individuals unwilling to accept the state practice of forced disappearances should be entitled to bring their claims to international bodies. Further building on this decision, the Court has since noted that family members of the disappeared are often themselves direct victims of cruel, inhumane, and degrading treatment because they have been denied access to justice and have lived with the uncertainty of not knowing the whereabouts of their loved ones.[34]

The case also helped to depoliticize the human rights discourse in the hemisphere. By framing the issue in terms of human rights abuses and not politics, the case reinforced the idea that human rights apply regardless of the political context or the regime in power. By following a judicial process based on a treaty, and issuing an impartial decision grounded in the rule of law, the Court circumvented sovereignty concerns and the politics that generally accompanied human rights discussions in the hemisphere.

B Barrios Altos v. Peru (*2001*)

1 Brief Factual Overview

The case of *Barrios Altos* involves extrajudicial killings in the context of Peru's fight against terrorism. The analysis of the case is particularly significant because it addresses amnesty laws enacted by the Peruvian government for the purposes of preventing investigations of crimes and protecting human rights violators.

The events that led to this case occurred on November 3, 1991, when six armed members of the military entered a building in the Barrios Altos neighborhood in Lima, Peru, while the victims were having a fundraising party. The armed group ordered everyone to drop to the floor and opened fire indiscriminately.[35] As a result, fifteen people were killed and another four were injured. The incident was linked to the *Grupo Colina*, a division within the Peruvian army that acted as a death squad in the fight against terrorism. Information

34 *See* 19 Merchants v. Colombia, Merits, Reparations and Costs, Judgment, Inter-Am. Ct. H.R. (ser. C) No. 109, ¶ 229 (July 5, 2004); Juan Humberto Sánchez v. Honduras, Preliminary Objections, Merits, Reparations and Costs, Judgment, Inter-Am. Ct. H.R. (ser. C) No. 99, ¶ 101 (June 7, 2003); Blake v. Guatemala, Merits, Judgment, Inter-Am. Ct. H.R. (ser. C) No. 48, ¶ 38 (Jan. 22, 1999); Bámaca-Velásquez v. Guatemala, Merits, Judgment, Inter-Am. Ct. H.R. (ser. C) No. 70, ¶ 160 (Nov. 25, 2000).

35 *See* Barrios Altos v. Peru, Merits, Judgment, Inter-Am. Ct. H.R. (ser. C) No. 75, ¶ 2(b) (Mar. 14, 2001).

gathered later from different sources suggested that prior to this incident a series of terrorist attacks attributed to Sendero Luminoso (the Shining Path) may have triggered the military attack. The validity of these claims, however, was never proven before the Inter-American Court.

Although the events occurred in 1991, the first judicial investigation into the incident did not occur until 1995. This investigation was then suspended after the Peruvian Congress issued Law No. 26479, which "exonerated members of the army, police forces and also civilians who had violated human rights or taken part in such violations from 1980 to 1995 from responsibility."[36]

After several attacks on the constitutionality of the amnesty laws, and fearing that a judicial decision striking down the laws was forthcoming, the Peruvian Congress passed Law No. 26492, "directed at interfering with legal action in the *Barrios Altos* case," adding that the amnesty law could not be reviewed by any judicial authority. Consequently, judicial actions challenging the constitutionality of the amnesty laws in question were abandoned and pending investigations were closed.

Victims and their lawyers, supported by the legal staff of non-governmental organizations, brought this before the Inter-American system in 1995. Peru's first response to the case was to defend the amnesty laws, claiming that they were exceptional measures adopted based on the urgent need to fight terrorism in the country. The Commission rejected this argument and filed a petition with the Court on June 8, 2000 in light of Peru's refusal to investigate the claims and compensate the victims.

In the proceedings before the Court, the Peruvian government, after unsuccessfully trying to withdraw its recognition of the Court's contentious jurisdiction, recognized its international responsibility in the case for the violations of Articles 4 (right to life), 5 (right to personal integrity), 8 (right to due process), and 25 (access to justice) of the American Convention. The Court additionally declared that Articles 1 and 2 of the Convention had been violated. The Court, again reacting favorably to the efforts of the victims, lawyers, and the Commission, expanded on the incompatibility of amnesty laws with the Convention, stating that,

> [t]his Court considers that all amnesty provisions, provisions on prescription and establishment of measures designed to eliminate responsibility are inadmissible, because they are intended to prevent the investigation and punishment of those responsible for serious human rights

---

36 *Id.* ¶ 2(i).

> violations such as torture, extrajudicial summary or arbitrary executions, and forced disappearances, all of them prohibited because they violate non-derogable rights recognized by international human rights law.[37]

Furthermore, the Court added that "self-amnesty laws lead to the defenselessness of victims and perpetuate impunity; therefore, they are manifestly incompatible with the aims and spirit of the Convention."[38]

2 Impact on Social Change

The Inter-American Court's rejection of amnesty laws as "manifestly inconsistent" with the Convention has had significant effects in the region. Non-governmental organizations and lawyers have used this decision to strengthen their arguments against amnesty laws. For example, in 2005, Argentina's Supreme Court ruled on the unconstitutionality of amnesty and pardon laws based on Inter-American law and jurisprudence.[39] Further, in Chile, the courts adopted the theory of "the continuing crime" (*delito continuado*) as a way to exclude the application of amnesty laws in a context where the latter had been declared in violation of the Inter-American human rights norms.[40]

The jurisprudence of the Inter-American system on this issue has also had a broader impact given the pervasiveness of impunity in the region, which can shield offenders from investigation and punishment through both the adoption of amnesty laws and also *de facto* measures. Impunity is indivisible: it pervades the legal system as a whole, sending the message that even the most abhorrent crimes can be shielded from investigation or punishment. In fighting to reject amnesty laws, victims and human rights defenders persuaded the Court to uphold the duty to investigate and punish human rights violations, as stated in Article 1.1 of the American Convention. The efforts of the attorneys in this case, and of all other human rights advocates involved, led the Court to its decision, which reinforced that individuals need to live in a system that secures and guarantees protection of their internationally-protected rights. Impunity directly prevents fulfillment of that State obligation.

---

37 *Id.* ¶ 41.

38 *Id.* ¶ 43.

39 *See* Argentine Supreme Court, Recurso de hecho deducido por la defensa de Julio Hector Simon en la causa Simon, Julio Hector y otros s/privacion ilegitima de la libertad, etc., Causa No. 17.768, Judgment, June 14, 2005.

40 *See* Claudio Grossman, *The Inter-American System of Human Rights: Challenges for the Future*, 83 IND. L. J. 1267, 1276 (2008).

C Mayagna (Sumo) Awas Tingni Community v. Nicaragua (*2001*)

1 Brief Factual Overview

The Awas Tingni, an indigenous community of approximately 630 individuals, have inhabited land on the Atlantic coast of Nicaragua for generations. That land is rich in timber and other natural resources. For more than half a century, the tribe had requested that the government demarcate their land. Nonetheless, Nicaragua had failed to do so.

The concerns of the community regarding land titling and demarcation intensified when the government of Nicaragua granted Maderas y Derivados de Nicaragua S.A. (MADENSA), a Dominican company, permission to enter the Awas Tingni's lands and inventory the tropical forest resources in preparation for large-scale logging. In December 1993, a concession for logging on approximately 43,000 hectares of land was finalized with MADENSA. At the time, the World Wildlife Fund and the University of Iowa College of Law assisted the Awas Tingni community in negotiations with the government and MADENSA. As a result, an agreement was signed in May 1994, providing for economic benefits for the community. Additionally, the government committed itself to commencing the process of identifying, demarcating and titling the lands.

The government's commitment to this process proved illusory, as it was already engaged in discussions with Sol del Caribe (SOLCARSA), another logging company from South Korea, in a similar project. When SOLCARSA won a concession to log Awas Tingni land, the community decided to take legal action, both domestically and internationally.

After several attempts, the community managed to get SOLCARSA's concession revoked in domestic courts. However, the titling and demarcation of the community lands were still pending. The lack of government cooperation in this regard and its failure to comply with the Commission's recommendations guaranteed that the Commission would bring the case to the Inter-American Court. The petition requested that the Court order Nicaragua to establish and implement a procedure that would result in the prompt demarcation and specific recognition of Awas Tingni's communal lands, and to provide monetary compensation to the Awas Tingni for the infringement of their property rights.

The Court's proceedings illustrated the fundamental difference between the government's and the indigenous people's views about the ownership of land and resources. The Nicaraguan government advanced the traditional paradigm of state "dominance over territory, a perspective in which is absent a desire to understand accurately and fully the dimensions and significance of the indigenous presence,"[41] while the Awas Tingni stressed communal ownership of the land based on their traditional fishing and hunting use since time immemorial.

In the end, the Court accepted the Awas Tingni's claim and ruled that the community was entitled to the recognition of property rights over their lands. The Court found that Nicaragua had failed to guarantee the rights expressly recognized in its constitution and legislation, and that there were no adequate and effective remedies for indigenous peoples to claim such rights in the domestic arena. The Court thus found that the failure to implement the rights expressly granted by a State's domestic legal order violated the American Convention.

Additionally, the lawyers in the case successfully argued, and the Court accordingly found, a violation of the right to property set forth in Article 21 of the Convention. In its analysis of Article 21 the Court further found, inter alia, that: 1) there is a right to communal property; and 2) indigenous peoples are entitled to their traditional lands based on their use (e.g., fishing and hunting) since time immemorial. For the Court a narrower conception of rights in domestic law did not trump broader treaty obligations.[42] According to the Court:

> Through an evolutionary interpretation of international instruments for the protection of human rights, taking into account applicable norms of interpretation and pursuant to article 29(b) of the Convention—which precludes a restrictive interpretation of rights—it is the opinion of this Court that article 21 of the Convention protects the right to property in a sense which includes, among others, the rights of members of the indigenous communities within the framework of communal property, which is also recognized by the Constitution of Nicaragua.[43]

Reacting favorably to the efforts of the Awas Tingi community and to those of their advocates, the Court stressed that "the close ties of indigenous people with the land must be recognized and understood as the fundamental basis of their cultures, their spiritual life, their integrity, and their economic survival."[44] It concluded that "[a]s a result of customary practices, possession of the land should suffice for indigenous communities lacking real title to property

41 S. James Anaya & Claudio M. Grossman, *The Case of Awas Tingni v. Nicaragua: A New Step in the International Law of Indigenous Peoples*, 19 ARIZ. J. INT'L & COMP. L. 1, 11 (2002).

42 The Mayagna (Sumo) Awas Tingni Community v. Nicaragua, Merits, Reparations and Costs, Judgment, Inter-Am. Ct. H.R. (ser. C) No. 79 (Aug. 31, 2001).

43 *Id.* ¶ 148.

44 *Id.* ¶ 149.

of the land to obtain official recognition of that property, and for consequent registration."[45]

2 Impact on Social Change

The Awas Tingi community, in the process of defending its native lands, mobilized non-governmental organizations that supported the rights of indigenous populations in the region, thus leading to the first international decision to recognize the right to communal property. It was also the first international decision to recognize indigenous law and custom as sources of enforceable rights and obligations. The Court, having been persuaded by the attorneys in the case, reiterated the right of indigenous peoples to live freely within their territory, and acknowledged their legal, cultural, and social background as an indigenous community. Since the decision in the *Awas Tingni* case, several cases before the Court have recognized the special character of indigenous populations and their collective rights, based on the American Convention.[46]

In addition, the social exclusion of indigenous peoples—including relatively high rates of illiteracy and poverty in comparison to the rest of society—has led to the Commission's creation of a Special Rapporteur on the Rights of Indigenous Peoples.[47] The purpose of that position is to promote the recognition of the rights of indigenous groups by setting standards and initiating cases before the Inter-American organs. The landmark Awas Tingni case codified the rights of indigenous populations in the Inter-American system and additionally supported the work of the Special Working Group to prepare the proposed UN Declaration on the Rights of Indigenous Peoples.

---

45 *Id.* ¶ 151.

46 *See, e.g.*, Case of the Saramaka People. v. Suriname, Preliminary Objections, Merits, Reparations and Costs, Judgment, Inter-Am. Ct. H.R. (ser. C) No. 172 (2007); Case of the Yakye Axa Indigenous Community v. Paraguay, Interpretation of the Judgment of the Merits, Reparations, and Costs, Judgment, Inter-Am. Ct. H.R. (ser. C) No. 142 (2006); Case of the Sawhoyamaxa Indigenous Community v. Paraguay, Inter-Am. Ct. H.R. (ser. C) No. 146 (2006); Case of the Yakye Axa Indigenous Community v. Paraguay, Merits, Reparations and Costs, Judgment, Inter-Am. Ct. H.R. (ser. C) No. 125 (2005); Case of Yatama v. Nicaragua, Preliminary Objections, Merits, Reparations and Costs, Judgment, Inter-Am. Ct. H.R. (ser. C) No. 127 (2005); Case of the Plan de Sánchez Massacre v. Guatemala, Reparations, Judgment, Inter-Am. Ct. H.R. (ser. C) No. 105 (2004); Inter-Am. Comm'n H.R., Annual Report, ch. 2, at ¶¶ 55–63, OEA/Ser.L/V/II.130, doc. 22 (Dec. 29, 2007).

47 *See Judgments of the Inter-American Court*, ORGANIZATION OF AMERICAN STATES, http://www.oas.org/en/iachr/indigenous/decisions/ia_court_hr.asp (listing all judgments of the Inter-American Court involving rights of indigenous people from 1991 to 2014).

D General Usón-Ramírez v. Venezuela

1 Brief Factual Overview

On March 30, 2004, a fire erupted in a detention cell at Fort Mara, Venezuela. The fire, which killed two soldiers,[48] was believed to have been intentional.[49] Following these atrocious deaths, on April 16 and May 10, 2004, respectively, retired General Francisco Usón Ramírez commented on the possibility that these fires may have been intentional during a television interview about the National Armed Forces. The National Armed Forces then sued Mr. Usón Ramírez for slander in military court, leading to Mr. Usón Ramírez's deprivation of liberty, as he was sentenced to five years and six months in prison.

The General and his attorneys, supported by the Inter-American Commission on Human Rights, brought this case before the Inter-American Court on Human Rights on October 21, 2008. The main conflict in the case was reconciling the General's right to freedom of expression and the Armed Forces' purported inherent right to the defense of their honor under Venezuelan domestic laws.[50] The General's attorneys successfully argued that the Venezuelan law under which he was sentenced did not have a legitimate purpose, despite it being successfully codified in accordance with domestic procedures.

In November 2009, the Inter-American Court on Human Rights found that the Venezuelan contempt law under which the former General was convicted of "slander against the National Armed Forces" was far too vague to meet the legality threshold of Article 13 of the American Convention.[51] The Court ruled that the statute failed to meet the legality requirement because it did not clearly establish the elements of the crime, nor did it specify the *mens rea* needed for conviction. Further, the harsh criminal sanction against Usón-Ramírez was disproportionate to the goal of protecting the military's honor, according to the Court, which added that proportionality should guide the behavior of the state when exercising its punitive power.[52]

The Court emphasized that it is in the public's best interest that the government be freely subject to public scrutiny.[53] The Court emphasized that

48 Usón Ramírez v. Venezuela, Case 12.554, Inter-Am. Comm'n H.R., ¶ 39, n.14 (July 25, 2008).

49 *Id.* (stating that the Venezuelan Fire Department issued a statement indicating the fire could have been intentional).

50 Usón-Ramírez v. Venezuela, Preliminary Objections, Merits, Reparations and Costs, Judgment, Inter-Am. Ct. H.R. (ser. C) No. 193, ¶ 45 (Nov. 20, 2009).

51 *Id.* ¶¶ 38, 56–57.

52 *Id.* ¶ 87.

53 *Id.* ¶ 83.

opinions and reports about the government should be allowed into the public discourse with great latitude to foster a "truly democratic society."[54]

Unfortunately, the Court did not rule that criminal sanctions for speech violated the American Convention.[55] The Court found that Venezuela does have a legitimate interest in protecting the military's honor and that imposing some liability on freedom of expression may be justified.[56] The Court also did not exclude criminal sanctions for slander against government entities; it simply set the bar high.[57] To date, however, the Court has not, in any of its decisions, ruled that contempt laws—laws such as the one in dispute here, which criminalize "offensive" expression directed at public officials—are *per se* in violation of the American Convention, but in no concrete case did the Court find that such laws have been justified when applied to an individual. [58] Additionally, the Convention establishes rights for individuals, such as the protection of honor. Accordingly, institutions, including the armed forces, are not covered by the Convention. Accordingly, the Court should exclude situations where expression of an opinion is charged as "slander against the National Armed Forces," as in the Usón-Ramírez case.[59] Legitimate national security concerns in the framework of a democratic society could be taken into account for the purposes of determining liability, but there is no place in the American Convention to resort to honor concepts in order to protect institutions.[60]

2 Impact on Social Change

Following this trial, Venezuela denounced the American Convention on Human Rights via a letter to the Secretary General of the OAS dated September 6, 2012. Despite Venezuela's withdrawal from the Court's jurisdiction, this particular case portrayed the inherent value of the regional human rights system in the narrative of fighting for human rights. In this case, the victim and his

54 *Id.*

55 *Id.*

56 *Id.* ¶ 66.

57 *Id.* ¶¶ 56, 66, 69, 83, 87; *see also* Tristán-Donoso v. Panama, Preliminary Objections, Merits, Reparations and Costs Judgment, Inter-Am. Ct. H.R. (ser. C) No. 193, ¶ 112 (Jan. 27, 2009) (reiterating the same jurisprudential approach).

58 *See also id.*; Ivcher-Bronstein v. Peru, Merits, Reparations and Costs, Judgment, Inter-Am. Ct. H.R. (ser. C) No. 74 (Feb. 6, 2001); "The Last Temptation of Christ" (Olmedo-Bustos et al.) v. Chile, Merits, Reparations and Costs, Judgment, Inter-Am. Ct. H.R. (ser. C) No. 73 (Feb. 5, 2001).

59 Usón-Ramírez v. Venezuela, Preliminary Objections, Merits, Reparations and Costs, Judgment, Inter-Am. Ct. H.R. (ser. C) No. 193, ¶ 38 (Nov. 20, 2009).

60 *See* American Convention, *supra* note 3, art. 13(2)(b), 27.

lawyers denounced the role of military tribunals in judging civilians and exposed disproportionate sanctions, which furthered the narrative that issues of public importance should not be censored and that freedom of expression is a "cornerstone upon which the very existence of a democratic society rests."[61] The approach taken by authorities towards freedom of expression serves as a social barometer of what direction change might take. Traditionally, serious economic, political, social, and security problems have been used to justify authoritarianism and validate the rejection of a pluralistic view of society for which freedom of expression is essential. In contrast to strong-men who govern without checks and balances, or the case of political or military vanguards who purport to "lead their nations or people," a human rights framework offers an alternative that the rule of law, including the right to free expression, represents both the values of human dignity and a path of action to confront societal problems.

IV Conclusion

The cases summarized in this paper are evidence of a process where victims, their lawyers, and NGOs worked to achieve justice and influence social developments through impact litigation, relying on regional human rights norms and procedures in a context where, domestically, all venues have been closed. These various cases involved specific societal issues of crucial significance, including forced disappearances, impunity and amnesty laws, the rights of indigenous populations, and limits on freedom of expression. Exposing and delegitimizing the criminal practice of forced disappearances reduced the political space for dictatorial regimes to resort to criminal behavior as a way of annihilating and intimidating their opposition.[62] It led also, ultimately, to processes of democratic transition that those dictatorial regimes could not survive. While the rejection of amnesty laws has not resulted in the imprisonment of every human rights oppressor, its message has not lacked significance. There are hundreds of human rights violators now serving sentences following a process of accountability, driven by international norms and strengthening internal domestic efforts to reject impunity.[63] The decision analyzed in this

---

61 Compulsory Membership in an Association Prescribed by Law for the Practice of Journalism (Arts. 13 and 29 American Convention on Human Rights), Advisory Opinion OC-5/85, Inter-Am. Ct. H.R. (ser. A) No. 5, ¶ 70 (Nov. 13, 1985).

62 *See supra* section III(A).

63 *See supra* section III(B).

paper regarding the rights of indigenous populations has brought further legitimacy to the territorial claims of indigenous populations by solidly grounding them in law.[64] The decision regarding freedom of expression mentioned in this article, as well as other decisions adopted in the Inter-American System in this domain, has helped to develop democratic values in the Western Hemisphere, limiting the ability of States to curtail people's ability to freely express their ideas.[65]

In some cases, the efforts of victims and their attorneys and the Court's decisions never translated into immediate action or immediate change. Rather, the decisions were part of a process of delegitimizing regimes and creating space for political and legal action that sometimes spread over a vast period of time. These efforts provided an important narrative that strengthened the ability of internal domestic groups to affect change.

The reliance on legal norms and the adjudicatory process served to depoliticize many issues, pushing the dialogue to an evidence-based, technical, and arguably more objective forum that allowed significant progress in shaping the region's political landscape. The spill-over effects of relying on hard international law norms thus went beyond the individual cases to a general reinforcement of the rule of law and democracy. More specifically, some of the norms announced by the regional system have also influenced the development of domestic laws, regional treaties, and international instruments like the UN Declaration on the Rights of Indigenous Peoples.

However, the regional and international human rights systems continue to be somewhat limited by the existence of two conflicting visions of human rights: one where human rights are seen as the instrument for achieving positive social change, and another where traditional human rights frameworks at the international level are considered a threat to a State's sovereignty, as exposed in *Usón-Ramírez v. Venezuela*. The evolution of the Inter-American System as a forum for expressing the aspirations of society has provided important space for action while legitimizing laws empowering actors fighting for social change.

The cases discussed above would not have been possible without the contribution of civil society organizations and their lawyers. As noted before, a community of practice consisting of a variety of stakeholders in the system, such as NGO leaders, public interest lawyers, activists, and academics, emerged using the mechanisms existing in the Inter-American System to expose societal

---

64 *See supra* section III(C).

65 *See supra* section III(D).

issues through an international framework and influence the national domain. While there are legitimate differences among civil society actors in how they view the system, they all resort to it to expose domestic situations, channeling claims through the system and seeking implementation of the system's decisions.[66] The attorneys and NGOs zealously pushed to expand the space for civil society through the Court's jurisprudence. The quality of their legal work, the diligence and rigor of their preparatory work and their ability to act transnationally, among other factors, led to the expansion of democratic values in the Western Hemisphere, and inspired such an expansion across the globe.

These efforts were by no means easy. There were instances where witnesses were threatened and even seriously harmed or killed in an effort to silence them.[67] The victims' representatives, however, continued to fight zealously not only for their clients, but also for the larger goal of promoting valuable social change and seeking full State compliance with the decisions adopted by the system's organs. In this respect, it is important to note that compliance with reparations and compensation decisions have been easier than measures of investigation and punishment of violations of human rights.[68] Additionally, the system can be criticized for the slow handling of cases requiring NGOs to tolerate delays in processing their petitions, and in granting new measures that have yet to be finalized. As the cases rarely finish with a decision—compliance with judgments is heavily monitored—their role and dedication were instrumental to the social changes perpetuated by the Inter-American Court's decisions in the four cases outlined above.

---

66 It is also important to note that different government structures also have shown different positions involving the system (e.g. last year after the conclusion of the process to strengthen the system, there were some governments that wanted to reduce the ability of the Commission to enact its own regulations.) In addition, within governments themselves, different actors show different degrees of acceptance of the Commission and Court's decisions.

67 *See Clients: Zenaida Velásquez Rodriguez*, THE CENTER FOR JUSTICE AND ACCOUNTABILITY, http://cja.org/what-we-do/litigation/reyes-v-lopez-grijalba/clients/ ("Witnesses scheduled to testify against the government began to receive death threats. Although the IACHR pleaded with the government to protect them, two witnesses were killed. Miguel Angel Pavon was assassinated following his testimony about the pattern of abuses perpetrated by security forces in Honduras. Sergeant José Isaias Vilorio, a member of the security forces who may have been involved in Manfredo's disappearance, was killed on a public street 13 days before he was scheduled to testify.").

68 For example, if we look at the use of amnesty laws in the region throughout history, we have seen that immediate compliance was not achieved but the issue remained valid and strengthened by the legitimacy of a decision under the Inter-American system. As a result, we see how societies like Chile, Argentina, and Peru, that resisted the illegality of amnesty, ended up abolishing or re-interpreting their position later on.

Further, some states, under the pretext of "strengthening the system", attempt instead to weaken it. Their attempts included (1) shifting the role of the Commission from mostly handling cases to engaging in educational activities; (2) limiting the power of the Commission to issue provisional measures; (3) efforts to move the headquarters of the Commission from Washington D.C., the site of the OAS, to other countries; (4) limiting resources to the system as a whole, thus constricting the ability of the Commission and the Court to react promptly and handle petitions in a timely fashion. As a result of the latter, the President of the Commission, James Cavallaro, cancelled two sessions of hearings, its 159th and 160th sessions, which had been scheduled for July and October of 2016. The financial support of States has always been one of the biggest limits in allowing the Inter-American Commission and Court to carry out their mandates. To put this issue in perspective, while the Council of Europe receives 40% of the total budget of the Union, the Inter-American human rights system receives only 6% of the total budget of the OAS.

The Commission and the Court, aided by external advocates, have been generally successful in stopping attempts to weaken the system. Crucial in this respect has been the role of states who opposed extreme measures designed to weaken the system, as well as the leadership of the current Secretary General of the OAS, Luis Almagro. The mobilization of civil society has been essential to limit what they see as a critical space to channel societal demands for justice when domestically it has not been possible to prevent or properly repair human rights violations.

CHAPTER 4

Children's Rights: Social Change through the Application of Hard and Soft International Law

*Ann Skelton**

I Introduction

This chapter begins with a detailed discussion of hard and soft international law pertaining to children, a background necessary to understand the three case studies that describe campaigns and strategies to bring about social change through the application of hard and soft international law. The case studies all relate in some way to the criminal justice system. The first tells the story of how a gap in the Convention on the Rights of the Child (CRC) pertaining to children of imprisoned parents has been filled through borrowing from regional charters, general comments, resolutions and jurisprudence. The second case study is about the minimum age of criminal responsibility. Again, a weak area in the CRC, bolstered through a General Comment which had good and bad effects, leading to a new wave of debates about how to approach the minimum age question. The final case study tells the surprising story of the use of the CRC by the U. S. Supreme Court to outlaw the death penalty and limit life without parole for offenders who were children at the time of the offence—this despite the fact that the United States remains the only country in the world that has not ratified the CRC.

II Overview of International Law Pertaining to the Child

A *Convention on the Rights of the Child*

1 History of Children's Rights and the Making of the Convention on the Rights of the Child

The Convention on the Rights of the Child was adopted by the United Nations General Assembly in 1989—the first comprehensive hard international law instrument on children's rights. The idea that children were deserving of special

* Professor of Law at the University of Pretoria, holder of the UNESCO Chair: Education Law in Africa, and a member of the UN Committee on the Rights of the Child.

 | DOI:10.1163/9789004417021_005

protection in international law had germinated almost 70 years earlier, when British social pioneer Eglantyne Jebb[1] penned a document which became the Geneva Declaration of the Rights of the Child, adopted by the League of Nations in 1924.[2] It contained only five briefly stated principles, focused largely on protection of the child. This was followed, thirty-five years later, by a United Nations Declaration on the Rights of the Child. This document contained ten principles, and was more 'rights' oriented. Adam Lopatka, who chaired the working group that later drafted the CRC observes that:

> In the years between the two world wars, a contemporary concept of childhood was developed. At its core is the conviction that the child is an autonomous person who has his or her own needs, interests and rights; and that he or she is not only an object of care and concern but also a subject whose interests and rights should be respected.[3]

This idea was then taken up and developed by sociologists,[4] and became the subject of child rights movements.[5] But that is only half of the story. While some activists pushed for stronger child rights with increased autonomy or agency in mind, others wanted rights to protect the idea of childhood as a phase of innocence.[6] Phillip Veerman has pointed out that during the twentieth century

---

1 Eglantyne Jebb (1876–1928) founded Save the Children in a public launch at the Albert Hall in 1919. The initial focus was on children affected by the First World War, but Jebb soon turned her attention to making child protection a worldwide issue. *See further* CLARE MULLEY, THE WOMAN WHO SAVED THE CHILDREN: A BIOGRAPHY OF ELGANTYNE JEBB, THE FOUNDER OF SAVE THE CHILDREN (2009).

2 BRIAN MILNE, RIGHTS OF THE CHILD: 25 YEARS AFTER THE ADOPTION OF THE UN CONVENTION 2–3, 163 (2015), points out that calls for a charter for children had been made even earlier by Janusz Korczak (a Polish Jewish paediatrician and author whose real name was Henryk Goldszmit). Korczak ran an orphanage in a Warsaw ghetto and was last seen accompanying 190 children to Treblinka; a court has recently declared that he died on 7 August 1942. *See further* JTA, *Jewish Doctor Janusz Korczak Died With 190 Children at Treblinka*, FORWARD (Mar. 30, 2015), http://forward.com/news/breaking-news/217654/jewish-doctor-janusz-korczak-died-with-190-childre/.

3 OHCHR, LEGISLATIVE HISTORY OF THE CONVENTION ON THE RIGHTS OF THE CHILD (2007) at xxxvii, in the foreword by Adam Lopatka, http://www.ohchr.org/Documents/Publications/LegislativeHistorycrc1en.pdf.

4 THE SOCIOLOGY OF CHILDHOOD: ESSENTIAL READINGS LONDON BATSFORD ACADEMIC AND EDUCATIONAL (Chris Jenks ed., 1982).

5 THE RIGHTS OF CHILDREN (Bob Franklin ed., 1986).

6 The different arguments are discussed by PHILIP VEERMAN, THE RIGHTS OF THE CHILD AND THE CHANGING IMAGE OF CHILDHOOD 8–10 (1992).

those seeking to improve children's rights shifted from the language of 'needs' towards the language of 'rights'. In a fascinating discussion of the process that began in 1948 and culminated in 1959 in the UN Declaration on the Rights of the Child, Veerman demonstrates that the idea for a binding charter was promoted by the communist countries. "The Russian representative, Mr Sapozhnikov, expounded that the Declaration on the Rights of the Child should not only include general principles but also duties of the State and proceedings leading to the realisation of the rights."[7] The representative of the United States in the Third Committee complained that "Communist delegates pressed for welfare-state provisions." Most of these amendments were rejected on the ground that interference in the domestic affairs of individual countries must be avoided. The Soviet motions sought to provide for free health services and free education at every level, and to outlaw child labour.[8] The United States made it clear that they would only support the declaration "in absence of any specific provision for implementation and international enforcement."[9] The Chinese delegate characterised the debate as being a divide between those who viewed the child as being a responsibility of the state, and those who saw him as being a responsibility of the individual.[10] In the end, the Western view prevailed, and resulted in the non-binding, rather weakly stated UN Declaration on the Rights of the Child. But it was a step forward, and it led to consensus building on the nature of children's rights over the coming years.

Children's rights awareness slowly began to grow, and the need for a binding treaty on children's rights became increasingly apparent. According to Veerman, the 1960s was an active time for the development of child rights advocacy in the United States,[11] including class action suits being brought by the Youth Law Centre in San Francisco in the late 1970s.[12] The children's liberation movement flourished during the 1960s and 70s. This was a part of the children's rights movement that demanded agency for children through the right to vote, work, choose their own guardians, and have access to information.[13] In 1973 the International Labour Organisation adopted Convention No. 138 concerning

7 *Id.* at 164.

8 Paul Hofmann, *UN Body Backs Childs' Charter*, N. Y. TIMES (Oct. 20, 1959), *cited in* VEERMAN, *supra* note 6, at 165.

9 *Id.* at 164.

10 *Id.*

11 C. Johnson, *Child Advocacy in the United States: The Children's Defence Fund*, *in* UNDERSTANDING CHILDREN'S RIGHTS 187, 187–98 (Eugeen Verhellen ed., 1996).

12 Veerman points to the work of attorney Mark Soler, who worked on juvenile justice cases.

13 JOHN C. HOLT, ESCAPE FROM CHILDHOOD: THE NEEDS AND RIGHTS OF CHILDREN (2013); RICHARD E. FARSON, A BILL OF RIGHTS FOR CHILDREN (1974).

the minimum age for admission to employment. Although binding on signatory states, this Convention covered a very narrow issue. It may, however, have moved states towards a positive mode regarding hard international law commitments to children. As far as informal standard setting was concerned, several regional and local charters of children's rights had been written,[14] and the establishment of the world's first ombudsman for children, in Norway, was under discussion.[15] However, there is little evidence of co-ordination of these efforts and some writers who were close to the process view the gap between the 1959 Declaration and the initiation of a binding Convention as a period of silence.[16]

Following a United Nations resolution,[17] 1979 was declared "The International Year of the Child"—it marked 20 years since the adoption of the 1959 Declaration. Cantwell observes that the International Year of the child sharpened the focus of debates about children's rights and instigated "an unprecedented amount of information on child rights issues' into the public domain."[18] In that year, Poland submitted a proposal for a convention on the rights of the child, which was adopted by the General Assembly at its 34th session. Some of the 'official' reasons why, by this time, there was a need for hard rather than soft international law regarding children can be gleaned from a resolution issued by the Human Rights Council on the "Question of a Convention on the Rights of the Child."[19] The resolution gives several reasons why it viewed the drafting of a comprehensive, binding convention on children's rights to be a priority. Firstly, nineteen years had elapsed since the Declaration on the Rights of the Child and states parties had developed socio-economic policies taking that declaration into account—so presumably this meant they were now ready to take on obligations. Secondly, there was a need to strengthen the care and wellbeing of children worldwide. Thirdly, there was a special need to assist children

---

14 *See, e.g.*, The White House Children's Bill of Rights, 1970; The Charter of Rights of the Arab Child (adopted by the Jordanian cabinet in 1984); Declaration of the Rights of the Child in Israel (1979).

15 Malfrid G. Flekkoy, *An Ombudsman for Children: Quality Requirements*, *in* Verhellen (ed.), *supra* note 11, at 175.

16 Geraldine Van Beuren, *International Children's Rights: A Stop-go History*, *in* Verhellen (ed.), *supra* note 11, at 313; Nigel Cantwell, *The Convention on the Rights of the Child, Vini, Vici … Et Vinci? in* Verhellen (ed.), *supra* note 11, at 386.

17 G.A. Res. 31/169, (Dec. 21, 1976).

18 Nigel Cantwell, *The Origins, Significance and Process of the Drafting of the CRC*, *in* CONVENTION ON THE RIGHTS OF THE CHILD: GUIDE TO THE TRAVAUX PERPARATOIRES 19, 21 (Sharon Detrick ed.,1992).

19 Commission on Human Rights Res. 29 (XXXIV) (March 8, 1978).

in developing countries. Cantwell points out that a move had already begun within the UN to provide for 'special rights' over and above those in the Universal Declaration, for vulnerable groups such as women and the disabled, and that this provided support for the idea of a children's rights treaty.

Despite this apparently fertile soil, the proposal for a binding convention was not initially met with much enthusiasm, from either states or non-governmental organisations. The delegate for the International Union for Child Welfare (one of the largest child rights NGOs at the time) was dubious about a binding convention. Speaking in the discussion in the Commission on Human Rights,[20] she pointed out that the Geneva Declaration of the Rights of the Child promulgated in 1924 had taken six years to achieve its unanimous acceptance. She was also concerned that at the time that the UN Declaration on the Rights of the Child had been adopted in 1959, many African countries had been colonies, and she was concerned about whether, as independent nations, they would agree to a binding Convention. Too hasty a process, she said, could possibly exclude eighty percent of the worlds' population, and deprive them of the few rights they had.[21] Cantwell recalls that the NGOs were not enthusiastic because they were worried about moving from a situation where there was wide acceptance of the 1959 Declaration—towards a situation of uncertainty about whether a Convention that superseded the Declaration would be ratified by sufficient nations. The NGOs wanted a conference to be able to discuss the suggestion of a binding Convention. They supported Canada in asking that more time be taken so that better consensus could be reached.[22] Kelly Weisberg recorded the concern that a Convention, though binding, could weaken the moral force of the 1959 Declaration, but she acknowledged that rejecting the idea of a Convention, once the UN had resolved to draft one, would also do harm.[23] UNICEF made no contribution to the debate at that time—Van Beuren observed that instead of roaring like a lion in support of child rights as the sector had come to expect it to, it squeaked like a mouse.[24] Cantwell confirms this, but records that UNICEF's "total lack of

20 U.N. Doc. E/CN.4/SR1471 (Mar. 13, 1978).

21 Mrs. Underhill (International Union of Child Welfare) quoted in the report of the Discussion in the Commission on Human Rights in OHCHR, LEGISLATIVE HISTORY OF THE CONVENTION ON THE RIGHTS OF THE CHILD (2007) at sec1:42.

22 Nigel Cantwell, *18 Candles: The Convention on the Rights of the Child Reaches Majority*, OHCHR, http://www.ohchr.org/Documents/Publications/crc18.pdf.

23 Kelly Weisberg, *The Rights Of The Child in the Western World*, 1978 REV. OF THE INT'L COMMISSION OF JURISTS 21, 43–51, *cited in* VEERMAN, *supra* note 6.

24 Van Beuren, *supra* note 16, at 316.

interest in the exercise was nonetheless happily to be remedied before the end of the drafting process."[25]

Cynthia Price Cohen provides a substantive reason for the lukewarm response to the resolution.[26] She observes that the draft Convention which had been tabled by Poland as part of their proposal for a Convention was very similar to the 1959 Declaration. At the initial discussion, several states pointed out that it contained many deficiencies, and that a new Convention would have to be more comprehensive. This led to the Commission rejecting the first draft because it was too vague to be legally enforceable. Poland then drafted a second model Convention which was significantly different, being double in length, with twenty substantive articles. This document was used as a guide for further drafting, although all the articles were amended, and several others were added.[27]

An open-ended working group of member states was established and began its work in 1979. Initially, state participation in the drafting process was weak. NGOs were involved from the beginning, but it was not until 1983 that they consolidated their efforts by establishing an NGO *ad hoc* group on the drafting of the Convention, with logistical assistance from UNICEF's Geneva office. Gradually, enthusiasm for the process began to build, and it is now widely recognised that the NGOs played a highly significant role in the drafting process.

The working group, chaired by Adam Lopakta of Poland, operated on the basis of consensus, which caused the drafting process to be slow and, according to Cantwell, caused some proposals to be abandoned, even though there was a clear majority supporting them. However, the positive outcome of this approach was that it meant the draft text finally submitted by the working group was unanimously agreed, except for the issue of financial support for the committee on the rights of the child. This facilitated the acceptance of the Convention by the UN system, and may have contributed to its subsequent ratification successes.[28]

Ten years after the working group began drafting, the final version was transmitted through the Economic and Social Council. On November 20, 1989 (the thirtieth anniversary of the 1959 Declaration on the Rights of the Child) the General Assembly adopted the United Nations Convention on the Rights of

25 Cantwell, *supra* note 18, at 21.

26 Cynthia P. Cohen, *Drafting of the United Nations Convention on the Rights of the Child, in* Verhellen (ed.), *supra* note 11, at 325.

27 Poland also submitted another more carefully drafted version to the 1980 meeting of the open-ended working group.

28 Cantwell, *supra* note 22, at 22–23.

the Child (hereafter CRC), and it entered into force on September 2, 1990. Apart from being the first comprehensive binding instrument on children's rights, the CRC was also notable for the fact that it was the first treaty that brought together social, economic and cultural rights with political and civil rights, all in the same instrument—and treated them as indivisible.[29] The CRC was fundamentally different from the earlier declarations in that it viewed children not as passive recipients of special care and treatment, but as rights bearers.

2 Ratification and Legal Status

The CRC has been an unrivalled success in terms of ratification. Ratification was rapid and is now near universal. On October 1, 2015 Somalia became the 196th state to ratify the Convention, leaving the United States the only country in the world that has not ratified it.[30] The legal status of the CRC, like that of all treaties, differs from state to state. A study published by Child Rights International Network (CRIN) in January 2016 found that ninety-four countries have fully incorporated the CRC into national law, while a further twenty-nine have incorporated it with reservations that have a limiting effect. Just under half of the 196 countries that have ratified allow the CRC to be directly enforced in the courts, which allows children to challenge laws and practices that violate their rights under the CRC. Many other countries use the CRC as a tool for interpretation of national law and practices by courts of law.[31] The CRC has been interpreted and augmented by Optional Protocols and General Comments issued by the Committee on the Rights of the Child. The impact of hard and soft international laws relating to children's rights in the courts will be discussed in more detail below.

B *Other Binding Treaties That Directly Affect Children's Rights*

Children benefit from general provisions in many other human rights treaties.[32] The only other public international law conventions that have been developed dealing solely with children's rights at an international level are the

---

29 *Id.*

30 *Hailing Somalia's ratification, UN renews calls for universalization of the* CRC, U.N. NEWS (Oct. 2, 2015), www.un.org/apps/news/story.asp?NewsID=52129.

31 CRIN, *Rights, Remedies And Representation: A Global Report On Access To Justice For Children* (2016), https://home.crin.org/issues/access-to-justice/rights-remedies-and-representation-a-global-report-on-access-to-justice-for-children.

32 Notably the International Convention on Civil and Political Rights (ICCPR), the international Convention on Economic, Social and Cultural Rights (ICESCR) (particularly education), Convention to End Discrimination Against Women, the Convention to End Racial Discrimination, CPRD and the CRSR.

ILO Convention 138 on the Minimum Age for Admission to Employment and Work[33] and the ILO Convention 182 on the Worst Forms of Child Labour.[34] These self-evidently have a narrow scope compared with the CRC.

In the field of Private International Law, the Hague Conference has produced several treaties that relate directly to children.[35] These treaties operate only between the countries that have ratified them, but are also used by courts to flesh out provisions in the CRC, and to lobby for or guide the drafting of domestic laws.[36] Two Hague Conventions that closely relate to CRC are the Convention on Intercountry Adoption and the Convention on the Civil Aspects of International Child Abduction.[37]

C *Regional Charter on Children's Rights*

At the regional level, the African Charter on the Rights and Welfare of the Child (hereafter ACRWC) was adopted by the African Union[38] in 1990.[39] At first reading it appears to be similar to the CRC but in fact contains significant differences in wording of certain clauses. In some respects the ACRWC provides a higher level of protection than the CRC,[40] and in some respects it is weaker.[41]

---

33 This convention came into force on June 19, 1976 (more than a decade before the CRC), and has been ratified by 169 states, *see ILO Conventions and Recommendations on Child Labour*, ILO, http://www.ilo.org/ipec/facts/ILOconventionsonchildlabour/lang--en/index.htm.

34 This convention came into force on Nov. 19, 2000 (a decade after the CRC), and has been ratified by 180 states, *see id.*

35 Hague Convention on the Civil Aspects of International Child Abduction, Oct. 25, 1980; Hague Convention on Protection of Children and Co-operation in Respect of Intercountry Adoption, May 29, 1993; Hague Convention on Jurisdiction, Applicable Law, Recognition, Enforcement and Co-operation in Respect of Parental Responsibility and Measures for the Protection of Children, Oct. 19, 1996; Hague Convention on the International Recovery of Child Support and other Forms of Family Maintenance, Nov. 23, 2007.

36 The Hague Conference on Private International Law produces 'Guides to Good Practice,' which are a very useful to guide courts, law makers, and lobbyists.

37 *Id.*

38 At that time, it was called the Organisation of African Unity.

39 The pace of ratification of the ACRWC was slow, causing it to come into operation only in 1999, nine years after adoption. As of September 30, 2016, 45 African states have ratified it.

40 For example, Art. 30—dealing with the children of imprisoned mothers—does not have a counterpart in the CRC.

41 For example, the juvenile justice provisions are weaker in the ACRWC than the CRC, the former lacking important protections such as a ban on the use of the death penalty or life imprisonment without parole. For a more a general discussion on the ACRWC and its similarities and differences to the CRC *see* B.D. Mezmur, *The African Children's Charter*

Significantly, the ACRWC has a built-in communications procedure. The Committee of Experts on the Rights and Welfare of the Child has considered four matters in recent years,[42] which means that a regional jurisprudence is gradually emerging. The Committee has also issued five General Comments.[43] The first of these, on the children of imprisoned parents, is relevant to one of the case studies to be discussed later in this chapter. Although other regions have not produced child rights charters or conventions, the CRC has been used in communications to regional treaty bodies, and this will be discussed below.

D *Optional Protocols to the CRC*

There are three optional protocols to the CRC. The first two were issued in 2002, in an attempt to strengthen aspects of the CRC. The first protocol is on the involvement of children in armed conflict.[44] It deals with one of the issues that had been controversial during the drafting of the CRC —the minimum age of recruitment.[45] The protocol bans compulsory recruitment into the armed forces of anyone below the age of eighteen years, but it allows voluntary recruitment at the age of fifteen years. The second optional protocol deals with the sale of children, child prostitution, and child pornography.[46] The third optional protocol establishes a communications procedure for the CRC.[47] This

---

versus the UN Convention on the Rights of the Child: A zero-sum game?, S. AFR PUBLIC L. 1 (2008).

42 *Michelo Hansungule and Others (On Behalf of Children in Northern Uganda) v. The Government of Uganda*, Commc'n No. 001/Com/001/2005; Institute for Human Rights and Development in Africa (IHRDA) and Open Society Justice Initiative on behalf of children of Nubian descent in *Kenya v. Kenya*, Decision No.002/Com/002/2009; *The Centre for Human Rights (University of Pretoria) and La Rencontre Africaine Pour la Defence des Droits de L'homme (Senegal) v. Government of Senegal*, Decision No. 003/com/001/2012; *Institute for Human Rights Development in Africa v. Malawi*, Commc'n No. 004/com/001/2014.

43 General Comment on Art. 30 of the ACRWC (Children of caregivers facing imprisonment) 2013; General Comment on Art. 6 of the ACRWC (Name and Nationality) 2014; General Comment on Article 31 (Responsibilities of the child) 2017; Joint General Comment on Ending Child Marriage (2017); General Comment on Article 1 (State party obligations and systems strengthening for child protection) 2018.

44 Optional protocol to the U.N. Convention on the Rights of the Child on the involvement of children in armed conflict, adopted and opened for signature, ratification and accession on May 25, 2000.

45 Cantwell, *supra* note 22, at 26.

46 Optional protocol to the U.N. Convention on the Rights of the Child on the Sale of Children, Child Prostitution and Child Pornography, *adopted and opened for signature, ratification and accession* May 25, 2000, 2171 U.N.T.S. A-27531.

47 Optional Protocol to the Convention on the Rights of the Child on a Communications Procedure, *adopted and opened for signature, ratification and accession* February, 2012.

is a space in which jurisprudence is developing, but so far the Committee has only considered twenty two communications, but has a pending case list of ninety four.[48]

E *Soft Law Related to the* CRC

1 Rules and Guidelines

The application of the criminal justice system to children, whether offenders or victims, is the cluster of rights which has produced the most soft international law in the form of international instruments. While the CRC was being drafted, there were parallel processes going on which culminated in the UN Standard Minimum Rules for the Administration of Juvenile Justice (1985) known as the Beijing Rules, the UN Standard Minimum Rules for the Protection of Juveniles Deprived of their Liberty (1990) known as the JDLs or the Havana Rules, and the UN Guidelines for the Prevention of Juvenile Delinquency (1990) known as the Riyadh Guidelines. These instruments are not binding but they provide significantly more detail than the CRC, and have frequently been referred to in case law.[49] Much later, the UN Guidelines on Justice in Matters Involving Child Victims and Witnesses of Crime (2005) were adopted. These guidelines spell out a set of practical measures to be taken to protect child victims and witnesses during the various phases of the criminal justice system. These have been used in international, regional and domestic fora, to assist in the interpretation of the CRC. Examples will be given later in the chapter.

The Beijing Rules deserve special mention because they have proved very influential. It should be noted that, unlike the other guidelines and rules mentioned here, they were drafted prior to the CRC, and while some of the contents are repeated in the CRC, the Rules are more detailed than the Convention. The idea of the Rules arose at the Sixth UN Congress on the Prevention of Crime and the Treatment of Offenders in Caracas, Venezuela.[50]

See further Trevor Buck & Michael Wabwile, *The Potential and Promise of Communications Procedures under the Third Protocol to the Convention on the Rights of the Child*, 2 (2) INT'L HUM R. LAW REV. 205 (2013).

48 As at 2 September 2019, Views have been issued in six cases, six have been discontinued and 10 were ruled inadmissible. Further information is available at http://juris.ohchr.org/en/search/results?Bodies=5&sortOrder=Date.

49 For a detailed discussion of their use in case law, in particular South Africa and India, *see* LITIGATING THE RIGHTS OF THE CHILD: THE UN CONVENTION ON THE RIGHTS OF THE CHILD IN DOMESTIC AND INTERNATIONAL JURISPRUDENCE 13–51 (Tom Liefaard & Jaap. E. Doek eds., 2015).

50 U.N. Dep't of Int'l Econ. and Social Aff., Report of the Sixth United Nations Congress on the Prevention of Crime and the Treatment of Offenders, Caracas, Venezuela, Aug. 25—Sep. 5, 1980, A/CONF.87/14/Rev.1 (1981).

The Congress called for the development of model rules on juvenile justice administration. The Crime Prevention and Criminal Justice Branch of the UN requested Professor Horst Schüler-Springorum to develop an initial draft. The Rules were presented and discussed at the inter-regional preparatory meeting for the Seventh UN Congress on the Prevention of Crime and the Treatment of Offenders in Beijing. The report notes that some amendments were agreed upon, and it was resolved to call the rules the UN Standard Minimum Rules for Juvenile Justice.[51] They were adopted by the UN General Assembly in 1985. The subsequent influence of the Beijing Rules is partly due to the fact that the CRC subsequently adopted several of their key provisions, notably the minimum age of criminal responsibility, and detention as a measure of last resort, therefore rendering them binding. An interesting feature of the Beijing Rules is that they contain a built-in commentary under each rule, which provides a useful aid to interpretation. This makes them attractive to lawyers and judges, and is another probable reason why the Beijing Rules feature prominently in court precedents.

2 Resolutions

UN Resolutions as separate documents are issued by the Security Council, General Assembly, and Economic and Social Council. Human Rights Council resolutions are issued as individual documents. There are a bewildering array of resolutions, made on a wide range of children's issues such as administration of justice, alternative care, birth registration and right to nationality, children of incarcerated parents, children living and working on the street, education, health, and migration.[52] Resolutions often a conduit for advocacy work being done by bodies such as UNODC, UNICEF, the Office of the Secretary General, or by special rapporteurs. NGOs may be involved in their development, through making comments.[53] Once passed, they can also be used in further advocacy work by UN bodies and by governments and NGOs.

---

51 Report of the Interregional Preparatory Meeting for the Seventh U.N. Congress on the Prevention of Crime and the Treatment of Offenders on Topic IC 'Youth, Crime and Justice' Beijing 14–18 May 1984, U.N. Doc. A/CONF.121/IPM/1 (June 27, 1984).

52 For a list of resolutions on child rights adopted by the HRC, for example, go to https://www.childrightsconnect.org/list-of-child-rights-resolutions-adopted-by-the-hrc/.

53 On the role of NGOs in soft and hard international lawmaking, *see* M. Noortmann, *Non-governmental Organisations: Recognition, Roles, Rights and Responsibilities*, *in* NON-STATE ACTORS IN INTERNATIONAL LAW 205, 205–223 (Math Noortmann et.al. eds., 2015).

3 General Comments of the CRC Committee

The UN Committee on the Rights of the Child has issued twenty four general comments to date.[54] The purpose of the General Comments is to provide an authoritative interpretation of the rights contained in the articles and provisions of the CRC and the optional protocols. The Committee selects a 'theme' that it considers to require elucidation, and through a consultative process develops a detailed comment.[55] General Comments are not binding, even on parties that have ratified the Convention. However, they are sometimes used by Courts to enhance interpretation of the Convention. In some instances, General Comments fill in gaps that are left by the CRC, a typical role that soft law plays. An example of this will be referred to in the case study on the minimum age of criminal responsibility, below.

F *General Use of Hard and Soft International Law in Litigation*

1 International

At the international level, in the absence of a communications procedure under the CRC, which was only established in April 2014, international treaty body jurisprudence on children's rights was nevertheless developed through the individual complaints procedures of other treaty bodies that are coordinated by the Office of the High Commissioner for Human Rights.[56] There are ten such treaty bodies.[57] Examples of cases include matters concerning a child's right to registration and preservation of identity,[58] the right of the child to maintain contact with both parents,[59] the child's right to respect for family life,[60] protection from violence,[61] protection in the context of pregnancy and

54 The General Comments can be found at http://www.ohchr.org/EN/HRBodies/CRC/Pages/CRCIndex.aspx.

55 CRIN, *CRC General Comments*, https://www.crin.org/en/library/publications/crc-general-comments.

56 A. de Zayas, *The CRC in Litigation under the ICCPR and CEDAW, in* LITIGATING THE RIGHTS OF THE CHILD, *supra* note 49, at 177–191.

57 The other 9 besides the UNCROC are the Human Rights Committee (CCPR), Committee on Economic Social and Cultural Rights (CESCR), Committee on the Elimination of Racial Discrimination (CERD), Committee on the Elimination of Discrimination Against Women (CEDAW), Committee Against Torture (CAT), Sub-committee on the Prevention of Torture, Committee on Migrant Workers (SPT), Committee on the Rights of Persons with Disabilities (CRPD), Committee on Enforced Disappearances (CED).

58 Art. 4 of the ICCPR, *Darwina Rosa Monacho de Gallicchio and Ximena Vacario v. Argentina*, HRC Case No. 400/1990.

59 Art. 17 of the ICCPR, *LP v. Czech Republic*, HRC Commc'n No. 946/2000.

60 Children of Immigrants, *Winata et al v. Australia*, HRC Commc'n No. 930/2000.

61 Art 24. of the ICCPR, *SVP v. Bulgaria*, HRC Commc'n No. 31/2011.

choice of termination,[62] protection from female genital mutilation,[63] and detention.[64] An important case regarding abortion was heard by CEDAW,[65] and there are examples of the CAT hearing matters where children's deportation was found unlawful where they were facing the threat of torture[66] or female genital mutilation.[67]

2 Regional

The main task of the European Court of Human Rights (ECtHR) is to adjudicate on the application of the European Convention on Human Rights (ECHR) and the European Social Charter, which both contain brief references to children's rights. According to Ursula Kilkelly the ECtHR has used the CRC "to inform the interpretation of general human rights standards to children."[68] Helen Stafford's analysis of the European Court of Justice's jurisprudence on child rights, by contrast, shows that the Court of Justice has failed to embrace the CRC fully.[69] However, Stafford makes the claim that in recent years the EU has increasingly endorsed the key principles of the CRC, and its accompanying guidance in the form of soft international law. The EU Agenda for the Rights of the Child (2011) has expressly indicated that EU action must ensure respect for the CRC.

The CRC has also been used in the Inter-American human rights system. Monica Feria-Tinta has pointed out that the Court has adopted an approach to interpretation that the corpus juris of international human rights law comprises a set of international instruments, including treaties, conventions, resolutions, and declarations. This has resulted in the Inter-American Court drawing not only on the CRC but also on the Beijing Rules, the Riyadh Guidelines and the 1990 UN Standard Minimum Rules for Non-custodial Measures (the Tokyo Rules). It has also considered the provisions providing protection to children in times of war in the 1949 Geneva Convention and the 1977 Additional Protocols.

---

62 Art 24. of the ICCPR, *Karen Noelia Huamán v. Peru*, HRC Commc'n No. 1153/2003.

63 Art 24. of the ICCPR, *Diene Kaba v. Canada*, HRC Commc'n No. 1465/2006.

64 Art 9. and 24 of the ICCPR, (Immigration) *Ali Aqsar Bakhtiyari et al v. Australia*, HRC Commc'n No. 1069/2002; (Indigenous children) *Corey Brough v. Australia*, HRC Commc'n No. 1184/2003.

65 Zayas, *supra* note 57, at 177–191.

66 *T.A. v. Sweden*, Commc'n No. 226/2003; *C.T. and K.M. v. Sweden*, Comc'n No. 279/2005.

67 *F.B. v. The Netherlands*, Commc'n No. 613/2014, *adopted* Nov. 19, 2015.

68 Ursula Kilkelly, *The CRC in Litigation under the ECHR, in* LITIGATING THE RIGHTS OF THE CHILD, *supra* note 49, at 193–209.

69 H. Stafford, *The CRC in Litigation under EU Law, in* LITIGATING THE RIGHTS OF THE CHILD, *supra* note 49, at 211–230.

Furthermore, the court has used concluding observations of the Committee on the Rights of the Child in some of its cases. The case of *Massacre of Mapiripan*[70] was about a terrorist act against civilians, including children, by a paramilitary organization. The Inter-American Court drew attention to the Concluding Observations of the Committee on the Rights of the Child that had been handed down to Colombia in 2000, in which the Committee expressed its concern about the effects of armed conflict on children in that country, in particular acts committed by paramilitary groups. The Inter-American Court found that Colombia had an obligation to prevent situations that lead to the breach of the right to life of children within its borders. Despite being aware of the risks to children, having had that pointed out by the CRC Committee, Colombia had failed to protect the children.

The Inter-American Court also referred to concluding observations of the Committee on the Rights of the Child in the case of *Vargas Areco* which concerned a child soldier, recruited into the Paraguayan armed forces at the age of fifteen, who was then shot and killed while he was fleeing from the army camp.[71] The Court pointed out that when Paraguay had reported to the Committee on the Rights of the Child in 1997, the concluding observations had pointed out that despite legal restrictions to the contrary, children below eighteen years were being recruited, and when the country reported again in 2001, the committee had recommended that Paraguay put a stop to recruitment of children under eighteen into the armed forces and police. In its judgment, the court also welcomed a new declaration signed by the then President of Paraguay that was intended to replace the earlier one deposited with the ratification of the Optional Protocol to the CRC on the use of child soldiers in armed conflict. The earlier declaration had set the age of recruitment at sixteen years. The new declaration set it at eighteen years.

G *Conclusion of Overview*

The above overview gives a sense of the overwhelming quantity of soft and hard international law on children's rights. This includes binding and non-binding international and regional instruments, as well as resolutions and general comments. International law also includes child rights jurisprudence, which has emerged across numerous treaty bodies, at both the international and regional levels. The courts are guided not only by hard law, but also make frequent use of different kinds of soft law such as rules, guidelines and

70 The Massacre of Mapiripán v. Colombia, Judgment, Int-Am. Ct. H.R. (series C) No. 134 (Sept. 15, 2005).

71 Vargas Areco v. Paraguay, Judgment, Int-Am. Ct. H.R. (series C) No 155 (Sept. 26, 2006).

general comments to interpret the law, build a child rights jurisprudence and to sometimes close gaps in the hard international law. The examples of the Inter-American courts show that even concluding observations to states parties are sometimes used to show that the State had prior knowledge of a problem before it reached crisis point, thus adding to State accountability. The remainder of the chapter will focus on how this plethora of legal resources has been and can be used to advocate for social change for children. The possibilities are endless, but three case studies are offered as illustrations of the role that soft and hard international law can play in social change for children.

III Case Studies

A *Case Study One: Children of Imprisoned Parents*

Children of imprisoned parents are not specifically mentioned in the CRC. This has meant that soft law has had an important role to play in developing the rights of this group of children. The considerable gains in this field have been achieved through a process of litigation, UN resolutions, and comparative developments through the African Committee of Experts on the Rights and Welfare of the Child. South African courts were the first to consider constitutional court litigation on this issue, coming from a children's rights perspective. In the 2007 case of *S v. M (Centre for Child Law as Amicus Curiae)*,[72] the Constitutional Court considered the role of the law in the protection of children whose primary caregivers were facing imprisonment. The Court mentioned the CRC in relation to the best interests of the child as a primary consideration (which is in any case framed more robustly as the paramount consideration in the South African Constitution) but relied more heavily on the African Charter on the Rights and Welfare of the Child, article 30 which is titled 'Children of imprisoned mothers' and which provides at article 30(1) that non-custodial sentences should always be a first resort for such mothers. Relying on this provision, together with a child's right to family and parental care, the court found that careful consideration should be given to the best interests of the child when sentencing a primary caregiver. Where possible, a non-custodial sentence should be preferred.

The Quaker United Nations Office (QUNO), had been working on this issue since 2005. A paper published by QUNO in April 2006 indicates that they were attempting to bring about change for women prisoners and their children, by

---

72 *S v. M*, 2008 (3) SA 232 (CC).

lobbying the CRC Committee to ask about this issue in the reporting processes, and to include it in concluding observations.[73] The paper indicates that the Committee started to do this in 2005. It is not apparent that QUNO had its sights set on a binding convention, it was seeking either a general comment or a resolution. Following *S v. M*, QUNO galvanised their work on this topic—and shifted focus to a gender neutral perspective, children of incarcerated parents (as in *S v. M*, which spoke of children of sentenced primary caregivers, rather than mothers).[74] Their lobbying paid off. On December 24, 2009, two years after the judgment was handed down, the UN General Assembly passed a resolution on the 'Rights of the Child' aimed at strengthening efforts of member states to promote children's rights.[75] The resolution has a specific heading entitled *'Children of person alleged to have infringed or recognized as having infringed penal law'*. Under this heading, paragraph 47 states the UN General Assembly:

> Also calls upon States to give attention to the impact of parental detention and imprisonment on children and, in particular:
>
> To give priority consideration to non-custodial measures when sentencing or deciding on pretrial measures for a child's sole or primary caretaker, subject to the need to protect the public and the child, and bearing in mind the gravity of the offence;
>
> To identify and promote good practices in relation to the needs and physical, emotional, social, and psychological development of babies and children affected by parental detention and imprisonment.[76]

This was the first UN document to specifically include a provision on the children of incarcerated parents.

The UN Committee on the Rights of the Child has themed 'days of general discussion' from time to time. On September 30, 2011 the theme of the Committee's 'day of general discussion' was 'Children of incarcerated parents.'

---

73 Lauren Townhead, *Women in Prison and Children of Imprisoned Mothers: Recent Developments in the United Nations Human Rights System*, EUROPEAN COMMISSION (April, 2006), https://ec.europa.eu/justice/grants/results/daphne-toolkit/en/file/322/download?.

74 Oliver Robertson, *Collateral Convicts: Children of Incarcerated Parents: Recommendations and Good Practice from the UN Committee on the Rights of the Child Day of General Discussion* (2012).

75 G.A. Res. 63/241 Rights of the Child (Mar. 13, 2009).

76 *Id.*

The case of *S v. M* was highlighted in the plenary session of this day of general discussion.[77]

Following the day of general discussion, a resolution was adopted by the Human Rights Council,[78] also entitled 'Rights of the child.' Below the heading 'Children of incarcerated parents' is paragraph 69 which calls upon States:

> To give priority, when sentencing or deciding on pre-trial measures for a pregnant woman or a child's sole or primary caregiver, to non-custodial measures, bearing in mind the gravity of the offence and after taking into account the best interest of the child.[79]

QUNO and other NGOs, notably Penal Reform International,[80] worked with the UNODC to ensure the inclusion of these gains into the more formal soft law instrument, the United Nations Rules for the Treatment of Women Prisoners and Non-custodial Measures for Women Offenders (the Bangkok Rules), adopted by the UN General Assembly in 2011.[81] The Rules include the following relevant rule:

> Non-custodial sentences for pregnant women and women with dependent children shall be preferred where possible and appropriate, with

77 Robertson, *supra* note 74. According to Oliver Robertson, "[t]his was the first time that any part of the UN system had looked in any detail at the issue of children affected by parental involvement in the criminal justice system, and it attracted unprecedented interest and engagement."

78 Human Rights Council Res. 19/37 Rights of the Child (April 19, 2012).

79 The remainder of paragraph 69 deals with the consideration of best interests of the child in deciding whether and how long a child should be incarcerated with an imprisoned mother; to allow children access to their incarcerated parents through regular and private meetings; the right of children to have their best interests considered in all decisions made about their incarcerated parent; to be informed of transfers or petitions for pardons, and where parents are to be executed; to be provided with information about the execution and to allow a last visit.

80 Penal Reform International and Quaker United Nations Office, *Briefing on the UN Rules for the Treatment of Women Prisoners and Non-Custodial Measure for Women Offenders ('Bangkok Rules')*, www. quno.org/sites/default.files/resources/ENGLISH_Briefing on Bangkok Rules.pdf.

81 G.A. Res. 65/229 (Mar. 16, 2011). These Rules are considered to be "soft law." Although not binding on States, such Rules have been given weight by South Africa Courts—*see, e.g.*, the use of the Rules and Guidelines pertaining to child offenders (*Centre for Child Law v. Minister of Justice* 2009 (6) SA 632 (CC) at ¶ 61) and to child victims and witness (*Director of Public Prosecutions, Transvaal v. Minister of Justice* 2009 (2) SACR 130 (CC) at ¶ 13).

> custodial sentences being considered when the offence is serious or violent or the woman represents a continuing danger, and after taking into account the best interests of the child or children, while ensuring that appropriate provision has been made for the care of such children.

This new rule, together with the resolutions described above, closes a gap in the CRC itself, which does not contain any specific provision about children of incarcerated parents, although the right 'not to be separated from a parent' is a key provision included in article 9(1) of the CRC.[82] Although paragraph 9(4) acknowledges that separation may result from action initiated by the State, such as imprisonment, the Article is mainly aimed at situations where children are removed from their parents due to abuse or neglect.

As explained above, the African Charter has a specific provision relating to children of imprisoned mothers. In 2013, the African Committee of Experts on the Rights and Welfare of the Child (ACERWC) issued their first General Comment, entitled *General Comment no 1: (Article 20 of the African Charter on the Rights and Welfare of the Child) on "Children of Incarcerated and Imprisoned Parents and Primary Caregivers."*[83]

Expressly drawing inspiration from *S v. M*, the General Comment starts with the following quotation from Sachs J:

> Every child has his or her own dignity, If a child is to be [...] imagined as an individual with a distinctive personality, and not merely as a miniature adult waiting to reach full size, he or she cannot be treated as a mere extension of his or her parents, umbilically destined to sink or swim with them.[84]

82 States parties shall ensure that a child shall not be separated from his or her parents against their will, except when competent authorities subject to judicial review determine, in accordance with applicable law or procedures, that such separation is necessary for the best interests of the child.

83 South African Courts have acknowledged General Comments in their judgments, *see, e.g., Governing Body of the Juma Musjid Primary School and Others v. Essay N.O. and Others* (Centre for Child Law and Another as Amici Curiae) 2011 (8) BCLR 761 (CC) in which the Court referred to general comment 13 issued by the Committee on Economic, Social and Cultural Rights; and Director of Public Prosecutions; *Transvaal v. Minister of Justice* 2009 (2) SACR 130 (CC) in which the Court referred to the UN Committee on the Rights of the Child's general comments 3 and 5.

84 *S v. M*, 2008 (3) SA 232 (CC) at ¶ 18. The word omitted from the original is 'constitutionally'.

The General Comment interprets article 30 as being more broadly applicable—that 'mother' should be read as 'caregiver' and that 'imprisonment' should include pre-trial detention and any custodial measures.[85] This is a good example of soft law being consciously used to expand the ambit of hard law. The General Comment requires State Parties to "take an individualised, qualitative approach that is nuanced and based on actual information about incarcerated parents/caregivers and children."[86] The General Comment urges States Parties to put in place policy, legislative, administrative and judicial measures to ensure the protection of children whose parents are facing imprisonment.[87]

Under the heading "The scope and nature of Article 30" the General Comment points out that the words 'special treatment' mentioned in the lead in to article 30 "implies a much higher level of obligation for States Parties than that required in ordinary circumstances."[88] The General Comment, under the same heading, goes on to require that States parties "ensure that a non-custodial sentence will always be *first* considered when sentencing such mothers" (emphasis added).[89] The General Comment[90] sets out an implementation framework for Article 30, expressly based on *S v. M.*[91]

This case study demonstrates an intricate and complex weaving of hard and soft international law in the development of rights protection for a specific group of children. It is clear that QUNO saw the lack of protection in the CRC and lobbied for recognition of the problem by the UN through concluding observations and a general day of discussion, and the development of soft international law to fill the gap. The South African case did not aim primarily at filling the lacuna, but having found it, the litigators bridged the gap by relying on the ACRWC. The Constitutional Court intentionally broadened the scope beyond the wording of Article 30 of the ACRWC in its application of the Charter to South African law, by extending it beyond mothers, using the gender neutral terminology "children of primary caregivers facing imprisonment"—an interesting approach in that M, the applicant in *S v. M*, was female. The court thus did not need to make this extension for the case itself, but it approached the matter from an equality perspective.[92] The original lacuna in the CRC has been

85 ACERWC General Comment no. 1, ¶ 13.
86 ACERWC General Comment no. 1, ¶ 15.
87 ACERWC General Comment no. 1, ¶ 24(a).
88 ACERWC General Comment no. 1, ¶ 33.
89 ACERWC General Comment no. 1, heading 3.1.1.
90 ACERWC General Comment no. 1, ¶ 36.
91 *S v. M*, 2008 (3) SA 232 (CC) at ¶ 36.
92 In this regard, the Court may have been developing the law from its earlier judgment in *President of the Republic of South Africa v. Hugo* 1997 (4) SA 1 (CC). In that case, a

bridged through borrowing from the ACRWC and the development of UN declarations, which paved the way for inclusion of a clause in the Bangkok Rules. Litigation at the domestic level played an important role in interpretation and broadening of the ACRWC article 30, which has flowed back into soft international law through the ACRWC General Comment on the subject.

B *Case Study Two: the Use of the General Comment in Relation to Age and Criminal Responsibility*

Article 40(3) of the CRC provides that state parties should establish a minimum age below which a child will be presumed not to have criminal responsibility. The gist of Article 40(3) is that there must be a minimum age of criminal responsibility (MACR). Whatever age this minimum age should be was left in the hands of countries who are parties to the treaty. The ambiguous wording and inadequate nature of article 40(3) begs for clarity and expansion. In 2007, the Committee on the Rights of the Child issued General Comment 10 (GC 10) on Juvenile Justice, which has remedied this to some extent by shedding light on Article 40(3).

GC 10 interprets Article 40(3) as saying that children who commit an offence at an age that is below the set age of the particular country cannot be held criminally responsible.[93] The implication is that children may factually be capable of committing crimes but lack the capacity to be held accountable for that crime.[94] GC 10 goes on to interpret Article 40(3) to mean children who are at the age of the established MACR of a particular country or above, but younger than eighteen years, can be held criminally liable and can be charged formally for an offence; but the processes and procedures involved therein must comply with the provisions of the CRC,[95] so they are to be differentiated from adults.

Referring directly to the Beijing Rules, GC 10 states as follows:

> Rule 4 of the Beijing Rules recommends that the beginning of the MACR shall not be fixed at too low an age level, bearing in mind the facts of emotional, mental and intellectual maturity. In line with this, the Committee

presidential decree allowing the early release of imprisoned mothers was unsuccessfully challenged by an imprisoned father. The court found the discrimination to be fair, due to the fact that mothers still carry most of the burdens (and joys) of caring for children. In *S v. M* the court emphasized care-giving (as opposed to bread-winning), rather than gender.

93 CRC General Comment no. 10, ¶ 30.

94 *Id.* ¶ 31.

95 *Id.*

> has recommended States parties not to set an MACR at a too low level and to increase the existing low MACR to an internationally acceptable level. From these recommendations, it can be concluded that a minimum age of criminal responsibility below the age of twelve years is considered by the Committee to be internationally unacceptable. States parties are encouraged to increase their lower MACR to the age of twelve years as the absolute minimum age and to continue to increase it to a higher level.[96]

So it is clear that the Beijing Rules (which set the principle but did not set a minimum age) provided the impetus to the Committee developing soft law, firstly through its own concluding observations, and then through the more formal route of a general comment.[97] The Committee encouraged countries to set their MACR at a minimum of twelve years and to strive to incrementally increase their MACR.[98] As for those countries whose MACRs are higher than the recommended age of twelve, the Committee clearly indicated that this is not an invitation to lower that age.[99] The Committee recommended that exceptions are not made to the set MACR to lower the age of criminal responsibility regardless of the nature or gravity of offence which the child might have committed.[100] Finally, in those instances where the age of the child cannot be obtained or where there is no proof of the child's age in order to determine whether or not that child is below or above the MACR, such child is not to be held criminally responsible.[101]

Since that adoption of the CRC and Article 40(3), the following patterns have been seen in MACRs, around the world: In the sixteen years between 1990 (the first year of operation of the CRC) and 2007 Brazil, Peru, El Salvador, Australia, Costa Rica, Honduras, Indonesia, Barbados, Ghana, Bolivia, Spain, Afghanistan, Paraguay, Chile, Ireland and Bangladesh, took the positive step of increasing their MACRs.[102] However, on the negative side, countries such as

---

96 *Id.* ¶ 32.

97 The shades of less/more formal and informal soft/hard law are difficult to define. A general comment is more formal in that it is meant to apply to all parties, while concluding observations may be seen as less formal as it is addressed to a specific country, but is a form of precedent setting. For more on the complexity of this subject see Joost Pauwelyn, *Informal International Lawmaking: Framing The Concept*, *in* INFORMAL INTERNATIONAL LAWMAKING (J. Pauwelyn *et al.* eds., 2012).

98 CRC General Comment no. 10, *supra* note 93, at ¶ 32.

99 *Id.* ¶ 32.

100 *Id.* ¶ 34.

101 *Id.* ¶ 35.

102 DON CIPRIANI, CHILDREN'S RIGHTS & MINIMUM AGE OF CRIMINAL RESPONSIBILITY: A GLOBAL PERSPECTIVE 111 (2009).

Andorra, France, Nepal, Mauritania, Slovakia, Georgia, and Japan decreased their MACR within the same time period.

In the first few years following 2007 (the introduction of GC 10), the following countries decreased their MACRs: Georgia, Japan, the Czech Republic, and the Philippines. The following countries increased their MACRs: Bahrain, Belize, Bhutan, Burundi, Cambodia, France, Indonesia, Jordan, Kenya, Lebanon, Lesotho, Malawi, Maldives, Namibia, Oman, Samoa, South Africa, Swaziland, Tanzania, and Thailand.[103] Thus it appears that GC 10 initially had a very positive effect.

However, it is concerning that since the issuing of General Comment 10, several countries have lowered their MACR, despite the Committee having warned against this. Those countries are Denmark,[104] Georgia,[105] Panama,[106] and Hungary.[107] Several others are debating Bills or policies that aim to lower the MACR.[108] In Brazil, there was significant civil society mobilization against a bid to reduce the MACR from eighteen down to sixteen.[109] In a public statement, a civil society coalition called on the government of Brazil not to go ahead with the planned change to the law, saying that it would violate Brazil's obligations under the CRC. It mentioned articles 37 and 40, as well as General Comment no 10. In July 2015, the lower house of the Brazilian Congress narrowly rejected the proposed amendment.[110]

---

103 *Id.* at 111.

104 CRC Concluding Observations of 2011: "The Committee expresses its deep concern on the lowering of the age of criminal responsibility from 15 years to 14 years."

105 CRC Concluding Observations of 2008: "The Committee deeply regrets the decision of the State party to lower the MACR from 14 to 12."

106 Panama reduced the minimum age from 14 to 12. CRC concluding observations of 2011: The Committee criticized the change and recommended "that the state bring the juvenile justice system fully in line with the Convention by increasing the age of criminal responsibility."

107 Hungary lowered the minimum age from 14 to 12 for homicide and other serious offences. CRC Concluding Observations of 2014: "The Committee criticized the change and recommended that Hungary increase the minimum age of criminal responsibility to 14 for even the most serious offences."

108 Prominent among these are a number of South American countries, namely Argentina, Bolivia, Brazil Mexico, Peru and Uruguay. Phillipines also has a Bill in Parliament to lower the MACR. High profile crimes have seen similar initiatives in India and Spain. See a full list of all the countries at https://www.crin.org/en/home/what-we-do/policy/stop-making-children-criminals.

109 PEC 171. For a discussion of the Bill, *see* S. Aman, *Selective Adulthood: Brazil Moves to Lower Age of Criminal Responsibility* (May 29, 2015), www.coha.org.

110 *Brazil Rejects Lowering Age of Criminal Responsibility*, BBC (July 1, 2015), www.bbc.com/news/world-latin-america-33343361.

Of course, this wave of attempts to lower the MACR was not what the Committee on the Rights of the Child expected to happen. But the General Comment and its specific mention of the age of twelve has subsequently been blamed for the sudden rush of countries rushing to lower the MACR.[111]

This has prompted some prominent civil society advocates to adopt a fairly radical new stance. A leading promoter of this is the Child Rights International Network (CRIN), calling for a debate that "gets beyond pragmatism and compromise."[112] They urge a way forward that separates the concept of responsibility from that of criminalization. The nub of their concern is that the UN Committee's call for a MACR of not less than twelve years has been misused by some states which previously had a MACR of older than twelve years to support law reform to reduce the age. CRIN proposes that we should stop focusing on *criminal* responsibility. Children should be held responsible, and this is in line with the trends in restorative justice, which is widely promoted in child justice. But should this 'responsibility' be *criminal*?[113] Council of Europe Commissioner, Thomas Hammarberg, has called for a complete shift in the MACR debate to one in which children below eighteen should be held responsible, but not criminally responsible.[114]

However, there are some who believe that there remains a need, in the interim, to continue to incrementally raise the MACR as far as possible. In 2011 the Inter-American Commission on Human Rights issued a report entitled "Juvenile justice and human rights in the Americas."[115] The report reiterates Hammarberg's call for a new debate separating the concepts of 'responsibility' and 'criminalization,' but recognizes that excluding children totally from the criminal justice system (whilst holding them accountable and guaranteeing due process) is a complex matter that may take some time to implement. Thus, continued pragmatism is required, and the Commission "urges states to progressively raise the minimum age under which children can be held responsible in the juvenile justice system towards eighteen years of age."[116]

111 CRIN, *Stop Making Children Criminals*, https://archive.crin.org/en/home/what-we-do/policy/minimum-ages/stop-making-children-criminals.html.

112 *Id.*

113 CRIN, *Age Is Arbitrary: Setting Minimum Ages*, Discussion Paper (2017), https://archive.crin.org/sites/default/files/discussion_paper_-_minimum_ages.pdf.

114 Hammarberg's position is cited in CRIN, *supra* note 113, at 8–9.

115 The report was written by the Inter-American Commission's rapporteur on children's rights, Paulo Pinheiro, the former UN special rapporteur on violence against children.

116 Inter-American Commission on Human Rights, *Juvenile Justice and Human Rights in the Americas*, http://www.cidh.org/countryrep/JusticiaJuvenileng/jjtoc.eng.htm.

The Committee on the Rights of the Child revised General Comment no. 10, which was adopted (as General Comment no. 24 on the rights of children in child justice systems) in 2019. In it, the Committee now recommends that states raise the age to 14 years, citing new knowledge obtained from development science about child and adolescent development. The Committee adds that although the setting of a minimum age of criminal responsibility at a reasonably high level is important, an effective approach also depends on how each State deals with children above and below that age.[117]

The story of the MACR is an example of where the international instrument is vague, and the treaty body decided to spell out a minimum standard that provides more clarity in a General Comment. It was in part successful, with many states raising the MACR, but appears to have also contributed to some states lowering the age. CRIN has been particularly critical about how the Committee decided on the age of twelve in the first place. Apparently, the age was decided on by calculating the world average MACR. The CRIN paper rebuked the Committee for setting policy based on an average approach.[118] This points to a possible disadvantage of using general comments as a means of soft law development. The process of drafting is a fairly closed process carried out by experts. Although in recent years the CRC Committee has allowed more participation by civil society through allowing drafts to be circulated for comment, states parties are generally not included in the process. This may be the reason for the lack of 'buy in' by some member states. Indeed, the chairpersons of the treaty bodies agreed in 2015 that opportunities for states, NGOs, UN Agencies, and NHRIs to comment on General Comments would be the standard method going forward, and this was the method followed by the Committee in recent years.[119] However, one can appreciate better with hindsight why the CRC (and the Beijing Rules) did not set a specific minimum age.

117 General Comment no. 24 on Children's rights in child justice systems (2019), paras 21 to 23.

118 CRIN, *supra* note 113.

119 At the 27th meeting of Treaty Body Chairs held in Costa Rica in 2015, the Chairpersons acknowledged the importance of consultation for the "transparency, legitimacy and publicity of general comments." It was observed that posting draft General Comments on the OHCHR website and inviting comment from States Parties, NGOs, NHRIs, UN Agencies, and other interested bodies and persons was to be the general practice going forward. Submissions will be taken into account but the final responsibility for drafting rests with the Committees (A/70/302 at ¶¶ 21–25).

C *Case Study Three: the Use of the CRC in United States, Despite Non-Ratification*

In 2015, Somalia and South Sudan ratified the CRC, leaving the United States the only country in the world yet to ratify the Convention.[120] One reason for the resistance of United States with regard to the ratification of the CRC was the fact that ratifying would oblige the state to abolish the death penalty, which until 2005 was applicable to children in some twenty-two States in the USA.[121]

Despite this however, there has been a shift since 2005 regarding the application of the UNCRC in relation to the issue of the death penalty and life imprisonment for offenders who were below the age of 18 years at the time of commission of the offence. The case of *Roper v. Simmons*[122] has been hailed as a breakthrough in the American juvenile justice system.[123] In this case, a seventeen-year-old (Christopher Simmons) and his friend (a child younger than Christopher) committed a pre-meditated murder.[124] Christopher was convicted and sentenced to the death penalty.

Many years later, his sentence was overturned on appeal in a case that abolished the death penalty for offenders below the age of eighteen at the time of the offence. The Supreme Court focused on the difference between adults and youths. The court particularly looked at the behavioral patterns of youths and held that unlike adults, youths are unable to anticipate the imminent consequences of their actions. The problem of peer pressure and the potential of youths to reflect on the consequences of their actions in the future were also considered.[125] The court concluded that children were less culpable than adults.[126] The constitutional provision on which the Court based its opinion was the Eighth Amendment provision against cruel and unusual punishment.[127] The Court declared the death penalty to be unconstitutional insofar as it applied to offenders who had been children at the time of the offence.

---

120 *Hailing Somalia's ratification, UN renews calls for universalization of the CRC*, U.N. NEWS (Oct. 2, 2015), www.un.org/apps/news/story.asp?NewsID=52129.

121 Bernadine Dohrn, *The Surprising Role of the CRC in a Non-State-Party, in* LITIGATING THE RIGHTS OF THE CHILD, *supra* note 49, at 75.

122 *Roper v. Simmons*, 543 U.S. 551 (2005).

123 Dohrn, *supra* note 121, at 77.

124 C. L. Scott, Roper v. Simmons *Can Juvenile Offenders be Executed?*, 33 J. AM. ACAD. PSYCHIATRY L. 547–548 (2005).

125 *Roper v. Simmons*, 543 U.S. at 563.

126 *Id. at* 570 (2005).

127 Elizabeth Scott, et al, *Juvenile Sentencing Reform in a Constitutional Framework*, 2016 TEMPLE L. REV. 675.

And so it was that article 37 played a vital role in the U. S. Supreme Court's striking down of the juvenile death penalty. Article 37 of the CRC abolishes the death penalty and life without parole in respect of offenders who were children when the crimes were committed. Ironically, this article has been identified as one of the main stumbling blocks to ratification of the CRC by the United States.[128] Veteran U.S. child rights activist Bernadine Dorhn has described as "astounding" the fact that the majority judgment in *Roper* "discussed the international isolation on the question of the juvenile death penalty, citing article 37 of the CRC."[129] The court mentioned that none of the countries which had ratified the CRC made reservations in terms of article 37 and further, that since 1990, only seven countries had subjected juvenile offenders to the death penalty whilst other countries had completely abolished this form of punishment for juvenile offenders and others had publicly rejected the execution of juvenile offenders.[130] These factors were all relevant to the court's evaluation of "evolving standards of decency" which it is enjoined to consider when deciding matters that engage the Eighth Amendment. But evolving standards of decency usually focuses on consensus within the US, not beyond it. In *Roper*, however, the Court found as follows: "In sum, it is fair to say that the United States stands alone in a world that has turned its face against the juvenile death penalty." The Court concluded "[t]hat the opinion of the world community, while not controlling our outcome, does provide respected and significant confirmation of our own conclusion."[131]

The *Roper* judgment and the citation of article 37 of the CRC was the beginning of a turnaround for the United States juvenile justice system. This surprising development means that article 37 of the CRC has been integrated into United States constitutional law.[132] The *Roper* case paved the way for cases such as *Graham v. Florida*,[133] where the court held that sentencing juveniles to life without parole for a non-homicide felony is unconstitutional—highlighting the plight of those who did not in fact kill a person, but were convicted of a

128 *Why Won't America Ratify the UN Convention on the Rights of the Child?*, THE ECONOMIST (Oct. 7, 2013), http://www.economist.com/blogs/economist-explains/2013/10/economist-explains-2.

129 Dohrn, *supra* note 121, at 79.

130 *Roper v. Simmons*, 543 U.S. 551, 573 (2005).

131 *Id.* Justice Scalia could not have disagreed more. In his dissent, he roundly rejected the majority's use of international law to confirm its finding of a national consensus, stating that '"[a]cknowledgement' of foreign approval has no place in the legal opinion of this Court."

132 Dohrn, *supra* note 121, at 79–80.

133 *Graham v. Florida*, 560 U.S. 48 (2010).

felony murder in which someone else did the killing.[134] This case affirmed the link between the CRC and the Eighth Amendment, with the court finding that " 'the United States now stands alone in a world that has turned its face against' life without parole for juvenile non homicide offenders" and that life without parole for a child offender gives them "no hope." The *Graham* court again affirmed that the "climate of international opinion" and "global consensus" was relevant to consideration of the Eighth Amendment.[135]

It is significant, here, that the CRC is hard international law, and that it has been so widely ratified—tending towards customary international law.[136] It is notable that where the *Roper* Court refers to the CRC and its express prohibition of capital punishment of children, it also mentions that the International Covenant on Civil and Political Rights (ICCPR) contains a similar provision (though the United States had entered a reservation regarding this article),[137] as does the American Convention on Human Rights, and the African Charter on the Rights and Welfare of the Child. However, the non-binding Beijing Rules are not mentioned in *Roper*, although the Rules also contain the same express provision prohibiting the juvenile death penalty.

The achievements in linking the CRC to the eighth amendment were not produced by the Court alone. There were organized networks of lawyers, researchers and advocates who worked tirelessly to place *amicus briefs* before the courts. Even they seem slightly surprised by their own success, as summed up by Dorhn, who numbered amongst them: "Few recognized that an unfunded and ragtag network of human rights advocates and youth justice litigators would abolish the juvenile death penalty in the US."

It must be acknowledged that the influence of international law was not the only factor in this sea-change—Former director of the Juvenile Law Centre,

134 The case of *Miller v. Alabama*, 132 S. Ct. 2455 (2012), extended the application of the effect of the Graham judgment further by holding that the mandatory sentencing of juveniles to life without parole without consideration their age and circumstances is unconstitutional. It did not expressly refer to the CRC.

135 *Graham v. Florida*, 560 U.S. at 51 (quoting *Roper v. Simmons*, 543 U.S. at 578).

136 Wide ratification, decisions of international tribunals and legal academic opinion all point towards the recognition of the CRC as customary international law. See Amanda Lloyd "*A Theoretical Analysis of Children's Rights in Africa: An Introduction to the African Charter on the Rights and Welfare of the Child,*" 2002 AFR. HUM. RTS. L. J. 11.

137 The court notes at paragraph 13 of the *Roper* judgment that the petitioner (superintendent of the prison) relies on the fact that when the United States ratified the ICCPR, it made a reservation regarding the prohibition of death penalty for juveniles below 18 years. The court found that the reservation "at best provides faint support for the petitioner's argument" because it was passed in 1992 and since then five states (of the United States) had abandoned capital punishment for juveniles.

Bob Schwartz has described the "developmental framework"—based largely on brain science and new knowledge on the development of the adolescent brain—that "would represent a paradigmatic shift in juvenile justice. It would change our world."[138]

Furthermore, while the idea that 'kids are different' caught the public imagination and was even cited in former President Obama's important speech about criminal justice reform,[139] this wave of enthusiasm may be reaching its sell-by date. Indeed, Obama's abolition of solitary detention for juveniles,[140] and his acts of clemency, which have inspired the release of twelve former child offenders in New York State,[141] may signal the end of the winning spree for child rights advocates. The Trump Administration promises to be tough on crime, and will almost certainly not ratify the CRC.

IV Conclusion

The case studies have shown that the interplay between hard and soft international law is not linear. It is a complex weave of binding treaties with non-binding instruments. Jurisprudence can arise from the application of international law, but as illustrated in the children of primary caregivers facing imprisonment example, jurisprudence can also feed back into international and regional law, providing principles and content for General Comments and resolutions. The rights of children of primary caregivers of children facing imprisonment were not specifically dealt with in the CRC which prompted work on the issue by NGOs such as QUNO (although it was initially framed in a more gendered manner as children of imprisoned mothers). In a parallel development, the counsel for the *amicus curiae* in the South African Constitutional Court case of *S v. M* noticed that gap and martialed article 30 of the other hard law treaty on children's rights applicable in the region, the ACRWC, to bridge it. The Court used the provision, and through interpretation reframed it as

138 Robert G. Schwartz, *Preface*, 88 (4) TEMPLE L. REV. 615 (2016).

139 Ursula Kilkelly, *Advancing the Rights of Young People in Juvenile Justice: The Impact of the Juvenile Law Centre*, 88 (4) TEMPLE L. REV. 629 (2016).

140 Michael D. Shear, *Obama bans Solitary Confinement of Juveniles in Federal Prisons*, N.Y. Times (Jan. 26, 2016), https://www.nytimes.com/2016/01/26/us/politics/obama-bans-solitary-confinement-of-juveniles-in-federal-prisons.html?.

141 *Governor Cuomo Grants First-Ever Conditional Pardons to More Than 100 New Yorkers Convicted of Crimes at Ages 16 and 17* (Dec. 30, 2016), https://www.governor.ny.gov/news/governor-cuomo-grants-first-ever-conditional-pardons-more-100-new-yorkers-convicted-crimes-ages.

a gender-neutral provision (although the applicant in the case was in fact a mother). This gender neutral version was taken up by QUNO which shifted the focus of their campaign to "children of imprisoned parents." The subsequent themed day of general discussion was an opportunity for the development of the standard, and the relevant provisions in two declarations as well as the Bangkok Rules are good examples of soft law filling the gap in the CRC. In an interesting flourish, the African Committee of Experts took inspiration from the *S v. M* court's reliance on article 30 of the ACRWC, and expanded its scope in a modernized interpretation through its General Comment no 1.

The second case study on the MACR demonstrates how the attempt to set standards in a General Comment where the CRC and the Beijing Rules were lacking had both positive and negative outcomes. The recommendation of a minimum age of criminal responsibility at twelve years, which was intended by the Committee to be a floor, also became a ceiling. With hindsight, it is apparent that the original drafters of the CRC may have had good reason to set what seemed a vague standard. The mixed response to this aspect of GC 10 is difficult to read. The drafting of general comments is a fairly closed process conducted by experts, and this may explain the lack of buy-in by some states. A UN resolution may have proved more successful as it involves states parties and has a more formal soft international law status. A standout out feature of the minimum age recommendation of twelve years in GC 10 is the effect that this has had on the debates on MACR. Some child rights activists have used the negative effects as a spring-board for a more radical campaign to move away from compromises about the age of 'criminal' responsibility towards a more restorative notion of responsibility for child offenders.

The final case study shows the effect of international law even in a non-ratifying state, which has embedded the international law principles into domestic law through jurisprudence. It is apparent that the hard international law nature of the CRC, as well as its wide ratification, gave it a cogency that the U.S. Supreme Court could attach weight to despite the fact that the United States is not bound by it. The *Roper* court made reference to other hard international law that contained similar provisions but did not mention the Beijing Rules, though the Rules also contain a prohibition of the juvenile death penalty. Creating domestic precedents out of international instruments that have not been ratified is no easy task. The concerted efforts of human rights lawyers, juvenile justice advocates and researchers have achieved a great deal. However, time will tell whether the sea-change will persist into the next administration.

CHAPTER 5

The International Criminal Court and the Use of Hard Law in the Quest for Accountability for Core International Crimes

*Angela Mudukuti**

> Our hope is that, by punishing the guilty, the ICC will bring some comfort to the surviving victims and to the communities that have been targeted. More important, we hope it will deter future war criminals, and bring nearer the day when no ruler, no State, no junta and no army anywhere will be able to abuse human rights with impunity.
>
> KOFI ANNAN[1]

1 Introduction

Hard international law is essential to ensure accountability for core international crimes.[2] Whilst core international crimes can be prosecuted at the

---

* Angela Mudukuti (LLM) is a Zimbabwean human rights lawyer specializing in International Criminal Law and currently with the Wayamo Foundation. She was previously with the International Criminal Court, the Southern Africa Litigation Centre, and Cherif Bassiouni at the Siracusa International Institute for Criminal Justice and Human Rights and holds and LLB and LLM.

1 U.N. Secretary-General, Address to the Mexican Congress, U.N. Doc. SG/SM/8171 (Mar. 21, 2002) ("The argument in [favor] of aid has now been won"), https://www.un.org/press/en/2002/sgsm8171.doc.htm.

2 Core international crimes include genocide, crimes against humanity, and war crimes as defined by the Rome Statute. UN General Assembly, Rome Statute of the International Criminal Court arts 6–8, July 17, 1998, 2187 U.N.T.S. 90, https://www.icc-cpi.int/nr/rdonlyres/ea9aeff7-5752-4f84-be94-0a655eb30e16/0/rome_statute_english.pdf [hereinafter *Rome Statute*]. For the purposes of this paper the crime of aggression will not be discussed. The ICC has only had jurisdiction over the crime of aggression since July 2018 when it entered into force. At the time of writing there had been no litigation at the ICC pertaining to the crime of aggression.

 | DOI:10.1163/9789004417021_006

domestic level, it is the happenings at the international level, namely the International Criminal Court (ICC), that forms the main component of this chapter. The ICC is arguably the most ambitious permanent international project embarked on in the name of justice and accountability, and it vividly displays both the challenges and the advantages of using hard international law. This chapter will assess the ICC's (and thus hard international law's) contribution to accountability for core international crimes including the associated challenges and opportunities. This chapter does not contend that soft law cannot contribute positively to the discourse on international criminal law, but it posits that hard law, in this instance, has been indispensable to punishing perpetrators, providing justice for the victims, reparations and deterring future perpetrators.

II The ICC—a Manifestation of Hard International Law

Hard international law is understood to be binding in nature and includes treaties, protocols, covenants, or conventions that has been ratified or acceded to by states.[3] Due to its binding nature, hard international law is very difficult to negotiate, and consensus is hard to reach. The ICC is no different in this regard. It too is the result of hard negotiations and compromise.

The ICC is a court designed to secure accountability, combat impunity, deter would-be perpetrators and, through the Trust Fund for Victims (TVF), organise reparations—all of which are easier to achieve with hard international law structures that have binding power. The ICC is up and running now. However, the road to establishing an international accountability mechanism based on hard international law has been long and challenging.

A *The Road to a Permanent International Accountability Mechanism*

Many commentators trace the origins of the ICC to 1872 when Gustav Moynier, a founder of the International Committee of the Red Cross, suggested that a permanent court be established to respond to crimes committed during the Franco Prussian War.[4] The suggestion was echoed in 1919

---

3 Statute of the International Court of Justice, Art. 38, June 26, 1945, 59 Stat. 1055, 33 U.N.T.S. 993; International Commission of Jurists et al., *Human Rights Standard: Learning from Experience*, 11, http://www.ichrp.org/files/reports/31/120b_report_en.pdf.

4 Coalition for the International Criminal Court, http://www.iccnow.org/?mod=icchistory [hereinafter *Coalition for the ICC*].

by the drafters of the Versailles Treaty (mostly technical experts and politicians from France, Britain, Japan, the USA and Italy), who thought an *ad hoc* international court should be established to try German war criminals for the transgressions of World War I.[5] The Versailles Treaty originally provided for the prosecution of what would be referred to today as "war criminals" including Emperor Wilhelm II,[6] and it mandated Germany to extradite "all persons accused of having committed an act in violation of the laws and customs of war".[7] Germany never fully accepted the provision allowing prosecution and never truly implemented it. Germany also managed to water down the duty to extradite war criminals. They ultimately held only domestic trials.[8]

The next vital moment in the history of international criminal justice came in the wake of the Second World War. The victorious Allied Forces decided to hold high level Nazis accountable and thus the International Military Tribunal at Nuremberg was established. The International Military Tribunal for the Far East (otherwise known as the Tokyo Tribunal) was created to hold senior Japanese military and political leaders accountable. Neither were ever intended to be permanent courts and by 1946 the Nuremberg trials were concluded, and the Tokyo trials came to an end by 1948.[9]

In 1948, the UN General Assembly adopted the Convention on the Prevention and Punishment of the Crime of Genocide which contained a call for criminals to be tried "by such international penal tribunals as may have jurisdiction"[10] and invited the International Law Commission (ILC) to analyse the possibility of creating such an institution.

---

5 *Id.*

6 Univ. of Glasgow, *Towards International Courts*, https://www.futurelearn.com/courses/ww1-new-world-order/2/steps/21579.

7 Peace Treaty of Versailles (Versailles Treaty) art. 228, June 28, 1919, ("[T]he German Government shall hand over to the Allied and Associated Powers, or to such one of them as shall so request, all persons accused of having committed an act in violation of the laws and customs of war, who are specified either by name or by the rank, office or employment which they held under the German authorities."), https://www.loc.gov/law/help/us-treaties/bevans/m-ust000002-0043.pdf.

8 Univ. of Glasgow, *supra* note 6.

9 U.S. DEP'T OF STATE, OFFICE OF THE HISTORIAN, THE NUREMBERG TRIAL AND THE TOKYO WAR CRIMES TRIALS (1945–1948), https://history.state.gov/milestones/1945–1952/nuremberg.

10 Convention on the Prevention and Punishment of the Crime of Genocide, Dec. 9, 1948, 78 U.N.T.S. 276 (entered into force Jan. 12, 1951); U.N. Office of Legal Affairs, *Why Do We Need an International Criminal Court?*, http://legal.un.org/icc/general/overview.htm.

The ILC did indeed draft a document in the early 1950s, but the Cold War interrupted this initiative and the General Assembly put the concept on ice in light of technical challenges such as finding a definition of the crime of aggression[11] and the development of an international code of crimes.[12]

The initiative was resurrected in 1989 by Trinidad and Tobago's Prime Minister Arthur Robinson. Trinidad and Tobago were deeply concerned about the effects of drug trafficking and hoped a court that had the necessary jurisdiction over this crime could be established. Robinson, with the help of ICC advocate Robert Woetzel, former Nuremberg Prosecutor Benjamin Ferencz, and international criminal law expert Cherif Bassiouni, drafted a motion for the General Assembly calling for the "establishment of an international criminal court with the jurisdiction to prosecute and punish individuals and entities who engage in inter alia, the illicit trafficking in narcotic drugs across national borders."[13] Their motion to the UN General Assembly thus re-invigorated the process of establishing a permanent accountability mechanism.[14]

The UN General Assembly adopted the motion and asked the ILC to resume its work on a draft document. The Rwandan Genocide, the conflicts in Bosnia-Herzegovina and Croatia, with their mass perpetration of crimes against humanity and war crimes inspired the UN to established two temporary *ad hoc* tribunals. This showed just how necessary a permanent mechanism was.[15]

In 1993 the ILC prepared a draft document under the guidance of Special Rapporteur James Crawford. Bassiouni gathered a number of non-governmental organisations who were referred to as the NGO Committee of Experts to review the document. This group met in Siracusa, Italy and worked on the draft. In general, NGOs have been accredited with positively influencing the process and to adding a layer of complexity.[16] Pearson writes that NGOs

---

11 Bassiouni writes that the crime of aggression or crime against peace at that time was the "first and most important crime" to be included in the draft and thus the failure of agree on a definition was "indispensable" and thus it significantly stalled the process. It was also used as a convenient political excuse to delay the entire process, according to Bassiouni. A DRAFT INTERNATIONAL CRIMINAL CODE AND DRAFT STATUTE FOR AN INTERNATIONAL CRIMINAL TRIBUNAL 7 (M. Cherif Bassiouni ed., 1987).

12 *Coalition for the ICC*, *supra* note 4.

13 BENJAMIN N. SCHIFF, BUILDING THE INTERNATIONAL CRIMINAL COURT 37 (2008).

14 U.N. Office of Legal Affairs, *supra* note 10.

15 *Coalition for the ICC*, *supra* note 4.

16 Zoe Pearson, *Non-Governmental Organizations and the International Criminal Court: Changing Landscapes of International Law*, 39(2)(ii) CORNELL INT'L L. J. 283 (2006) ("The overall picture of NGO involvement in these international fora is a positive one, with indications that these groups were able to significantly influence the substance and structure of the ICC negotiations. The ICC negotiations show the ability of a variety

brought recognised expertise to the discussions.[17] They also actively sought to ensure the preservation of victims' rights and emphasised the importance of issues such as gender-based crimes, the conscription of child soldiers, and reparations.[18]

The draft was presented to the UN General Assembly in 1994,[19] which established the Preparatory Committee[20] on the Establishment of the ICC to consolidate the draft statute. From 1996–1998 the Committee sat for six sessions with the goal of completing a document that could be adopted by States at a conference to be held in Rome, Italy.

They began with a preliminary document containing sixty-eight articles from the ILC. After nineteen weeks of meetings and drafting, the Preparatory Committee sent the document to the participants in the forthcoming conference. It contained 116 articles and 1,700 brackets with disputed and contentious language.[21]

The General Assembly convened the conference at its 52nd session. The Rome Conference, as it became known, took place from June 15 to July 17, 1998 in Rome, Italy. 160 countries and more than 200 NGOs were involved.[22] After five hard weeks of negotiations and discussions, 120 nations voted in favour of the adoption of the Rome Statute. Only seven nations voted against the treaty. They were Libya, Yemen, China, Israel, Iraq, Qatar, and the United States of America [23]. Twenty-one states abstained.[24]

---

of NGOs acting within network structures, autonomously and cooperatively, to further particular agendas and issues at the international level.").

17 *Id.* at 281.

18 Schiff, *supra* note 13, at 39.

19 *Id.* at 38.

20 *See* John Washburn, *The Negotiation of the Rome Statute for the International Criminal Court and International Law-making in the 21st Century*, 11 PACE INT'L L. REV. 361 (1999); G.A. Res. 50/46, U.N. GAOR, 50th Sess., Supp.No.49 at 307, U.N. Doc. A/50/46 (1995). For the background and history of the ICC issue at the United Nations, *see* THE STATUTE OF THE INTERNATIONAL CRIMINAL COURT: A DOCUMENTARY HISTORY 1–35 (M. Cherif Bassiouni ed., 1998); Roy Lee, *The Rome Conference and Its Contribution to International Law, in* THE INTERNATIONAL CRIMINAL COURT: THE MAKING OF THE ROME STATUTE 1–40 (Roy Lee ed., 1999).

21 Washburn, *supra* note 20, at 361. *See* Rep. of the Preparatory Committee on the Establishment of an Int'l Crim. Ct., U.N. Diplomatic Conference of Plenipotentiaries on the Establishment of an Int'l Crim. Ct., U.N. Doc. A/Conf. 183/2/ Add.1 (1998).

22 *Coalition for the ICC*, *supra* note 4.

23 Michael P. Scharf, *Results of the Rome Conference for an International Criminal Court.* 3(10) AM. SOC'Y OF INT'L L. (August 1998).

24 *Coalition for the ICC*, *supra* note 4.

The Prepartory Committee was also tasked with developing additional documents related to the elements of the crimes that would be subject to the jurisdiction of the court, and its rules of procedure and evidence.

Finally, on April 11, 2002, the 60th ratification required to bring the Statute into force was deposited. July 1, 2002 marks the official entry into force of the Rome Statute.

After the legal establishment of the ICC, the practical elements of running the court had to be dealt with, which included hiring staff and other operational elements. During this time, additional states acceded to the Statute. To date the ICC has 122 State Parties to the Rome Statute, of which 33 are African States, 18 Asia-Pacific States, 18 Eastern European States, 28 Latin American and Caribbean States, and 25 are from Western European and other States.[25]

III The ICC's Positive Impact

While it is difficult to quantify impact[26] and there are varied interpretations and understandings of what constitutes impact, for the purposes of this

---

25 Assembly of States Parties, https://asp.icc-cpi.int/en_menus/asp/states%20parties/Pages/states%20parties%20_%20chronological%20list.aspx.

26 In 2015, the Open Society Justice Initiative (OSJI) published a briefing paper, entitled Establishing Performance Indicators for the International Criminal Court, after the Assembly of States Parties in requested that the Court develop such indicators. In the OSJI Briefing Paper 2015 they highlight the complexities of establishing such indicators for judicial institutions. They note that, "While the notion of performance indicators is relatively simple, the actual process of developing performance indicators may be rather complex. There are also specific complexities that relate to development of performance indicators for judicial institutions. Measuring the performance of such institutions differs from other organizations because the "end product" is the criminal justice process itself. Excellence is therefore measured by the quality and integrity of each step, each action, from the first awareness of possible crimes through the final appeal following a trial and verdict. Justice may be done through a conviction or through a prosecutorial decision to decline prosecution for lack of evidence. In either case, it is the quality of the process that guarantees that the outcomes are right. Despite these challenges, national judicial institutions in several countries have been able to develop performance indicators. The ICC can draw inspiration and lessons from such experiences. In addition, developing indicators for the ICC presents some unique challenges. In order to be meaningful and intelligible to outsiders and allow for accurate self-reflection by the ICC itself, indicators must reflect on the Court's work as one institution ("court-wide indicators"). This may be difficult because the Court's three organs (Presidency and Chambers, Office of the Prosecutor and Registry) have traditionally operated separately. While there have been efforts in recent years to implement a one-court principle that aims to bring the three organs together, the institutional culture of each organ operating as a separate entity may present challenges

chapter the positive impact of the ICC will include the unique and active participation model for victims, convictions (from the perspective of victims and the Office of the Prosecutor), reparations, and deterrence.

A. *Victim Participation at the ICC*

Drawing from the civil law system and seeking to avoid the criticism levelled against the International Criminal Tribunal for the former Yugoslavia and International Criminal Tribunal for Rwanda that had no such victim participation model, the ICC developed a system that international criminal law expert Christine Chung refers to as "a major innovation."[27] Others have called it "one of the most notable aspects"[28] of the Rome Statute. It has also been suggested that active victim participation could restore the victims' dignity and facilitate a process of reconciliation and fact finding.[29]

The Rome Statue allows for the extensive legal participation of victims, not just as witnesses for prosecutors or defence teams, but as active participants. This is enshrined in Article 68.[30] Rules 87–93 of the ICC Rules of Procedure and Evidence further detail the provisions of victim participation.[31] Victims, for purposes of the Rules of Procedure and Evidence, are defined as:

> (a) … natural persons who have suffered harm as a result of the commission of any crime within the jurisdiction of the Court;
>
> (b) Victims may include organizations or institutions that have sustained direct harm to any of their property which is dedicated to religion, education, art or science or charitable purposes, and to their historic

---

for the indicators project." Open Soc'y Just. Initiative, *Establishing Performance Indicators for the International Criminal Court; Briefing Paper*, (Nov. 2015), https://www.opensocietyfoundations.org/sites/default/files/briefing-icc-perforamnce-indicators-20151208.pdf.

27 Christine H. Chung, *Victims' Participation at the International Criminal Court: Are Concessions of the Court Clouding the Promise?*, 6 NW. J. INT'L HUM. RTS. 459, 459 (2008).

28 Charles P. Trumbull IV, *The Victims of Victim Participation in International Criminal Proceedings*, 29 MICH. J. INT'L L. 777, 778 (2008).

29 *Id.* at 777.

30 *Rome Statute*, *supra* note 2, art. 68 ("Where the personal interests of the victims are affected, the Court shall permit their views and concerns to be presented and considered at stages of the proceedings determined to be appropriate by the Court and in a manner which is not prejudicial to or inconsistent with the rights of the accused and a fair and impartial trial. Such views and concerns may be presented by the legal representatives of the victims where the Court considers it appropriate, in accordance with the Rules of Procedure and Evidence.").

31 ICC Rules of Procedure and Evidence, Rule 85(a), https://www.icc-cpi.int/iccdocs/pids/legal-texts/rulesprocedureevidenceeng.pdf.

monuments, hospitals and other places and objects for humanitarian purposes.[32]

Participation, which is subject to the judges' discretion, can include making opening and closing statements, giving testimony, and questioning other witnesses through legal counsel. The ICC was the first[33] international criminal tribunal to recognize this form of participation in proceedings.[34]

This practice is partly inspired by the civil legal systems, which allow a victim to act as "*partie civile.*"[35] Under the doctrine of "*partie civile,*" a victim may, through their legal counsel, or through the prosecution, provide evidence in the criminal trial "which the victim deems necessary for the subsequent pursuit of damages in civil proceedings."[36]

According to the 1999 UN Handbook on Justice for Victims, in Argentina, victims are allowed to have legal counsel who is mandated to act as a "victim-prosecutor."[37] This includes cross-examination of witnesses, making closing statements, reviewing evidence, and even making recommendations to the investigative magistrate.[38]

While the ICC's model of victim participation is definitely worthy of recognition, it has been criticized over the course of the Court's existence because only a limited number of victims have actually been able to participate. In addition, some have argued that the potential long-term harm done to victims of ICC situation countries (including those who take part in the trial and those who do not get the opportunity to do so) is still unknown,[39] raising questions about the value of the model itself.

32 *Id.*

33 *See* Conference Summary: Victim Participation in International Criminal Justice at a Crossroads: A Promising Route Forward? (Feb. 28, 2018), https://www.law.ox.ac.uk/centres-institutes/centre-criminology/blog/2018/02/victim-participation-international-criminal.

34 Chung, *supra* note 27, at 459.

35 Gerard J. Mekjian & Mathew C. Varughese, *Hearing the Victim's Voice: Analysis of Victims' Advocate Participation in the Trial Proceeding of the International Criminal Court,* 17 PACE INT'L L. REV. 1, 16 (2005).

36 Gerard J. Mekjian & Mathew C. Varughese, *Hearing the Victim's Voice: Analysis of Victims' Advocate Participation in the Trial Proceeding of the International Criminal Court,* 17 PACE INT'L L. REV. 1, 17 (2005).

37 CRIMINAL PROCEDURE: A WORLDWIDE STUDY 45 (Craig Bradley ed., 1999); U.N. OFFICE FOR DRUG CONTROL & CRIME PREVENTION, HANDBOOK ON JUSTICE FOR VICTIMS 39 (1999) [hereinafter *Handbook on Justice*].

38 Bradley, *supra* note 37, at 45; *Handbook on Justice, supra* note 37, at 39.

39 Chris Tenove, *Victim Participation at the ICC—What is the deal?,* (Nov. 22, 2013), https://justiceinconflict.org/2013/11/22/victim-participation-at-the-icc-whats-the-deal.

B *Convictions*

As a court of law, convictions are part and parcel of the process; however, when assessing the question of convictions at the ICC, one must begin by acknowledging that the ICC is composed of four different organs (Office of the Prosecutor (OTP), the Registry, the Presidency, and the Judicial Divisions) and that convictions are a measure of success for only one of those organs—the OTP. Convictions can be viewed as successes from the OTP's perspective given that the Office of the Prosecutor of the ICC is mandated to hold those who are deemed most responsible to account. For convictions to be credible, it is indispensable that the process leading to the conviction include thorough investigations, due process, fair trials, transparency, and sound judicial reasoning.

Despite the OTP having only secured three convictions at the time of writing, as discussed below these convictions have been important for victims and affected communities because these convictions have resulted in the granting of reparations to them.

1 Lubanga

The ICC's first conviction was that of Thomas Lubanga Dyilo, the former leader of the Union of Congolese Patriots (UPC) militia group, from the Democratic Republic of Congo (DRC). His war crime (enlisting and conscripting children under the age of fifteen years and using them to participate actively in hostilities)[40] was perpetrated during the Ituri conflict.[41]

Ituri, a region in the north-eastern parts of the DRC, has been ravaged by conflict since 1999. This conflict is so catastrophic that it has been called the most devastating since World War II.[42] The conflict continues today albeit at a different level of intensity. At the heart of it is ethnic tension, and competition for natural resources. In 2006 the BBC reported that at least 60,000 people had died since 1999 as different rebel groups fought each other and the DRC government for control.[43] The DRC government referred the situation to the

40 ICC, Case Information Sheet: The Prosecutor v. Thomas Lubanga Dyilo, https://www.icc-cpi.int/CaseInformationSheets/LubangaEng.pdf [hereinafter *Lubanga Case Info Sheet*].

41 Prosecutor v. Lubanga, ICC-01/04-01/06, Judgment and Sentence, (2012), https://www.icc-cpi.int/drc/lubanga.

42 INT'L CTR. FOR TRANSITIONAL JUST., *Democratic Republic of Congo: Impact of the Rome Statute and the International Criminal Court* (May 2010), https://www.ictj.org/sites/default/files/ICTJ-DRC-Impact-ICC-2010-English.pdf.

43 BBC NEWS, *Eastern DR Congo Rebels to Disarm*, (Nov. 30, 2006), http://newsvote.bbc.co.uk/mpapps/pagetools/print/news.bbc.co.uk/2/hi/africa/6158331.stm.

ICC in 2004. The ICC investigated crimes against humanity and war crimes committed since the Rome Statute came into force on July 1, 2002 and focused on Eastern DRC, the Ituri region and the North and South Kivu Provinces.

After a preliminary examination and further investigations, the ICC, indicted Thomas Lubanga, and five other rebel leaders, including Germain Katanga who was also convicted.

On March 14, 2012, Lubanga was found guilty of the war crime of enlisting and conscripting children under the age of fifteen years and using them to participate actively in hostilities.[44] By this point, Lubanga had been in the ICC detention centre since 2006.

On July 10, 2012, he was sentenced to a total of fourteen years of imprisonment, but time served in custody was subtracted. The conviction and sentence were confirmed by the ICC Appeals Chamber in December 2014. One year later, Thomas Lubanga was transferred to a prison in the DRC where he is to serve the remainder of his sentence.

The fact that victims and witnesses were able to tell their stories, to be heard and to receive justice is an example of the powerful impact institutions backed by hard international law can make. In their closing statement, the legal representative for victims noted that "the main concern of the victims participating in this trial was the establishment of the truth and the punishment of the individuals who were the cause of their victimisation."[45]

This case has also contributed significantly to international criminal law jurisprudence, as it is the first international case involving the use of child soldiers. It provides legal clarity on the specific features of the conscription and enlistment and use of child soldiers in conflict.[46] The case has raised awareness about the plight of children in conflict and that their conscription, enlistment, and use in combat is a war crime.[47]

Lubanga's trial is also significant as it is the first trial to reach the phase of reparations (an issue which will be addressed below).

44 *Lubanga Case Info Sheet*, *supra* note 40.

45 INT'L JUST. MONITOR, Summary of the Closing Statements in the Prosecutor v. Thomas Lubanga Dyilo, https://www.ijmonitor.org/2011/11/summary-of-the-closing-statements-in-the-prosecutor-v-thomas-lubanga-dyilo/.

46 Triestino Mariniello, "Prosecutor v. Thomas Lubanga Dyilo: The First Judgement of the International Criminal Court's Trial Chamber" INT'L HUM. RTS. L. REV. 137–147, 138 (2012).

47 HUM. RTS. WATCH, *First Verdict at the International Criminal Court: The case of the Prosecutor vs. Thomas Lubanga Dyilo*, 4, (2012), https://www.hrw.org/sites/default/files/related_material/2012_DRC_Lubanga.pdf.

Despite these positive aspects, Lubanga's trial was not without blemishes as the Office of the Prosecutor (OTP) made several costly mistakes that were deemed to have jeopardised the rights of the accused. The trial was set to begin on June 13, 2008 but was delayed for five months due to the OTP's failure to disclose potentially exculpatory evidence to the accused's legal representation. This resulted in the Trial Chamber's decision to issue a formal stay of proceedings until the disclosure issue was settled.[48] The Trial Chamber also ordered Lubanga's release on this basis on July 3, 2008.[49] The OTP appealed the release and the Appeals Chamber reversed the release order on October 21, 2008. The trial continued before Trial Chamber I but hit another snag in July 2010 when, despite a court order to that effect, the OTP failed to disclose the identity of an intermediary[50] who had been implicated in suspected witness tampering. On July 15, 2010, Trial Chamber I ordered a stay of proceedings and Lubanga's release due to fair trial concerns.[51] The Appeals Chamber reversed the stay of proceedings and the release order on the grounds that the Trial Chamber made a mistake when it imposed the stay of proceedings without considering other options, like sanctions on the prosecutor for failure to comply with the order to reveal the identity of the intermediary in question.[52] These complications prolonged the trial significantly. It took five years to try one man, from the commencement of the trial in 2008 to conviction in 2012.

2 Katanga

Germain Katanga, former leader of the Patriotic Resistance Force in Ituri, another armed group operating in Ituri, was convicted and found guilty on March 7, 2014. The judgement is final as both the prosecution and defence withdrew their appeals. He was convicted as an accessory to one count of crimes against humanity (murder) and four counts of war crimes (murder, attacking a civilian population, destruction of property and pillaging). He was sentenced to twelve years imprisonment.[53] Human rights activist working with victims stated that

---

48 INT'L JUST. MONITOR, *Lubanga Judgment—The Prosecution's Investigation and Use of Intermediaries*, (Aug. 20, 2012), https://www.ijmonitor.org/2012/08/lubanga-judgment-the-prosecutions-investigation-and-use-of-intermediaries/.

49 INT'L JUST. MONITOR, *Trial Monitor Timeline*, https://www.ijmonitor.org/thomas-lubanga-timeline/.

50 Intermediaries (individuals and organizations) were used by the OTP to contact witnesses and often acted as liaisons between the ICC and the affected communities on the ground.

51 INT'L JUST. MONITOR, *Lubanga Judgment, supra* note 48.

52 *Id.*

53 Prosecutor v. Katanga, ICC-01/04-01/07, Order on victim reparations, (Mar. 24, 2017), https://www.icc-cpi.int/drc/katanga.

"We welcome this second guilty verdict issued by the ICC as it brings hope of reparations to victims. The decision comes at the right time for the people of Ituri, as well as for all the affected communities in Irumu, Bunia, and the surrounding area, which unfortunately are still plagued by violence."[54] However, others were dissatisfied with the sentence and the failure to convict him for rape and sexual slavery.[55]

Many[56] question and criticise the ICC's DRC trials. They point to the following issues in their criticisms: selection of crimes; selection of geographical areas investigated; the fact that members of the current DRC government have not been investigated; and whether all victims have been taken into account.[57] This further amplifies the difficulty of quantifying and assessing impact. Whilst those questions and issues are valid, it would be inaccurate to say that no impact has been made. As will be explained below, reparations have been vital for many communities.

---

54 Olivia Bueno, *In Ituri, Katanga Verdict Viewed as a Limited Success,* (Mar. 2014), https://www.ijmonitor.org/2014/03/in-ituri-katanga-verdict-viewed-as-a-limited-success/.

55 *Special Issue of Legal Eye on the ICC,* (May 2014), https://www.ijmonitor.org/2014/05/icc-partially-convicts-katanga-in-third-trial-judgment-acquitting-katanga-of-rape-and-sexual-slavery/ ("ICC partially convicts Katanga in third Trial Judgment, acquitting Katanga of rape and sexual slavery").

56 For example, "The main criticism of the court pertains to the prosecutorial and investigative strategy of the Office of the Prosecutor. One of the primary criticisms of the ICC's investigations in the DRC cases is that they lack representativeness, reflecting only part of the conflict, in terms of both affected victims and temporal scope. The proceedings also revealed deficiencies in respect of fair trial principles, especially those related to the rights of defendants. These principles, considered fundamental in national and international law, are guaranteed by the Rome Statute of the ICC and the ICC's Rules of Procedure and Evidence (RPE), in particular those regulating evidence. When these principles are violated, the consequences can be catastrophic for the defence as well as the prosecution, and they can undermine the fairness of the entire trial. Any violation of fair trial principles can thus cause interruptions and delays and even impede the prosecution of alleged perpetrators for the sum of their crimes. Indeed, this occurred in the DRC cases, when the gathering of evidence, use of intermediaries, and application of the exception of confidentiality and nondisclosure were called into question." Reflections on ICC Jurisprudence Regarding the Democratic Republic of the Congo Drawing Lessons from the Court's First Cases ICTJ Briefings available at https://www.ictj.org/sites/default/files/ICTJ-Briefing-DRC-ICCReflections-2014.pdf accessed 29 June 2018 and DR Congo: ICC Charges Raise Concern Joint letter to the Chief Prosecutor of the International Criminal Court available at https://www.hrw.org/news/2006/07/31/dr-congo-icc-charges-raise-concern.

57 INT'L CTR. TRANSITIONAL JUST., *Democratic Republic of Congo: Impact of the Rome Statute and the International Criminal Court*, https://www.ictj.org/sites/default/files/ICTJ-DRC-Impact-ICC-2010-English.pdf.

3 Al Mahdi Case

The ICC has also brought justice for intentional attacks on historic monuments and buildings dedicated to religion in Timbuktu, Mali. The Northern Mali Conflict began in 2012 as tensions between the north and southern parts of Mali increased and as Islamist groups such as Assan Edine, battled for control of the north. Assan Eddine is a movement allegedly associated with Al Qaeda.[58]

Mali requested the Court's intervention and as a result Ahmad Al Mahdi Al Faqi, an alleged member of Assane Edine, was charged with war crimes including attacking a mosque and nine mausoleums.[59] In an unprecedented turn of events, Al Mahdi pled guilty. His is the third case to progress to the reparations phase after Lubanga and Katanga. The Al Mahdi case is the first case before the ICC to deal with cultural heritage law and it is hoped that his conviction will serve as a form of deterrence. El-Boukhari Ben Essayouti, who, in conjunction with UNESCO oversaw the reconstruction of the Sidi Yahia mosque (the mosque that was laid to waste by Al Mahdi and reopened in 2016), hoped that Al Mahdi's trial would show "to everyone that in the same way that we cannot kill another person with impunity, we cannot just destroy a world heritage site with impunity either."[60]

4 Acquittals and Non-Confirmation of Charges

One cannot talk about convictions without mentioning acquittals and failure to confirm charges. Acquittals are a failure from the victim's perspective as well as that of the OTP, but they are an inherent and vital part of a fair criminal justice system and a reflection of the judges' legal opinion on the evidence put before them. Justice and due process require that the accused be acquitted if the prosecutor has failed to prove guilt beyond reasonable doubt. The ICC judges have acquitted four people thus far. Laurent Gbagbo and Charles Ble Goude from the Ivory Coast, (at the time of writing) were acquitted by Trial Chamber 1 but the OTP indicated that it would consider its options[61]

---

58 ICC, Al Mahdi Case, Case Information Sheet, https://www.icc-cpi.int/CaseInformationSheets/Al-MahdiEng.pdf.

59 ICC, Al Mahdi case: Reparations Order Becomes Final, (Mar. 8, 2018), https://www.icc-cpi.int/mali/al-mahdi.

60 Africa Times, Mali Dedicates Restored UNESCO Mosque at Center of ICC Case, (Sep. 2016), https://africatimes.com/2016/09/20/mali-dedicates-restored-unesco-mosque-at-center-of-icc-case/.

61 "The Prosecution has the right to appeal this decision … We will be carefully analysing the written decision of the Trial Chamber I and its reasons when they become available and assess the appropriate next steps" Statement of the ICC Prosecutor,

after the full judgment is released. The other two are Mathieu Ngudjolo Chui and Jean Pierre Bemba. Bemba was initially convicted and then acquitted on appeal.[62]

The Democratic Republic of Congo's Jean Pierre Bemba, was found guilty of crimes against humanity (including murder and rape) and war crimes, by the Trial Chamber on June 21, 2016.[63] The crimes were allegedly committed in the Central African Republic during a time when Bemba was the military commander of the Movement for the Liberation of Congo. This case is particularly important as it was the first ICC trial judgement to find a perpetrator guilty under the doctrine of command responsibility[64] and the first to provide a conviction for sexual violence. Sexual violence is rampant in conflict situations and is yet to be thoroughly handled by the international community or its courts. The Bemba judgment was a significant step in the right direction as it sent a clear message that rape, and other forms of sexual violence will not go unpunished.

However, the conviction was overturned on appeal on June 8, 2018, and Bemba was acquitted of crimes against humanity.

The confirmation of charges phase is when charges presented by the Prosecutor are either confirmed or not, and occurs prior to the commencement of the actual trial.[65] Charges were not confirmed against Callixte Mbarushimana, Abu Garda, Kenya's Mohammed Hussein Ali and Henry Kiprono Kosgey. Charges were vacated against Kenya's William Samoei Ruto and Joshua Arap Sang and charges were withdrawn in the case of current Kenyan President Uhuru Kenyatta.[66]

Fatou Bensouda, following today's decision by Trial Chamber I in the case of Laurent Gbagbo and Charles Blé Goudé, (Jan. 15, 2019), https://www.icc-cpi.int/Pages/item.aspx?name=190115-otp-stat-gbagbo.

62 ICC, Closed stage, https://www.icc-cpi.int/Pages/closed.aspx [hereinafter *ICC Closed Stage*].

63 Prosecutor v. Bemba, ICC-01/05-01/08, Majority decision of Appeals Chamber acquitting Bemba from charges of war crimes and crimes against humanity, https://www.icc-cpi.int/car/bemba#17.

64 *Rome Statute*, *supra* note 2, at art. 28.

65 *Id.* at art. 61 ("Subject to the provisions of paragraph 2, within a reasonable time after the person's surrender or voluntary appearance before the Court, the Pre-Trial Chamber shall hold a hearing to confirm the charges on which the Prosecutor intends to seek trial. The hearing shall be held in the presence of the Prosecutor and the person charged, as well as his or her counsel.").

66 *ICC Closed Stage*, *supra* note 62.

C *Reparations and the Trust Fund for Victims*

At the ICC reparations are only awarded when a conviction is secured. When the accused is deemed indigent, (for purposes of reparations) by the Court, reparations are provided by the Trust Fund for Victims (TFV). The TFV, created in 2004 by the Assembly of States Parties, is also mandated to provide reparative assistance to victims and their families. This reparative assistance is not dependent on a conviction.

The TFV was created in terms of article 79 of the Rome Statute[67] and its mandate is twofold as it is designed to:

1) provide reparative assistance to victims and their families in ICC situations through programmes of psychological rehabilitation, physical rehabilitation, and material support and;
2) implement judicial reparations awards ordered against a convicted person by the Court.[68]

The assistance mandate of the TFV means that it provides "psychological rehabilitation, physical rehabilitation, and material support" to victims and their families in ICC situation countries. This part of their mandate is not connected to particular cases before the Court but to situations identified by the Court. This allows the Fund to act in a timely manner and to respond to the pressing needs of the affected communities. It also allows them to assist a wider range of victims not just those who have a connection to a specific case before the ICC. [69]

The TFV's second responsibility is to "implement judicial reparations awards ordered against a convicted person by the Court." This process is naturally dependent on a conviction and can only be conducted after a conviction has been secured. The TFV uses a combination of monetary contributions from public and private donors, and court-ordered fines and forfeitures to assist affected communities.[70]

---

67 *Rome Statute, supra* note 2, at Art. 79(1) ("A Trust Fund shall be established by decision of the Assembly of States Parties for the benefit of victims of crimes within the jurisdiction of the Court, and of the families of such victims."); *Id.* at Art. 79(2) ("The Court may order money and other property collected through fines or forfeiture to be transferred, by order of the Court, to the Trust Fund."); *Id.* at Art. 79(3) ("The Trust Fund shall be managed according to criteria to be determined by the Assembly of States Parties.").

68 Trust Fund for Victims (TFV), *Background Information,* https://www.trustfundforvictims.org/sites/default/files/inline-files/TFV%20Background%20Information_1.pdf.

69 *Id.*

70 TFV, *Strategic Plan 2014–2017,* (Aug. 2014), https://www.trustfundforvictims.org/sites/default/files/imce/1408%20TFV%20Strategic%20Plan%202014–2017%20Final%20ENG.pdf.

In the Lubanga matter, the first reparations order was issued in August 2012 but numerous appeals seeking clarity were filed by the all parties and an amended order for collective reparations was handed down by the Appeals Chamber in 2015. Lubanga's liability for reparations was set at ten million USD, despite him being deemed indigent.[71] This leaves the financial matters in the hands of the TFV.[72] Four-hundred-thirty-seven persons submitted files in support of their reparations claims and 425 of them were recognised as being direct or indirect victims eligible for collective reparations.[73]

Direct victims, according to the Chamber, have experienced "material, physical and/or psychological damages",[74] whilst indirect victims had to show, amongst other factors, "a personal relationship or connection to the direct victim in addition to establishing harm."[75]

The TFV has designated that money will go towards psychological rehabilitation, physical rehabilitation and socio-economic measures, including helping victims establish sustainable livelihoods.[76] The TFV will also handle symbolic reparations and this includes building commemoration centres. Medical treatment for victims is also on the list of issues to be dealt with by the TFV.

Katanga was also deemed indigent[77] by the Trial Chamber on March 24, 2017 and reparations were set at one million USD in total. The court awarded individual reparations to the recognised 297 victims, "namely compensation in the form of a symbolic award of USD 250, and collective reparations designed to benefit individual victims, in the form of support for housing, support for an income-generating activity, support for education and psychological support."[78]

---

71 Wairagala Wakabi, *Lubanga's Financial Liability for Reparations Set at US$ 10 Million*, INT'L CTR. TRANSITIONAL JUST., (Dec. 15, 2017), https://www.ijmonitor.org/2017/12/lubangas-financial-liability-for-reparations-set-at-us-10-million/.

72 *Id.*

73 Pearl Eliadis, *Case Comment: Lubanga: New Direction in Reparations Liability from the ICC*, KIRSCH INS, (Mar. 2018), http://www.kirschinstitute.ca/lubanga-new-direction-in-reparations-liability-from-the-icc/.

74 *Id.*

75 *Id.*

76 Wairagala Wakabi, *How the Trust Fund for Victims will Spend 1 Million Euros on Collective Reparations in Congo*, INT'L CTR. TRANSITIONAL JUST., https://www.ijmonitor.org/2017/02/how-the-trust-fund-for-victims-will-spend-e1-million-on-collective-reparations-in-congo/.

77 Prosecutor v. Katanga, ICC-01/04-01/07-3728, Order for Reparations pursuant to Article 75 of the Statute, ¶ 118 (Mar. 7, 2014), 118, https://www.icc-cpi.int/CourtRecords/CR2017_05121.PDF.

78 *Id.*

The TFV decided to "complement" in full the one million USD value of the reparations awards.[79]

The significance of reparations cannot be overstated. Victims from the Katanga case stated that, "We want to erase the image of war. These reparations are expected and will help us."[80] Reparations represent an important outcome as they allow victims and affected communities to rebuild their lives. Without the existence of hard international law, there would be no ICC and probably no TFV, which would deprive victims of much needed support under the TFV's assistance mandate.

The TFV identified 15.8 million people in need in Ituri, North Kivu, and South Kivu and has already provided: physical rehabilitation including medical referral services for fistula repair and reconstructive surgery; psychological rehabilitation including trauma counselling; and material support including education grants in terms of their assistance mandate.[81]

In the aforementioned Al Mahdi case, the ICC Trial Chamber VIII judges made a reparations order on August 17, 2017.[82] The Court concluded that Al Mahdi is liable for 2.7 million euros in expenses covering individual and collective reparations. Given that Al Mahdi is indigent, the TFV was directed to "complement" the reparations award and to develop a draft implementation plan.[83]

In the case of Jean Pierre Bemba, though the victims will no longer receive reparations, they were not forgotten as the TFV issued a statement a few days after his conviction was overturned indicating that it intends to accelerate the launch of its victims' assistance programme for victims in the Central

---

79 TFV, *Reparations Orders*, https://www.trustfundforvictims.org/en/what-we-do/reparation-orders, (stating that this reparations order was appealed and mostly confirmed by the Appeals Chamber, save for an order to reassess some applicants on March 8, 2018).

80 Radio Canal Révélation, *Reactions from the Local Population to Reparations in the Katanga Case*, https://www.ijmonitor.org/2017/07/reactions-from-the-local-population-to-collective-reparations-in-the-katanga-case/, (recording of Village Chief of Nyakeru, which is located approximately eleven miles to the south of the town of Bunia. Bunia is the district capital of Ituri Province. Reproduced by the Open Society Justice Monitor, originally compiled by Radio Canal Révélation, a radio station based in Bunia, Democratic Republic of Congo (DRC)).

81 TFV, *Assistance Programmes*, https://www.trustfundforvictims.org/en/what-we-do/assistance-programmes.

82 ICC, *Al Mahdi case: ICC Trial Chamber VIII Issues Reparations Order*, (Aug. 17, 2017), https://www.icc-cpi.int/Pages/item.aspx?name=pr1329.

83 *Id.*

African Republic. This programme will include, "physical and psychological rehabilitation as well as material support for the benefit of victims and their families."[84] Therefore, even though the conviction was overturned and there will be no formal reparations, at least some assistance will still be provided to the victims.

D *Deterrent Effect*

In addition to striving to deliver justice and provide reparations, promote due process, establish an important historical record,[85] and promote the rule of law, the deterrent effect of the ICC should also be considered.

It has been said that the prosecution of international crimes can "dissuade forever, others who may be tempted in the future to perpetrate such atrocities by showing them that the international community shall not tolerate the serious violations of international humanitarian law and human rights."[86] This is an important consequence of the ICC's work and thus an important function of hard law. Although scholars[87] cannot agree on whether one can actually quantify deterrence, and there is much debate as to whether issuing penalties can have a dissuasive effect on potential perpetrators.

Whilst there is no empirical evidence, one can speculate that the prosecution of the war in Syria, for example, might have been different if the ICC had the requisite jurisdiction[88] to investigate and prosecute timeously.

84 TFV, Press release: *Following Mr Bemba's acquittal, Trust Fund for Victims at the ICC Decides to Accelerate Launch of Assistance Programme in Central African Republic* (June 13, 2018), https://www.trustfundforvictims.org/en/news/press-release-following-mr-bemba%E2%80%99s-acquittal-trust-fund-victims-icc-decides-accelerate-launch.

85 Jennifer Schense and Linda Carter, Int'l Nuremberg Principles Academy, *Two Steps Forward, One Step Back: The Deterrence Effect of International Criminal Tribunals* (2016), 1, http://www.nurembergacademy.org/fileadmin/media/pdf/publications/DETERRENCEPUBLICATION.pdf.

86 Prosecutor v. Rutaganda (Judgment), ICTR Trial Chamber ICTR-96-3-T, 455 (Dec. 6, 1999).

87 Courtney Hillebrecht, *The Deterrent Effects of the International Criminal Court: Evidence from Libya*, 42:4 INT'L INTERACTIONS 616, 616–43 (2016); Christen Romero Philips, *The International Criminal Court & Deterrence: A Report to the Office of Global Criminal Justice, U.S. Department of State*, STAN. L. SCH. L. & POL'Y LAB, (June 2016); Jo, H., & B, Simmons, *Can the International Criminal Court Deter Atrocity?* 70(3) INT'L ORG. 443, 443–475 (2016).

88 There are three ways in which the ICC can exercise jurisdiction: a self-referral, a UNSC referral and a *proprio motu* action. Given that Syria is not a member of the Rome Statute, a *proprio motu* investigation and a self-referral are unlikely, leaving the UNSC referral as the only option.

Syria has been in a state of turmoil since 2011 with millions dying and fleeing to other countries. Syria is not a signatory to the Rome Statute and thus the only way in which the situation can come before the Court is if the United Nations Security Council refers the matter to the ICC. Thus far the UNSC has failed to make such a referral due to the political dynamics at play, a good example of how the ICC's work is hindered by the UNSC's political nature.

Whilst there has been no ICC referral, the International, Impartial and Independent Mechanism on crimes committed in the Syrian Arab Republic (IIIM) was established by a UN General Assembly resolution[89] in 2016 and it is mandated "to collect, consolidate, preserve and analyse evidence; and to prepare files to facilitate and expedite fair and independent criminal proceedings in national, regional or international courts, in accordance with international law."[90]

At the time of writing it is too early to determine the effectiveness of the IIIM and therefore it remains to be seen how this mechanism, established by a "soft international law" UN General Assembly resolution will fare. The IIIM complements the work of the United Nations Independent International Commission of Inquiry on the Syrian Arab Republic[91] that was established on August 22, 2011 by the Human Rights Council.[92] The Commission is mandated to collect information on all alleged violations of international human rights law since March 2011 in the Syria. The Commission was also tasked with establishing "the facts and circumstances that may amount to such violations and of the crimes perpetrated and, where possible, to identify those responsible with a view of ensuring that perpetrators of violations, including those that may constitute crimes against humanity, are held accountable."[93] The Human Rights Council extended the Commission's mandate for one year on 19 March, 2018.[94]

---

89 G.A. Res. 71/248, (Dec. 21, 2016), https://iiim.un.org/mandate/.

90 U.N. HUM. RTS. OFF. OF THE HIGH COMM'R, *International, Impartial and Independent Mechanism on International Crimes Committed in the Syrian Arab Republic* (Feb. 27, 2017), *available at* https://www.ohchr.org/EN/NewsEvents/Pages/DisplayNews.aspx?NewsID=21241.

91 U.N. HUM. RTS. OFF. OF THE HIGH COMM'R, *About the Independent International Commission of Inquiry on the Syrian Arab Republic*, https://www.ohchr.org/EN/HRBodies/HRC/IICISyria/Pages/AboutCoI.aspx.

92 G.A. Res. S-17/1, http://www.ohchr.org/Documents/HRBodies/HRCouncil/CoISyria/ResS17_1.pdf.

93 U.N. HUM. RTS. OFF. OF THE HIGH COMM'R, *supra* note 91.

94 G.A. Res. A/HRC/37/L.38, http://undocs.org/A/HRC/37/L.38.

However, the Commission has suffered a number of setbacks including the resignation of former prosecutor and commissioner Carla del Ponte[95] on 6 August, 2017. Citing a lack of political will from the UNSC and the frustration of no accountability for war crimes committed, Del Ponte resigned leaving the Commission with only two commissioners until the appointment of Hanny Megally on October 13, 2017.[96]

The same lack of political will at the UNSC has prevented a referral of the situation in Syria to the ICC. Several UNSC members have voiced support for an ICC referral including France, the United Kingdom, South Korea, Luxembourg and Argentina. But it is the veto powers wielded by the permanent members, the United States of America, China and Russia that block the referral.[97]

A referral could be a vital step in bringing an end to the grave violations of human rights in Syria and could provide renewed hope for victims that their suffering will not go unnoticed. The threat of imminent prosecution by an international court and knowledge that evidence is being collected for this purpose could dissuade foot soldiers and leaders from the further perpetration of war crimes. It would also send a clear message to all perpetrators that core international crimes will not go unpunished and this could be a form of deterrence that could at the very least reduce or curb the rampant perpetration of core international crimes. [98]

If the ICC were able to investigate and indict those most responsible for the bloodshed and war crimes, the proliferation of the conflict could be prevented.[99] For example, if any of those suspected of having committed international crimes are caught in neighbouring ICC signatory states, that state would be duty bound to arrest the suspected perpetrator for subsequent transfer to the ICC.

---

95 REUTERS, *Syria Investigator del Ponte Quits, Blaming U.N. Security Council*, (Aug. 6, 2017), https://www.reuters.com/article/us-mideast-crisis-syria-investigator-idUSKBN1AM0P4.

96 U.N. HUM. RTS. OFF. OF THE HIGH COMM'R, *Human Rights Council President Appoints Hanny Megally of Egypt to Serve on Commission of Inquiry on the Syrian Arab Republic*, (Oct. 13, 2017), https://www.ohchr.org/EN/NewsEvents/Pages/DisplayNews.aspx?NewsID=22234&LangID=E.

97 HUM. RTS. WATCH, *Q&A: Syria and the International Criminal Court*, https://www.hrw.org/news/2013/09/17/qa-syria-and-international-criminal-court#3.

98 *Id.*

99 JUST. INFO., *If the ICC Had Jurisdiction in Syria, It Might Save Many Lives: Interview with Kenneth Roth of Human Rights Watch* (July 16, 2018), https://www.justiceinfo.net/en/tribunals/icc/38014-bbb.html.

Granted it would take a combination of solutions to solve the crisis in Syria, but accountability, via the only permanent international criminal court and a powerful hard international law tool could make a significant difference. However, all is not lost, as domestic courts in Europe, for example, are making use of universal jurisdiction laws to seek justice for core international crimes committed in Syria.[100]

IV ICC's Inherent Hard International Law Challenges

In addition to its success, the ICC has also been plagued with challenges related with its hard international law foundation.

A *Membership and Case Selection*

Challenges include the inability to secure global buy-in in terms of membership. The United States, China and Russia, three of the five permanent members of the United Nations Security Council, refuse to sign the Rome Statute. Other powerful nations like India also choose to remain outside the system. The lack of universal membership jeopardises the legitimacy of the ICC[101]. This can be attributed to a number of factors, but the binding nature of hard international law is definitely one of those factors. The idea of being subjected to the Court's jurisdiction in such a binding manner is a challenging and politically sensitive move for many nations. For example, the United States has gone to great lengths to prevent their nationals from being subjected to the Court's jurisdiction including signing into law what is colloquially known as the "Hague Invasion Act." Its formal name is the American Service Members Protection Act of 2002,[102] and it authorises the use of, "all means necessary and appropriate to free US or allied personnel detained by or on behalf of the ICC."[103] This includes military force. It also allows for the withdrawal of American military support from countries that have opted to ratify the Rome Statute

100 EUR. CTR. FOR CONST. AND HUM. RTS. (ECCHR), *Press Release: Arrest Warrant Against Jamil Hassan is a Milestone and Good News for All Affected by Assad's Torture System* (Aug. 6, 2018), https://www.ecchr.eu/nc/en/press-release/arrest-warrant-against-jamil-hassan-is-a-milestone-and-good-news-for-all-affected-by-assads-torture-system/.

101 Catherine Gegout, *The International Criminal Court: Limits, Potential and Conditions for the Promotion of Justice and Peace*, 34:5 THIRD WORLD Q. 800, 800–818 (2013).

102 American Service-Members' Protection Act of 2002, Title 2 of Pub.L. 107–206, H.R. 4775, 116 Stat. 820 (2002).

103 *Id.* § 2008.

and it limits the participation of US troops in UN peacekeeping missions if immunity from prosecution for US troops is not provided.[104] Though these stipulations can be waived by the President in favour of "national interests,"[105] they are a poignant example of how far the United States is willing to go to avoid the binding hard law nature of the Rome Statute.

The failure to secure the membership of all countries, in itself is a weakness and it also has a knock-on effect as it limits the countries in which the Court can work thereby limiting its jurisdiction, reach, and potential impact.

In addition to the limited membership, accusations of selective justice have plagued the Court because all of the cases that have reached the trial phase are African cases. Cases stem from situations in the Democratic Republic of Congo, Uganda, the Central African Republic, Mali, Sudan, Côte d'Ivoire, Kenya, and Libya.[106] The prevalence of African cases before the ICC can be attributed to the fact that the African block constitutes the biggest regional block of signatories and a vast number of the African cases came to the court by way of self-referral.

A self-referral is when a signatory to the Rome Statute asks the Prosecutor of the ICC to intervene and investigate.[107] Uganda, the Central African Republic (on two occasions), Democratic Republic of Congo, and Mali requested the Court's intervention.

Gabon was the last African nation to request the Court's assistance.[108] Gabon's government requested that the OTP "open an investigation without delay" into the events beginning from May 2016 with "no specific end date."[109] On September 29, 2016, the Prosecutor announced the opening of a preliminary examination. The preliminary examination was closed on September 21, 2018, as the Prosecutor concluded that the available information "did not provide a reasonable basis to believe that the acts allegedly committed in Gabon in the context of the 2016 post-election violence, either by members of the

---

104 *Id.* § 2005.

105 *Id.* § 2005(c) 3; *Id.* § 2007(b).

106 ICC, *Situations Under Investigation*, https://www.icc-cpi.int/pages/situation.aspx.

107 *Rome Statute*, *supra* note 2, at Art. 14 ("A State Party may refer to the Prosecutor a situation in which one or more crimes within the jurisdiction of the Court appear to have been committed requesting the Prosecutor to investigate the situation for the purpose of determining whether one or more specific persons should be charged with the commission of such crimes.").

108 ICC, *Preliminary Examination: Gabon*, https://www.icc-cpi.int/gabon.

109 *Id.*

opposition or by the Gabonese security forces, constitute crimes against humanity within the meaning of the Rome Statute of the ICC."[110] The Prosecutor also stated that the information available does "not provide a reasonable basis to believe that the crime of incitement to genocide was committed during the election campaign."[111]

There are two other ways in which a case can come before the ICC. As mentioned above, the United Nations Security Council can refer a matter to the ICC[112] and the Prosecutor can exercise his or her jurisdiction *proprio motu*[113] in a member state. The UNSC referred the situations in Libya and Darfur, Sudan to the ICC.

Côte d'Ivoire warrants further explanation as it signed the Rome Statute in 2003[114] but did not ratify until 15 February 2013. Therefore, it was not considered a member of the Rome Statute when, on 14 December 2010 and 3 May 2011 President Alassane Ouattara, recognised the jurisdiction of the ICC. As a result, and for the sake of legal clarity, the Prosecutor sought authorisation from the Pre-Trial Chamber to open a *proprio motu* investigation on 23 June 2011. Authorisation was granted on 3 October 2011.[115]

Kenya and Burundi are the purest examples of the use of the prosecutor *proprio motu* powers.[116] Despite the existence of self-referrals there are still those who remain adamant that the ICC is "targeting"[117] Africa. This is a position that is both inaccurate and lacks nuance as it fails to take into account the facts

---

110 *Id.*

111 *Id.*

112 *Rome Statute*, *supra* note 2, at art. 13(b) ("A situation in which one or more of such crimes appears to have been committed is referred to the Prosecutor by the Security Council acting under Chapter VII of the Charter of the United Nations ... ").

113 *Id.* at art. 15(1) ("The Prosecutor may initiate investigations *proprio motu* on the basis of information on crimes within the jurisdiction of the Court").

114 *See* ICC., Declaration of Recognition of the ICC's Jurisdiction, (translated from French), https://www.icc-cpi.int/NR/rdonlyres/FF9939C2-8E97-4463-934C-BC8F351BA013/279779/ICDE1.pdf (containing signature of Mamadou Bamba, Minister of Foreign Affairs of the Government of former President Laurent Gbagbo); *See also* No. 02/11, Corrigendum to Decision Pursuant to Article 15 of the Rome Statute on the Authorisation of an Investigation into the Situation in the Republic of Côte d'Ivoire, (Nov. 15, 2011), https://www.icc-cpi.int/CourtRecords/CR2011_18794.PDF.

115 No. 02/11, Situation in the Republic of Côte d'Ivoire, https://www.icc-cpi.int/cdi.

116 No. 01/09, Situation in the Republic of Kenya, https://www.icc-cpi.int/kenya; No. 01/17, Situation in Burundi, https://www.icc-cpi.int/burundi. Despite Burundi's withdrawal from the ICC, the ICC still has jurisdiction over crimes committed between April 26, 2015 and October 26, 2017 before withdrawal became effective.

117 ICC Forum, *Is the ICC Targeting Africa Inappropriately?* (Mar. 2013-Jan. 2014), https://iccforum.com/africa.

stated above. That being said, the universal application of justice is vital to the sustainability of the system and therefore it remains important for the Court to expand the geography of its docket.

The fact that the ICC also has preliminary examinations outside of Africa has also done nothing to silence the critics. The most interesting preliminary examinations would be those involving the United States of America (USA) and the United Kingdom (UK). The OTP is examining, *inter alia,* the alleged crimes committed by British troops in Iraq and requested the judge's permission to turn the preliminary examination of alleged crimes in Afghanistan into an investigation. This includes examining the conduct of US troops in the Afghanistan situation. Unfortunately, on 12 April 2019 the judges denied the Prosecutor's request. However an appeal has been filed by the OTP. Other non-African preliminary examinations include, Columbia, Bangladesh/Myanmar, Ukraine, Venezuela and the Philippines. The only non-African situation that is at the investigation phase is Georgia.

B *Withdrawal*

In addition to lack of universal membership and allegations of selective justice, the ICC has also suffered the loss of two of its members-Burundi and the Philippines. In 2016, Burundi, the Gambia, and South Africa all submitted their notices of withdrawal to the United Nations Secretary General, which effectively begins the process of withdrawal from the ICC.

Under new leadership, the Gambia changed its mind. South Africa's notice of withdrawal was revoked by the North Gauteng High Court on procedural grounds. Efforts to withdraw were reinvigorated when the South African Minister of Justice, announced at the 16th Annual Assembly of States Parties that South Africa still intends to withdraw and that it will follow proper Constitutional and procedural processes to do so. Calls for withdrawal, at the time of writing, seem to have subsided in South Africa after the government spoke predominantly of constructive engagement during the 2018 Assembly of States Parties.

Burundi's withdrawal from the ICC became effective on 27 October 2017[118] whilst the Philippines submitted its notice of withdrawal on 17 March 2018 and its withdrawal became effective on 17 March 2019.[119]

---

118 U.N. Secretary-General, Withdrawal: Burundi, C.N.805.2016.TREATIES-XVIII.10 (Depositary Notification), (Oct. 28, 2016), https://treaties.un.org/doc/Publication/CN/2016/CN.805.2016-Eng.pdf.

119 ICC, *Press Release: 20 March 2018 ICC Statement on The Philippines' Notice of Withdrawal: State Participation in Rome Statute System Essential to International Rule of Law*, (Mar. 20, 2018), https://www.icc-cpi.int/Pages/item.aspx?name=pr1371.

C *Where Even Hard International Law Fails*

Without universal support, the ICC's impact will always be limited. Wavering support from member states has also presented challenges for the ICC and thus shows that the even hard international law has its limits. The failure to arrest former Sudanese president Omar al Bashir is a prime example.

Former President Bashir is wanted by the ICC for genocide, war crimes and crimes against humanity allegedly perpetrated in Darfur, Sudan. The first warrant for arrest for Bashir was issued on 4 March 2009, the second on 12 July 2010.[120] He has been at large since then and has proved very difficult to arrest. The ICC has no police force of its own and thus relies on member states to cooperate and arrest those who are wanted by the Court. Thus far, ICC member states, Nigeria, South Africa, Malawi, Djibouti, Uganda, the Democratic Republic of Congo, and Chad, have failed to arrest Bashir (whilst he was present on their respective territories), despite being legally obligated to do so. The hard international law duty to arrest him exists, but for various reasons ranging from complex customary international law immunity concerns to diplomatic and political concerns, states have failed to arrest Bashir.

The ICC has other challenges including allegations of inefficiency,[121] trial irregularities,[122] and limited funding. However, these matters fall out of the scope of this chapter.

V Conclusion

Despite its challenges and weaknesses, the ICC remains a crucial part of the international criminal justice framework and a good example of the importance of hard international law. Hard international law provides a solid foundation for the investigation and prosecution of perpetrators of egregious crimes. Thus, although challenging, agreeing on a hard international law instruments is fundamental for effective international criminal justice. Without

---

120 ICC, *Alleged Crimes (Non-Exhaustive List) ("Bashir Case")*, https://www.icc-cpi.int/darfur/albashir/pages/alleged-crimes.aspx.

121 Jessica Hatcher-Moore, *Is the World's Highest Court Fit for Purpose?*, THE GUARDIAN, (Apr. 5, 2017), https://www.theguardian.com/global-development-professionals-network/2017/apr/05/international-criminal-court-fit-purpose.

122 *See, e.g.*, BBC NEWS, *First ICC accused—DR Congo's Lubanga—'to be freed,'* (July 15, 2010), https://www.bbc.com/news/world-africa-10650399.

it, accountability initiatives are unlikely to survive. As seen with the ICC, even with the existence of a hard international law accountability initiatives are still subjected to various forms of interference and hindrance. However, how much worse would the situation be without this hard international law instrument?

CHAPTER 6

The Hard Choices in Promoting Environmental Access Rights

*Natalia Gomez Peña** and *David B. Hunter***

1 Introduction

This chapter analyzes the evolution in international law of three environmental governance norms known collectively as environmental access rights: (1) the right to access environmental information; (2) the right to participate in environmental decisions that affect your life and livelihood; and (3) the right of access to justice in environmental disputes. Rooted in general human rights norms, these access rights (also sometimes referred to as transparency, inclusivity, and accountability have been promoted as fundamental to good environmental governance and the achievement of sustainable development.[1] In this context, they emerged first as global and then regional soft law and subsequently were enshrined in two regional treaties (Europe and more recently Latin America and the Caribbean). This chapter tracks the evolution of these environmental access rights from soft to hard international law, with a primary focus on the recent developments in Latin America.

* Civil society representative in the negotiations of the regional agreement on access to information, participation and justice in environmental matters in Latin America and the Caribbean. Ms. Gomez currently works as Advocacy Officer with CIVICUS: World Alliance for Citizen Participation.

** Professor of Law at the American University's Washington College of Law.

1 *See, e.g.*, International Law Association, Accountability of International Organisations, Berlin Conference Final Report (2004), 8 (defining good governance with respect to international organizations as including "the following elements: transparency in both the decision-making process and the implementation of the ensuing institutional and operational decisions; a large degree of democracy in the decision-making process; access to information open to all potentially concerned and/or affected by the decisions at stake; the well-functioning of the international civil service; sound financial management; and appropriate reporting and evaluation mechanisms").

 | DOI:10.1163/9789004417021_007

II The Rio Declaration and the Emergence of Environmental Access Rights

Public participation, access to information and access to judicial review have long been cherished by environmental advocates, particularly from the United States.[2] These access rights existed in human rights law[3] but their emergence in the international environmental context depended on the confluence of two issues. First, the opening of the former Soviet bloc revealed widespread environmental contamination in many industrialized countries. With relatively strong environmental standards, the region's severe environmental degradation was seen as largely resulting from the lack of public dialog. Environmental advocates did not want to leave access rights to the whim of each country in the future; the advocates wanted a global framework to set a minimum standard for these access rights. Second, the rise of a globalized environmental

---

2 *See, e.g.,* David B. Hunter, *The Emerging Norm of Transparency in International Environmental Governance*, in RESEARCH HANDBOOK ON TRANSPARENCY 343, 344–47 (P. Ala'i & R. Vaughn, eds.) (2016).

3 The environmental access rights to information, participation, and justice are in many ways specific and more detailed applications of widely accepted human rights norms. The right to access government-held information is rooted in Article 19 of the Universal Declaration on Human Rights and repeated in the International Covenant on Civil and Political Rights (ICCPR): '[e]veryone shall have the right to freedom of expression; this right shall include freedom to seek, receive and impart information and ideas of all kinds . … ' United Nations, International Covenant on Civil and Political Rights, 999 U.N.T.S. 171 (Mar. 23, 1976), art. 19; *see also* Report of the Special Rapporteur, Promotion and protection of the right to freedom of opinion and expression, UN Doc. E/CN.4/1998/40, 28 January 1998, ¶ 14. Inter-American Declaration of Principles on Freedom of Expression, 108th Regular Session, 19 October 2000, ¶ 3; African Commission on Human and Peoples' Rights, Declaration of Principles on Freedom of Expression in Africa, 32nd Session, 17–23 October 2002, pt. IV. With respect to the right of participation, Article 25 of the ICCPR states that "[e]very citizen shall have the right and the opportunity … to take part in the conduct of public affairs, directly or through freely chosen representatives." ICCPR, *supra* note 3, at art. 25; *see also* The European Ombudsman, *European Code of Good Administrative Behavior* (Luxembourg: Office for the Official Publications of the European Communities, 2005), art. 16. ('[e]very member of the public shall have the right, in cases where a decision affecting his rights or interests has to be taken, to submit written comments and, when needed, to present oral observations before the decision is taken'). With respect to judicial review, article 10 of the 1948 Universal Declaration of Human Rights provides that "Everyone is entitled in full equality to a fair and public hearing by an independent and impartial tribunal, in the determination of his rights and obligations and of any criminal charge against him." United Nations, Universal Declaration of Human Rights, UN G.A. Res. 217 A(III) (10 December 1948), art. 10; see also Council of Europe, Convention for the Protection of Human Rights and Fundamental Freedoms (Rome, 4 November 1950; entry into force 3 September 1953), art. 6(1).

movement was pushing for greater participation in international environmental processes more generally. Among the issues they promoted was the right to participate in environmental decision-making at all levels. The convergence of these two trends came together initially at the 1992 Earth Summit.

A *The Earth Summit and the Rio Declaration: Greening Access Rights*

The first important adoption of access rights to the environmental context came as part of the *Rio Declaration on Environment and Development* adopted at the 1992 "Earth Summit." The Earth Summit was the largest gathering of world leaders in history; it also marked the emergence of the global environmental movement as a key force in global environmental policy. In the words of Peter Sand: "the 'participatory revolution' at Rio ... served as a powerful reminder of the legitimate claim of civil society to take part in international decision-making,"[4] The unprecedented "participat[ion] revolution" evidenced at Rio was the physical manifestation of the demands for environmental access rights in the text of the *Rio Declaration.*

Initially, organizers hoped that a binding Earth Charter would emerge from the United Nations Conference on Environment and Development (UNCED), As negotiations progressed, it became clear that a binding set of principles of environmental law was not realistic, or it would have come only with significantly weaker substantive text. The governments asked the UNCED Preparatory Committee to focus on a non-binding declaration of general principles instead. Antecedent global instruments, most notably the 1972 Stockholm Declaration, largely did not include access rights, but two regional Ministerial Declarations (from Europe and from Asia) did emphasize the importance of public participation and led to the inclusion of access rights in the document.[5] As the negotiations reached their conclusion, the final compromise text was negotiated by a small, closed group of sixteen countries, eight developed countries and eight developing countries.[6] This small group negotiated the final text, which was submitted to and adopted (unchanged) by the Earth Summit.

---

4 *See* Peter H. Sand, *The Evolution of International Environmental Law*, in THE OXFORD HANDBOOK OF INTERNATIONAL ENVIRONMENTAL LAW (J. Brunnee, D. Bodansky & E. Hey, eds. 2007).

5 *See* Bergen Ministerial Declaration on Sustainable Development in the ECE Region, *adopted* May 16, 1990, UN Doc A/CONF.151/PC/10, annex 1, ¶ 6; Bangkok Ministerial Declaration on Environmentally Sound and Sustainable Development in Asia and the Pacific, adopted October 16, 1990, UN Doc A/CONF.151/PC/10, annex 2, ¶ 27.

6 The North was represented by the United States, Portugal, Netherlands, Germany, Australia, Norway (alternating with Sweden), Japan and Russia. The South was represented by Pakistan, India, Iran, Brazil, Mexico, Nigeria, Tanzania and China. *See* Ambassador Tommy Koh, *The*

Although the public would be highly visible at the Earth Summit in 1992, civil society was not particularly active in the negotiations of the *Rio Declaration*. Partly, this was because the process of negotiating a text with legal principles, even a non-binding text, was still seen as within the sole province of government legal experts. Civil society lawyers with international environmental law expertise were just appearing in international fora and the methods for incorporating their participation was part of the dynamic changes happening around the Earth Summit. Endorsed by virtually every country in the world, the *Rio Declaration* ultimately reflected a global political consensus of the legal and policy principles for achieving environmentally sustainable development. The *Rio Declaration* codified or launched many emerging principles in the field of international environmental law, including the environmental access principles found in Principle 10:

> Environmental issues are best handled with the participation of all concerned citizens, at the relevant level. At the national level, each individual shall have appropriate access to information concerning the environment that is held by public authorities, including information on hazardous materials and activities in their communities, and the opportunity to participate in decision-making processes. States shall facilitate and encourage public awareness and participation by making information widely available. Effective access to judicial and administrative proceedings, including redress and remedy, shall be provided.[7]

Principle 10's impact on subsequent legal developments has been profound.[8] It reshaped what was thought to be the structure of international environmental law, because rather than addressing relatively discrete transboundary or global environmental threats or processes, this principle was almost entirely aimed at shaping *how* national environmental law would be made. Principle 10 was thus closer to human rights than to previous environmental treaties. Indeed, to

---

Earth Summit's Negotiating Process: Some Reflections on the Art and Science of Negotiating, in N. ROBINSON, ED., AGENDA 21: EARTH'S ACTION PLAN, vi, et seq. (1993).

7 U.N. Conference on Environment and Development, *Rio Declaration on Environment and Development*, U.N. Doc. A/CONF.151/26 (Vol. 1) (Aug. 12, 1992); 31 I.L.M. 874 (1992), princ. 10, http://www.un.org/documents/ga/conf151/aconf15126-1annex1.htm.

8 *See, e.g.*, Jonas Ebbesson, *Principle 10: Public Participation*, in JORGE E. VIÑUALES, THE RIO DECLARATION ON ENVIRONMENT AND DEVELOPMENT: A COMMENTARY (Oxford Press, 2015).

some extent, Principle 10 simply repackaged generally accepted human rights and applied them to the specific context of environmental rights.

Principle 10 confirmed the central importance of access rights to the pursuit of Rio's vision of sustainable development. Environmental protection was not just a technical exercise comfortably left to scientists and other experts, but depended also on the active involvement of an informed public. Given the importance of access rights to civil society's effective participation in environmental matters, civil society prioritized the post-Rio dissemination and uptake of Principle 10.[9] This was particularly true in Europe where Principle 10 contributed to the increasing momentum for expanding the right of public participation and the access rights associated with it. The political integration of western and eastern Europe after the Cold War, mixed with the devastating environmental legacy of the Soviet era, offered an opportunity to create the first continent-wide conversation about the future of pan-European environmental policy. The governments launched a series of "Environment for Europe" Ministerial conferences, which would provide a multi-stakeholder framework for governments, civil society, and others to discuss access rights in Europe—beginning with the first Ministerial in 1991, which emphasized the importance of public participation for sustainable development.[10] In 1993, the second Ministerial called for the United Nations Economic Commission for Europe (UNECE) to "draw up proposals for legal, regulatory and administrative mechanisms to encourage public participation in environmental decision-making."[11]

The UNECE, with substantial participation of the public, subsequently drafted the *Guidelines on Access to Environmental Information and Public Participation in Environmental Decision-making* (*Guidelines*). The *Guidelines* were endorsed by the Third "Environment for Europe" Ministerial.[12] The Ministerial also authorized the UNECE to negotiate a binding "regional convention on public participation … with the appropriate involvement of NGOs."[13] The *Guidelines* served as the blueprint for the future convention with the negotiating committee explicitly declaring that the convention should have the same

9 David Banisar et al., *Moving from Principles to Rights: Rio 2012 and Access to Information, Public Participation, and Justice*, SUSTAINABLE DEV. L. & POL'Y 12, no. 3, 8 (2012) at 10.

10 UNECE, First Ministerial Conference "Environment for Europe" (1991), https://www.unece.org/env/efe/historyofefe/history.en1991_01.html.

11 ¶UNECE, *The Aarhus Convention: An Implementation Guide*, U.N. Doc. ECE/CEP/72, at 24 (1998), https://www.unece.org/fileadmin/DAM/env/pp/implementation%20guide/english/part2.pdf. [hereinafter Aarhus Implementation Guide].

12 Declaration by the Ministers of Environment of the Region of the United Nations Economic Commission for Europe ¶ 42 (Oct. 25, 1995).

13 *Id.* ¶ 47.

scope as the *Guidelines*. The Ministerial's reference to NGOs in the authorizing language assured that the negotiations would have unprecedented participation of civil society.

Less than two years later, negotiators agreed to the *UNECE Convention on Access to Information, Public Participation in Decision-making, and Access to Justice in Environmental Matters*,[14] known more commonly as the "Aarhus Convention," after the Danish town where the Fourth Ministerial "Environment for Europe" Conference adopted the Convention on June 25, 1998. The treaty entered into force in 2001.[15] It was open for signature by any country, and, as of June 2019, forty-seven countries had ratified the Convention.[16]

III The UNECE Aarhus Convention

The Aarhus Convention clearly and explicitly aimed at implementing Principle 10's soft law norms through the adoption of a binding regional treaty. It sets forth a binding framework for national laws in the same broad categories as Principle 10: access to information, participation, and access to justice. The Aarhus Convention's overall objective reflects the human rights ancestry of Principle 10's environmental access rights. The Aarhus Convention links these access rights to the emerging right to a healthy environment:

> In order to contribute to the protection of the right of every person of present and future generations to live in an environment adequate to his or her health and well-being, each Party shall guarantee the rights of access to information, public participation in decision-making, and access

---

14 UNECE, Convention on Access to Information, Public Participation in Decision-making and Access to Justice in Environmental Matters, UN Doc. ECE/CEP/43 (Aarhus, Denmark, 25 June 1998), http://www.unece.org/env/pp/documents/cep43e.pdf [hereinafter Aarhus Convention]. On the Aarhus Convention in general, *see* Veit Koester, *The Convention on Access to Information, Public Participation in Decision-Making and Access to Justice in Environmental Matters (Aarhus Convention)*, in *MAKING TREATIES WORK: HUMAN RIGHTS, ENVIRONMENT AND ARMS CONTROL*, EDS GEIR ULFSTEIN, ET AL, 179–217 (2007); Marc Pallemaertz, *The Aarhus Convention on Access to Information, Participation in Decision-Making and Access to Justice in Environmental Matters: A Model for Engaging the Disenfranchised in Decision-Making through the Institutionalization of Procedural Rights?*, in ENGAGING THE DISENFRANCHISED: DEVELOPING COUNTRIES AND CIVIL SOCIETY IN SUSTAINABLE DEVELOPMENT GOVERNANCE, ED. JESSICA GREEN (2005).

15 Council Decision 2005/370, 2005 (L124) 1 (EC).

16 For an update on the status of ratifications for the Aarhus Convention, *see* UNECE, *Status of Ratification*, http://www.unece.org/env/pp/ratification.html.

> to justice in environmental matters in accordance with the provisions of this Convention.[17]

The "hardening" of the Principle 10 norms is not simply a matter of them being incorporated into a binding instrument. The Aarhus Convention obligates Parties to adopt a relatively detailed rights-based framework in their national laws. For example, Aarhus defines environmental information broadly to include human health and safety.[18] Aarhus requires information to be provided in electronic format, if requested. It also bars national requirements that requesters have to prove a specific interest,[19] and it identifies some environmental information that Parties must provide.[20] In matters of participation, Aarhus requires the public be notified early of its opportunities to participate,[21] requires decision making processes include reasonable timeframes for meaningful participation, and links meaningful participation to the obligation to provide relevant information before a decision is made.[22]

The Convention also included a relatively robust compliance process, at least when compared to most environmental agreements. The compliance mechanism can be triggered by non-state actors and has been used in several instances to enhance a country's compliance. The Aarhus Compliance Committee is a non-confrontational, non-judicial, and consultative body composed of independent experts. It reviews the compliance of parties to the Convention.[23] A unique characteristic of the Aarhus Compliance Committee is that it allows the public to send communications to the Committee regarding a party's compliance. The Committee then examines the merits of the case and adopts its findings in a report, that, in cases of non-compliance, contains recommendations for the meeting of the parties, or if the Party agrees, can be sent directly to the concerned Party.

Through the successful negotiations of the Aarhus Convention, environmental democracy advocates were able to shift the access rights from a general soft international law norm to a regionally binding framework with significant detail that nearly fifty countries were committed to implementing in national law. The negotiations benefited from the relative economic and socio-political

17 Aarhus Convention, *supra* note 14, at art. 1.
18 Aarhus Convention, *supra* note 14, at art. 2.
19 Aarhus Convention, *supra* note 14, at arts. 1, 2.
20 Aarhus Convention, *supra* note 14, at arts. 5.2 5.3.
21 Aarhus Convention, *supra* note 14, at arts. 6.2, 6.4.
22 Aarhus Convention, *supra* note 14, at arts. 6.3, 6.6.
23 Aarhus Convention, *supra* note 14, at art. 15.

homogeneity of Europe. Western Europe's historical commitment to democracy and human rights joined with strong impulses in Eastern Europe for a rapid democratic transition and integration into the west to create favorable political winds for the Aarhus negotiations. The countries also shared relatively industrialized economies with strong and politically active environmental movements. Civil society organizations (CSOs) were a driving force in shaping Aarhus both because access rights were a high priority for civil society and because civil society was, and is still, viewed as a particularly legitimate and authoritative voice on issues relating to transparency, participation, and accountability.[24]

Fresh from the relatively quick back-to-back victories at Rio and Aarhus, civil society advocates turned to the question of how to implement environmental access rights in other regions. One obvious approach was to try to replicate the Aarhus Convention, either in other regions or globally. After all, every country in the world had endorsed Principle 10 as part of the *Rio Declaration* and Aarhus provided a detailed substantive framework for implementing Principle 10. Several factors conspired to make a global treaty difficult. A real possibility existed that the framework set out in Aarhus would be significantly diluted in global negotiations with countries from Asia and Africa rejecting a model based on western principles of governance and human rights. In addition, South America in the early 1990s did not have long traditions of democratic governance in the environmental context that would lead them to be champions among developing countries.

Second, environmental democracy was not conceptually a good fit for a global treaty. Issues like climate change or ozone depletion were clearly transboundary issues that required global cooperation to address. Access rights and environmental democracy, on the other hand, were inherently internal issues relating more to how governments operate with respect to their citizens than to transboundary environmental impact. In that regard, the conceptual basis for the environmental democracy treaty had to be rooted more in human rights than transboundary environmental harm. Moreover, efforts at Rio to internationalize environmental administration in developing countries—for example in setting minimum environmental standards—in the absence of transboundary impacts had been fiercely opposed by developing countries as a neocolonial attack on sovereignty. In that context, CSOs active on the issue decided that trying to strengthen national or regional implementation of the

24 Aarhus Implementation Guide, *supra* note 11, at 2 (2000).

principles—that had already been agreed to in the *Rio Declaration*—was a better option than pursuing a global treaty.[25]

Although more acute with respect to a global inititaive, these obstacles also impeded any momentum for the rapid replication of a regional treaty outside the European context. Europe's pending expansion of the European Union provided a framework that drove a harmonized approach to environmental standards more generally and would have led to enhanced access rights in the region, even absent the Aarhus Convention. Aarhus clearly benefited from the strong interest of both governments and civil society in the successful political and economic integration of eastern and western Europe. No similar tailwinds were driving regional integration in Africa, Asia, or South America.

These factors did not immediately deter civil society from exploring a binding global treaty or multiple regional treaties—but no clear political opportunities existed in the short-term. With no single clear path forward for binding approaches that would not weaken the norms emerging in Aarhus, environmental democracy advocates turned to longer term strategies for building support over time, including both international soft law techniques, such as the Bali Guidelines,[26] and national level techniques, most notably the World Resource Institute's (WRI's) Access Initiative and its associated Partnership for Principle 10.

IV The WRI Access Initiative and Partnership for Principle 10: Building Capacity and Consensus (Slowly)

In 2000, after considering different avenues for promoting environmental access rights, the WRI launched The Access Initiative (TAI)—a concerted effort to promote access rights through a global network of active and expert CSOs.[27] TAI now boasts 248 members, including individuals and organizations, all over the world.[28] The network is led by a core team composed of six organizations

25 The author, David Hunter, participated in the civil society strategy discussions, which would ultimately lead to the creation of the Access Initiative as an alternative strategy to the push for a global treaty.

26 *See infra* text accompanying notes 36–44.

27 *See, e.g.*, World Resources Inst., What We Do, Project Directory, The Access Initiative (TAI), https://www.wri.org/our-work/project/access-initiative-tai.

28 The Access Initiative, *Core Team Report to the TAI Network 2014–2016*, Paris, France, at 9. https://accessinitiative.org/sites/default/files/core_team_report_paris2014-2016.pdf.

representing the different regions of the world and the World Resources Institutes (WRI) serves as the Secretariat of the network.

WRI and its partner organizations work primarily at the national level but with a shared commitment to a global framework based on Principle 10. TAI developed a set of uniform indicators for monitoring countries' implementation of the access rights under Principle 10; these indicators were used to benchmark a country's laws and performance.

To build international political will for the implementation of access rights, TAI promoted a Partnership for Principle 10. Announced at the 2002 World Summit on Sustainable Development and formally launched in 2003, the Partnership for Principle 10 was a coalition of governments, international organizations, and civil society groups committed to the implementation of Principle 10.[29] The Partnership was built around a common set of commitments that aimed to accelerate the implementation of Principle 10 in each country.[30] With partners from eleven governments, more than thirty CSOs and four UN system organizations,[31] the Partnership for Principle 10 was the first non-regional exercise to promote access rights implementation through international cooperation among various stakeholders.[32]

The Partnership for Principle 10 proposed that all members commit to the shared objectives of the partnership to conduct independent evaluation of policies and practices and to collaborate with other members. Members also agreed to undertake specific commitments to improve their own performance regarding access rights.[33] The Partnership also had an important component of mobilizing resources to fund activities related to the implementation of Principle 10 in various countries. Two examples of the specific commitments of members were Uganda's access to information legislation, adopted in 2005,

---

29 *See* Partnerships for the SDGs, *Partnership for Principle 10*, https://sustainabledevelopment.un.org/partnership/?p=1600.

30 *Id.*

31 Governments at the Partnership for Principle 10: Bolivia, Chile, European Commission, Hungary, Italy, Mexico, Sweden, Uganda, Ukraine, United Kingdom and United States. International Organizations: IUCN-World Conservation Union, United Nations Development Program, United Nations Environment Program and World Bank. *See*: Partnership for Principle 10, *Commitments for Action: Moving towards transparent and accountable governance*. Annual report 2004/2005. Doc. No.1/2005 CoW/London (on file with the authors).

32 Partnership for Principle 10, *Commitments for action moving towards transparent and accountable governance*, Annual Report 2006/2007. Doc. No. 1/2007 (on file with the authors).

33 *Id.*

and the open dialogue between civil society and government organizations in Mexico.[34]

The insight of the Partnership for Principle 10 was the direct focus on the end goal which was to change national laws to protect access rights. A treaty was an indirect way of reaching that goal when compared to working directly with countries willing to adopt and implement reforms. By demonstrating success in some countries, the Partnership for Principle 10 served as an important step in building momentum for what would become negotiations of the Latin American treaty on environmental democracy. The Partnership contributed to a boost in membership of Latin American organizations to the TAI coalition to conduct national assessments for access rights legislation.[35] It also built important bridges, creating the space for the first dialogue between countries in the region and CSOs that were part of the TAI network. The CSOs and governments from Mexico and Chile, in particular, created effective alliances that later became an important input for the Latin American Principle 10 process.

A *The Bali Guidelines: the Struggle for Access Rights Implementation*

Responding to concerns from governments that they had no consensus model for national legislation on Principle 10, especially in those countries that had no access to information or participation laws, TAI made the strategic decision to promote a soft law approach to model legislation.[36] TAI hoped that willing governments could develop common standards through an international process that could build support for legislative changes in more reluctant countries.[37]

The resulting 2010 Bali Guidelines for the Implementation of Principle 10 (Bali Guidelines) were negotiated under the auspices of the United Nations Environment Program (UNEP) and adopted in a special session of the Global Ministerial Environmental Forum—UNEP's governing body.[38] The Bali Guidelines provide guidance for governments on how to implement Principle 10 in their national legislation.[39] For some, the adoption of the Bali Guidelines

---

34 *Id.*

35 According to the 2006/2007 report of the Partnership for Principle 10, there were 20 organizations in Latin America conducting national Principle 10 assessments by that year.

36 Interview by Marcos Orellana with Carole Excell, Acting Director Environmental Democracy Practice, WORLD RESOURCES INST. (June 2017) (on file with the Authors).

37 *Id.*

38 UNEP, Putting Rio Principle 10 into Action: An Implementation Guide for the UNEP Bali Guidelines for the Development of National Legislation on Access to Information, Public Participation and Access to Justice in Environmental Matters, October 2015, at 6 [hereinafter *Bali Implementation Guide*].

39 *Id.*

eighteen years after the signing of the *Rio Declaration* proves how slow UN bodies have been in addressing access rights.[40] But the Guidelines also reflected civil society's incremental strategy to use a soft international law catalyst to advance national legislation with a long-term goal of building support for (or at least weakening resistance to) a future binding agreement. Governments supported the adoption of the guidelines precisely because it was a non-binding soft international law instrument, which was seen positively as a non-intrusive mechanism for the upward harmonization of national laws on access rights.[41]

Unfortunately, limited financial resources and a lack of political will has hurt implementation of the Bali Guidelines. For example, it was not until 2015 that UNEP was able to publish the implementation handbook for the Bali Guidelines.[42] The lack of knowledge about the existence of the Guidelines and the lack of training for government officials on how to use them have significantly decreased their potential impact.[43] Nonetheless, the Bali Guidelines have become a practical tool for civil society to use as an international standard to demand better national legislation. They evaluate access rights legislation against the Bali Guidelines and "name and shame" lagging governments before the international community.[44] In this way, environmental rights advocates improve national legislation, and, as more countries conform their national legislation to this international standard, opposition to regional or global binding instruments arguably declines.

V The Road to a Latin American and Caribbean Treaty on Principle 10

The adoption of the Bali Guidelines built momentum for a discussion on environmental democracy at the 2012 United Nations Conference on Sustainable Development, or Rio +20, in 2012. The Conference brought governments together to renew the political commitment made at the 1992 Earth Summit and, among other things, strengthen the institutional framework for sustainable development.[45]

40 Banisar et al., *supra* note 9, at 4.

41 Banisar et al., *supra* note 9, at 4.

42 *Bali Implementation Guide, supra* note 38, at 6.

43 *Bali Implementation Guide, supra* note 38, at 10.

44 *See* Environmental Democracy Index, https://environmentaldemocracyindex.org/about/.

45 *See* Sustainable Development Knowledge Platform, About the Rio+20 Conference, https://sustainabledevelopment.un.org/rio20/preparatoryprocess.

Environmental access rights were central to this discussion of strengthening the institutional framework for sustainable development. Implementing the governance system envisioned at Rio back in 1992, which included effective implementation of Principle 10, was viewed as a critical starting point for the discussions. This was reinforced by civil society's continued emphasis on accountability, participation, and transparency in environment-related decision-making. Civil society argued that effective implementation of Principle 10 required a rights-based approach where governments commit to establishing and operationalizing legal rights that enable and protect affected people.[46]

To many observers, strengthening a rights-based approach to Principle 10 required new international instruments.[47] Many proposals regarding Principle 10 were discussed during preparation for Rio +20, including a universal global instrument, regional instruments and encouraging more countries to join the Aarhus Convention.[48] The Brazilian delegation among others led the call for a universal convention, but the proposal did not find support from enough governments and faced opposition from large countries like the United States, China, and Russia.[49] Also, as in 1992, some environmental democracy advocates viewed the global convention as dangerous because gaining support from many countries would necessarily lead to lower substantive standards, particularly if the instrument was going to be both universal and binding.[50]

As the prospects for a global instrument dimmed, civil society sought to capitalize on the support of the Brazilian delegation, plus the support of other Latin American countries that had joined Brazil, to push for a regional convention for the Latin American and Caribbean region.[51] The LAC region was farther ahead than many other regions in the adoption of access rights. The Organization of American States (OAS), for example, had launched a non-binding action plan to support countries in implementing Principle 10 as early as 2001.[52] In 2010, the OAS released its Model Law on Access to Information which proved to be a useful tool for governments and civil society in promoting access rights. The OAS would continue to be a positive voice throughout the period, making transparency and associated rights of participation a central

46 Banisar et al., *supra note* 9, at 2.

47 Interview with Carole Excell, *supra* note 36.

48 Banisar et al., *supra note* 9, at 10.

49 Interview with Carole Excell, *supra* note 36.

50 Banisar et al., *supra note* 9, at 10.

51 Interview with Carole Excell, *supra* note 36.

52 OAS Unit for Sustainable Development and Environment, *Inter-American Strategy for the Promotion of Public Participation in Decision-Making for Sustainable Development*, at 2 (2001), https://www.oas.org/dsd/PDF_files/ispenglish.pdf.

piece of their engagement with member countries with respect to sustainable development.

In addition, the TAI network was especially strong in the LAC region, and some partners made direct submissions during consultations in Rio + 20, working closely with several supportive governments on the matter.[53] In pre-Rio + 20 negotiations, for example, both Chile and Jamaica made submissions responding to the public call by the UN Department of Economic and Social Affairs (UNDESA). In those submissions, these countries proposed a regional convention on Principle 10 to address the gaps in the region in the implementation of access rights.[54]

A *The LAC Declaration on Principle 10: a Road Map for a Regional Environmental Democracy Agreement*

For the LAC region, the June 2012 Rio + 20 meeting, formally the United Nations Conference on Sustainable Development, was a turning point for broader recognition of the need for a binding instrument to strengthen access rights in the region. After the hard work of the preparatory negotiations and with the leadership of the Chilean delegation, ten LAC countries signed the Declaration on the Application of Principle 10 of the *Rio Declaration on Environment and Development* (the LAC Declaration).[55] The LAC Declaration recognized that the rights of access to information, participation, and justice in environmental matters are essential for promoting sustainable development, democracy, and a healthy environment for all individuals.[56] Latin American and Caribbean States recognized that advancing the implementation of access rights was critical for meeting the environmental challenges of the region.[57]

The signing of the LAC Declaration was a major success for TAI partners in the region and marked the beginning of a long negotiation process that

---

53 Interview with Carole Excell, *supra* note 36.

54 Lalanath de Silva and Jeremy Wates, *Globalizing Environmental Democracy: A Call for International Action* (May 2012), http://www.unep.org/civil-society/Portals/24105/documents/perspectives/ENVIRONMENT_PAPERS_DISCUSSION_7.pdf.

55 The initial signatory countries were: Chile, Costa Rica, Dominican Republic, Ecuador, Jamaica, Mexico, Panama, Paraguay, Peru and Uruguay. *See* U.N. Conference on Sustainable Development Rio + 20. Declaration on the application of Principle 10 of the Rio Declaration on Environment and Development. U.N. Doc. A/CONF.216/13/(Vol.I), item 10 (Jul.25, 2012) [hereinafter LAC Declaration on Principle 10].

56 *Id.* ¶ 2.

57 Marcos Orellana, *Democracia Ambiental y Desarrollo Sostenible: Hacia un Instrumento regional sobre Derechos de Acceso*. FARN Informe Ambiental Anual (2014), at 44, http://farn.org.ar/archives/16501.

would ultimately lead to the world's second environmental democracy treaty. In the LAC Declaration, countries committed to have an open negotiating process with significant public participation, which was a major win for the TAI network. This would allow for civil society to have a central role in the upcoming negotiations.[58] Achieving the LAC Declaration was itself a key accomplishment that required proponents to overcome three major concerns. First countries expressed concern about the lack of resources, both financial and human, for the elaboration and implementation of a new convention. Second, some observers questioned the need for a separate LAC regional convention, as Aarhus was open to all the countries in the world. Third, skeptics questioned the ultimate effectiveness of the future convention, given the weak implementation of Principle 10 at the national level in some countries of the region.[59]

The intergovernmental negotiations and the work done by civil society allowed for these issues to be addressed and to build consensus for the LAC Declaration's adoption.[60] A regional convention could arguably respond better to the specific needs and characteristics of the region. Latin America is particularly beset by environment and development conflicts. The region is home to many biodiverse ecosystems and hundreds of indigenous and tribal communities, and at the same time, it is a region that has become the most dangerous place on earth for environmental defenders.[61] The high rate of conflict could arguably be mitigated by a regional agreement that particularly addresses the three elements of Principle 10. An international framework that ensures the rights of people to take part in development decisions could reduce conflicts by creating space for dialogue and specific protections for environmental defenders who risk their lives every day. The hope was that a LAC convention could help resolve the region's many environmental conflicts by promoting better standards on access rights and providing a collaborative approach for their implementation.[62]

A regional instrument could provide a common benchmark of minimum standards for a region with diverse legislation.[63] Such a benchmark would

---

58 LAC Declaration on Principle 10, *supra* note 55, ¶ 6.

59 Orellana, *supra* note 57, at 49.

60 Orellana, *supra* note 57.

61 Global Witness, *Defenders of the Earth: Global Killings of Land and Environmental Defenders on 2016*, at 8, https://www.globalwitness.org/en/campaigns/environmental-activists/defenders-earth/.

62 Report on the Situation of Environmental Human Rights Defenders, U.N. Doc. A/71/281, ¶ 22 (Aug. 3, 2016) (Report by Michael Forst, the Special Rapporteur on the situation of human rights defenders).

63 Interview with TAI director 2017.

pressure governments to make necessary changes in their national legislation, but it would do so in a framework of cooperation.[64] Although the possibility of a compliance mechanism was important to civil society, just as important was that a regional convention could provide targeted financial and other resources to build the capacity of those governments whose failure to implement access rights did not reflect unwillingness as much as a lack of institutional capacity.

The LAC Declaration was a renewal of the political commitment made originally in 1992 and a recognition that LAC States still experienced implementation gaps on access rights that needed to be addressed. Signatory countries committed to explore the feasibility of a regional instrument to ensure the full implementation of access rights.[65]

After two years of preliminary work, in November 2014, the countries that signed the Declaration initiated the negotiations under the auspices of the UN Economic Commission for Latin America and the Caribbean (ECLAC) that served as the technical secretary.[66] The negotiation process was characterized as "one of the most important steps at the international level to protect and promote environmental democracy."[67] The process was gaining momentum in the region and by the end of the negotiations in March 2018, twenty-four countries were participating in the negotiation committee.[68]

On March 4, 2018, the process that was initiated back in 2012 with the LAC Declaration concluded in Costa Rica with the adoption of the Regional Agreement on access to information, public participation, and justice in environmental matters in Latin America and the Caribbean, known as the Escazú Agreement, because of the region of San Jose, Costa Rica where it was adopted. The treaty is a milestone as the first human rights and environment treaty of the region and the first treaty in the world to specifically recognize the role of environmental human rights defenders and commit parties to their protection. The treaty also reflected the hard work of the region's activists that

64 Orellana, *supra* note 57, at 49.

65 *Id.*

66 U.N. ECLAC, *Fourth meeting of the focal points appointed by the Governments of the signatory countries of the Declaration on the application of Principle 10 of the Rio Declaration on Environment and Development in Latin America and the Caribbean*, art. 3 (Nov. 6, 2014), http://repositorio.cepal.org/bitstream/handle/11362/37214/S1420707_en.pdf?sequence=1 [hereinafter Santiago Decision].

67 Statement by United Nations experts on the ECLAC's negotiation of a regional instrument on environmental democracy (Oct 22, 2015): http://www.ohchr.org/EN/NewsEvents/Pages/DisplayNews.aspx?NewsID=16630&LangID=E#sthash.yiDuDPu1.dpuf.

68 On August 4, 2017 on the Seventh meeting of the negotiation committee Saint Lucia became signatory of the declaration becoming State number 24 to join the process.

successfully transformed the political will reflected in the soft-law LAC Declaration into the binding obligations of a regional agreement.

B *The ECLAC-Escazú Agreement*

Discussions on the nature of the agreement were hanging in the balance until the last moment as parties were striving for consensus on the substantive norms. Most of the countries participating in the negotiations had publicly expressed their support for a legally binding convention before, but a small minority led by Colombia and Mexico repeatedly showed reluctance to adopt a legally binding instrument.[69] In the last negotiation meeting the parties, led by the Costa Rican presidency and the Chilean co-presidency, managed to convince the small opposition group to agree to a binding agreement by trading-off a few of the substantive standards that were still being negotiated. Reunited in Escazú, Costa Rica, on Saturday evening, March 3, 2018, the negotiating committee burst into large applause when the final text of the Regional Agreement was unanimously adopted by the twenty-four countries that were members of the committee.

Activists generally achieved their objective of a regional environmental democracy convention, with a strong set of obligations that commit countries to guarantee access rights and take measures for their effective implementation. Additionally, the Escazú Agreement includes a committee to support implementation and compliance which follows the Aarhus model. The Escazú Committee however cannot yet receive communications from the public, as the Aarhus Committee does. Countries couldn't agree on this issue and decided to postpone this discussion for the first Conference of the Parties.

In terms of standards and legal obligations, the Escazú Agreement adopts the Aarhus Convention's model of three substantial pillars of environmental democracy: the right to access information, the right of participation, and the right to access to justice in environmental matters, but, significantly, it adds a new pillar on the rights of environmental human rights defenders.[70] The inclusion of environmental human rights defenders as a new pillar in the Escazú

69 *See* Natalia Gomez Peña, *Un balance desalentador deja la 7ª ronda de negociaciones sobre democracia ambiental en América Latina y el Caribe* (Aug 4, 2017), http://www.ambienteysociedad.org.co/es/un-balance-desalentador-deja-la-7a-ronda-de-negociaciones-sobre-democracia-ambiental-en-america-latina-y-el-caribe/.

70 U.N. ECLAC, *Regional agreement on access to information, public participation and justice in environmental matters in Latin America and the Caribbean*, UN Doc. arts. 4–9 (Escazú, Costa Rica, 4 March 2018), https://treaties.un.org/doc/Treaties/2018/03/20180312%20 03–04%20PM/CTC-XXVII-18.pdf [hereinafter Escazú Agreement].

Agreement is a direct international legal response to social reality, as the region has become the most dangerous place in the world for environmental rights defenders.[71] The recognition of the role of defenders and the obligation to protect them is included in the general obligations section,[72] and in a specific article, which creates a regimen of protection for environmental human rights defenders.[73]

The Escazú Agreement develops a stronger and more direct relationship with human rights law. As in the Aarhus Convention, the Escazú Agreement's ultimate goal is to strengthen democracy and sustainable development, but with a more visible component of human rights protection.[74] The Escazú Agreement's objective links environmental democracy rights to the realization of the right to live in a healthy and sustainable environment.[75] The Escazú Agreement is based on the premise that access rights were already recognized by countries in various international soft law instruments,[76] and therefore the objective of this Agreement should be the full and effective implementation of those rights.[77] As well, the Escazú Agreement reinforces the idea of participatory governance, in which people have the right to participate in an effective and informed manner in the matters that affect them. This is significant in the context of increasing attacks on civic space in the world.

In the Escazú Agreement, the articles on the three pillars of environmental democracy are clearly drafted as rights for people to exercise, while in comparison in Aarhus, the drafting of the pillars does not use the word "rights" but instead stresses the obligations of parties.[78] At the same time the Escazú Agreement clearly states that each party has to guarantee each one of the rights it protects. The Escazú Agreement also includes specific references to the obligation of parties to guarantee the right of every person to live in a healthy environment;[79] to a reaffirmation of human rights instruments and the responsibility of States to respect, protect, and promote human rights;[80] and to the obligation to apply human rights principles, such as equality and

---

71 Global Witness, *supra* note 61.

72 Escazú Agreement, *supra* note 70, at art. 4.6.

73 *Id.* art. 9.

74 *Id.* at pmbl., ¶ 4.

75 *Id.* Article 1.

76 *See* Rio Declaration on Environment and Development, *supra* note 7; LAC Declaration on Principle 10, supra note 55.

77 Escazú Agreement, *supra* note 70, at art. 1.

78 *See id.* art. 4–9.

79 *Id.* art. 4.1.

80 *Id.* pmbl. ¶ 5.

non-discrimination,[81] non-regression,[82] and the pro-persona principle,[83] in the implementation of the agreement.

The Escazú Agreement aims to unify the availability of access rights across the LAC region. Latin America and the Caribbean have major differences in standards and access rights legislation, with Latin America having a more developed framework of regulations than the Caribbean region. For example, countries such as Grenada and the Bahamas do not have access to information laws,[84] while countries such as Argentina and Brazil even have specific laws to access environmental information.[85] The standards set by the Escazú Agreement aim to equilibrate these differences among regions and the agreement proposes a minimum standard of rights that parties should guarantee for all their citizens. As a minimum standard, nothing in the Escazú Agreement prevents parties from including more favorable rights in their legislation or in any other international instrument that the country signs.[86]

The Escazú Agreement's provisions on access to environmental information (articles 5 and 6), [87] public participation (article 7), [88] and access to remedies

81 Escazú Agreement, *supra* note 70, at art. 3.a.

82 *Id.* art. 3.c.

83 *Id.* art. 3.k.

84 Economic Commission for Latin America and the Caribbean (ECLAC), Access to information, participation and justice in environmental matters in Latin America and the Caribbean: towards achievement of the 2030 Agenda for Sustainable Development, LC/TS.2017/83, 46–47 (2018).

85 *Id.*

86 Escazú Agreement, *supra* note 70, at art. 4.7.

87 *Id.* art. 6. Article 6 on access to environmental information states the presumption of public character of environmental information; the right of the public to request information without demonstrating any special interest and to be informed of the right to appeal if the information is not delivered; the obligations of States to facilitate access to information for individuals or groups in vulnerable situations, and the conditions that should be applicable when States deliver information. Article 7 establishes the obligations of States when generating and disseminating environmental information, including the obligation of public authorities to proactively collect and publicize the environmental information they possess, and that information is available in accessible formats.

88 *Id.* art 8. Article 8, on public participation in environmental decision-making, establishes the commitment of parties to implement inclusive participation mechanisms for environmental decision-making which will apply to decisions on conservation, use, exploitation and management of natural resources. In these mechanisms people should have the right to access the relevant information necessary to participate, to exercise their right to participate since the beginning of the processes to have the possibility to influence the decision, and to have reasonable times to exercise their participation.

(article 8),[89] are based on both soft and hard international instruments. For example, the provisions of access to information include important standards from the jurisprudence of the Inter-American Court of Human Rights regarding, inter alia, the legality principle applicable to restrictions of access to information, the maximum disclosure principle, and the burden of proof for parties when establishing restrictions to access to information.[90] The Escazú Agreement also includes standards from the OAS Inter-American Model Law on Access to Information.[91] Among those standards are the possibility to make a request of information without providing any justification, the right to appeal when access to information is denied, and the obligations of active transparency that require parties to publish and disseminate certain information.[92]

The standards of the Inter-American System of Human Rights are also reflected in the section of the Escazú Agreement on access to participation. The jurisprudence of the Court in this matter has mainly developed in the context of indigenous peoples and their right to consultation.[93] The Agreement's approach to the right to participate recasts the jurisprudence to establish that participation must be informed, effective, and prior to the decision.[94]

The widespread inequality in the region necessitated specific provisions for persons and groups in vulnerable situations. Throughout the negotiations, the recognition of the region's diversity committed States to negotiate a treaty that would recognize diversity and support the groups most affected by socio-environmental conflicts.[95] Unfortunately, as one of the compromises made at the end to convince the "opposition group" to accept a binding instrument, the

---

89 *Id.* art. 9. Article 9 introduces the right of every person to access environmental justice through judicial or administrative procedures, in a timely, effective and transparent manner. This right should be ensured for individuals to have the mechanisms to demand protection of their rights to information and participation, or challenge any action that affects the environment.

90 Claude Reyes v. Chile. Merits, Reparations and Costs, Judgment, Inter-Am. Ct. H.R. (ser. C), ¶ 89–92(Sep.19, 2006).

91 Adopted by the General Assembly of the Organization of American States on June 8, 2010. See: OAS, Model Inter-American Law on Access to Public Information, AG/RES. 2607 (XL-O/10), (June 8, 2010), https://www.oas.org/dil/AG-RES_2607-2010_eng.pdf [hereinafter Model Inter-American Law].

92 *Id.* art. 5.

93 *See, e.g.*, Saramaka v. Suriname, Merits, Reparations and Costs, Judgment, Inter-Am. Ct. H.R. (ser. C), (Nov.28, 2007); Case of the Mayagna (Sumo) Awas Tingni Community v. Nicaragua, Merits, Reparations and Costs, Judgment, Inter-Am. Ct. H.R. (ser. C, Vol 79), (Aug. 31, 2001).

94 Escazú Agreement, *supra* note 70, at art. 7.4, 7.6.

95 *See* LAC Declaration on Principle 10, *supra* note 55.

parties included an intentionally ambiguous definition of persons and groups in vulnerable situations that will likely lead to problems of interpretation.[96] The definition of persons or groups in vulnerable situations includes all persons or groups that face more obstacles to exercise access rights because of conditions defined by each country. This ambiguous definition was the result of hard negotiations between countries that balked at including more protective language as they realized this negotiation would end with a binding agreement. Nonetheless, the Escazú Agreement, in various provisions, commits parties to support persons and groups in vulnerable situations in the exercise of their access rights. Additionally, the Escazú Agreement specifically supports indigenous communities and ethnic groups in the exercise of their access rights.[97]

The Escazú Treaty also reflects some steps back from Inter-American standards and the Aarhus Convention. Countries chose not to establish a clear, limited, and standardized system of exceptions to available information for the whole region and instead allowed each country to apply its own legislation when denying access to information.[98] Additionally, both the Inter-American Model Law and Aarhus establish a category of information whose access can never be denied by the States, but the Escazú Agreement failed to include this provision.[99]

In general, the Escazú Agreement provides a robust set of standards that will positively impact the region. However, the Treaty also included many weak provisions that diminished the effect of its binding nature. During the negotiations, some countries constantly tried to attach conditions based on their national legislation, and they succeed in a few cases. For instance, in the case of the provision that recognizes broad standing in defense of the environment, one of the major wins in the Escazú Agreement, countries at the last minute

96 Escazú Agreement, *supra* note 70, at art. 2.e.

97 *See id.* arts. 5.4, 6.6.

98 Escazú Agreement, *supra* note 70, at art. 5.5. *See* Model Inter-American Law, *supra* note 91, at art. 41; Aarhus Convention, *supra* note 14, at arts. 4.3, 4.4.

99 In the sixth version of the draft text Article 6.7 stated that information concerning factors that negatively affect the environment and human health and safety would not be considered as being exempt from disclosure. This article, which was deleted by States in the negotiation in Argentina, allowed that information of fundamental importance for the protection of the right to health and a healthy environment was always brought to the attention of the citizens. Similar articles are included in other instruments of international law such as the Aarhus Convention, which states that information on emissions of pollutants to the environment should always be delivered, and the Inter-American model law on access to information, which states that in no case access to information may be denied in cases of serious violations of human rights or crimes against humanity.

added that broad standing would be recognized "in accordance with domestic legislation."[100] Additionally, various obligations, especially those in Article 6 that refer to active transparency, have a soft law feel with conditional text such as to "the extent possible within available resources,"[101] or that parties should "use their best endeavors" to comply with an obligation.[102]

The institutional framework of the Escazú Agreement includes a clearing house, a voluntary fund, a committee to support implementation and compliance, and a secretariat that will be exercised by ECLAC.[103] The Escazú Agreement's approach to compliance follows the general approach of the Aarhus compliance committee as a non-adversarial, non-judicial, consultative organ, but in at least one aspect it took a significant step backward. In the original draft text, the compliance committee could consider communications from members of the public regarding the compliance of parties to the treaty.[104] This is included in the Aarhus Convention and was approved by the first Aarhus Conference of the Parties.[105] However, this power was dropped as part of the compromise to ensure the binding nature of the LAC Treaty.[106] Ultimately, the rules relating to the structure and functioning of the committee under the LAC Treaty will be determined by the first COP.[107] How communications from the public will be treated is expected to be one of the main points for discussion at the first COP.

The LAC process entered a new phase after the treaty opened for signature and ratification on September 27, 2018. In this regard, the treaty states that the Agreement will be open for signature to the thirty-three countries of Latin American and the Caribbean and that it will enter into force when the eleventh instrument of ratification is deposited.[108] Advocates are now working to achieve the signature and ratification of the instrument in each one of their countries. The political context of this new phase has changed as various

---

100 Escazú Agreement, *supra* note 70, at art. 9.3.c.

101 *See id.* art. 6.1.

102 *Id.* art. 6.7.

103 *Id.* art. 12–26.

104 U.N. ECLAC, *Text Compiled By The Presiding Officers Incorporating The Language Proposals From The Countries On The Preliminary Document On The Regional Agreement On Access To Information, Participation And Justice In Environmental Matters In Latin America And The Caribbean Eighth Version*, LC/L.4059/Rev.8, at art. 19.4, (Jan. 22, 2018), https://repositorio.cepal.org/bitstream/handle/11362/39051/37/S1800064_en.pdf.

105 Aarhus Convention, *supra* note 14.

106 Escazú Agreement, *supra* note 70, at art. 18.

107 *Id.* art. 18.1.

108 Escazú Agreement, *supra* note 70, at art. 21–22.

countries in the region are going through elections, including Costa Rica and Chile, the main governmental forces behind the Agreement, which means that many governments are signing and ratifying an agreement that was negotiated by their predecessors. The real impact of the Escazú Agreement for the region will be seen after the treaty enters into force and the implementation of the instrument begins. Hopefully, like Aarhus, it becomes useful both for governments and citizens to strengthen civic space and prevent socio-environmental conflicts.

The Escazú Agreement is a major win for civil society in the LAC region and for the TAI network that energized the process since the beginning. For civil society, the process is an example of the possibilities that citizens have to advocate and promote change in the international arena. Civil society, reunited in the TAI network, made a conscious decision to first advocate for the Latin American and Caribbean Principle 10 Declaration, and to build the political support and the necessary capacities to then negotiate a hard-law instrument. From 2012 to 2014 activists worked to get their countries to sign onto the Declaration and build the necessary capacities to start the negotiation process in May 2015. This was also an important time to build confidence with government representatives and advocate for the adoption of inclusive modalities of participation.

The Escazú Agreement is also a product of the work of progressive countries, like Chile and Costa Rica, that led the negotiations since 2012 and worked closely with civil society partners. Along with Chile and Costa Rica, the work of the delegates from Panama, Trinidad and Tobago, Brazil, and Argentina, in different stages of the negotiation, was very important to achieving the Agreement. For the international law community, the negotiation is a great example of the catalytic effect a soft international law instrument can have in terms of promoting political support among countries and forming a base of support for developing a binding treaty. Additionally, the negotiation set a new benchmark for the role of civil society in multilateral processes and gave important lessons on participation modalities that can be replicated and strengthened in the future.

C *The LAC P10 Process: New Modalities for the Participation of Civil Society in International Negotiations*

The negotiations of the Escazú Agreement established innovative modalities for the participation of civil society that directly influenced the outcome of the process. In the 2012 LAC Declaration, countries committed to an open process with significant participation from the interested public.[109] The modalities for the participation of the public, constructed with the input of civil society, were

109 LAC Declaration on Principle 10, *supra* note 55.

adopted in 2013.[110] TAI played a major role in the approval of these modalities by organizing civil society and advocating through its members in the region for strong standards for the participation of the public.

The modalities of participation, following the precedent set in the Aarhus negotiations, allowed civil society to participate directly at the negotiating table with governments. When the negotiation committee was formed in 2014, the governments invited the public to designate two official representatives to maintain a dialogue with the presiding officers.[111] This invitation led to an election procedure through the regional public mechanism created by ECLAC where two civil society representatives were elected as principals and four as alternates. The civil society representatives could present text proposals to the plenary that, when supported by at least one government, were incorporated into the negotiating text. Instead of only advocating in the shadows, civil society representatives were able to address the whole plenary with their proposals.

The elected representatives led the dialogue between governments and civil society and contributed to the creation of a civil society advocacy strategy that primarily convened around the TAI network. These civil society diplomats made strategic alliances with progressive governments that adopted civil society proposals, such as Chile, Costa Rica, Panama, and Peru, and they gathered support from other states to achieve greater results when advocating for better standards.

Civil society organizing around the TAI network was particularly important in moments where the negotiations were losing their course. In August 2017 when the Seventh Negotiation Committee convened in Buenos Aires, Argentina, civil society successfully objected to countries lowering the standards for access to information, by announcing that they would abandon the meeting if the situation was not corrected in the next meeting.[112] In the last meeting of the committee in Escazú, Costa Rica, civil society successfully demanded the adoption of a binding treaty that did not allow parties to make reservations.

---

110 ECLAC, Third meeting of the negotiating committee of the regional agreement on access to information, participation and justice in environmental matters in Latin America and the Caribbean, Annex 1 Modalities of Participation for the Public, (April, 8 2016), https://repositorio.cepal.org/bitstream/handle/11362/40413/S1600323_en.pdf?sequence=1&isAllowed=y.

111 Santiago Decision, *supra* note 66, at 6.

112 *See* Marcos Orellana, *Civil Society Groups Threaten to Walk Out of Latin America Environment Talks: Lack of Rights Guarantees at Buenos Aires Negotiations Raises Concern* (Aug. 21, 2017), https://www.hrw.org/news/2017/08/21/civil-society-groups-threaten-walk-out-latin-america-environment-talks.

The practice of the Committee also allowed the public to organize alternative side-events to raise major topics for discussion. For example, in 2016, the public organized a panel with three environmental human rights defenders from the region with the objective of showing the negotiators the importance of including specific protection for them. They made the plight of human rights defenders a high priority throughout the rest of the negotiations, even holding an intervention in 2018 in remembrance of the two-year anniversary of the assassination of Honduran indigenous activist Berta Caceres. In addition, the Committee also established a panel of independent experts, one for each right, who contributed to clarifying the conceptual doubts of the negotiators and constantly advocated for the adoption of the best standards in international law.[113]

Civil society faced many challenges, including a lack of funding and resources, that directly impacted civil society's effectiveness. The unwillingness of governments to adopt progressive positions was also hard to overcome. Nonetheless, many civil society proposals were adopted by countries. The process contributed to the capacity-building of many organizations and advocates in the region, and even of government representatives that also learnt to have a more direct relationship with civil society representatives.

Active civil society participation in the Escazú negotiations was possible because of the mechanisms and rules that countries adopted, after heavy advocacy from activists. Nonetheless, the formal dynamics of an international negotiation required certain technical expertise and continued commitment that may have limited the possibilities of grass-roots activists to participate. More often, civil society participants came from organizations based in the capital cities.

The formalities of a treaty negotiation forced civil society to adopt a more diplomatic tone that sometimes may have been counterproductive, as it caused civil society to defer more direct and strong actions that may have been more effective. Civil society-elected representatives became the "official diplomats" for the public, which required them to adopt less direct argumentation in order to reduce the risk of being seen as obstructive by countries, and therefore, providing them with an excuse to exclude civil society. In some ways, civil society won a voice at the table but with many conditions on what would be said and how it should be said. Civil society agreed to this because of the extraordinary possibility of a having a chair at the negotiating table. Therefore,

113 From 2014 to 2017, the Panel was composed by Silvia Capelli, Promoter of Justice from Rio Grande do Sul (Brazil), Marcos Orellana, Adjunct Professor at George Washington Law School, and Winston Anderson, Judge of the Caribbean Court.

they mostly followed the "diplomatic behavior" and achieved a large influence in the final text, while also speaking clearly and directly against countries who were taking regressive positions.

VI Lessons Learned from the Evolution of Access Rights

Since emerging on the global agenda in the 1992 *Rio Declaration*, access rights have followed an uneven path towards their progressive elaboration and effective implementation. Analyzing this path reveals important lessons for the relationship between social change and international law. The adoption of Principle 10 in 1992, the Aarhus Convention in 1994, the Bali Guidelines in 2010, and the recently adopted Escazú Agreement in March 2018, all reflect civil society leadership in shaping international law as a tool to drive social change. The access rights process also shows the interplay between soft and hard international law instruments that over time provide a range of opportunities to guarantee more rights to people.

One observation that emerges relates to the role of major UN Summits in the evolution over time of environmental access norms. These UN Summits created major opportunities where civil society could build political will for social change among governments, even if it was motivated by avoiding embarrassment in the international community. Beginning with the 1992 Earth Summit's endorsement of Principle 10, the UN Summits created focal points for progress. The Partnership for Principle 10 was announced at the 2002 WSSD and the LAC Declaration was signed at Rio +20. These processes kept momentum going on the development of norms, and they offer points in time to focus multiple stakeholder's attention on progress.

The *Rio Declaration* in 1992 was a sign of important political commitment by countries, and it gave birth to a new system of governance where citizen participation was recognized as essential for better environmental decisions. The challenge was how this general commitment would be taken up and implemented. The same momentum that led to Principle 10 also led to almost immediate operationalization for Europe in the binding Aarhus Convention. The example of Aarhus as a hard international law instrument with strong standards set a benchmark for future developments and contributed to promoting interest for a binding instrument in the LAC process among countries of that region.

Throughout the continuing evolution of environmental access rights, we see the advocates challenged by the clear trade-off between the "bindingness" of the instrument and the relative strength of the substantive norms. The

Aarhus Convention set a rare baseline of relatively strong standards in a binding instrument with a relatively robust compliance mechanism. This benchmark influenced the future evolution of access rights. At several points, proponents have opted not to pursue a binding instrument because they feared the standards would be significantly lower than those in Aarhus. Having Aarhus sitting there, open to any country to join, leaves a clear alternative option for the long-term view of what is possible, making a compromise on substance-for-enforceability less appealing.

Yet, the globalization of Aarhus as a universal binding set of norms ran into opposition that led civil society both to work regionally and to embrace the value of global soft law negotiations. The soft law Bali Guidelines helped to globalize Principle 10 as well as to build the expertise of civil society in promoting access rights. The greater informality of UNEP's process led to an enhanced role for civil society and provided it with opportunities to build strategic alliances with some governments. The Aarhus model, and the experience gained by Latin American civil society advocates at Bali, combined to shape the Latin American process.

The Bali Guidelines in retrospect were a crucial moment for civil society who directly participated in the negotiations through the TAI network. The Guidelines, although slow in their implementation, are being used as a universal benchmark to evaluate legislation around the world and promote the improvement of standards.[114] They supplanted the Aarhus Convention as the benchmark in many ways precisely because they purported to be universal. The expectations after the Bali Guidelines were for all States to adopt a legal framework for access rights even if the obligation was not enforceable and if practice lagged. Civil society used the Guidelines as a benchmark to evaluate national laws and when presenting international proposals to governments, for example in the LAC negotiations.

In this way, Principle 10, the Bali Guidelines, and even the OAS's Inter-American Model Law on Access to Information, all soft international law instruments, created the climate for a hard international law instrument in Latin America modelled in many ways after the hard international law Aarhus Convention.[115] As mentioned above, the process in Latin America started with a Declaration proposed by the government of Chile and then signed by nine other governments. This Declaration was result of TAI partners work in Latin America that successfully advocated before their governments. The

114 *See* Interview with Carole Excell, *supra* note 36.

115 *Id.*

Declaration committed States to start a process that could lead to the adoption of an international treaty. This soft and ambiguous Declaration launched a process that delivered, in 2018, the second environmental democracy treaty in the world.

The evolution toward a LAC instrument highlights many complexities in the choice between hard and soft international law instruments, as well as the related choice in this context between regional and global approaches. Perceived and real differences among regions have made it difficult to build a global consensus for how to apply access rights. Europe's homogeneity and shared experience allowed it to reach a consensus rapidly on strong access rights. Likewise, shared experiences and values led the LAC region to pursue a regional approach, both considering Europe's success and the perceived reluctance of other regions to commit to global negotiations.

The Escazú Agreement is an interesting example of the impact of civil society and international lawyers in producing social change in international law. The modalities of public participation inspired by the Aarhus model really marked a before and after for the participation of civil society in international negotiations. As Aarhus, the Escazú Agreement includes a strong set of regulations, but it also exemplifies how countries and advocates may have to compromise to achieve a legally binding instrument.

CHAPTER 7

The Hard Choice for Soft Commitments in the Climate Change Regime

*David B. Hunter**

I Introduction

Climate change is the defining environmental issue of the 21st century. Climate change has now been linked to unprecedented and deadly heatwaves on every continent; the reduction of ice in Greenland, the Arctic, and Antarctica; rising sea levels; the bleaching of coral reefs; more extreme weather, including stronger cyclone and hurricanes, more severe floods in some regions, and more severe droughts in others; and multiple changes in the range and behavior of wildlife.[1] These are the impacts we can already observe. The extent of future impacts depends substantially on how effective the world is in curtailing the future emissions of carbon dioxide and other greenhouse gases (GHG s).[2]

International negotiations to address climate change have continued largely unabated since the late 1980s. The resulting climate regime is a complex mixture of binding and non-binding instruments, evolving over time through annual negotiations that take place in a highly politicized and public way. The latest major addition in the evolution of the regime was the 2015 Paris Agreement, negotiated in front of thousands of observers and joined by virtually every country in the world.

Although the climate regime covers a wide range of issues, the central issue in the negotiations is how to curb net GHG emissions—or in the regime's vernacular, how to *mitigate* climate change. This chapter focusses on the regime's treatment of mitigation commitments, culminating in the Paris Agreement

---

* Professor of Law at the American University's Washington College of Law.

1 *See generally* Intergovernmental Panel on Climate Change (IPCC), Syntheses Report of Working Groups I, II and III to the Fifth Assessment Report of the Intergovernmental Panel on Climate Change (R.K. Pachauri & L.S. Meyer, eds.,) (2014) [hereinafter IPCC Fifth Assessment Report].

2 *See generally id.;* IPCC, Global Warming of 1.5°C: An IPCC Special Report on the Impacts of Global Warming of 1.5°C Above Pre-Industrial Levels, Summary for Policymakers (V. Masson-Delmotte, et al., eds.) (2018).

 | DOI:10.1163/9789004417021_008

and its compromise that situated voluntary mitigation commitments in a hard law instrument.[3] The regime's path to the Paris Agreement's compromise has not been linear. It has included hard law instruments, like the UN Framework Convention on Climate Change (UNFCCC)[4] and the now largely abandoned cap-and-trade system of the Kyoto Protocol;[5] soft law instruments like the Copenhagen Accord;[6] and instruments of uncertain status, like decisions from the Conferences of the Parties (CoP).

Examining the evolution of the regime's approach to mitigation can thus provide insights on the various roles of hard and soft international law, the trade-offs between the two, and how hard and soft international law can be complementary within a single treaty regime. After summarizing the climate negotiations' approach to mitigation commitments over time, this chapter evaluates the regime's evolution through a hard/soft international law lens.

II Evolution of the Climate Regime

Given the high stakes, complexity, and divergent interests involved in the climate negotiations, it is no wonder that the climate regime is taking years to develop. Scientific research and associated demands for international action to address climate change coalesced in the late 1980s.[7] By 1990, the United Nations authorized an Intergovernmental Negotiating Committee on Climate to begin formal discussions of a binding global treaty, which would culminate in the 1992 Framework Convention on Climate Change.[8]

To set mitigation commitments under a climate regime, two basic questions had to be addressed. First, what level of global mitigation (i.e. reduction of net greenhouse gases) is necessary to prevent significant harm from climate

3 *See* G.A. Res. 1/CP.21, Paris Agreement (Dec. 12, 2015).

4 United Nations Framework Convention on Climate Change, art. 4(2), May. 9, 1992, 1771 U.N.T.S. 107 [hereinafter UNFCCC].

5 Kyoto Protocol to the United Nations Framework Convention on Climate Change, Dec. 11, 1997, 37 I.L.M. 22 [hereinafter Kyoto Protocol].

6 UNFCCC, The Copenhagen Accord, Dec. 2/Cp.15, U.N. Doc. FCCC/CP/2009/11/Add.1, at 5 (Dec. 18, 2009) [hereinafter Copenhagen Accord].

7 *See, e.g.*, Stat. of the Int'l Conference of the Changing Atmosphere: Implications for Glob. Sec. (1988); Philip Shabecoff, *Global Warming Has Begun, Expert Tells Senate*, N.Y. TIMES, June 24, 1988, https://www.nytimes.com/1988/06/24/us/global-warming-has-begun-expert-tells-senate.html.

8 G.A. Res. A/Res/4512, Protection of Global Climate for Present and Future Generations of Mankind (Dec. 21, 1990).

change? Second, how would the responsibility for achieving that level of mitigation be allocated among the countries? The first question was thought to be primarily a scientific question—the second, a question for diplomacy.

A *Power and Interest in the Climate Negotiations*

Since the beginning, the climate negotiations have been highly public and highly politicized. Every country in the world participates in the negotiations and the rule of decision remains one of consensus. It is convenient to divide the parties into developed and developing blocs, and to some extent this division explains Parties' positions within the negotiations. However, this bi-polar approach masks significant differences within the blocs. For example, the oil-producing countries oppose any strong, binding commitments and generally try to slow the regime's development. By contrast, the small island states faced with an existential threat from climate change are generally the strongest supporters of strong binding commitments. The other state parties generally align along a continuum between these two positions, depending frequently on their particular resource base or energy mix. For example, Argentina, with significant hydropower resources, was willing to take on binding commitments before other middle-income countries. South Africa's negotiating positions reflected their heavy dependence on coal. Brazil focused on how the negotiations addressed forests' role in the carbon cycle because of the potential impact on its massive Amazon forest.

State party positions are also influenced by the active participation of non-state observers to the negotiations. The primary venue for the formal climate negotiations, the annual Conferences of the Parties (CoPs), take place under the watchful eye and with the active participation of literally thousands of representatives from civil society organizations, private companies, the media, and academia.[9] The presence of these non-state actors at times gives the negotiations a carnival-like feeling, as environmental activists stage mini-protests, give out "fossil" awards, publish daily satires to prod the negotiators, and wear matching brightly colored t-shirts with cutting slogans. The non-state actors also provide significant expertise, often with scientists, lawyers, and economists who have followed the entire thirty years of negotiations.[10]

---

9 For a discussion of the role of non-state actors in the climate negotiations, *see* UCLA Sch. of Law, Kal Raustiala & Natalie L. Bridgeman, *Nonstate Actors in the Global Climate Regime*, Research Paper No. 07–29 (2007), https://papers.ssrn.com/sol3/papers.cfm?abstract_id=1028603#.

10 Civil society's participation in the climate regime is generally quite similar to that described in Chapter 8 by Patricia Lambert regarding the International Tobacco Control Treaty. As noted therein, civil society organizations experienced with climate change

Even though many of the small negotiating sessions are formally closed to non-state actors, non-state actors have a variety of ways to inject their perspectives into the negotiations. Many CSO or industry representatives are part of official delegations; others are sought out by the negotiators in the hallways. Non-state actors publish documents that may be distributed officially or unofficially to all the parties, and many parties hold daily briefing sessions for exchanges with non-state actors.

Like the state parties, non-state actors take a wide range of approaches to the issues of the nature and strength of mitigation commitments. Oil and gas company representatives are closely and quite visibly aligned with the positions of the oil-producing countries.[11] Representatives of the solar and wind power industries or from the insurance industry often take positions on mitigation, more closely aligned with the small island states.[12] Environment and development advocacy groups also take a range of approaches, with, for example, some interested in promoting a carbon trading system that would allow industry greater flexibility[13] and others taking a rights-based approach that emphasizes immediate, ambitious, and binding commitments, closely and visibly aligned with the small island states.[14] Non-state actors thus generally align with those states that match their interests, ideology, and to a lesser extent

negotiations brought their tactics to the tobacco negotiations. *See* Patricia Lambert, *infra* ch. 8 in this volume.

11 The role of the fossil-fuel industry in global climate policy is well documented. *See, e.g.*, ERIK M. CONWAY & NAOMI ORESKES, MERCHANTS OF DOUBT (2010).

12 *See, e.g.*, Solar Energy Indus. Ass'n, *Initiatives: Climate Change*, https://www.seia.org/initiatives/climate-change; Adnan Z. Amin, Int'l Renewable Energy Agency, *Renewables are the Key to a Climate-Safe World*, https://www.irena.org/newsroom/articles/2018/Nov/Renewables-are-the-key-to-a-climate-safe-world; J. of the Am. Inst. of Architects, *Insurance and Climate Change: Risk too Great to Ignore*, Oct. 4, 2017, https://www.architectmagazine.com/practice/insurance-and-climate-change-risk-too-great-to-ignore_o; United Nations Development Program (UNDP), Small Island Nations at the Frontline of Climate Actions, Sept. 18, 2017, https://www.undp.org/content/undp/en/home/news-centre/news/2017/09/18/small-island-nations-at-the-frontline-of-climate-action-.html.

13 *See, e.g.*, Envtl. Defense Fund, *How Cap and Trade Works*, https://www.edf.org/climate/how-cap-and-trade-works (June 15, 2019); Bob Sussman, Brookings Inst., *The Return of Cap and Trade is Good News for U.S. Climate Policy*, Oct. 21, 2015, https://www.brookings.edu/blog/planetpolicy/2015/10/21/the-return-of-cap-and-trade-is-good-news-for-u-s-climate-policy/.

14 *See, e.g.*, Cent. for Int'l Envtl. Law & Friends of the Earth, *Is World Trade Law a Barrier to Saving Our Climate?* (Sept. 2009) https://www.ciel.org/Publications/ClimateTradeReport_foee-ciel_sep09.pdf.; Indigenous Environmental Network, *Carbon Offsets Cause Conflict and Colonialism*, May 18, 2016, https://www.ienearth.org/carbon-offsets-cause-conflict-and-colonialism/.

identity—although these alliances may shift from one issue to the next. Non-state actors work to build coalitions first within similar interest groups (e.g., environmental advocacy groups)[15] and also across interest groups (e.g., environmentalist/industry coalitions).[16] In this way, non-state and state actors are all trying to build power in the negotiations by aligning with those with similar interests.

With respect to the question of whether the mitigation commitments should be embodied in hard or soft international law, most environmental advocacy groups supported strong hard international law commitments as important to achieving the social goal of reduced greenhouse gas emissions. Over time, however, the trade-off in the climate negotiations became more evident and intractable: achieving clear binding commitments would reflect and demonstrate greater political commitment from the Parties, but it might come at the price of (1) weaker commitments and/or (2) less universal adoption of commitments. Different advocacy groups would make different calculations of these trade-offs over time. But, in general, as discussed further below, those stakeholders seeking strong climate mitigation shifted towards the view that sacrificing the hardness of mitigation commitments was a price worth paying to gain more universal and more immediate action.

B *The* UNFCCC

At the outset of the climate change negotiations in the late 1980s, both state and non-state participants expected that scientific assessments by the Intergovernmental Panel on Climate Change (IPCC) would lead to a scientifically determined global cap on net emissions of GHG s. This global cap would be set at a level that would avoid the worst climate change impacts. The overall cap would then be allocated through internationally negotiated national emission caps (called mitigation targets and timetables). Informed by past approaches in other environmental negotiations, parties understood that the industrialized countries would be expected to accept binding mitigation targets first, and that the developing countries would accept binding targets a decade or so later.[17] The negotiated targets and timetables would reflect accepted principles

15 The largest network of climate advocacy organizations is the Global Climate Action Network, http://www.climatenetwork.org/about/members (stating that the Climate Action Network has 1100 members in over 120 countries).

16 *See, e.g.* Ceres, www.ceres.org/about-us (last visited June 15, 2019); The Climate Group, www.theclimategroup.org (last visited June 15, 2019).

17 This approach was affirmed in the principle of common but differentiated responsibilities adopted in the UNFCCC and Rio Declaration. *See* UNFCCC, *supra* note 4, at art. 3(1); *see also* U.N. Conference on Environment and Development., *Rio Declaration on Environment*

of equity and of common but differentiated responsibilities. The negotiations generally followed this approach through the 1992 UNFCCC and the 1997 Kyoto Protocol.

The UNFCCC has been ratified by virtually every country in the world, including all of the major contributors to climate change. The Convention provides the framework under which subsequent climate negotiations have proceeded. Importantly, it established the institutional architecture for the progressive development of the regime through subsequent decisions, protocols, or amendments. The Convention vests overall policy-setting authority in the annual Conference of the Parties, day-to-day operations in the Secretariat, financial grant-making in the Global Environment Facility, and technical reviews in a scientific and technical subsidiary body. All of these entities are controlled and staffed by state actors, although non-state actors can influence their behavior through the wide range of practices described generally above.

The Convention's objective and its principles have been particularly vital in shaping future negotiations. The Convention's objective, found in Article 2, requires the parties to collectively achieve "stabilization of GHG concentrations in the atmosphere at a level that would prevent *dangerous anthropogenic interference* with the climate system."[18] This objective is the standard by which the parties' commitments under the climate regime are measured. The parties are required periodically to evaluate whether implementation of the Convention's commitments are adequate to meet this overall objective. These periodic evaluations (and the inevitable conclusions that we have not made enough progress) provide the factual predicate for the parties' decision to negotiate stronger commitments over time—negotiations that have led, for example, to the Kyoto Protocol and the Paris Agreement.

The UNFCCC also set forth principles for guiding these future negotiations, the two most important of which proved to be the principle of common but differentiated responsibilities (CBDR) and the principle of equity. The CBDR principle justifies treating developed and developing countries differently under the climate regime because developed countries have disproportionately contributed to climate change, and they command a disproportionate amount of economic resources. This principle explains the relative nature of the respective commitments of developed and developing countries, including, for example, why only developed countries were obliged to reduce emissions under the Kyoto Protocol. Similarly, the principle of equity implied that any

and Development., U.N. Doc. A./CONF.151/26(Vol.I), Principle 7 (Aug.12, 1992), http://www.un.org/documents/ga/conf151/aconf15126-1annex1.htm.

18 UNFCCC, *supra* note 4, at art. 2 (emphasis added).

allocation of a global cap would have to be fair between countries and implicitly recognized that the current allocation was unfair. These two principles highlighted the difficult political task of reaching agreement over how to allocate the relative amounts each party would be able to emit under a global cap.

The UNFCCC is undeniably a binding treaty, and thus is considered by all to be a hard international law instrument.[19] Yet, the UNFCCC's language was intentionally negotiated to avoid any specific binding mandates, at least with respect to reducing GHG emissions. Article 4(1) places certain general requirements on all Parties, including that they adopt policies and measures to mitigate climate change, while "taking into account their common but differentiated responsibilities and their specific national and regional development priorities, objectives, and circumstances." Article 4(2) subjects developed countries (referred to as the Annex I countries) to additional requirements, including most notably the obligation to "adopt national polices and take corresponding measures on the mitigation of climate change, by limiting anthropogenic emissions of greenhouse gases and protecting and enhancing greenhouse gas sinks and reservoirs." This requirement to adopt a national policy was not tied legally to any specific target, although such plans were to be adopted "*with the aim of* returning individually or jointly to their 1990 levels" by the end of the decade.[20]

These provisions resulted from a compromise designed to maintain the universal participation of all parties. All parties agreed that the UNFCCC should be a treaty, but the United States and the oil-producing countries opposed any specific target and timetable for reducing GHG emissions. By contrast, Europe and others sought clear numerical targets. The result was a binding instrument and a clear numerical target referenced as a goal—not an obligation. The Parties also did not agree to any mechanism to enforce the goal. The United States only agreed to the target (1990 levels by 2000) because it was written in soft, aspirational language.[21]

Most observers accepted the lack of hard, clear commitments in the UNFCCC because the Convention was primarily intended to establish a framework

---

19 Treaties are one of the sources of international law identified in Article 38 of Charter of the International Court of Justice (ICJ). Statute of the ICJ, June 26, 1945, 59 Stat. 1055, 33 I.N.T.S. 933, art. 38 (hereinafter ICJ Statute). They are binding on those State parties that have ratified the agreement and the agreement has entered into force. *See generally* Vienna Convention on the Law of Treaties, Jan. 27, 1980, 1155 U.N.T.S. 331 [hereinafter Vienna Convention].

20 UNFCCC, *supra* note 4, at art. 4(2)(b) (emphasis added).

21 *Id.*

under which future binding mitigation targets would be adopted in ensuing protocols. This framework-protocol approach to treaty negotiations was a deliberate strategy, largely patterned after the Montreal Protocol regime's successful response to the threat of ozone depletion.[22] The plan was to adopt increasingly strict, binding targets over time, with developed countries committing first.

C *The Kyoto Protocol: Binding Commitments on Developed Countries*

This basic plan for establishing binding emission targets appeared to be on track in the few years immediately following the UNFCCC's entry into force. The Convention required the parties to "review the adequacy" of the developed countries' commitments, "in light of the best available scientific information and assessment on climate change and its impacts."[23] Most everyone came to the first meeting of the Conference of Parties (CoP) in 1995, expecting the developed countries to step up their level of commitments. The resulting "Berlin Mandate" committed developed countries to negotiate a binding instrument with clear targets and timetables for reducing net GHG emissions by the third CoP scheduled for December 1997 in Kyoto, Japan.[24]

After a tumultuous and difficult negotiation, the 1997 Kyoto Protocol established binding reduction targets for all developed (or "Annex 1") countries. Developed country parties to the Protocol agreed to reduce GHG emissions on average about 5% below their 1990 levels. The reduction targets were to be met over a five-year commitment period—from 2008 to 2012—which was to be followed by subsequent commitment periods with progressively stricter emission targets.[25]

The Kyoto Protocol is clearly hard international law. It is in the form of a treaty, has mandatory clear language imposing commitments, and creates a process for monitoring, reporting, and sanctioning non-compliance. Whether this approach was effective in achieving the goal of reducing GHG emissions and what lessons it presents for understanding the value of hard law approaches are both complex questions. On the one hand, the binding commitments appeared to reflect high levels of political commitment with which most developed countries tried hard to comply. Particularly in Europe, the Kyoto

---

22 *See* Bryan A. Green, *Lessons from the Montreal Protocol: Guidance for the Next International Climate Change Agreement*, 39:1 ENVTL. L. 253–83 (2009).

23 UNFCCC, *supra* note 4, at art. 4.2(d).

24 *See* UNFCCC, *Rep. of the Conference of the Parties on its First Session, Held in Berlin* FCCC/CP/1995/7/Add.1, (June 6, 1995) [hereinafter *Berlin Mandate*].

25 *See* Kyoto Protocol, *supra* note 5, at annex I.

Protocol commitments led to wholesale changes in the law and ultimately to significant reductions in their emissions.[26]

The binding nature of the Kyoto commitments was also critical for the Kyoto Protocol's famous "cap-and-trade" approach and ultimately for its most singular achievement—the creation of a global carbon market for the buying and selling of GHG emission credits. The "trade" in carbon emissions raised difficult and novel questions. On the supply side, questions of how to define, certify and account for carbon credits predominated. But on the demand side, the market depended on an enforceable cap on emissions. States had to be facing tight targets that were clear commitments to promise a high enough price to make potential suppliers of carbon credits take the necessary steps to participate in a market that was entirely the product of regulations. That a multi-billion-dollar market was created under Kyoto was a reflection of the strong signals sent by the high-profile *binding* commitments of the parties.

On the other hand, the presumably higher profile and greater consequences associated with binding commitments did not prevent countries from turning away from them. In the largest blow to the Kyoto Protocol, US President George W. Bush announced in 2000 that the United States would not proceed with ratification of the Protocol. This announcement led to an acrimonious split with other developed countries, particularly the European Union. The U.S. departure meant that the largest source of emissions would not be covered by the mitigation commitments. Given US domestic politics and its subsequent withdrawal from the Paris Agreement, the US failure to participate cannot be ascribed to the binding nature of the document. But the binding nature of the commitment did not seem to slow down the country's switch in position. Moreover, part of the rhetoric in the United States was that it should not make binding commitments if India and China were not going to do so as well.

Similarly, after a change in governments and facing potentially significant penalties for failing to meet its Kyoto target, Canada in 2011 announced that it would formally withdraw from the Protocol. Canada notably argued that the Protocol did not bind the world's largest two emitters, the United States and

26 *See, e.g.*, FEDERAL FOREIGN OFFICE OF THE GERMAN GOVERNMENT, https://www.auswaertiges-amt.de/en/aussenpolitik/themen/klima/-/243944 (reporting that "[t]he European Union has lived up to its commitment: In the period 2008–12, emission levels in the then 15 EU member states fell by an average of 12.2% against 1990 levels. . .[and] Germany did manage to reduce its emissions by an average of 23.6% in this period"); *see also* European Environment Agency, *Why did Greenhouse Gas Emissions Decrease in the EU between 1990 and 2012?* available at https://www.eea.europa.eu/publications/why-are-greenhouse-gases-decreasing/download.

China, and therefore could not work.[27] This was obviously intended to distract from Canada's impending non-compliance, but the point remains that the binding nature of Canada's commitments did not exert enough pressure to change its behavior toward the social goal of reduced GHG emissions. Instead, rather than meet its legal obligations, it left the regime.

Regardless of how it performed, the Kyoto Protocol was never meant to be an end-point of the climate regime. The Parties always contemplated that additional commitments would be required beyond those for the first reporting period that ended in 2012. As that date approached, the parties sought to develop a comprehensive, post-Kyoto agreement that would be acceptable to the divergent positions of the United States, China, and the Kyoto parties, as well as others. Ultimately, the parties would agree in what was referred to as the 2007 Bali Road Map to continue negotiations along two tracks: one among Kyoto parties aimed at a second binding commitment period under the Kyoto Protocol,[28] and the second aimed at a universal agreement under the UNFCCC that could include both the United States and developing countries.[29] The expected form and legal status of such a universal agreement was left deliberately ambiguous so that the United States would not block passage of the Work Plan. The first track ended in 2012 when Parties agreed to a second Kyoto commitment period (Kyoto II).[30] The second track ultimately led through the Copenhagen Accord to the Paris Agreement.

---

27 *See Canada Pulls Out of Kyoto Protocol*, THE GUARDIAN (Dec. 12, 2011), https://www.theguardian.com/environment/2011/dec/13/canada-pulls-out-kyoto-protocol.

28 *See* UNFCCC, Ad Hoc Working Group on Further Commitment for Annex I Parties under the Kyoto Protocol, Fourth Session, *Report of the Ad Hoc Working Group on Further Commitments for Annex I Parties Under the Kyoto Protocol*, ¶ 22, U.N. Doc. FCCC/KP/AWG/2007/5 (Feb. 5, 2008).

29 *See* Conference of the Parties to the United Nations Framework Convention on Climate Change, Bali, Indon., Dec. 3–15, 2007, *Report of the Conference of the Parties—Addendum, Part Two: Action Taken by the Conference of the Parties at its Thirteenth Session*, Dec. 1/CP.13, U.N. Doc. FCCC/CP/2007/6/Add.1 (Mar. 14, 2008) [hereinafter *Bali Action Plan*].

30 In the end, thirty-seven countries, including most of Europe, Australia, and Kazakhstan, agreed to take a second round of binding commitments under the Kyoto Protocol, known as "Kyoto II." *See* Conference of the Parties serving as the meeting of the Parties to the Kyoto Protocol, Amendment to the Kyoto Protocol, Decision 1/CMP.8 (Dec. 8, 2012) [hereinafter the Doha Amendment]. Several original Parties to the Kyoto Protocol, most notably Russia, Japan, New Zealand, and Canada, refused to take a second round of commitments; three of the four (excluding Russia) had not been able to meet their Kyoto targets. The Kyoto II Parties agreed in aggregate to reduce their overall emissions by at least 18 percent below 1990 levels during the second commitment period (2013 to 2020). The participating parties in Kyoto II were by definition those willing to continue under the binding cap-and-trade approach of the Kyoto Protocol. The binding nature of

D Copenhagen and the Bottom-Up Bridge to the Paris Agreement

The second negotiating track under the Bali Road Map sought a comprehensive agreement under the UNFCCC that would (1) bring the United States back into the UN process for addressing climate change and (2) outline the future obligations, if any, of developing countries. The parties aspired to reach new commitments by 2009 in Copenhagen that would reflect, among other things, "a shared vision for long-term cooperative action, including a long-term global goal for emission reductions, to achieve the ultimate objectives of the Convention."[31]

In the lead-up to Copenhagen, the legal form of any agreement was a central discussion point.[32] Many climate advocates hoped for a new binding "Copenhagen Protocol" that imported most, but not all, parts of the Kyoto Protocol. This offered a relatively clean solution, but one that clearly lacked sufficient support for ratification by the U.S. Senate. China and other developing countries also strongly resisted binding commitments. The leading alternative option to a binding Protocol was to implement stronger commitments through a series of decisions by the UNFCCC's CoP. This would not require ratification by any of the parties, but the legal status of CoP decisions is open to question.[33] One promising variation was Australia's pledge-and-review approach.[34]

---

the commitments was never at issue; by contrast, the choice between a hard or soft law approach would be central to the second track of negotiations.

31 *Bali Action Plan*, *supra* note 29.

32 For excellent treatments of the choices of possible legal forms for the mitigation commitments at Copenhagen, *see* DANIEL BODANSKY, LEGAL FORM OF A NEW CLIMATE AGREEMENT: AVENUES AND OPTIONS (Pew Center on Climate Change, April 2009); Jacob Werksman & Kirk Herbertson, *The Legal Character of National Actions and Commitments in a Copenhagen Agreement: Options and Implications*, World Resources Inst. Working Paper (Nov. 2009).

33 Under the Vienna Convention on the Law of Treaties, COP decisions may be viewed as binding interpretations of the treaty. *Vienna Convention*, *supra* note 19. *See* Jacob Werksman, *"Taking Note" of the Copenhagen Accord: What It Means*, WORLD RESOURCES INST., (Dec. 20, 2009), http://www.wri.org/stories/2009/12/taking-note-copenhagen-accord-what-it-means; Werksman & Herbertson, *supra* note 32. Under U.S. domestic law, however, the DC Circuit has ruled that decisions made by Parties to the Montreal Protocol created no legal obligation on EPA to regulate the production and consumption of methyl bromide, an ozone depleting substance. *NRDC v. EPA, 464 F. 3d 1 (D.C. Cir. 2006)*. For a critique of the decision, *see John H. Knox, Natural Resources Defense Council v. Environmental Protection Agency. 464 F. 3d 1*. United States Court of Appeals for the District of Columbia Circuit, August 29, 2006, 101 AM. J. INT'L. L. 471, 474 (2007).

34 *See* Tomilola Akanle et al., *Summary of the Copenhagen Climate Change Conference* 12:459, EARTH NEGOTIATIONS BULLETIN (2009), available at https://enb.iisd.org/vol12/enb12459e.html.

Patterned loosely after the way tariff schedules are created under the World Trade Organization, each country would make some commitment to mitigate climate change based on factors such as their economic status and historical contribution to climate change. Industrialized countries would be expected to accept mandatory, economy-wide emissions caps, while developing countries could choose from the full range of policy options, including energy intensity targets or sectoral targets.

This approach would ultimately substantially influence the Copenhagen Accord. Ignoring the long-standing negotiating procedures for UN climate conferences, a small group of six countries[35] essentially negotiated and announced the Copenhagen Accord, including a non-binding pledge-and-review approach to mitigation, with limited input from the other Parties.[36] President Obama even publicly announced the agreement before many delegates had had a change to read it, let alone analyze or discuss it. The closed-door process incensed many delegates, particularly those from developing countries. Several countries objected that this was an undemocratic circumvention of the U.N. negotiations, which prioritize consensus and broad participation. Ultimately, the Copenhagen Conference of the Parties neither adopted nor endorsed the Accord, but merely "took note" of it. This reflected the lowest level of formal recognition, and, according to the UNFCCC Secretariat, the Accord's provisions would "not have any legal standing within the UNFCCC process even if some Parties decide to associate themselves with it." [37]

The Copenhagen Accord clearly lacked any legal status at all, and its provisions were non-binding, but the Accord would garner significant political support. Despite the procedural irregularities and political outcry at the time, nearly 150 countries would express their general support for the Accord by the time the Parties met again the next year in Cancun. Countries also took specific steps to begin implementing different parts of the Accord, including for example provisions relating to deforestation and financing. As a result, the

35 The only countries in the room were Brazil, Russia, India, China, South Africa (the BRICS countries), and the United States. Missing were some of the largest emitters (e.g., the European Union, Japan, and Australia) and those arguably most affected by climate change (e.g., the island states or the poorest states). *See* Radoslav S. Dimitrov, *Inside UN Climate Change Negotiations: The Copenhagen Conference*, 60:6 REV. OF POL. RES. (2010).

36 John Vidal et al., *Low Targets, Goals Dropped: Copenhagen Ends in Failure*, THE GUARDIAN (Dec. 18, 2009), https://www.theguardian.com/environment/2009/dec/18/copenhagen-deal.

37 UNFCCC Secretariat, Notification to Parties, Communication of Information Relating to the Copenhagen Accord (June 14, 2010).

Accord largely set the framework for subsequent negotiations leading up to and including the 2015 Paris negotiations.

Despite its controversial genesis and non-binding status, the Copenhagen Accord signaled a fundamental shift away from Kyoto's cap-and-trade approach to a pledge-and-review approach. Under this approach, countries would be invited to make a pledge of what they were intending to do at the national level to address climate change; their efforts to meet that pledge would be reviewed but not enforced. This re-direction meant that commitments would not be negotiated and agreed between countries nor enforced internationally—they would be primarily a matter of national policy, enforced if at all within the respective national legal systems.

By setting out a flexible vision for mitigation commitments, Copenhagen garnered widespread support among both developed and developing countries. This in turn unblocked less controversial issues that had been fully negotiated but were being held up pending an overall agreement. This enabled significant progress with respect to such issues as deforestation, financing, and adaptation.

The non-binding Copenhagen Accord was essentially proof of concept for the pledge-and-review approach. Coupled with this blue-print for handling mitigation and given the momentum built in Cancun on other issues, the governments decided once again to try for a comprehensive agreement. The 2011 Durban Platform, like the Berlin Mandate and the Bali Action Plan before it, set forth the official negotiating framework and timetable that the parties hoped would lead to an agreement in 2015 in Paris. The Durban Platform reflected the swirling debate over what should be the legal form of any agreement; the Parties decided "to develop a protocol, another legal instrument or an agreed outcome with legal force under the Convention applicable to all Parties."[38]

Although the exact legal form of the hoped-for agreement was deliberately left unclear, it was clear that the Parties were focused on the pledge-and-review approach unveiled in Copenhagen. In 2014, each Party was invited in the run-up to Paris "to communicate to the secretariat its intended nationally-determined contribution (NDC) towards achieving the objective of the Convention as set out in its Article 2."[39]

38 UNFCCC, Establishment of an Ad Hoc Working Group on the Durban Platform for Enhanced Action, Decision 1/CP.17 (2011) [hereinafter Durbin Platform].

39 UNFCCC, *Report of the Ad Hoc Working Group on Durban Platform for Enhanced Action*, U.N. Doc. FCCC/CP/2014/L.14 (Dec. 13, 2014). Each Party's intended nationally determined contribution (NDC) was expected to "represent a progression beyond the current undertaking of that Party." *Id.* at ¶ 10. The Party should consider them "fair and ambitious,

As Parties announced their intended NDCs, they were compiled on the Secretariat's website. Most important was the joint announcement by China and the United States of their intended NDCs in the Fall of 2014. The announcement by the two largest contributors to climate change that they would take significant steps to curb greenhouse gases built political momentum for acceptance of the pledge-and-review approach in Paris. By the end of the Paris negotiations, 186 countries had announced an intended NDC in support of the overall objectives of the Agreement.

E *The Paris Agreement*

The Paris Agreement was rightly heralded as a significant advance in the world's effort to address climate change, particularly because for the first time all countries agreed to take steps to prevent climate change, including the largest two emitters—China and the United States. The Agreement sits within the framework established by the UNFCCC. Under the UNFCCC, the objective of global climate negotiations is to "prevent dangerous anthropogenic interference" (known as (DAI)), which is defined in terms of avoiding significant damage to natural ecosystems, food security and economic development.[40] To meet the objective of avoiding DAI, the Paris Agreement sets an overall mitigation target "to hold the increase in the global average temperature to *well below* 2°C above pre-industrial levels and *to pursue* efforts to limit the temperature increase to 1.5°C above pre-industrial levels. ... "[41] The "well below 2°C" temperature goal reflects the governments' consensus of the maximum level of temperature increase that would still give the world a reasonable chance of avoiding significant harm from climate change. Rather than trying to meet the temperature goal by setting a global carbon cap with binding national targets and timetables, each country would pledge what they were willing to do by submitting their own NDC.[42]

The Parties anticipated that the initial NDCs would leave an "ambition gap"—the difference between the emissions reductions resulting from what the Parties had pledged to do and the total emissions reductions needed to achieve the 2°C temperature goal.[43] The Parties agreed to review their NDCs

---

in light of its national circumstances, and how it contributes towards achieving the objective of the Convention as set out in its Article 2." *Id.* at ¶ 14.

40 UNFCCC, *supra* note 4, art. 2.

41 Paris Agreement, *supra* note 3, art. 2(1)(a) (emphasis added).

42 *Id.* art. 4(2).

43 The United Nations issues an annual report assessing progress in closing the emissions gap. *See, e.g.*, UN ENVIRONMENT, EMISSIONS GAP REPORT 2018. UN Environment reports that fully implementing the current NDCs would meet only one-third of the

and communicate "successive" NDCs every five years, beginning in 2020.[44] The Parties are not allowed to backslide on their commitments. Each Party's successive NDC should "represent a progression beyond the Party's then current [NDC] ... and reflect its highest possible ambition".[45] The Parties envisioned adopting a "Paris Rulebook," before the second round of NDCs that would harmonize methodologies for disclosing, measuring, reporting and verifying NDCs so that future contributions would reflect comparable measurements of baseline emissions and estimated reductions.[46]

In addition to the near-term progress anticipated via the NDCs, the Parties also explicitly agreed to two mid-term goals on the path to achieving the ultimate temperature goal: (1) to achieve a "global peaking" of GHG emissions "as soon as possible"; and (2) "to achieve a balance between anthropogenic emissions by sources and removals by sinks of greenhouse gases in the second half of this century".[47] As a tangible step to operationalize these mid-term goals, the Parties were invited to submit "long-term low GHG development strategies" by 2020.[48]

F *The Hybrid Nature of the Paris Agreement*

The Paris Agreement certainly meets the form of hard international law as it is an international treaty but its mitigation commitments do not meet the tests of precision, obligation and delegation[49] since they lack clear, mandatory language and a robust approach to enforcement. Indeed, the Parties carefully crafted the language for the NDCs and mid-term mitigation commitments to ensure that the specific commitments were not binding as a matter of international law. In this sense, the Paris Agreement reflects a hybrid approach with the key normative requirement written in non-mandatory language in order to give maximum flexibility to the Parties to tailor their commitment

---

necessary emissions reductions. UN ENVIRONMENT, EMISSIONS GAP REPORT 2017, at xiv (2017) [hereinafter EMISSIONS GAP REPORT 2017].

44 Paris Agreement, *supra* note 3, art. 4(2); UNFCCC Decision 1/CP.21, FCCC/CP/2015/10/Add.1, ¶ 23–24 (Dec. 12, 2015) [hereinafter Paris CoP Decision] (the Parties *request* a new NDC from those having 2025 as their target date and only *urge* a new NDC in 2020 from those having 2030 as a target date).

45 Paris Agreement, *supra* note 3, art. 4(3).

46 *Id.* art. 4(13). Significant elements of the Paris Rulebook were adopted by the Parties at the 2018 CoP in Katowice, Poland.

47 *Id.* art. 4(1).

48 Paris CoP Decision, *supra* note 44, ¶ 36; *see also* Paris Agreement, *supra* note 3, art. 4(19).

49 *See* Kenneth W. Abbott & Duncan Snidal, *Hard and Soft Law in International Governance*, 3 INT'L ORG. 421 (2000).

to their specific national situation. Parties are required to submit NDCs, but the commitments are only those that they *intend* to achieve; the Parties never commit to achieving their NDCs.[50] And the NDCs for developed countries only *should* be an economy-wide cap on emissions.[51] To highlight the point, the United States intervened in the last plenary because in its view "shall" had errantly replaced "should" in the key paragraph relating to developed countries' NDCs.[52] In addition to the non-mandatory wording, the Agreement also lacks any process for compelling a Party to implement its NDC or sanctions for non-compliance. Nor does the Agreement explicitly require Parties to ensure compliance with the NDC under national law.

III Emerging Considerations from Early Implementation of the Paris Agreement

The Paris Agreement entered into force on November 4, 2016. In 2018, the Parties approved the first elements of the "Paris Rulebook," which aims to ensure a common baseline for measuring, comparing, monitoring, and reporting on future NDCs.[53] Given the early stage of implementation, it is impossible to determine whether the Paris Agreement will be effective in curbing climate change. Nonetheless, some initial observations are possible.

A *Implementation Challenges: US Withdrawal and a Lack of Ambition*

The hybrid structure of Paris was designed to allow the United States, China, and both developed and developing countries to join in a unified approach to reducing GHGs. The strategy was initially vindicated, at least to the extent that almost all countries ratified the Agreement and announced an NDC. As of June 2019, 185 countries had ratified the Agreement.[54] Many of these countries would not have accepted an agreement with binding mitigation commitments.

50 Paris Agreement, *supra* note 3, art. 4(2).

51 *Id.* art. 4(4).

52 John Vidal, *How a 'Typo' Nearly Derailed the Paris Climate Deal*, The Guardian, Dec. 12, 2015 (describing the controversy over whether the language was an honest mistake or a last minute ploy by the United States to weaken the language).

53 UNFCCC, *Report of the Conference of the Parties on Its Twenty-Fourth Session*, U.N. Doc. FCCC/CP/2018/10/Add.1 (Mar. 19, 2019). The Parties deferred decisions on other issues including the rules for managing forests and agricultural lands and whether to adopt a stronger temperature target.

54 UNFCCC, Paris Agreement—Status of Ratification, https://unfccc.int/process/the-paris-agreement/status-of-ratification.

Although such widespread participation is encouraging, subsequent developments have been mixed. Maintaining the non-binding nature of NDCs was apparently not enough to guarantee U.S. participation. In June 2017 President Trump announced that the United States would withdraw from the Paris Agreement.[55] Under the Agreement, the United States cannot officially withdraw until November 2020 and remains a Party.[56] On a positive note, the U.S. exodus does not seem to have triggered any other countries to abandon the Agreement.

Perhaps more troubling is that the non-binding nature of the NDCs has not yet incentivized sufficiently ambitious commitments. By all accounts the cumulative pledges fall significantly short of the total emissions reductions needed to achieve the Paris Agreement's 2°C goal. The United Nations estimates that fully implementing the current NDCs would achieve only one-third of the emissions reductions necessary to achieve the temperature goal.[57] The Parties anticipated the initial "ambition gap" and established a process for increasing NDCs over time. The Parties agreed to provide new, increasingly ambitious NDCs every five years beginning in 2020.[58]

On a macro-level, the Agreement intended to send long-term signals that governments are committed to shifting from fossil fuels to renewables and other alternatives over the next few decades. And the market is responding. In 2016, clean energy accounted for 61.5% of new generating capacity, surpassing all new oil, coal and natural gas generation. [59] Despite these positive trends in global energy investment, global *emission* trends suggest that implementation of the NDCs may be stalled; indeed, as of 2018 relatively few countries appear

---

55 Michael D. Shear, *Trump Will Withdraw U.S. From Paris Climate Agreement*, N.Y. Times, June 1, 2017.

56 Because withdrawal is not permitted under the Agreement until three years after it entered into force (i.e. November 4, 2016), the Trump Administration will presumably submit its withdrawal again on or after November 4, 2019, which will then take effect one year after receipt (i.e. no sooner than November 4, 2020). Until then, the United States is officially still a Party to the Agreement. *See* U.N. Status of Treaties, https://treaties.un.org/Pages/ViewDetails.aspx?src=TREATY&mtdsg_no=XXVII-7-d&chapter=27&clang=_en (last visited Aug. 28, 2019).

57 EMISSIONS GAP REPORT 2017, *supra* note 43, at xiv.

58 Paris Agreement, *supra* note 3, art. 4(2); Paris CoP Decision, *supra* note 44, ¶¶ 23–24 (the Parties *request* a new NDC from those having 2025 as their target date and only *urge* a new NDC in 2020 from those having 2030 as a target date).

59 OFFICE OF ENERGY PROJECTS, FEDERAL ENERGY REGULATORY COMMISSION, ENERGY INFRASTRUCTURE UPDATE (Dec. 2016), available at https://www.ferc.gov/legal/staff-reports/2016/dec-energy-infrastructure.pdf [hereinafter FERC ENERGY INFRASTRUCTURE UPDATE 2016].

clearly on track to meet their NDCs.[60] For example, after two years of declining emissions, U.S. emissions increased in 2018 by 3.4 percent to a new peak.[61]

The tepid record of implementation and the US withdrawal beg the question of whether binding mitigation commitments would improve compliance and implementation. The monitoring and reporting regimes for compliance with the NDCs is anticipated to be as robust as if the commitments were binding.[62] The only difference then is the availability of sanctions. However, in both the case of binding and non-binding instruments sanctions would be primarily limited to naming-and-shaming. And, as discussed above, And given the failure of the threat of sanctions to compel compliance with the Kyoto Protocol, there was reason to doubt the added value of ensuring binding commitments for improving compliance with the Paris Agreement. Arguably naming and shaming may be more effective in the case of binding norms because of the higher profile and perceived deeper commitment when countries accept binding norms, but this effect may be less important given the already high profile of the climate commitments.

B *Hardening the Paris Commitments through National Law*

Because the Paris Agreement invokes non-obligatory language for the NDCs and other mitigation aspects, the Parties clearly sought to avoid state-to-state enforcement of the Agreement under international law. The Agreement's architecture, based as it is on nationally determined commitments, implicitly relies on the national laws for any enforcement that is going to occur.

Although the Agreement has just entered into force, in some countries commitments under the Paris Agreement are already being treated as binding under national law and subject to judicial review.[63] For example, a New Zealand court held that the NDC was subject to judicial review under New Zealand's administrative law, although Court ultimately deferred deciding on the adequacy of the NDC in part because an incoming government had announced it

60 *See infra* note 61.

61 Chris Moody & Brady Dennis, *U.S. Greenhouse Gas Emissions Spiked in 2018—And It Couldn't Happen at a Worse Time,* THE WASH. POST (Jan. 8, 2019) (resulting partly from the United States having abandoned pursuit of its NDC in conjunction with President Trump's announced withdrawal).

62 Most notable is UN Environment's annual review of NDC implementation. U.N. ENVIRONMENT PROGRAMME (UNEP), THE EMISSIONS GAP REPORT 2018, https://www.unenvironment.org/resources/emissions-gap-report-2018.

63 Judgment of Mallon J, *Sarah Thomson v. Minister of Climate Change Issues,* CIV 2015-485-919 [2017] NZHC 733, at ¶ 133–34 (Nov. 2, 2017) [hereinafter *Thomson v. New Zealand*].

would revisit the NDC within a year.[64] In 2017, a South African court recently invalidated the approval of a proposed coal-fired power plant, in part because the environmental assessment had not assessed whether the "proposed project fits South Africa's peak, plateau and decline trajectory [for GHG emissions] as outlined in the NDC."[65]

Such judicial review and use of NDCs by national courts is not particularly surprising as many NDCs include commitments that must be operationalized through national law. What is more surprising is the use of the Paris Agreement's overall mitigation framework, including the temperature targets and the mid- and long-term mitigation goals, as a framework for evaluating the government's other obligations under national or international law, particularly under human rights law. Under this approach, the Paris Agreement's temperature targets and longer term mitigation goals informs the courts' deliberations regarding a country's human rights obligations in climate-related cases. The Agreement's non-binding mitigation targets are not the source of the legal obligation; instead the targets provide the factual background from which courts can calculate, for example, a country's equitable share of climate mitigation efforts necessary to avoid catastrophic climate change impacts and by implication to meet their human rights obligations. Underlying this strategy is a linkage between the Paris Agreement's consensus view that holding temperatures "well below 2°C" is necessary to meet the objective of the climate regime—i.e., to avoid "dangerous anthropogenic interference" (DAI) with the climate system so as to ensure food security,

64 *Id.* at ¶¶ 133–34 (Nov. 2, 2017) [hereinafter Thomson v. New Zealand]. The High Court of New Zealand rejected the government's arguments opposing judicial review, finding that the importance of climate change required judicial scrutiny over political decisions. More specifically, the Court first rejected the government's argument that the adequacy of its climate targets were too "political" for judicial review because they involved balancing many socioeconomic factors. The Court also rejected the government's argument that because the NDCs were made pursuant to an international agreement, the courts should not intervene in the executive branch's exercise of its foreign relations authority. A similar case in Ireland challenges the country's 2017 National Mitigation Plan as exceeding Ireland's equitable share of the global carbon budget implicitly reflected in the Paris Agreement. As of January 2019, the pleadings in the case have not been made public but the action is described at the Friends of the Irish Environment's website. *See* https://www.climatecaseireland.ie/climate-case/.

65 Judgment, In the matter of EarthLife Africa Johannesburg, Applicant, and the Minister of Environmental Affairs, First Respondent, et al, S. Afr. H. Ct., Civ. No. 65662/16, at ¶ 90 (Gauteng Div., Pretoria: Mar. 8, 2017); *see also* Leonie Joubert, *Court Stalls New Coal Plan in South Africa,* ENERGY TRANSITION: THE GLOBAL ENERGIEWENDE (Oct. 10, 2017), https://energytransition.org/2017/10/court-stalls-new-sa-coal-mega-station/.

stable ecosystems and sustained economic development. Failing to meet the UNFCCC objective would also fail to protect associated human rights. Put another way, any "emissions gap" in meeting the Paris Agreement's mitigation commitments also reflects a gap in what countries must do at a minimum to reach a safe level of emissions for protecting human rights.[66]

The leading case taking this approach is *Urgenda v. The Netherlands*.[67] In *Urgenda*, a Dutch environmental group alleged that the Netherlands' inadequate action to prevent climate change violated the government's obligation to protect its citizens' rights to life and to family life under Dutch law and the European Convention of Human Rights.[68] In evaluating the government's duty of care, the Court used the Paris commitments as references to conclude that at least a 25 to 40 percent reduction of CO2 is not an "overly pessimistic starting point[] for establishing the State's duty of care." [69] The Court traced the 25–40 percent reduction target through the long negotiating process that led to the Paris Agreement and concluded that:

> The State has known about the reduction target of 25–40% for a long time. The IPCC report which states that such a reduction by end-2020 is needed to achieve the 2°C target (AR4) dates back to 2007. Since that time, virtually all COPs (in Bali, Cancun, Durban, Doha and Warsaw) have referred to this 25–40% standard and Annex I countries have been urged to align their reduction targets accordingly. This may not have established a legal standard with a direct effect, but the Court believes that it confirms the fact that at least a 25–40% reduction of CO2 emissions as of 2020 is required to prevent dangerous climate change.[70]

---

66 *See, e.g.*, World Bank, *Turn Down the Heat: Why a 4°C Warmer World Must Be Avoided* (2012). http://documents.worldbank.org/curated/en/865571468149107611/Turn-down-the-heat-why-a-4-C-warmer-world-must-be-avoided.

67 Ruling of Oct. 9, 2018, The State of the Netherlands v. Urgenda Foundation, Hague Ct. of App., Case No. 200.178.245/01 (Oct. 9, 2018) [hereinafter Urgenda App. Dec.].

68 *See generally* Eleanor Stein & Alex Geert Castermans, Case Comment, *Urgenda v. The State of the Netherlands: The "Reflex Effect"—Climate Change, Human Rights, and the Expanding Definitions of the Duty of Care*, 13 McGill J. Sust. Dev. L. 303, 305 (2017); Josephine van Zeben, *Establishing a Governmental Duty of Care for Climate Change Mitigation: Will Urgenda Turn the Tide?*, 4 TRANSNAT'L ENVTL L. 339, 341 (2015).

69 Judgment of June 24, 2015, Urgenda Foundation v. The Netherlands, The Hague D. Ct., Chamber of Comm. Aff., C/09/456689/HA ZA 13–1396, at ¶ 50 (June 24, 2015)] [hereinafter Urgenda Dist. Ct. Judgment].

70 *Id.* at ¶ 51.

Based on this analysis, the court held that the State's duty of care to protect the rights of its citizens required the State to reduce its emissions by at least 25 percent from 1990 levels by the end of 2020.[71] The court did not hold that the Paris Agreement created a legally binding obligation; rather the court invoked the Paris Agreement's temperature goals, as well as the science underlying those goals, as evidence of the level of action necessary to meet a legal obligation rooted in Dutch law and the European Convention on Human Rights. Viewed in this light, soft commitments in the Paris Agreement define what mitigation efforts are necessary to ensure protection of the right to life or other human rights.

IV Conclusion: Exploring the Shift from Hard to Soft Commitments

Drawing broad conclusions about hard and soft international law from the evolution of the climate regime's mitigation commitments may be dangerous given its *sui generis* nature. Nonetheless, we can draw some potential lessons regarding the choice and effectiveness of adopting hard versus soft international law, at least in the context of the adoption of non-binding standards in a binding treaty regime.

Since the late 1980s, civil society and states all agreed that climate change would be addressed through a binding treaty, and indeed given the successful negotiation of the UNFCCC in 1992, the arc of the primary climate negotiations was always within the traditional form of a treaty. As suggested by the above discussion, the early vision envisioned an orderly sequence of protocols negotiated over time with sequentially stronger targets and timetables backed up by a robust enforcement mechanism and sanctions. Thus, the soft commitments in the UNFCCC readily fit within the overall aim of the negotiators to create the institutional and broad policy framework in anticipation of future mandatory targets. That vision vanished after the United States withdrew from the Kyoto Protocol.

As it became clear that the climate regime would not fit neatly into the Framework-Protocol structure, the Parties engaged in a long and frustrating discussion over the legal form and relative "hardness" of the mitigation commitments.[72] The general expectation of binding commitments can be seen in how the Parties consistently framed their major negotiations in ways that preferred

---

71 *Id.* at ¶ 76.

72 *See* Bodansky, *supra* note 32; Werksman & Herbertson, *supra* note 32.

binding obligations. This was true for the Berlin Mandate that led to the Kyoto Protocol,[73] the Bali Action Plan that framed the Copenhagen Accord,[74] and the Durban Platform that led to the Paris Agreements.[75] If a consensus existed that the instrument should be binding, exactly what form the agreement was expected to take became less clear over time. As reflected in the Durban terms of reference for the Paris talks, parties agreed to "develop a protocol, another legal instrument or an agreed outcome with legal force under the Convention applicable to all Parties."[76] What "legal force" meant was open to interpretation and allowed significant flexibility in shaping the negotiations.

The ambiguity of this language reflected the growing understanding that the negotiations were unlikely to result in a clean Protocol with binding mitigation caps. Europe and the remaining Kyoto II Parties were operating under such a system and generally motivated to expand it. The United States and China, among others, however, had abandoned that approach and were actively seeking another way. Civil society and many countries—particularly island states and others hard hit by climate change—consistently sought targets in binding form. But many also realized that the value of a binding agreement like Kyoto would not be worth the price of losing the participation of China and the United States. Particularly after what was seen as the failure in Copenhagen to build consensus for a Kyoto-like approach, most countries shifted to support the pledge-and-review approach—at least when compared to continued stalemate. This shift from a focus on binding caps to the non-binding pledge-and-review approach reflected a shifting view of the relative trade-offs between hard and soft commitments.

The debate over the legal status of the commitments came to a head in the lead-up to Copenhagen because it was there that the need for a formula for engaging both China and the United States came to the forefront. A leading NGO think tank, the World Resources Institute (WRI) clearly framed the trade-offs. For a norm to be binding it had to be in the legal form of hard international law, have targets written in clear mandatory language, and have an institutional mechanism for enforcement.[77] According to WRI, evidence suggests such a norm in international environmental agreements reflected the "highest political commitment" and typically resulted in better outcomes because of the higher profile and greater consequences for non-compliance. The trade-off

73 *Berlin Mandate*, *supra* note 24.

74 *Bali Action Plan*, *supra* note 29.

75 Durbin Platform, *supra* note 38.

76 *Id.*

77 *See* Werksman & Herbertson, *supra* note 32.

was that fewer parties would participate and commitments would be lower.[78] As the negotiations dragged on, over time the calculus regarding that trade-off shifted toward acceptance of the soft law commitment.

A *The Softer Pledge-and-Review Approach Avoided the Impossible Question of How to Equitably Allocate a Hard Cap*

Inherent to the binding cap approach was a politically impossible question to answer—how should a global cap on the right to emit GHG s be allocated? What level should each country be permitted to emit? What principles should govern the choice? Citing the principle of equity in the UNFCCC, developing countries argued that the allocation should be made on a *per capita* basis. Industrialized countries rejected this out of hand, offering vague formulas based on efficiency that would allocate more to those countries who could produce more output per ton of carbon emitted. The gulf between these positions and the many differences at the national level left little hope for a principled approach to an overall allocation.

Moreover, the general approach set forth in the UNFCCC, based on principles of equity and common but differentiated responsibilities (CBDR) between developed and developing countries, was arguably outdated in a world in which rapidly industrializing countries, like China, are becoming significant GHG emitters. The United States was clear that it no longer supported a bipolar division of developed and developing countries as contemplated under the UNFCCC.[79] The United States did not wholly reject the CBDR principle but argued rather that China—due to its growing economic power and status as the largest annual emitter—and other middle-income countries should not be treated the same as sub-Saharan Africa. China and others should now take on

---

78 *Id.*

79 *See* Todd Stern, U.S. Special Envoy for Climate Change, Keynote Address, Brookings Conference: Energy and Climate Change 2010: Back to the Future (May 18, 2010): [T]he idea that "common but differentiated responsibilities and respective capabilities" requires a different regime for developing and developed countries on every particular, whether mitigation, transparency or any other issue is completely unfounded. On its face, the phrase expresses the notion of a continuum of responsibilities and capabilities among countries. It does not legislate an unbridgeable divide between developed and developing countries. It does not prevent differentiation among developing countries or among developed countries. It does not say that China should be treated like Chad even though its capacities are closer to members of the OECD. It does not say that the lineup of countries in 1992 can never evolve. Most important, it does not trump the core objective of the Framework Convention itself: that we must act to avoid dangerous climate change.

the responsibility of avoiding climate change along with the United States and Europe.[80]

A focus on the largest current emitters makes sense, of course, but that is not the whole picture. Historical emissions and the benefits derived therefrom are also critical to consider. China and India, among others, argued that "atmospheric resources are the common wealth of humankind" and that wealthy countries had inequitably benefited from using the existing atmospheric space and thus limited the emission space available to developing countries.[81] In their view, the initial allocation of emission limits should reflect an obligation of developed countries to pay compensation for the disproportionate use of our common atmospheric heritage.

The wide philosophical gap between these approaches assured a broad gap among countries in arriving at a mutually agreed set of mitigation targets. With the shift in approach to CBDR, no overarching consensus principles existed for organizing a global allocation of the limited emissions pie. Expecting countries to negotiate binding emission caps absent some agreed overall approach was probably unrealistic given the complexity and high stakes at issue. Because fossil fuel consumption (and thus GHG emissions) was historically linked to a country's economic growth, negotiating emission caps was equated to negotiating caps on a country's future rates of economic growth. Seen in this light, it appears naïve to think that top-down negotiations of national emissions caps would ever have succeeded.

The experience with the Copenhagen Accord demonstrated that the more flexible, non-binding pledge-and-review approach offered a way out of this thicket. It avoided the need for a global agreement on each country's binding mitigation target. The Parties gave up the goal of negotiating clear mandatory commitments in recognition that achieving such a consensus had not been possible in the past twenty years of negotiations—and was unlikely to be achieved in the next twenty years. Avoiding the most difficult diplomatic task would embrace action by all parties while allowing other important parts of the climate regime to move forward.

In this way, the softer pledge-and-review approach also responded to a growing sense of urgency; the time to act on climate change was running out. Diplomatic brinksmanship over the legal architecture that might lead to prolonged negotiations on the hope of a stronger regime might have seemed appropriate in the 1990s, but it seemed foolish by 2015. The sentiments were effectively

---

80 *Id.*

81 CHRISTOPH SCHWARTE & EMILY MASSAWA, EQUITY ISSUES IN THE CLIMATE CHANGE NEGOTIATIONS (Aug. 2009), http://pubs.iied.org/pdfs/G03002.pdf.

summed up by the challenge of young NGO observers who had taken to sitting silently in the plenaries with neon shirts that read "you've been negotiating my whole life; quit talking and start acting," The pledge-and-review approach was action-oriented. Countries focused on what they *were willing to do,* be it a little or a lot—rather than on negotiating future commitments.

B *Non-Binding Commitments Did Increase Participation, at Least for Now*

The decision to adopt only non-binding mitigation commitments in Paris reflected a deliberate and highly scrutinized choice in favor of greater participation with more countries agreeing to at least some mitigation commitments. The Parties gave up the opportunity to have international state-to-state oversight and formal enforcement of the commitments, potentially with sanctions. The question is whether this trade-off improved the overall effectiveness of the global climate regime.

This compromise undoubtedly increased the number of countries that agreed to take some mitigation commitments in the Agreement and probably resulted in more substantial commitments even from those who were likely to accept binding commitments. Although using participation in the Kyoto framework as a comparative reference point is not without caveats,[82] the second phase of Kyoto (Kyoto II) was negotiated roughly in parallel to the negotiations that led to Paris. Only 37 countries agreed to make binding commitments in Kyoto II. Although several reasons contributed to the relatively low participation in Kyoto, the vastly larger number (185) that have agreed to adopt NDCs under the Paris Agreement suggests the non-binding and flexible approach to commitments succeeded in expanding participation. Numerically, the difference largely reflects the participation of developing countries, most of which made their first mitigation commitment of any type at Paris.

Most importantly, the approach appealed to the two largest emitters—the United States and China—whose participation in the climate regime was critical. Together, the countries emit more than forty percent of annual global emissions.[83] Both countries offered meaningful and substantive commitments and sent a signal of cooperation early in the run-up to Paris. For different reasons,

---

82 *See, e.g.,* Agus P. Sar, *Developing Country Participation: The Kyoto-Marrakech Politics,* HAMBERG INST. OF INT'L ECON. (2005), https://papers.ssrn.com/sol3/papers.cfm?abstract_id=868988.

83 *See* T. A. Boden, et al, *National CO2 Emmisions from Fossil-Fuel Burning, Cement Manufacture, and Gas-Flaring, 1751–2014* (Carbon Dioxide Information Analysis Center, 2017).

neither the United States nor China would have joined if the mitigation commitments had been binding.[84]

Moreover, the evidence suggests that Parties who were always willing to accept binding targets (i.e. those who participated in Kyoto II) were willing to increase their commitments in the context of the pledge-and-review approach. The willingness to increase commitments was less about the non-binding nature of the commitments than it was about willingness to do more as an incentive for more universal participation in a comprehensive approach. For example, in the run-up to Copenhagen, Australia conditioned its promise to "reduce its greenhouse gas emissions by 25% from 2000 levels by 2020 if the world agrees to an ambitious global deal capable of stabilizing levels of greenhouse gases in the atmosphere at 450 ppm CO2-eq or lower."[85] Absent such a global deal, Australia would only commit to reduce "emissions by 5% below 2000 levels by 2020. … " Similarly, the European Union agreed that "as part of a global and comprehensive agreement for the period beyond 2012," it would move to "a 30% reduction by 2020 compared to 1990 levels, provided that other developed countries commit themselves to comparable emission reductions and that developing countries contribute adequately according to their responsibilities and respective capabilities."[86] Japan agreed "to 25%

84 Without a doubt, the Paris Agreement would not have its current shape were it not for the need to accommodate the United States. Most countries reluctantly realized that, having rejected the Kyoto Protocol, the United States was not likely to reverse its position and ratify an upgraded "Paris Protocol." Any reasonably informed observer understood that any instrument that imposed binding mitigation targets on the United States was unlikely to garner the two-thirds vote of the U.S. Senate required for ratification, even if the Administration strongly supported it. The choice then was to negotiate a binding treaty that no one believed the United States could ratify—or look for some other option. The Obama Administration identified pledge-and-review as a clear option early and focused like a laser on bringing other countries along. The Obama Administration also had a clear view on how they could avoid Senate ratification by using the President's authority to sign binding executive agreements with other countries. Under this approach, the United States could not agree to any new binding substantive commitments, but it could agree to binding procedural or interpretive provisions that involved sharing information or simply interpreted existing provisions in the UNFCCC. The pledge-and-review fit this architecture in ways a binding cap never could. The Paris Agreement's carefully crafted mix of binding procedural obligations and non-binding mitigation commitments allowed room for US participation.

85 Warwick J. McKibbin et al., *Comparing Climate Commitments: A Model-Based Analysis of the Copenhagen Accord*, HARVARD PROJECT ON INT'L CLIMATE AGREEMENTS 6 (June 10, 2010), https://www.belfercenter.org/sites/default/files/files/publication/McKibbin-DP-June2010-final.pdf.

86 *Id.*

reduction from 1990 levels, assuming the establishment of a fair and effective international framework in which all major economies participate and on agreement by those economies on ambitious targets."[87] These countries used the promise of more ambitious targets in an effort to expand the number of countries committed to address climate change, but did not expressly require the commitments to be legally binding.

C *The Added Enforcement Value of Binding Commitments Is Unclear*

One of the benefits of binding commitments is that they reflect stronger political commitment to the norm and that potential consequences from non-compliance would result in more compliance. But experience with the Kyoto Protocol implementation, as well as environmental agreements more generally, highlighted the shortcomings of formal enforcement and sanctions in gaining compliance with binding targets.[88] The Kyoto Protocol had clear commitments and an enforcement mechanism, yet this did not prevent Canada, for example, from going essentially unsanctioned after announcing it would simply withdraw from the Protocol rather than face any potential sanctions for non-compliance.[89]

The relative ineffectiveness of sanctions in the Kyoto context was not lost on the Paris negotiators. Why accept lower substantive commitments to secure a binding architecture if sanctions were not available and credible on the back end? Moreover, the growing consensus regarding enforcement in the environmental context more generally relies less on sanctions for non-compliance and more on *facilitating* compliance through financial support, technology transfers, and constructive dialogue over a period of time.[90] Ultimately, naming and

---

87 *Id.*

88 *See* Werksman & Herbertson, *supra* note 32 (discussing the trade-offs between better performance under a clear, binding cap and universal participation under a system with variable mitigation commitments). The relative lack of success in establishing effective enforcement mechanisms with sanctions in the Kyoto Protocol (or most other environmental agreements for that matter) slowly led advocates to question the added value of negotiating binding commitments. Whether binding or non-binding commitments, the primary sanctions available were some form of "naming and shaming." To be certain, some greater shaming ability attached to binding instruments, but the question was whether that advantage warranted lengthened negotiations or significant sacrifice in the substance of the commitments.

89 *See Canada Pulls Out of Kyoto Protocol*, *supra* note 27.

90 *See* ENGAGING COUNTRIES: STRENGTHENING COMPLIANCE WITH INTERNATIONAL ENVIRONMENTAL ACCORDS (Edith Brown Weiss & Harold K. Jacobson eds (1998);.ABRAM CHAYES & ANTONIA HANDLER CHAYES, THE NEW SOVEREIGNTY: COMPLIANCE WITH INTERNATIONAL REGULATORY AGREEMENTS (1995).

shaming countries in non-compliance and disqualifying such countries for regime benefits, such as financial support, are the primary formal sanctions available in international environmental law. Even these sanctions are seen as limited and counter-productive at least where the non-compliant party is willing, but unable, to comply. Moreover, naming, shaming and the withdrawal of regime benefits may still be available as incentives even if the commitments are not in a binding form.

From this perspective, the distinction between binding and nonbinding commitments with respect to enforceability does not appear as significant in practice as once thought. What matters more is building a robust system of facilitative mechanisms as well as transparent reporting procedures to permit all stakeholders to monitor compliance and to participate in both facilitation and naming/shaming activities. Note, too, that 100% compliance of all countries all the time is not required to achieve the overall objectives of most environmental regimes, including climate change. Thus, we would expect that whatever slippage in performance results from the voluntariness of the commitments could be more than offset by broader and more ambitious commitments in the first place.

Moreover, the institutional and procedural architecture for monitoring compliance coupled with the high profile of the Paris Agreement arguably makes the commitments as binding *de facto* as if they were legally mandatory. At least in the climate context, giving up binding norms with the potential for formal state-to-state enforcement and the availability of sanctions does not seem like it compromised the regime's effectiveness in reducing net GHG emissions. Given how closely the climate regime is scrutinized, naming and shaming remains the primary enforcement approach, and one that does not appear to be significantly weakened because the commitments are not mandatory.

D *International v. National Enforcement of the NDCs*

Abandoning hard international law commitments meant abandoning the possibility of state-to-state enforcement in a compliance system established under the regime or in some other international forum. In place of international enforcement, the Agreement relies on enforcement of the NDCs at the national level. Although the Paris Agreement does not require the NDCs be made binding in national law, many countries have chosen to implement their NDCs through national law. As discussed above, these NDCs may be open to judicial review and may form the basis for enforcement against the state under national law. A focus on national level enforcement is particularly important in the climate context because addressing climate change ultimately requires changing the behavior of private companies, investors, and consumers—the role of the state is important primarily as a rule-maker and policy setter. The threat of international enforcement of nation-wide emission caps may pressure a state to act, but it does little to directly support national implementation or behavioral change in the regulatory target. By allowing NDCs that can reflect diverse national priorities and approaches, the Agreement arguably catalyzes a national discussion of appropriate commitments that may ultimately better socialize the norms and increase the likelihood of compliance at the national level. By requiring the setting of NDCs, the Agreement has created the opportunity for progressive development of nationally binding laws. And by providing transparency for reporting and monitoring results, the Agreement supports national level enforcement. It is too early to assess, but this hybrid approach may ultimately result in more hard domestic law being used to change conduct by the regulated private actors than would have occurred through a focus on hard international law that would only bind the State.

E *The Regime's Signaling Effect*

Addressing climate change will ultimately require a fundamental shift toward a cleaner economy, with far less dependence on coal and other fossil fuels. The non-binding nature of the NDCs could have softened the signal being sent regarding how committed governments are to this shift in the market. By establishing the temperature goal and associated mid-term goals, the parties to the Paris Agreement intended to signal their long-term commitment to a cleaner energy future. The Agreement also included mandatory procedures that reinforced their commitment, including the regularly scheduled progressive revision of the NDCs and the requirement that each Party is to submit long-term low-GHG development strategies.[91]

The combination of setting global goals and putting mandatory procedures in place for making progress toward the goals seems to be sufficient to send a clear signal to the market. The bindingness of the short-term national commitments as part of the Agreement's overall comprehensive and universally accepted approach does not appear to have eroded the long-term signals. Although we may not be able to predict what our precise energy mix will be in the future, the Agreement is clear that fossil fuels will be significantly less important.

---

91 *See* Paris CoP Decision, *supra* note 44, ¶ 36; *see also* Paris Agreement, *supra* note 3, art. 4(19).

The widespread participation of non-state actors and the massive publicity around Paris likely strengthened the signaling affect. Although formally only governments committed to a low-carbon future, in a very real sense industry, environmental advocates, and many other stakeholders committed as well.[92] With such broad societal consensus, the market signal was not significantly tempered by the non-binding nature of the NDCs. The momentum carried through as most countries quickly ratified the Agreement. Although difficult to prove quantitatively, any disappointment in failure to reach binding commitments did not appear to slow the overall momentum for a long-term market shift.[93]

F *The Symbiotic Relationship of Hard and Soft International Law in a Complex Regime*

The climate change regime provides an institutional architecture and policy framework intended to manage the complex and evolving problem of climate change over the long-term. In the context of such a regime, the interplay of hard and soft international law takes on a symbiotic relationship reflecting a long-term practical political calculus in furtherance of the (sometimes slow) evolution of the regime.

Although the periodic treaty negotiations (for example at Kyoto and Paris) garner most of the public's attention, the actual implementation and evolution of the regime depends as much on decisions of annual Conference of the Parties. The Parties are constantly negotiating CoP decisions, which are adopted by consensus at the annual meetings. Such decisions are not included in the sources of international law listed in the Charter of the ICJ, and most observers do not believe they are legally binding.[94] Nonetheless, the Parties treat the CoP decisions as at least politically binding, relying on them to operationalize the regime over time. For example, through these decisions, the Parties have operationalized the Green Climate Fund, the Adaptation Fund, the Clean

92 *See* Melissa Danzo, *Can Non-State Actors Save the Paris Climate Agreement?* 40 MICH. J. INT'L L. (2019), http://www.mjilonline.org/can-non-state-actors-save-the-paris-climate-agreement/#_ftn2; *see also* Karin Bäckstrand et al., *Non-State Actors in Global Climate Governance: From Copenhagen to Paris and Beyond* 26:4 ENVTL. POL. 561–79 (May 26, 2017), available at https://www.tandfonline.com/doi/full/10.1080/09644016.2017.1327485.

93 Reliance on solar, wind, and other non-renewable energy sources took off before and after the Paris negotiations. In 2016, for example, clean energy accounted for 61.5 percent of new generating capacity, surpassing all oil, coal, and natural gas generation. *See* FERC ENERGY INFRASTRUCTURE UPDATE 2016, *supra* note 59.

94 *See* ICJ Statute, *supra* note 19.

Development Mechanism, emissions trading, technology transfer, and myriad other institutions or policies. Negotiation of the decisions align the Parties in a shared collective development of the regime. This process is not dependent on the decision's legal status under the Charter of the ICJ, but on the legitimacy of and commitment to the CoP decisions as the primary mechanism for evolving the regime to manage the complexities of regulating climate change.

What emerges from an understanding of the CoP is that the progressive development of a regime is not dependent on the legal form of the decision, the clarity of the norm or its ability to be legally enforced. What is important is that the Parties recognize the legitimacy of the decisions and can be relatively certain that all Parties will act in accordance with them. This "reliance" factor is an important role for legal norms but reliance can also be engendered through credible soft international law processes as countries demonstrate their willingness to behave in accordance with them over time.

Reliance on CoP decisions for operationalizing the regime has its limits with regard to the long-term evolution of the regime, however. Because the scope of CoP decisions is limited to the underlying treaty instrument, they cannot impose additional substantive obligations on the Parties. The UNFCCC is a broad enough framework to allow for significant developments, but new mitigation commitments, absent another process adopted by the Parties, eventually required a new hard international law instrument like the Paris Agreement or Kyoto Protocol. As demonstrated by Paris the nature of the commitments could be soft, given that they are embedded in a regime with the institutional and policy framework for facilitating implementation. After all, what the climate regime seeks is actual reductions in emissions, not necessarily strong enforcement against non-compliant states. Enforced hard law standards are simply one tool to achieve reductions; the Paris Agreement embodies a different tool—non-binding, differentiated standards in a robust implementation framework. We will soon know whether it will be more effective in achieving the goal of reduced emissions.

CHAPTER 8

A Turning Point in a Slow Revolution: the WHO Framework Convention on Tobacco Control

*Patricia Anne Lambert**

1 Introduction

The World Health Organization (WHO) Framework Convention on Tobacco Control (FCTC), which entered into force on February 27, 2005 and is currently binding on 180 countries and the European Union, that are home to 90 percent of the world's people, is the first global public health treaty. The FCTC provides a unique example of how well-informed individuals and organizations from civil society, together with some willing governments, prevailed in their effort to create and adopt a hard law instrument that has completely altered the landscape not only for tobacco control, but also for global public health. Since its entry into force, the mere existence of the FCTC and its rapid and almost universal acceptance have strengthened and given renewed purpose to the movement for tobacco control that created it in the first place.

Ultimately, the story of the FCTC is a story of social change. It is the story of a unique battle by civil society, some governments, and a section of the WHO, working together against a powerful, immensely rich and unaccountable industry. The tobacco industry is the vector for the preventable diseases and death caused by the use of its addictive products—which it markets aggressively and shamelessly to all, including young people, despite irrefutable scientific evidence of their harm.

* Director of the International Legal Consortium at The Campaign for Tobacco Free Kids; former Board member of Action on Smoking for Health (USA) and the Framework Convention Alliance (FCA) ; former president of International Network of Women Against Tobacco (INWAT); and former Legal Advisor, Ministry of Health, Government of South Africa, in which capacity she represented South Africa as the Head of Delegation in the negotiations of the tobacco treaty. She also served as the representative of the African group of forty-six Member States on the Bureau that managed the negotiating process and as the co-chair (English) of the African Regional Group. These experiences strongly influenced her perspective on the FCTC's development and subsequent implementation. For their comments on earlier versions of this chapter, she is grateful to Kathy Mulvey, Kathy Shats, David Hunter, and Danny Bradlow, and for technical assistance to Kaitlin Donley and Katie Seifu.

 | DOI:10.1163/9789004417021_009

Emma Goldman, the American political activist, noted for her advocacy for workers' rights and women's empowerment, famously wrote, "[n]o real social change has ever been brought about without a revolution." By any standard, the revolution from a rapidly escalating tobacco epidemic to a new international set of norms for tobacco control may seem like a rather slow revolution, but it was a revolution nonetheless. The turning point was the negotiation, adoption, and entry into force of the FCTC.

This chapter traces the path of the revolution that culminated in the passage of the FCTC; examines the treaty as both a process and a product; examines the roles played by state and non-state actors, including the tobacco industry; highlights some exceptional features of the treaty; traces the development of the treaty through the work of the Conference of the Parties to the treaty (COP); describes the legal challenges to the treaty since its entry into force; and evaluates the relative success of the treaty over the past thirteen years.

A *The Creation of an Epidemic*

Today, there are more than one billion smokers in the world.[1] Tobacco use killed 100 million people in the 20th century. In the 21st century, one billion people could die from tobacco-related causes if current patterns of tobacco use continue.[2] Seen another way, tobacco kills more than six million people each year. By 2030, the number of tobacco-related deaths will increase to eight million per year.[3] Most of the carnage will unfold in low—and middle-income countries placing an ever-greater strain on health systems already over-burdened by other diseases.

By the middle of the twentieth century, tobacco use, and especially cigarette smoking, was iconic in Western society. Smoking was seen as sophisticated and as an indication that the smoker was living "the good life." Stars of stage and screen, athletes, and even doctors actively endorsed various cigarette brands.[4] Cigarette advertisements on billboards, on television, and in magazines showed us aspirational versions of ourselves: relaxing at home and in exotic places, playing with our children and pets, dancing under the stars, riding with cowboys, fishing, skiing, playing tennis, riding horses, and sunning ourselves

1 WORLD HEALTH ORGANIZATION (WHO), WHO REPORT ON THE GLOBAL TOBACCO EPIDEMIC 2015: RAISING TAXES ON TOBACCO (2015).

2 MICHAEL P. ERIKSEN ET AL., THE TOBACCO ATLAS (5th ed. 2015) (last visited Aug. 21, 2019).

3 WHO, *WHO Report On the Global Tobacco Epidemic 2011: Warning About the Dangers of Tobacco*, (2011).

4 ALLAN M. BRANDT, THE CIGARETTE CENTURY: THE RISE, FALL, AND DEADLY PERSISTENCE OF THE PRODUCT THAT DEFINED AMERICA (2007).

on the beach. Smoking, which had been a symbol of wealth in the early part of the century, had by mid-century spread to the middle and working classes.

The avalanche of advertising had the effect desired by the tobacco corporations. The number of tobacco users soared. By the 1950s, an estimated 66 percent of American adult males were regular smokers and the number of female smokers was rising at an alarming rate. Similar statistics were seen in Canada, Australia, European and other Western countries.

The first spark in the slow revolution was ignited in the 1930s, when scientists in Germany and the US linked smoking to cancer, but the advent of the Second World War limited the spread of the information.[5] After the war, however, in the early 1950s, a number of scientific studies conducted in the US and the United Kingdom definitively linked smoking to a higher risk of lung cancer, a disease that had previously been rare.[6]

The tobacco companies reacted swiftly. Despite being competitors in the marketplace, they came together to defend their product and their steadily growing profits. On December 14, 1953, the CEOs of the biggest tobacco companies in America met with public relations company Hill & Knowlton at the Plaza Hotel in New York City to plan how they were going to respond to the scientific research that linked cigarette smoking and lung cancer.[7] They agreed to set up and fund a committee to refute the growing body of science: the Tobacco Industry Research Committee (TIRC).

On January 4, 1954, TIRC released the "*Frank Statement to Cigarette Smokers*" in 448 newspapers across the United States. In it, the industry group stated that it took responsibility for people's health, that it would always cooperate with those who worked in public health, and that it believed that tobacco companies' products were "not injurious to health."[8]

This singular event marked the beginning of the tobacco industry's strategy of denial, deception, delay, and the creation of doubt about the health harms of its product. In a parallel strategy, the industry began to lobby policy makers and politicians to ward off any form of regulation of its product. The tobacco companies carried out these strategies for decades in the United States,[9] and

5 Hanspeter Witschi, *A Short History of Lung Cancer*, 64 TOXICOLOGICAL SCI. 4 (2001).

6 *Id.*

7 Allan M. Brandt, *Inventing Conflicts of Interest: A History of Tobacco Industry Tactics*, 102 AM. J. PUB. HEALTH 63 (2012).

8 Tobacco Industry Research Committee, *A Frank Statement to Cigarette Smokers*, N.Y. TIMES (Jan. 4, 1954), http://archive.tobacco.org/History/540104frank.html.

9 Jack E. Henningfield et al., *Tobacco Industry Litigation Position on Addiction: Continued Dependence on Past Views*, 15 TOBACCO CONTROL 4 (2006).

as globalization opened up new markets for tobacco products, they replicated their successful game plan to deceive the public and block policy action in middle- and low-income countries.

B A Slow Revolution and the Turning Point

In the years after the tobacco industry launched its campaigns of deception and political interference, three watershed events changed the course of tobacco control. The first was the publication of two high-level reports that causally linked smoking to lung cancer, other lung diseases including bronchitis, heart disease, and gastrointestinal problems. One report was released in 1962 by the Royal College of Physicians in the United Kingdom and the other in 1964 by the Surgeon General of the United States. Both reports were titled "Smoking and Health."[10] The reports prompted advocacy on smoking and health by non-state actors, including scientists, academics, and health professionals and eventual policy-making by some governments in high-income countries. Thus began a process of developing public health policies to reduce cigarette consumption. The policies included health warnings on cigarette packs, advertising bans, indoor smoking restrictions, and increases in taxation on tobacco products.

The second watershed event was a conference that drew the growing forces of tobacco control together. In 1967, the first *World Conference on Smoking and Health* was convened in New York City. Robert F. Kennedy, a Senator in the US Congress at the time, delivered the keynote address, an indication of the high profile of the meeting. The conference was convened every four years until 1987 and every three years thereafter. From 1990 onwards, however, it was known as the World Conference on Tobacco Or Health (WCTOH) to draw attention to the fact that tobacco use and health could not co-exist. The conferences provided a vital platform for scientists, policymakers, health professionals and other tobacco control advocates to exchange information, especially in the era before electronic communication. The regular occurrence of the conference and its global nature meant that tobacco control policies and new scientific evidence of the health and economic harms of tobacco could be disclosed, discussed and reviewed, not just by activists and advocates in high-income countries, but by those in low—and middle-income countries as well.[11]

---

10 Daniel Horn, *Smoking and Health: A Report of the Royal College of Physicians on Smoking in Relation to Cancer of the Lung and other Diseases*, 12 CA: A CANCER J. FOR CLINICIANS 111 (1962).

11 HEATHER WIPFLI, THE GLOBAL WAR ON TOBACCO: MAPPING THE WORLD'S FIRST PUBLIC HEALTH TREATY (2015) (providing a more in-depth account).

The third event, in 1970, occurred when the World Health Assembly (WHA), the norm-setting body of the WHO, adopted its first resolution on tobacco. The resolution was a remarkable shift in focus for the WHA, which had until then devoted its attention almost exclusively to issues like malaria, tuberculosis, smallpox, polio, hookworm, venereal diseases, maternal and child health, nutrition, and systems for the classification of diseases. The resolution included a "request" to smokers at future WHAs to refrain from smoking during meetings as well as a request to the Director-General to "consider" convening an expert group to recommend actions to discourage smoking.[12]

From the body mandated to take care of the health concerns of the people of the world, this was a tepid response, by any measure, to the strong scientific evidence presented in the UK and the US eight and six years before, respectively. But it marked the start of growing recognition that the WHO would have to shift some of its focus to tobacco use and associated non-communicable diseases, including cancer. It also marked the first time the world's public health body targeted a consumer product.

Together, these three events set in motion a revolution—albeit a slow one. Over the course of the next three decades, high-income countries like Australia, Canada, Finland, Norway, and Singapore adopted tobacco control measures such as restrictions on tobacco advertising, public education campaigns, and increased excise taxes to reduce tobacco consumption. Some of these policies were also taken up by a few middle-income countries.[13] And the revolution would continue at the international level with the negotiation of the FCTC, the first international treaty on public health and one of the most rapidly embraced treaties in the international legal system.[14]

II Laying the Groundwork for International Tobacco Control and the FCTC as a Global Good for Public Health[15]

When formal negotiations for the Convention by the 172 Member States of the WHO began in Geneva, Switzerland in October 2000, the application of

12 Health Consequences of Smoking, WHA Res. 23.32, 23d Sess., 14th plen. mtg., (May 19, 1970).

13 Derek Yach & Heather Wipfli, *A Century of Smoke*, 100 ANNALS OF TROPICAL MED. & PARASITOLOGY 465 (2006).

14 WHO, *History of the WHO Framework Convention on Tobacco Control* (Geneva, 2009).

15 Allyn L. Taylor & Douglas W. Bettcher, *WHO Framework Convention on Tobacco Control: A Global Good for Public Health*, 78 BULL. OF THE WORLD HEALTH ORG. 920 (2000).

hard international legal instruments to international health issues was still rudimentary, at best. Outside of some instances of multilateral cooperation in areas related to infectious diseases, public health, including tobacco control, was seen almost exclusively as a national concern.

However, over the previous decade, the ground had been prepared for the treaty-making initiative. Tobacco control had been persuasively promoted as a global public "good" alongside other issues directly related to public health such as preventing further environmental degradation, controlling the spread of infectious diseases, enhancing food security, and expanding access to the benefits of biotechnology. An international treaty on tobacco control came to be seen as the means to deliver the global public good.[16] Added to this, it was becoming apparent to everyone that the many soft international law resolutions on tobacco control adopted by the WHA over twenty-five years had been relatively ineffective in curbing the smoking epidemic in the face of rapid globalization. Many low—and middle-income countries were growing concerned as the tobacco industry focused its attention and marketing muscle on them. This is discussed in more detail below.

A *The World Health Organization and Its Normative Powers*

Established on April 7, 1948, the WHO[17] is designated as a specialized agency under the auspices of the United Nations (UN) and is tasked with the coordination of international health policy and activities.

The WHO Constitution states unequivocally that, "The enjoyment of the highest attainable standard of health is one of the fundamental rights of every human being without distinction of race, religion, political belief, economic, or social condition." It defines health as "a state of complete physical, mental, and social well-being and not merely the absence of disease or infirmity."[18]

The WHO Constitution grants the agency, through the WHA, the power to create both hard and soft international law. Article 19 enables it to adopt hard law treaties, Articles 21 and 23 enable it to adopt soft international law regulations, recommendations, and resolutions, and Article 63 enables it to monitor national health legislation.[19]

16 *Id.*
17 WHO, BASIC DOCUMENTS (43rd ed. 2001).
18 *Id.*
19 LAWRENCE O. GOSTIN, PUBLIC HEALTH LAW: POWER, DUTY, RESTRAINT (2008).

B *The Limits of a Soft International Law Approach to Tobacco Control*

Between 1970 and 1998 the WHA adopted 17 non-binding resolutions on different aspects of tobacco control. These resolutions were based on the work of more than eight WHO *ad hoc* expert committees, which consisted variously of scientists, public health experts, and advocates from civil society organizations, universities, and governments, and at least one lawyer, Professor Ruth Roemer from the University of California, Los Angeles.[20] In 1979, a report by the WHO Committee on Smoking Control proposed that the WHA should consider using its hard law treaty-making powers under Article 19 of the WHO Constitution to adopt an international convention to address the tobacco epidemic.[21] Neither the WHA nor the WHO, in its role as the secretariat, showed any interest in the idea. The idea would not resurface publicly until 1992 when Professor Allyn Taylor, while working on her doctoral dissertation at the School of Law at Columbia University, published an article arguing that the WHO should use its treaty making authority to develop a legal framework to assist its Member States in strengthening their public health measures.[22] The article came to the attention of Roemer, who reached out to Taylor and suggested that the legal framework she was advocating could be applied to tobacco control.[23]

Roemer campaigned for the idea at public health conferences and initiated discussions with senior staff in the WHO. She and Taylor believed that tobacco would make a good test case because of its policy history in the WHO. Roemer also tapped into the leadership of the significant global health movement that had been created by the regular WCTOH s. In particular, she reached out to Dr. Judith Mackay, who had been championing tobacco control in Asia for a number of years. Together, Roemer, Taylor, and Mackay introduced a resolution that was adopted at the Ninth WCTOH in Paris in 1994. The resolution called on national governments, Ministers of Health, and the WHO to "immediately initiate action to prepare and achieve an International Convention on Tobacco Control to be adopted by the United Nations."[24]

The idea of developing an international legal instrument for tobacco control was formally taken up by the WHA in 1995. The WHA passed a resolution

---

20 PAUL CAIRNEY, ET AL., GLOBAL TOBACCO CONTROL (2012).

21 WHO, *History of the WHO Framework Convention on Tobacco Control* (Geneva, 2009).

22 Allyn Lise Taylor, *Making the World Health Organization Work: A Legal Framework for Universal Access to the Conditions for Health*, 18 AM. J.L. MED. 301 (1992).

23 Ruth Roemer et al., *Origins of the WHO Framework Convention on Tobacco Control*, 95 AM. J. PUB. HEALTH 936 (2005).

24 Judith Mackay, *The Making of a Convention on Tobacco Control*, 81 BULL. OF THE WORLD HEALTH ORG. 551 (2003).

(WHA 48.11) that referenced the one adopted at the Paris conference, requesting the Director General of the WHO to report on "the feasibility of developing an international instrument such as guidelines, a declaration, or an international convention on tobacco control to be adopted by the United Nations."[25] Roemer and Taylor were then contracted to draft a report on various options for the implementation of WHA 48.11, which they presented to the WHO in July of the same year. It recommended the development and implementation of a framework convention and related protocols to promote global cooperation and national action for tobacco control.[26]

The idea met with significant opposition within the WHO. It had always seen itself as an institution at the service of its Member States, which provided it with direct financial support. Using Article 19 of its Constitution would alter that dynamic significantly by creating a hard international law instrument that would impose legally binding obligations on its Member States, which would then, presumably, have to report formally to the WHO on their domestic actions related to tobacco control. Opposition could also have been related to tobacco industry infiltration of the WHO, which was revealed in evidence from previously secret internal tobacco company documents a few years later.[27] Perhaps not surprisingly, then, the report was criticized as "ambitious to a fault." WHO officials called upon Roemer and Taylor to be "realistic." The officials suggested that the report be revised to recommend either the development of a WHO code of conduct—a soft law approach similar to the WHO International Code of Marketing of Breast-milk Substitutes that could be adopted as a resolution of the WHA[28]— or

25 WHA Res. 48.11, WHO, A48/1995?VR/12 (May 12, 1995).

26 Roemer, *supra* note 23, at 936.

27 WHO, Committee of Experts on Tobacco Industry Documents, *Tobacco Company Strategies to Undermine Tobacco Control Activities at the World Health Organization,* (July 2000) (*prepared by* Thomas Zeltner, David A. Kessler, Anke Martiny & Fazel Randera).

28 The WHO International Code of Marketing of Breast-milk Substitutes, adopted as a resolution of the WHA in 1981. The Code sought to address the general decline in breastfeeding around the world, a trend exacerbated by the aggressive marketing and promotion of breast-milk substitutes by companies such as Nestlé. In low-income countries, infants were frequently fed diluted or contaminated commercial formula, with disastrous health and economic consequences. For the first time, the WHA specified responsibilities not just for governments but also for non-state actors—including manufacturers and distributors of breast-milk substitutes, health workers, and non-governmental organizations. With the Code, advocates aimed to create a vehicle for translating soft international law standards for a large multinational industry into hard national law practice. However, in the decades following, implementation and compliance by member states has been low, with only one third having enacted legally binding measures encompassing the

a hard law treaty to be adopted under the auspices of the UN General Assembly.[29]

Roemer and Taylor were convinced that a soft law approach similar to previous WHA resolutions on tobacco control or the Breast-milk Substitutes Code would be ineffective. In addition, they contended that the WHO, as the specialized agency of the UN concerned with international public health and not the parent body, was the most appropriate forum for the negotiation of a public health treaty. They stood by their original recommendation and sent the final manuscript to the WHO in August 1995.[30]

As instructed by WHA resolution 48.11, the WHO Director-General summarized the key recommendations of the Roemer and Taylor report to the Executive Board of the WHO in January 1996. Despite strong opposition from the WHO secretariat, the Executive Board adopted a resolution, to be carried forward to the 49th WHA, which endorsed a hard international law solution to the tobacco epidemic. In consequence, in May 1996, the WHA adopted resolution 49.17 calling for the development of a WHO framework convention on tobacco control and related protocols.[31]

C *Four Critical Events Propel the Start of Negotiations*

Despite the mandate given to the WHO by the WHA in 1996, substantial opposition to the drafting of a hard law instrument by WHO officials—including legal counsel—slowed the momentum towards the actual drafting of the treaty. Then, in 1998, four critical events took place that propelled the treaty towards formal negotiations. The first event was the election of Dr. Gro Harlem Brundtland as the new Director-General of the WHO. Brundtland, a medical doctor, public health specialist, and experienced politician, had served as Norway's Minister of Health and its Minister for the Environment. She had served three terms as Norway's Prime Minister. Importantly, she had also been the chair of the UN's World Commission on Environment and Development, which convened between 1983 and 1987 and produced a report entitled "Our Common Future," also known as the Brundtland Report, in 1987. Having experienced

majority of the provisions in the Code. The continued widespread marketing of breast-milk substitutes around the world has been criticized and has led to calls for stricter regulatory frameworks and compliance mechanisms. *See generally* Leah Margulies, *The International Code of Marketing of Breastmilk Substitutes: A Model for Assuring Children's Nutrition Rights Under the Law,* 5 INT'L J. CHILDREN'S RTS. 419 (1997).

29 Roemer, *supra* note 23, at 936.

30 *Id.*

31 WHO, World Health Assembly Res. 49/17, (May 25, 1996), http://www.who.int/tobacco/framework/wha_eb/wha49_17/en/ (last visited June 14, 2019).

successful international negotiations first-hand, she was not intimidated by the treaty-making process in the way that some of the WHO staff had been when Roemer and Taylor initially approached them on developing the FCTC. On assuming office at the WHO, Brundtland, closely advised by key tobacco control advocates from several countries, made tobacco control and the development of the FCTC one of the goals of her administration.[32]

The second event was Brundtland's creation, in 1998, of a dedicated unit within the WHO: the Tobacco-Free Initiative (TFI). The TFI was a dynamic powerhouse from the outset. Brundtland gave it authority and a degree of autonomy unusual in the stiffly bureaucratic WHO and it had considerable resources. In addition to funding from the WHO regular budget (contributions from Member States), it had, at Brundtland's request, received significant funding from the United Nations Foundation/United Nations Fund for International Partnerships as well as extra-budgetary contributions from individual governments, including Canada, with a strong interest in the development of a tobacco control treaty.

The TFI was tasked with raising global awareness of the health problems caused by tobacco use, preparing WHO Member States for the treaty-making process, and creating partnerships with civil society organizations (CSOs) and other intergovernmental organizations (IGOs) like the Food and Agriculture Organization (FAO), the United Nations Children's Fund (UNICEF), and the World Bank. In addition, the TFI team created aggressive and innovative media advocacy and social marketing campaigns to highlight the dangers of tobacco use, the marketing strategies of the tobacco industry, and the urgent need for a coordinated global response to tobacco use. These campaigns helped to shift the focus at the government level to corporate accountability and the malfeasance of the tobacco industry.[33] The TFI set up two advisory committees, one on policy and strategy and the other on product regulation. These committees were comprised of experienced tobacco control advocates, including scientists, academics, policy advocates, and other civil society representatives, most of whom were already known to one another through attendance at one or more of the regularly held WCTOHs.[34]

At the WHO, the TFI was known for breaking norms.[35] It worked at a fast pace and with unusual urgency and creativity, nimbly circumventing traditional

32 Geoffrey B. Cockerham & William C. Cockerham, *International Law and Global Health, in* 16 LAW AND GLOBAL HEALTH: CURRENT LEGAL ISSUES (Michael Freeman et al., ed., 2014).

33 WIPFLI, *supra* note 11.

34 WHO, *History of the WHO Framework Convention on Tobacco Control* (Geneva 2009).

35 WIPFLI, *supra* note 11.

bureaucratic practices. It employed the services of creative advertising and marketing agencies and it funded civil society organizations directly, enabling them to participate fully in the treaty-making process.

The third critical event was the collaboration between the WHO and the World Bank that resulted in the publication of a World Bank report, *Curbing the Epidemic: Governments and the Economics of Tobacco Control*.[36] The report, prompted by the TFI, covered not only the global trends and health consequences of tobacco use but also the economic costs to national governments. The study outlined the evidence-based demand- and supply-side measures that governments could take to reduce tobacco consumption. It found that implementing the measures would be affordable, even in low-income countries, and would not significantly affect employment in most countries—refuting the tobacco industry's claims to the contrary. The economic analysis of tobacco use and benefits to government of tobacco control provided effective counter-arguments to the tobacco industry's position that increased tobacco regulation would be harmful to national economies.[37] The impact of the report was enhanced by a $500,000 grant from the Centers for Disease Control and Prevention (CDC), a US federal agency, for its global dissemination.

The fourth critical event was the settlement of lawsuits brought by state governments in the US against the tobacco industry. The attorneys general of the states of Mississippi and Minnesota had brought lawsuits against the tobacco companies in 1994 to recover health care costs related to tobacco use. Most of the other US states followed suit over the next four years. Only the Minnesota case, which was settled in May 1998, went to trial.[38] Six months later, forty-six states, five US territories, and the District of Columbia entered into the Master Settlement Agreement with the five largest tobacco companies. The agreement imposed prohibitions or restrictions on the sale, advertising, and promotion of cigarettes; dissolved the Tobacco Institute, the industry's lobbying arm;[39] and required the companies to pay the states billions of dollars annually in perpetuity.[40] In addition, the companies were compelled to release

36 Prabhat Jha & F. J. Chaloupka, THE WORLD BANK, *Curbing the Epidemic: Governments and the Economics of Tobacco Control* (1999).

37 Jeff Collin, *Tobacco Politics*, 47 DEV. 91 (2004).

38 *See, e.g.*, Minnesota Tobacco Control, https://www.publichealthlawcenter.org/topics/tobacco-control/minnesota-tobacco-control (last visited June 14, 2019).

39 Minnesota v. Philip Morris Inc., 1998 MN Dist. Ct. 2d CI-94–8565, https://www.publichealthlawcenter.org/topics/tobacco-control/tobacco-control-litigation/minnesota-litigation-and-settlement (last visited June 14, 2019).

40 Steven A. Schroeder, *Tobacco Control in the Wake of the 1998 Master Settlement Agreement*, 350 NEW ENG. J. MED. 293 (2004).

millions of pages of hitherto confidential internal documents. These proved to be a treasure trove that enabled health advocates, including the WHO, to have more insight into the industry's practices and strategies.

Using some of this information, a WHO panel of experts published a report in 2000,[41] which provided clear evidence that the tobacco industry had deliberately and strategically worked to undermine tobacco control efforts around the world. It had made financial contributions to politicians, published its own "junk science" questioning the health harms of tobacco use, distorted the WHO's research findings, and employed the media, front groups, and lobbying groups to subvert the WHO's tobacco-related activities.[42] It had attempted to reduce budgets for the WHO's scientific and policy activities related to tobacco control, worked to discredit the WHO through third-party critics, pitted other UN agencies against the organization, and used surrogates to influence WHO decisions.[43]

Under Brundtland's leadership and with the TFI's energy and strong convening authority, preparations for the negotiation of the FCTC proceeded swiftly. In May 1999, the 52nd WHA established a FCTC working group to prepare a report on proposed draft elements for a framework convention on tobacco control by the next year's WHA. The WHA also mandated the WHO to establish an Intergovernmental Negotiating Body (INB), open to all Member States, to negotiate and draft such a treaty.[44]

III Negotiations: The FCTC Takes Shape

A *From a Report to a Provisional Text*

The FCTC working group, which was open to all WHO Member States as well as civil society observers, met twice: in October 1999 and March 2000. Its task was to examine the existing scientific evidence and to make broad recommendations on the contents of the treaty. Over the course of the two meetings, the FCTC working group decided not only to produce a report with a list of recommended draft elements for inclusion in the treaty but also, with the help

41 WHO, Committee of Experts on Tobacco Industry Documents, *Tobacco Company Strategies to Undermine Tobacco Control Activities at the World Health Organization,* (July 2000) (*prepared by* Thomas Zeltner, David A. Kessler, Anke Martiny & Fazel Randera).

42 *Id.*

43 WIPFLI, *supra* note 11.

44 Towards a WHO Framework Convention on Tobacco Control, WHA Res. 52/18, (May 24, 1999).

of the TFI, to produce a provisional draft text of the treaty itself—in essence a template from which to initiate negotiations.

This was a remarkable achievement because during the meetings of the working group, vigorous disagreement arose. One group of delegates favoured binding obligations that would set high standards for the domestic implementation of tobacco control measures. Another group favored a weaker set of obligations on the basis that too many specific obligations might deter countries from supporting the treaty. A third group, the majority of the delegations, favored a strong but more general treaty that as many Member States of the WHO as possible could accede to. The working group's report artfully managed to reflect all views by including fairly detailed general comments as well as notes on each section of the provisional draft text.

The report, including the provisional draft text, was adopted by the 53rd WHA in May 2000, which then called for the FCTC negotiations to begin. At the first meeting of the Intergovernmental Negotiating Body (INB) in October 2000, as its first order of business, the draft provisional text was adopted and accepted as a starting point for the negotiations. The significance of this cannot be overstated. It takes time to write provisions and even more time to reach consensus. The WHO's mandate was to produce a treaty in six drafting sessions. Instead of having to construct a treaty from the ground up, negotiators were able to focus on achieving consensus on existing text. The agreed provisional draft text had resolved several issues at the working group stage, even before the negotiations began. The strong public health language in the preamble, objectives, and guiding principles[45] was difficult to refute and could be accepted by most countries because there were no obligations attached.[46]

1 Public Hearings

In order to ensure transparency, and facilitate greater buy-in, the WHO held public hearings on the two days immediately preceding the start of the negotiations, an unprecedented action. Some governments, the public health community, and the tobacco industry provided written and oral testimony. More than 500 submissions were received and representatives from 144 organizations gave oral testimony.[47]

45 WHO, *Proposed Draft Elements for a WHO Framework Convention on Tobacco Control: Provisional Texts with Comments of the Working Group*, Doc. A/FCTC/INB1/2 (July 26, 2000).

46 WIPFLI, *supra* note 11.

47 WHO, Tobacco Free Initiative, *Public Hearings on the WHO Framework Convention on Tobacco Control* (Oct. 12–13, 2000).

2 Tobacco Industry Opposition

The tobacco companies made their views on the draft of the FCTC known in submissions to the WHO, statements to their shareholders and partners, media interviews and presentations. Their views were not uniform but there were common threads: the treaty was unnecessary and fundamentally flawed; it would not achieve its objective; its draft provisions were unworkable or politically unfeasible; it would have a negative impact on international trade; it would be too expensive to implement; and it was an affront to national sovereignty. The chairperson of British American Tobacco (BAT), in the company's annual report, called the proposed FCTC "a developed world obsession being foisted on to the developing world."[48] The companies particularly decried the fact that they were not permitted to participate in the negotiations. They expressed their desire to cooperate with the WHO and national governments but only on condition that tobacco control measures accommodated adult smokers and were sensible and meaningful. They favored partnerships with national governments and the WHO on youth smoking prevention measures and suggested a voluntary regulatory scheme instead of a treaty.[49]

The tobacco industry was officially prohibited from participating in the negotiations—a decision supported by the report of the WHO Committee of Experts on Tobacco Industry Documents and reinforced by resolution WHA 54.18 on Transparency in Tobacco Control Process. Its representatives nevertheless succeeded in influencing the negotiations by working with industry-friendly governments on the composition of their national delegations and with private consultants and third-party organizations like the International Tobacco Growers' Association (ITGA) and the International Association of Airport Duty Free Stores (IAADFS), to promote the views of the tobacco industry, as outlined above.[50]

48 British American Tobacco (BAT), *Annual Review and Summary Financial Statement* (1999).

49 *See* The WHO'S Proposed Global Tobacco Treaty, Philip Morris Records, https://www.industrydocumentslibrary.ucsf.edu/tobacco/docs/msgw0074 (last visited July 19, 2018); Financial Statement for the Period 1-1-94 to 12-31-94 Tyrosine Phosphorylation of RNA Poymerase II, Council for Tobacco Research Records, https://www.industrydocumentslibrary.ucsf.edu/tobacco/docs/mgcw0077 (last visited July 19, 2018); R.J. Reynolds Tobacco Company's Pre-Hearing Submission., RJ Reynolds Records, https://www.industrydocumentslibrary.ucsf.edu/tobacco/docs/yswc0054 (last visited June 14, 2019); British American Tobacco's Submission to the WHO's Framework Convention on Tobacco Control, Philip Morris Records, https://www.industrydocumentslibrary.ucsf.edu/tobacco/docs/fklm0071 (last visited June 14, 2019).

50 WIPFLI, *supra* note 11.

3 Questions of Political Will

Over 170 Member States of the WHO participated in the six sessions of the INB held between October 16, 2000 and March 1, 2003 in Geneva, Switzerland. Not all states were committed to the process to the same degree and not all were anxious to develop a strong, effective treaty that would reduce tobacco use around the world. Ambassador Celso Amorim of Brazil, the original Chair of the INBs, divided the states into four groups: "Those who have done; those who want to do; those who want to but cannot; and those who do not want to do."[51]

"Those who have done" consisted mainly of high-income countries that had strong domestic tobacco control measures in place and had been instrumental in ensuring that the WHA was mandated to set the negotiation process in motion. These included Canada, Norway, Finland, and Australia. "Those who want to do" included a small group of middle-income countries that were in the process of implementing tobacco control measures and that believed that the FCTC would strengthen their domestic efforts. These included South Africa, Iran, and Thailand. "[T]hose who want to but cannot" consisted of a large group of countries, including most African countries, some countries from Central and South America and small island states in the Caribbean and Pacific regions, which had little knowledge of tobacco control measures and lacked the capacity to put such measures in place. The fourth group, those "who do not want to do" fought against strong tobacco control measures in the FCTC throughout the negotiations and at times threatened to derail the process altogether. These included the "Big Four"—Japan, Germany, China, and the United States—some of which were home to transnational and/or domestic tobacco companies and were heavily lobbied by the industry to block and/or weaken the treaty.[52]

During the negotiations a number of the delegations that were arguing for a strong, effective set of tobacco control measures became an informal alliance to counter the "Big Four." This alliance was aided greatly by the ability to draft regional positions during inter-sessional meetings held in the respective regions.[53] The African countries formed the first regional alliance shortly before the second session of the INB and proceeded thereafter to negotiate with a single voice. Together with other groups of low—and middle-income countries,

---

51 Yach & Wipfli, *supra* note 13, at 465.

52 ROSS HAMMOND & MARY ASSUNTA, THE FRAMEWORK CONVENTION ON TOBACCO CONTROL: PROMISING START, UNCERTAIN FUTURE (BMJ Publishing Group Ltd. 2003).

53 Katherine Deland, et al., *The WHO Framework Convention on Tobacco Control and the Tobacco Free Initiative*, *in* THE GLOBAL TOBACCO EPIDEMIC AND THE LAW 11, (Ad Mitchell & Tania Voon, ed., 2003).

the informal alliance provided a formidable counterforce to the "Big Four." In so doing, they significantly influenced the negotiations and raised the bar on key provisions of the treaty.[54] Internal corporate documents show that the tobacco industry sought to split WHO regions in its effort to derail and weaken the treaty.[55]

4 The Role of Civil Society

Treaty negotiations are, by definition, state-centric processes. In the case of the FCTC, however, the role of civil society was essential to the treaty.

Throughout the negotiations, empowered by WHA resolutions,[56] civil society organizations, including scientific experts, participated as energetic observers, playing a key role in the actual development of the treaty text. The TFI appointed a staff member to work directly with civil society, a process which facilitated and enhanced its access to government delegates and to the process. They adopted various strategies to influence the views of government delegates including organizing informative side events (with free meals to encourage attendance), supplying expert opinions and position papers, and adroit face-to-face lobbying in the corridors of the meeting.[57] Far from being coincidental, this was part of a carefully choreographed strategy by the WHO.

In 1998, as part of the pre-negotiation process, the WHO commissioned a series of technical briefing documents, including a paper on the mobilization of non-governmental organizations (NGOs). Drawing on lessons from the WHO Code on breast-milk substitutes, the landmine ban, and environmental conventions, Corporate Accountability, then known as Infact, argued in the paper that NGO involvement would result in a stronger treaty with a shorter timeline, that coordination of NGO participation would be key, and that NGOs' independence would enable them to set visionary goals and expand the horizons of what might be politically feasible.[58] Following this, in May 1999, a

54 Collin, *supra* note 37, at 91.

55 Stacy M. Carter, *Mongoven, Biscoe and Duchin: Destroying Tobacco Control Activism from the Inside.*, 11 TOBACCO CONTROL 2 (2002).

56 The enabling resolutions for the FCTC negotiations affirmed the value of civil society participation: Resolution WHA52.18 included multiple references to nongovernmental organizations, and Resolution WHA 53.16 in May 2000 called on the INB "to examine the question of an extended participation, as observers, of nongovernmental organizations ... ".

57 Hadii M. Mamudu & Stanton A. Glantz, *Civil Society and the Negotiation of the Framework Convention on Tobacco Control*, 4 GLOBAL PUB. HEALTH 150 (2009).

58 WHO, *Mobilizing NGOs and the Media Behind the International Framework Convention on Tobacco Control: Experiences from the Code on Marketing of Breast-milk Substitutes and Conventions on Landmines and the Environment*, WHO/NCD/TFI/99.3 (July 26, 2000).

symposium on the potential role of NGOs in the development of the FCTC provided a further critical step in the negotiations process. Participants, who came from both the Global North and the Global South, explored the idea of forming alliances that could incorporate smaller, less-resourced organizations from the Global South, keep them informed, and pursue joint work in several critical areas. These areas of collaboration included creating a public and political climate to support the treaty negotiations; exposing the bad acts and junk science of the tobacco industry; framing the issue of tobacco control around the need to protect children and young people from insidious and predatory tobacco advertising; and generally neutralizing the tobacco industry's influence on the treaty negotiations.[59]

Two global networks with significant worldwide influence coalesced during the negotiations: The Framework Convention Alliance (FCA), including more than 200 organizations from ninety-three countries, and the Network for Accountability of Tobacco Transnationals (NATT), including more than seventy-five organizations from fifty countries. These two alliances, initially formed around organizations from high-income countries and major international public health associations, made conscious efforts to recruit new members from low—and middle-income countries and, where necessary, to train them in lobbying as well as on the treaty context and content. This strategy has had a long-lasting impact on the later development of the FCTC by greatly increasing the number and strength of civil society organizations around the world that work to ensure the measures contained in the treaty are implemented by the governments that sign on to it.

During the negotiations, the FCA and the NATT produced daily bulletins containing a variety of materials including the latest scientific evidence on topics under discussion, expert opinions, position papers, and other relevant information. The NATT also made a remarkable contribution to the process by working with highly experienced and skilled lawyers from the environmental movement to produce a "gold standard" treaty text for consideration by government delegates. The text was of enormous benefit to many low—and middle-income countries in so far as it both provided them with a comprehensive vision of what a strong, effective treaty might look like and assisted them to advocate using legal treaty terminology.

Both the NATT and the FCA created a system for naming and shaming or praising country positions. The FCA, on the back page of its bulletin, awarded

59 NGO Forum for Health, Geneva, Switz., May 17, 999, *NGOs' Role in the Development of the Framework Convention on Tobacco Control.*

daily "Orchids" for countries supporting strong tobacco control measures and "Dirty Ashtrays" for countries that were diluting the text or attempting to derail the process. The NATT gave its "Marlboro Man" award to countries that took positions that would benefit the tobacco industry at the expense of public health. The "Big Four" achieved record numbers of negative awards while the low—and middle-income countries that were persistently espousing strong measures won bouquets of "Orchids."[60] These awards drew strong criticism from some governments, particularly the "Big Four". At the same time, they energized the alliance of low- and middle-income countries and those high-income countries that favoured strong, effective tobacco control measures.

Analysing the role of civil society at the conclusion of the negotiations, commentators wrote that it had acted as the "conscience of the negotiations,"[61] and had created an on-going "university of tobacco control."[62] It is therefore not unexpected that the significant role that civil society played in creation, adoption, and negotiation of the FCTC is acknowledged in the Preamble to the treaty, which "emphasizes the special contribution of ... civil society" and its future role is reflected in Article 4.7, which states that "[t]he participation of civil society is essential in achieving the objective of the Convention and its protocols."

The tactics used by NATT and the FCA during the FCTC negotiations drew heavily on the experiences and tactics of civil society in the earlier climate negotiations. This cross-fertilization of environmental and public health strategies is now also reflected in more recent public interest treaty negotiations like the Arms Trade Treaty,[63] the Paris Climate Agreement,[64] and the push towards a treaty to regulate international corporations,[65] suggesting an emerging practice for active civil society engagement in, and influence of, hard law negotiations.

---

60 Mamudu & Glantz, *supra* note 57, at 150; WIPFLI, *supra* note 11.

61 WIPFLI, *supra* note 11.

62 Yach & Wipfli, *supra* note 13, at 465.

63 Helena Whall & Allison Pyltak, *The Role of Civil Society in the International Negotiations on the Arms Trade Treaty*, 5 GLOBAL POLICY 453 (2014).

64 *See* Michael Jacobs, *High pressure for low emissions: How civil society created the Paris climate agreement,* (Mar. 23, 2016), https://www.ippr.org/juncture/high-pressure-for-low-emissions-how-civil-society-created-the-paris-climate-agreement (last visited June 14, 2019). *See also* David Hunter, Chapter 8 in this volume.

65 Carmen Steg, *A Powerful Civil Society Movement Pushes Forward the Treaty to Regulate International Corporations,* (Nov. 9, 2017), https://www.ciel.org/powerful-civil-society-movement-pushes-forward-treaty-regulate-international-corporations/ (last visited June 14, 2019).

IV The FCTC Emerges

During the closing plenary, Dr. Caleb Otto, the chief delegate from the tiny island of Palau, began his intervention with an infamous quote from an R.J. Reynolds executive: "We don't smoke the shit. We reserve that right for the young, the poor, the black, and the stupid."[66] He then went on to say: "Well, ladies and gentlemen, most of us who have gone through these treaty negotiations are from the poor nations, and we know that the tobacco industry has targeted us. I cannot change the color of my skin, so they are targeting me. We cannot prevent our children from passing through youth, so they'll target them. But we can stop them from calling us stupid with this FCTC."[67]

The sixth and final session of the INB concluded its work at around 3:00 A.M. on March 1, 2003. The negotiations had been long and hard-fought. Along the way they had generated a range of emotions in those involved—anger, frustration, and disappointment probably chief amongst them. But the prevailing mood in the room as the gavel was brought down on the final text to be forwarded for adoption by the WHA was one of euphoria and a sense of real achievement. Neither those fighting for the strongest possible set of tobacco control measures nor those who had worked assiduously to dilute them got everything they wanted but, on balance, the text was a definite victory for those countries that fought for a strong, comprehensive treaty.

Taken as a whole, the treaty provides enough hard law (with, arguably, some soft law elements) to tackle, in a meaningful way, the scourge of tobacco use and the epidemic that is steadily being spread across low—and middle-income countries by the tobacco industry. This is clearly reflected in the agreed-upon objective of the FCTC, which gives an indication both of the immensity of the problem and the fierce determination of the countries that fought for the strongest possible consensus text to tackle the problem:

> The objective of this Convention and its protocols is to protect present and future generations from the devastating health, social, environmental, and economic consequences of tobacco consumption and exposure to tobacco smoke by providing a framework for tobacco control measures to be implemented by the Parties at the national, regional and

---

66 Goerlitz Dep. 26, (Nov. 9, 1998), http://legacy.library.ucsf.edu/tid/ufro7aoo (last visited June 14, 2019).

67 DVD: Kelly Anderson, *Overcoming the Odds: A Story of the First Global Health and Corporate Accountability Treaty* (Infact 2004).

> international levels in order to reduce continually and substantially the prevalence of tobacco use and exposure to tobacco smoke.[68]

The WHA approved the final draft of the treaty in May 2003. By June 2004, when it closed for signature at the UN in New York, 168 states had signed on. It came into force on February 27, 2005, after it had been ratified by forty states. As of September 2019, the FCTC has been ratified by 180 countries and the European Union, which makes it a legally binding agreement for almost all countries in the world. Notable countries that have not embraced the FCTC include Indonesia, Argentina, the United States and Switzerland, headquarters of Philip Morris International and Japan Tobacco International.[69]

A *The Provisions of the FCTC*

The Preamble establishes the right of Parties to give priority to measures to protect public health; recognizes both the global nature of the tobacco epidemic and the scientific evidence of the health harms of tobacco use and exposure to tobacco smoke; emphasizes the need to be alert to efforts by the tobacco industry to undermine or subvert the treaty; and links the FCTC to the international human rights framework.[70]

Guiding principles enshrined in Article 4 of the treaty include the necessity for:

a) Every person to be informed about the health consequences of tobacco use and exposure to tobacco smoke;
b) Strong political commitment at government level;
c) International and regional cooperation;
d) Multisectoral commitment (which refers to a whole of government approach);
e) Civil society participation (as detailed above); and
f) Sustainable funding.[71]

Obligations contained in Article 5 of the Convention include the development of domestic tobacco control policies and legislation; the creation of national focal points for tobacco control; the formulation of guidelines and procedures

---

68 WHO Framework Convention on Tobacco Control, *adopted* May 21, 2003, 2302 U.N.T.S. 166 (entered into force Feb. 27, 2005), https://www.who.int/tobacco/framework/WHO_FCTC_english.pdf. [*hereinafter* FCTC].

69 Vienna Convention on the Law of Treaties, *opened for signature* May 23, 1969, 1155 U.N.T.S. 331, 8 I.L.M. 679.

70 FCTC, *supra* note 68, at pmbl.

71 *Id.*

for implementation; the creation of tools by each government to protect tobacco control policy from interference by the tobacco industry; the cooperation with regional and international intergovernmental organizations (IGOs); and the use of financial resources for effective implementation.

The treaty takes a comprehensive approach to tobacco control, addressing a wide range of policy areas, including pricing and taxation of tobacco products; protection from exposure to tobacco smoke; regulation of the contents of tobacco products and product disclosures; packaging and labelling; advertising, promotion and sponsorship; education and public awareness; tobacco dependence and cessation; illicit trade in tobacco products; protection of the environment; research and exchange of information; scientific and technical cooperation; and strengthening civil and criminal liability laws.

The notable absence in the treaty of any mention of international trade, particularly given that the subject of the treaty is an internationally-traded commodity, is notable. The question of whether public health or trade would prevail when the FCTC was examined for compatibility with other international agreements was hotly debated during the negotiations. Supported by civil society, the alliance of low- and middle-income countries fought for specific language that would prioritize public health over international trade policies when it came to tobacco control.[72] The African group sought to build on the 2001 Doha Declaration of the WTO Agreement on Trade-Related Intellectual Property Rights (TRIPs), which states that the TRIPs Agreement "does not and should not prevent Members from taking measures to protect public health ... the agreement can and should be interpreted in a manner supportive of WTO Members' right to protect public health."[73]

The "Big Four" and several other high-income countries vigorously opposed such provisions. Consensus was ultimately forged around what is now the first line of the Preamble to the FCTC: "The Parties to this Convention, *Determined* to give priority to their right to protect public health . ... " In addition, Article 2.2 provides that although the FCTC "shall in no way affect the right of Parties to enter into bilateral and multilateral agreements" on issues relevant to the FCTC, those agreements should be "compatible" with the obligations created by the FCTC. The expectation was that this language would ensure that Parties' obligations under the FCTC would be interpreted as being consistent with international trade obligations, as required by the Vienna Convention on the

72 Hadii M. Mamudu et al., *International trade versus Public Health during the FCTC Negotiations, 1999–2003*, 20 TOBACCO CONTROL e3 (2011).

73 WTO, Decision, DOHA Ministerial 2001: Declaration on the Trips Agreement and Public Heath, 41 I.L.M. 755 (2002).

Law of Treaties (VCLT).[74] Today, these provisions in the text and the intent underlying them provide Parties with vital tools to insulate their implementation measures against trade-related attacks.[75]

B *Governance and Development of the FCTC*

The FCTC established two bodies to oversee its functioning, the Conference of the Parties (COP) and a permanent Secretariat. As the governing body of the FCTC, the COP is the primary decision-making body for all treaty matters. Its tasks include reviewing implementation of the treaty; setting priorities; drafting and adopting implementation guidelines and protocols; adopting declarations, strategies, plans, programmes, policies, or any other measures deemed necessary for the full and effective implementation of the treaty; establishing any necessary subsidiary bodies; establishing working groups on particular aspects of the treaty; overseeing the work of the Convention Secretariat, which is housed within the WHO; and approving the Secretariat's budget and work plan.

The COP has met eight times since the FCTC entered into force and now meets regularly every two years.

The rapid negotiation and entry into force of the treaty appears to have foreshadowed its equally rapid development as a legal instrument. Between 2006 and 2016, the COP adopted Implementation Guidelines (IGs) for almost all of the substantive articles of the treaty and four declarations.[76] In addition, in 2012 the COP adopted its first additional hard international law instrument, a protocol to eliminate illicit trade in tobacco products, which entered into force on September 25, 2018.

C *A Hybrid of Soft and Hard Law*

Professor Allyn Taylor originally conceived of the FCTC as a series of hard international law instruments: a framework convention, to be negotiated by all the Member States of the WHO, would be followed by more detailed topic-specific protocols that would be negotiated by the parties to the framework convention.[77] The original framework convention would establish a "general

---

74 Vienna Convention on the Law of Treaties, May 23, 1969, 1155 U.N.T.S. 331, 8 I.L.M. 679 (1969).

75 The value of this preambular language was clearly illustrated in the adoption, at COP4, of the Punta del Este Declaration, which focused on strengthening the implementation and protection of public health policies in relation to tobacco control.

76 Philip Morris Brands Sàrl v. Oriental Republic of Uruguay, ICSID Case No. ARB/10/7 at [302] (July 2016).

77 Allyn L. Taylor, *An International Regulatory Strategy for Global Tobacco Control*, 21 YALE J. INT'L L. 257 (1996).

system of governance" for tobacco control and contain broadly stated goals. Each of the goals could then be elaborated through protocols as separate legally binding agreements, which could be either mandatory or optional for the parties to the framework convention.[78] At the time, this 'framework/protocol' approach was perceived to be the best way to obtain "political consensus and significant action on tobacco control."[79]

However, what emerged from the negotiations was more than a "general system of governance" with broad goals. It also contained a number of obligations and detailed provisions related to specific tobacco control policy measures like protection from exposure to tobacco smoke, packaging and labelling of tobacco products, and prohibitions on advertising and promotion of tobacco products, among others. In essence, the FCTC became a hybrid of hard and soft law elements containing both "shalls" and "shoulds" throughout its text.

The reason for its somewhat unusual hybrid composition goes back to the battles fought during the negotiations between the mainly low- and middle-income countries and the "Big Four" and other countries that did not want to support legally binding language. The low- and middle-income countries were concerned that it would take several years and a lot more funding to negotiate a set of detailed protocols and therefore pushed the INB relentlessly for binding language within the framework model. In consequence, the treaty includes both significant, overarching statements of principle as well as a range of substantive obligations for the implementation of national tobacco control policies.

D *Hard v. Soft Interpretations of the FCTC*

The legally binding nature of some provisions of the FCTC has sparked considerable dispute. Some argue that the FCTC purposefully includes ambiguous language to afford countries broad discretion in their implementation of tobacco control measures.[80] Likewise, there is dispute about the binding nature of the IGs with some countries, including China and Japan, arguing that the IGs are not binding and that they are obligated only to implement the tobacco control policy measures detailed in the actual text of the treaty.

78 This "framework/protocol" approach to treaty making has been the preferred strategy for complex environmental issues since the Montreal Protocol regime was developed between 1985–1990.

79 Daniel Bodansky, *The Framework Convention/Protocol Approach* 40, WHO/NCD/TFI/99.1, https://apps.who.int/iris/handle/10665/65355 (last visited June 14, 2019).

80 Lawrence O. Gostin & Devi Sridhar, *Global health and the Law*, 370 NEW ENG. J. OF MED. 1732 (2014).

A strong argument can be made, however, that the FCTC and its IGs do provide a legally binding framework for Parties to implement certain tobacco control measures.[81] Under the VCLT,[82] which codifies the customary law rules of treaty interpretation, the actual text of each provision of the FCTC should be interpreted in "good faith" and in the context of the treaty's objective, preamble, and principles. Furthermore, under Article 31(3) of the VCLT, the FCTC IGs, all of which were adopted by consensus at sessions of the COP, "*shall* be taken into account" as "subsequent agreements between the parties regarding the interpretation of the treaty or the application of its provisions."

Further reinforcing this view, Article 2.1 of the FCTC encourages Parties to the treaty to implement measures beyond those required in the treaty and emphasizes that "nothing in these instruments shall prevent a Party from imposing stricter requirements that are consistent with their provisions and are in accordance with international law." The treaty, then, is the "floor" for tobacco control measures domestically and internationally—not the "ceiling."

In this regard, Article 5 of the FCTC also sets out two critical obligations: "The Parties *shall* cooperate in the formulation of ... guidelines for the implementation of the Convention"[83] and "[t]he Parties *shall* ... adopt and implement *effective* legislative ... and other measures for preventing and reducing tobacco consumption, nicotine addiction and exposure to tobacco smoke."[84] The use of the descriptor 'effective' is particularly important because the science on nicotine addition, tobacco use, and the effects of tobacco marketing, among other aspects, is continually evolving. To ensure that governments continually use the best methods for reducing consumption of tobacco products, implementation of the treaty—the text of which was finalized in 2003—must be allowed to evolve through the development of IGs. Therefore, any apparent "soft law" language in either the treaty or the IGs is intended to allow room for continuously evolving scientific and technical standards. In this way, the treaty and the IGs set a "floor" or a baseline set of obligations that must be continuously assessed against new evidence and best practices.

In the past few years, various courts of law and international tribunals have substantiated this view and emphasized the integral relationship between the

81 Jonathan Liberman, *The Power of the WHO FCTC: Understanding its Legal Weight and Status*, *in* THE GLOBAL TOBACCO EPIDEMIC AND THE LAW, (Ad Mitchell & Tania Voon, ed., 2014).

82 Vienna Convention on the Law of Treaties, May 23, 1969, 1155 U.N.T.S. 331; 8 I.L.M. 679 (1969).

83 FCTC, *supra* note 68, Art. 5.4.

84 *Id.*

FCTC and its IGs. For example, Article 11 of the FCTC requires that warning labels on packages of tobacco products should cover "50 [percent] or more ... but no less than 30 [percent]" of each side of the pack. However, evidence gathered since the FCTC went into force has shown that larger warnings are more effective and in response, governments around the world have passed laws increasing the size to well above 50 percent, including up to 90 percent in some cases. The tobacco industry has challenged these laws, arguing that they are arbitrary or unjustifiable. In the vast majority of cases, courts have rejected these arguments on the basis that they do not align with the goals of the FCTC and its IGs.

In one case, the Sri Lankan Supreme Court specifically referred to the discretion in Article 2.1 for Parties to implement measures beyond those required by the treaty in defending larger warning labels.[85] Similarly, the Court of Justice of the European Union upheld a law requiring 65 percent warning labels and specifically referred to the recommendation in the IGs that Parties consider warnings larger than 50 percent and aim to cover as much of the display areas as possible, because the effectiveness of warnings increases with their size.[86] The Court also noted that the FCTC and its IGs have a "decisive influence" on the content of laws adopted pursuant to them.[87] The UK High Court also made a number of strong statements about both the FCTC and its IGs in a decision on plain packaging, describing them as important and relevant considerations, as a "consensus formed at the broadest of international levels, i.e. amongst 180 states worldwide" and that "under the FCTC ... contracting States were urged to go beyond the mandatory measures in the FCTC."[88] Finally, a key aspect of the ICSID Tribunal's determination in the Uruguay investment claim discussed below, was the fact that the challenged measures, which went far beyond the "hard law" obligations in the FCTC and its IGs, were "adopted in fulfillment

85 In the matter of Article 122(1)(b) of the Constitution [2015] S.C. (SD) No. 2/2015, https://www.tobaccocontrollaws.org/litigation/decisions/lk-00000000-in-the-matter-of-article-1221b (last visited June 14, 2019).

86 Case C-547/14, Philip Morris Brands SARL v. Sec'y of State for Health, ECLI:EU:C:2016:325 (May 4, 2016), *available at* http://curia.europa.eu/juris/document/document.jsf?text=&docid=177724&pageIndex=0&doclang=EN&mode=lst&dir=&occ=-first&part=1&cid=733433 (last visited June 14, 2019).

87 Case C-547/14, Philip Morris Brands SARL v. Sec'y of State for Health, ECLI:EU:C:2016:325 (May 4, 2016), *available at* http://curia.europa.eu/juris/document/document.jsf?text=&-docid=177724&pageIndex=0 (last visited June 14, 2019).

88 BAT et al., v. Sec. of State for Health [2016] EWHC 1169 (Admin), CO/2322/2015, CO/2323/2015, CO/2352/2015, CO/2601/2015 & CO/2706/2015, [258, 260, 370, 373, 464 & 901] (Queen's Bench Div.), https://www.judiciary.uk/wp-content/uploads/2016/05/bat-v-doh.judgment.pdf (last visited June 14, 2019).

of Uruguay's national and international legal obligations for the protection of public health."[89]

V The Impact of the FCTC

Following the conclusion of the negotiations, a senior vice-president for corporate affairs at Philip Morris International advised delegates attending a tobacco industry conference that whether or not the FCTC ever entered into force, it had already had a significant influence in that it had "accelerated the pace of regulation in individual countries."[90] That speaks for itself in regard to the impact of the FCTC from the perspective of the tobacco industry but it does not paint the whole picture. The FCTC has transformed tobacco control from a domestic public health issue to a topic of global importance. And, as predicted by Dr. Brundtland at the start of the treaty negotiations, it has created a public health movement that continues to advance effective tobacco control globally.

Today, not only tobacco control advocates but also significant numbers of people around the world recognise that tobacco products are not normal consumer products and that the industry that continues to manufacture and market them is contemptible. Through regular meetings of the COP, the FCTC has greatly strengthened the capacity of governments to implement effective tobacco control measures and to fight tobacco industry interference in policy making, and it continues to provide the platform essential for the sharing of experiences, expertise, and capacity among and between governments and civil society organizations. It has acted as a catalyst for the formation and subsequent strengthening of domestic and transnational civil society coalitions and it has brought new resources—political, financial and human—into the field.[91]

A *Official Ten-Year Assessment by the COP*

At its Sixth Session (October 2014), the COP mandated the Convention Secretariat to convene an Expert Group to conduct an impact assessment of the

---

89 Philip Morris Brands Sàrl v. Oriental Republic of Uruguay, ICSID Case No. ARB/10/7 at [302] (July 2016).

90 D. Davies, Senior V.P., Corp. Aff., Philip Morris Intl., Speech at TABEXPO: External Forces: Facing the Future (November 26, 2003).

91 Jonathan Liberman, *Four COPs and Counting: Achievements, Underachievements and Looming Challenges in the Early Life of the WHO FCTC Conference of the Parties*, 21 TOBACCO CONTROL 215 (2012).

FCTC. The report was presented at the Seventh Session of the COP in November 2016.[92] It reflected that in the ten years that the FCTC had been in force there had been "remarkable developments in global tobacco control," and while it would never be possible to identify precisely how many new tobacco control measures were directly or indirectly attributable to the treaty, and that implementation of the treaty was variable, the FCTC had played a "critical role as an authoritative and agreed catalyst and a framework for action." Furthermore, Parties that had implemented FCTC policy measures at high levels had experienced "greater reductions in smoking prevalence."

B *Legislation That References the FCTC*

In order to fulfil their treaty obligations, most Parties have had to pass or amend their domestic tobacco control legislation. This more narrow legal focus provides another measure of the impact of the FCTC. One hundred thirty-five laws from seventy-five countries and the European Union incorporate the FCTC in legislative objectives, definitions, and/or substantive provisions of their tobacco control legislation or policy, and a small number of laws contain multiple references to the FCTC. [93] The vast majority, more than 100 references, mention the FCTC in the preamble or introduction to the law, which states the law's overall purpose. Many of the references acknowledge that the country concerned has ratified the FCTC or is adopting the law in fulfilment of its FCTC obligations.

C *Legal Challenges to the Implementation of the FCTC*

Given the posture of the well-resourced tobacco industry, it is unsurprising that tobacco control measures have faced vigorous legal challenges—both domestic and international— since the FCTC went into force. The significant increase in litigation against tobacco control measures since 2005 when the Convention entered into force is not coincidental. Rather, it is a calculated strategy by tobacco companies, as illustrated by a statement made in 2010 by Louis Camilleri, Former Chair & CEO, Philip Morris International, that his company would "continue to use all necessary resources and extensive stakeholder

92 Conference of the Parties to the WHO Framework Convention on Tobacco Control, Delhi, India, November 7–12, 2016, *Impact assessment of the WHO FCTC: Report by the Expert Group*, http://www.who.int/fctc/cop/cop7/FCTC_COP_7_6_EN.pdf?ua=1 (last visited June 14, 2019).

93 *See* TOBACCO CONTROL LAWS, Home Page, http://www.tobaccocontrollaws.org/legislation/ (last visited June 14, 2019). (providing the Tobacco Control Laws' database containing laws from 205 countries and the European Union.).

engagement and, where necessary, litigation, to actively challenge unreasonable regulatory proposals."[94] And it goes almost without saying that in the eyes of the tobacco industry almost all regulatory proposals are, by their very nature, "unreasonable."

The FCTC has been a bulwark for evidence-based tobacco control measures around the world. It has been invoked successfully by governments defending their tobacco control measures from the tobacco industry and its associates; by civil society organizations in their efforts to hold their governments accountable to their obligations under the FCTC and compel higher standards for tobacco control measures; by domestic courts in handing down decisions on a variety of tobacco control measures; and by two Parties, Australia and Uruguay, in defending their tobacco control measures in the WTO and in arbitration at the International Centre for Settlement of Investment Disputes (ICSID) of the *World Bank, respectively.*[95]

The cases indicate a widespread acceptance of and reliance on the FCTC and its IGs when interpreting domestic tobacco control law. Judges and arbitrators have upheld the constitutionality of domestic tobacco control measures and reinforced the obligation of Parties to the FCTC to implement such measures. They have also referenced tobacco control measures both in the context of the promotion of a fundamental right to health and as a justification for limiting the tobacco industry's claims to freedom of expression, rights to property, the right to commerce, and the right to personal development.[96]

In relation to legal challenges to the FCTC and its IGs as hard international law, the growth in one particular tobacco control measure—plain or standardized packaging of tobacco products—is noteworthy. The measure, contained

---

94 Morgan Stanley Global Consumer & Retail Conference, New York, NY (Nov. 17, 2010), http://media.corporate-ir.net/media_files/IROL/14/146476/MorganStanleySLIDESFINAL1.pdf (last visited June 14, 2019).

95 Monique E. Muggli et al., *Tracking the Relevance of the WHO Framework Convention on Tobacco Control in Legislation and Litigation through the Online Resource, Tobacco Control Laws*, 23 TOBACCO CONTROL 457 (2013); MCCABE CENTRE FOR LAW AND CANCER & THE CAMPAIGN FOR TOBACCO-FREE KIDS, REPORT ON WHO FCTC IN LEGISLATION AND LITIGATION (2015), http://www.who.int/fctc/cop/FCTC-in-Legislation-and-Litigation-McCabe-Centre_TFK.pdf?ua=1 (last visited June 14, 2019); MCCABE CENTRE FOR LAW AND CANCER & THE CAMPAIGN FOR TOBACCO-FREE KIDS, REPORT ON WHO FCTC IN LEGISLATION AND LITIGATION (Aug. 2015), http://www.who.int/fctc/cop/FCTC-in-Legislation-and-Litigation-McCabe-Centre_TFK.pdf?ua=1 (last visited June 14, 2019).

96 *See, e.g.*, Muggli et al., *supra* note 95, at 457; MCCABE CENTRE FOR LAW AND CANCER & THE CAMPAIGN FOR TOBACCO-FREE KIDS, REPORT ON WHO FCTC IN LEGISLATION AND LITIGATION, *supra* note 95.

not in the treaty but in its IGs, was first implemented by Australia in December 2012, followed by the United Kingdom, France, Hungary, Norway, New Zealand, and Ireland. The measures were challenged domestically in Australia, the United Kingdom, France, and Norway and also referred to the European Union Court of Justice in cases of the United Kingdom and France. Initially, the legal challenges had a chilling effect on other countries, but resounding victories in domestic courts and in the EU Court of Justice have spurred countries to follow suit. As of September 2019, seven countries have fully implemented plain or standardized packaging measures; eleven have adopted laws but not implemented them, twelve countries are formally considering adopting plain or standardized packaging, and a further six countries have given a political commitment to do so. All of the judgements handed down both referred to the FCTC and its IGs as the most authoritative source of hard law on tobacco control measures and the most credible source of evidence for those measures and also underlined the fact that the governments concerned were merely giving effect to their obligations as Parties to the FCTC when they passed their laws.

In the ICSID matter, in February 2010, Philip Morris International (PMI) and its Uruguayan subsidiary, Abal Hermanos S.A., challenged the Uruguayan government's new packaging and labelling measures alleging a breach of a bilateral investment treaty (BIT) between Switzerland, where PMI is headquartered, and Uruguay. PMI claimed that Uruguay's measures negatively affected PMI's investment. Among other things, PMI claimed that its property had been expropriated by reducing the size of the area where it could display its trademarks; that it had a legitimate expectation that its intellectual property would be respected; that Uruguay had failed to protect its investments; that it had been treated unfairly and inequitably; and that Uruguay's tobacco measures were unreasonable and discriminatory. In July 2016, the Tribunal decided the case in favor of Uruguay on all points of the law, referring specifically to the FCTC as the evidence base for its decision, and it emphasized that there was, in light of the strength of the FCTC, no need for states to recreate that evidence base locally. In addition, PMI was ordered to pay the costs of the Tribunal and USD 7 million out of the USD 10 million that Uruguay had spent in defending its tobacco control measures.[97]

The WTO Panel that heard the dispute between Indonesia and the US in the case about clove- and menthol-flavored cigarettes referred extensively to the FCTC and to its IGs on the contents of tobacco products, even though neither

---

97 WHO FCTC Knowledge Hub on Legal Challenges to the WHO FCTC Implementation, *available at* http://www.mccabecentre.org/knowledge-hub/current/uruguaygraphics (last visited June 14, 2019).

country is a Party to the FCTC. The Panel referenced the IGs as drawing on "the best available scientific evidence and experience of the Parties." The fact that FCTC has been used in a matter where neither party had any obligation to implement the FCTC measures provides an outstanding validation of the treaty as a set of international norms for tobacco control.

In another matter before the WTO, Honduras, the Dominican Republic, Cuba, and Indonesia registered complaints against Australia's plain packaging measures, which effectively remove tobacco companies' logos from tobacco products for sale in Australia. The four countries argued that Australia's law breaches the WTO's General Agreement on Tariffs and Trade (GATT), its Agreement on Technical Barriers to Trade (TBT Agreement), and its Agreement on Trade-Related Aspects of Intellectual Property Rights (TRIPS) claiming that plain packaging measures are discriminatory, more trade restrictive than necessary, and unjustifiably infringe on trademark rights.[98] Relying frequently on the FCTC to support its findings, on June 28, 2018 the Panel rejected all grounds of the complaint and ruled that plain packaging contributes to Australia's objective of reducing tobacco use and exposure to tobacco smoke; is not more trade restrictive than necessary; and is not an unjustifiable encumbrance on the use of trademarks in the course of trade.[99] Honduras has filed an appeal but, given the findings of fact in the matter, it is unlikely that the appeal will succeed.

VI Conclusion

For more than fifty years, an ever-increasing body of scientific evidence pointed emphatically to tobacco products as the cause of significant death and disease. The initial response of the WHA to the growing epidemic was a series of seventeen largely ineffective soft international law resolutions passed over a period of almost thirty years. The bold decision to try to reverse the course of the epidemic by negotiating a hard international law instrument instead, marked the turning point for tobacco control. The speed with which states

98 An initial overview of the WTO panel decision in Australia—Plain Packaging, *available at* http://untobaccocontrol.org/kh/legal-challenges/initial-overview-wto-panel-decision-australia-plain-packaging/ (last visited June 14, 2019).

99 Panel Report, *Australia—Certain Measures Concerning Trademarks, Geographical Indication and other Plain Packaging Requirements applicable to Tobacco Products and Packaging*, WT/DS435/R, WT/DS441/R, (June 28, 2018), https://www.wto.org/english/tratop_e/dispu_e/435_441_458_467r_e.pdf (last visited June 14, 2019).

ratified the FCTC is indicative of an acute awareness of the increasing effects of globalization on public health generally and in particular of the need to find global solutions to the tobacco epidemic—solutions that include holding the tobacco industry accountable for deceptive and unethical practices that range from marketing to young people to direct interference in policy making.

The role of civil society before and during the negotiations was paramount to the development of the treaty. The prevailing idea that non-state actors have a greater role to play in soft international law processes and are handicapped in participating in the creation of state-centered hard international law is simply not supported by FCTC experience. The depth of scientific and legal knowledge within civil society, which was accepted and fostered by the WHO and a significant number of its Member States, enabled it to exert a powerful influence in the drafting of the FCTC and its IGs, and there is no reason for that to change as the treaty is implemented around the world.

The FCTC and its IGs present a unique case study in the ongoing debate about the operation and effectiveness of hard and soft international law approaches to international policy issues. The initial battle between legal scholars and the WHO, as the secretariat of the WHA, over the form that the agreement would take was later reflected on the floor of the negotiating room as governments put forward both hard and soft international law formulations of text depending on the extent to which they were being influenced by the tobacco industry and whether or not they had the political will to encapsulate the unequivocal scientific evidence into treaty obligations.

The battle has continued in domestic courts and international tribunals like the WTO and ICSID as the tobacco industry has challenged tobacco product packaging and labelling measures based on the FCTC and its IGs. Fortunately for the health of people around the world, courts and tribunals, citing the FCTC and its IGs as authority, have resoundingly upheld the right of governments to pass and enforce effective tobacco control measures and in so doing, have solidified the hard international law nature of the FCTC and its IGs.

The FCTC experience can leave little doubt that the development and adoption of hard international law instruments can effect enormous social change and that civil society has an essential role to play in the process.

CHAPTER 9

Soft International Law and the Promotion of Financial Regulation and Responsibility

*Daniel D. Bradlow**

1 Introduction

Finance was largely a domestic matter when the current arrangements for global economic governance were established. Financial institutions were—and still are—creatures of national law. They primarily raised funds from depositors and investors in their domestic markets and allocated funds to borrowers based in their home countries. Their limited amount of international financial activity was largely funded from their home market. This domestic focus meant that national authorities could effectively regulate their financial sectors.[1] Consequently, the mandates of the two international financial organizations established after the Second World War did not expressly deal with the regulation and supervision of financial markets and institutions. The International Monetary Fund (IMF) focused on international monetary affairs, and the International Bank for Reconstruction and Development, the oldest member of the World Bank Group, focused on development finance.[2]

---

* SARCHI Professor of International Development Law and African Economic Relations. Email: danny.bradlow@up.ac.za. The author presented earlier versions of this chapter at the Wits Institute for Social and Economic Research (WISER) and at the symposium on "Finding the Human Face of Finance" organized by the Business and Human Rights Initiative, U. Connecticut. He thanks all the participants in these events and David Hunter for their helpful comments on these earlier drafts. He also thanks Nthope Mapefane for her research assistance and Mallika Sen for her help in preparing the chapter for publication.

1 *See generally* CHRIS BRUMMER, SOFT LAW AND THE GLOBAL FINANCIAL SYSTEM: RULE MAKING IN THE 21ST CENTURY (2d ed. 2015).

2 *See* Articles of Agreement of the IMF, 60 Stat. 1401, 2 U.N.T.S. 39, https://www.imf.org/external/pubs/ft/aa/pdf/aa.pdf (last visited Aug. 21, 2019); International Bank for Reconstruction and Development; Articles of Agreement, 2 U.N.T.S. 134, http://siteresources.worldbank.org/EXTABOUTUS/Resources/IBRDArticlesOfAgreement_links.pdf (last visited Aug. 21, 2019). The third entity established after World War II to deal with the global economy, the General Agreement on Tariffs and Trade's mandate was promoting free trade in goods. *See* General Agreement on Tariffs and Trade [GATT], Oct. 30, 1947, 61 Stat. A-11, 55 U.N.T.S. 194, https://www.wto.org/english/docs_e/legal_e/gatt47_e.pdf (last visited Aug. 21, 2019). The GATT was

 | DOI:10.1163/9789004417021_010

This approach was consistent with past practice. Historically, public international law has not played a role in the supervision and regulation of finance. There are no treaties or customary international law principles that are specifically applicable to the regulation and supervision of financial markets or of financial institutions.[3] These activities were viewed as the prerogative of the sovereign state.

The national focus of financial regulation and supervision[4] had two important policy implications. First, governments could manage their financial sectors in ways that they believed were supportive of their own broad economic policy objectives. For example, they could utilize whatever indicators they thought appropriate to measure the safety and soundness of their banks, and they could decide for themselves what types of activities banks and other financial institutions could undertake.

Second, governments could decide how to allocate the risks associated with the social, environmental, and human rights impacts of the activities undertaken in their jurisdictions. They could allow the sponsors of these activities to externalize these risks and thereby socialize their associated costs, or they could compel financial institutions and their clients to account for them in the planning and budgeting of their transactions.

The expansion of international trade and investment that followed the end of the Second World War ultimately undermined these arrangements. It generated demand for and facilitated the internationalization of finance and financial institutions. This trend was further enhanced by the collapse of the Bretton Woods system of relatively fixed exchange rates, technological developments, and the deregulation of finance. The result was that those financial institutions that had the requisite resources and capacity were able to expand

---

the chapter on commercial policy in the Havana Charter that was drafted to establish the International Trade Organization (ITO). The ITO, which was never established, did not deal with financial regulation. *See* U.N. CONFERENCE ON TRADE AND EMPLOYMENT, FINAL ACT AND RELATED DOCUMENTS, U.N. Doc. E/CONF.2/78, U.N. Sales No. 1948.II.D.4, https://www.wto.org/english/docs_e/legal_e/havana_e.pdf (last visited Aug. 21, 2019).

3 Formally, the sources of public international law are conventions, customary international law, and general principles of international law. Judicial decisions and the writings of the most highly qualified publicists are subsidiary sources. *See* Statute of the International Court of Justice, art. 38, ¶ 1, https://treaties.un.org/doc/Publication/MTDSG/Volume%20I/Chapter%20I/I-3.en.pdf (last visited Aug. 21, 2019).

4 Financial regulatory frameworks consist of both the institutional arrangements and the substantive standards that guide the operations and conduct of the financial sector and that are used by financial regulators in supervising the financial institutions subject to their authority. In the interests of efficiency, this chapter uses the terms "financial regulation" to refer to both regulation and supervision.

the scale of their cross-border operations and to increase the number of markets and countries in which they did business.[5]

The globalization of finance made it more difficult for national regulators to continue effectively regulating their country's financial sectors. It meant that financial institutions could structure their activities to avoid national regulations that they found unduly burdensome. It also generated uncertainty about how national authorities should share supervisory authority over their financial institutions' international activities. For example, which country's authority should be responsible for regulating the US dollar-based activities of the branch of an Italian bank in London?[6] How could regulators ensure that they could deal with the international consequences of the collapse of a German bank with outstanding obligations to correspondent banks in the United States? [7] These changes also opened up opportunities for financial institutions to engage in regulatory arbitrage. For example, a bank that operated globally could design a multi-national corporate structure that ensured that no single national regulator had full access to information on the bank and its activities. As a result, significant parts of its overall operations would be effectively unregulated.[8]

These developments pushed national financial regulators to look for ways to collaborate on formulating international financial regulatory standards that would help them each meet their responsibility to oversee their own country's financial sectors. These standards could also help ensure that there was a level playing field for all financial institutions operating internationally. Given that these regulators did not have the authority to negotiate binding international agreements, they developed non-binding international standards. The international financial regulatory standards discussed in this chapter and their social change objectives are summarized in Appendix 1 to this chapter.

At the same time, civil society groups were becoming concerned about the conduct of financial institutions. They contended, for example, that financial

5 *See generally* BARRY EICHENGREEN, GLOBALIZING CAPITAL: A HISTORY OF THE INTERNATIONAL MONETARY SYSTEM (2008).

6 For general history on the development of the Eurodollar market *see, e.g.*, CHARLES KINDLEBERGER, A FINANCIAL HISTORY OF WESTERN EUROPE ch. 24 (6th ed. 2015); CHARLES GOODHART, THE BASEL COMMITTEE ON BANKING SUPERVISION: THE EARLY YEARS:1974–1997 (2011).

7 *See* Emmanuel Mourlon-Druol, *Trust is Good, Control is Better: The 1974 Herstatt Bank Crisis and its Implications for International Regulatory Reform*, 57 J. BUS. HIST. 311 (2015); GOODHART, *supra* note 6.

8 *See* INQUIRY INTO THE SUPERVISION OF BANK OF CREDIT AND COMMERCE INTERNATIONAL LJ BINGHAM, House of Commons Papers, 1992, https://archive.org/details/InquiryIntoTheSupervisionOfTheBankOfCreditAndCommerceInternational (last visited Aug. 21, 2019).

institutions were funding projects around the world that had significant negative social and environmental impacts[9]. They also noted that states appeared unable or unwilling to control these activities. The financial institutions' home states were reluctant to assert extra-territorial jurisdiction over these institutions because this would encroach onto the prerogatives of borrowers' home states. The latter group of states, on the other hand, were opposed to outsiders attempting to usurp their prerogatives to allocate the environmental and social risks associated with activities subject to their jurisdiction.

Civil society groups and their allies responded to this regulatory gap by developing international standards, which can be called international financial responsibility standards, clarified, *inter alia,* the social, human rights and environmental responsibilities of financial institutions.[10] Given that states showed limited interest in these initiatives, their proponents focused on formulating soft international law standards. They hoped that a combination of exposure to reputational risk and moral suasion would cause financial institutions and/or their regulatory authorities to comply with these standards. The international financial responsibility standards discussed in this chapter and their social change objectives are summarized in Appendix 2 to this chapter.

These two sets of international soft law standards offer useful insights into the factors affecting the efficacy of soft law as a vehicle for promoting change.

This chapter is divided into five sections. The second section will discuss soft international law instruments that establish common standards for the regulation and supervision of the financial sector (hereinafter "international financial regulatory standards"). The third section will discuss some soft international law initiatives dealing with the financial sector's responsibilities for managing the social and environmental impacts of their operations. (hereinafter "financial responsibility standards"). The fourth section draws some lessons about the use of soft law in promoting change. The final section is a conclusion.

II International Financial Regulatory Standards

The international standard setting bodies (SSBs) provide participating national financial regulators with a forum in which they can develop international

---

9 *See, e.g.,* World Commission on Environment and Development, *Our Common Future,* U.N. Doc. A/42/427, annex (1987); World Commission on Dams, *Dams and Development: A New Framework For Decision-Making,* (2000), https://archive.org/details/DamsAndDevelopmentANewFrameworkForDecision-making (last visited Aug. 21, 2019.

10 *See infra* Section III.

non-binding standards that either facilitate coordinated and efficient regulation of financial activity or express their views on best supervisory practices. They can each use the standards to adapt their own national regulatory framework so that it continues to effectively oversee safe and efficient financial sectors.

Since space does not permit a full discussion of all the SSBs, the paper focuses on four of the most prominent SSBs. The first three are the forums in which the regulators of the banking, securities, and insurance industries meet. The fourth is an inter-governmental task force dealing with the issues of anti-money laundering and counter-terrorist financing.

A *Basel Committee on Banking Supervision*

The most prominent SSB is the Basel Committee on Banking Supervision (BCBS), which is the "primary global standard-setter for the prudential regulation of banks."[11] Its members are representatives of independent supervisory agencies or central banks from twenty-eight countries. They are expected, but not legally obliged, to incorporate the standards that they have developed in the BCBS into their national laws and regulations.[12] In addition, despite its limited membership, the BCBS's mandate is to "strengthen the regulation, supervision and practices of banks worldwide."[13]

The BCBS has developed two prominent international standards. The first establishes a framework to promote the resilience of banks.[14] There have been three iterations of this standard. The most recent, Basel III, uses three tests—a risk-weighted capital to assets ratio, a liquidity coverage ratio, and a net stable funding ratio—to assess the adequacy of a bank's capital and funding

11 *See About the BCBS*, BIS, https://www.bis.org/bcbs/about/overview.htm?m=3%7C14%7C573 (last visited Aug. 21, 2019).

12 *See Implementation of the Basel Standards*, BIS, https://www.bis.org/bcbs/implementation.htm?m=3%7C14%7C587 (last visited Aug. 21, 2019).

13 *See About the BCBS*, BIS, https://www.bis.org/bcbs/about/overview.htm?m=3%7C14%7C573 (last visited Aug. 21, 2019).

14 *See* Basel Committee on Banking Supervision, *International Convergence of Capital Measurement and Capital Standards*, BIS (July 1988), http://www.bis.org/publ/bcbs04a.pdf (last visited Aug. 21, 2019); Basel Committee on Banking Supervision, *Basel II: International Convergence of Capital Measurement and Capital Standards: a Revised Framework*, BIS (June 2004), http://www.bis.org/publ/bcbs107.pdf (last visited Aug. 21, 2019); Basel Committee on Banking Supervision, *Basel III: A Global Regulatory Framework for More Resilient Banks and Banking Systems*, BIS (December 2010), http://www.bis.org/publ/bcbs189_dec2010.pdf (last visited Aug. 21, 2019).

arrangements.[15] It also establishes three criteria that investors and regulators can use to assess the robustness of financial institutions. These are the adequacy of its capital, its governance and risk management practices, and the quality of its public disclosures.[16]

The second is the Core Principles for Effective Banking Supervision,[17] which establishes twenty-nine principles with which all banking supervisory authorities should conform if they are to effectively implement their mandates to maintain safe and sound banks in their home countries. The principles deal with the powers and functions of banking supervisors and with their responsibilities relating to the governance of banks, their risk management practices, and compliance with supervisory standards.

B *International Organization of Securities Commissions*

The second SSB is the International Organization of Securities Commissions (IOSCO). Its membership consists of the regulators of securities markets in 115 jurisdictions.[18] It "develops, implements, and promotes adherence to internationally recognized standards for securities regulation."[19] Its most prominent standard is the IOSCO Objectives and Principles of Securities Regulation.[20] These thirty-eight principles are the organization's "main instrument to develop and implement internationally recognized and consistent standards of regulation, oversight, and enforcement."[21] IOSCO expects its members to incorporate these principles into their domestic regulatory frameworks. They deal with the powers and functions of the regulators of security markets, protection of investors, ensuring that securities markets are "fair, efficient and transparent,"[22] and the management of systemic risk in financial markets. IOSCO also promotes cooperation among security regulators in different countries.[23]

---

15 *See* Basel Committee on Banking Supervision, *Basel III: A Global Regulatory Framework for More Resilient Banks and Banking Systems*, BIS (December 2010), http://www.bis.org/publ/bcbs189_dec2010.pdf (last visited Aug. 21, 2019).

16 *Id.*

17 *See* Basel Committee on Banking Supervision, *Core Principles for Effective Banking Supervision*, BIS (Sept. 2012), http://www.bis.org/publ/bcbs230.pdf (last visited Aug. 21, 2019).

18 *See About International Organization of Securities Commissions [IOSCO]*, IOSCO, https://www.iosco.org/about/?subsection=about_iosco (last visited Aug. 21, 2019).

19 *Id.*

20 *See IOSCO Objectives and Principles of Securities Regulation*, IOSCO, https://www.iosco.org/about/pdf/IOSCO-Fact-Sheet.pdf (last visited Aug. 21, 2019).

21 *Id.*

22 *Id.*

23 *See, e.g.*, *IOSCO Multilateral Memorandum of Understanding*, FINANCIAL STABILITY BOARD, http://www.fsb.org/2012/05/cos_020501/ (last visited Aug. 21, 2019).

C *International Association of Insurance Supervisors*

The third SSB is the International Association of Insurance Supervisors (IAIS). It represents "insurance regulators and supervisors of more than 200 jurisdictions constituting ninety-seven percent of the world's insurance premiums."[24] Its goal is to promote consistent and effective regulation of the insurance industry in order to ensure that insurance markets are fair, safe, and stable. Its primary international standard is the Insurance Core Principles that sets out twenty-six principles for establishing an effective insurance supervisory authority that is independent, accountable, and transparent and that can promote a fair, safe, and stable insurance industry.[25]

D *Financial Action Task Force*

The fourth SSB is the Financial Action Task Force (FATF) to which representatives from thirty-five governments and two regional organizations belong. [26] An additional two countries and twenty-one organizations participate as observers in the work of FATF. Its objectives are "to set standards and promote effective implementation of legal, regulatory, and operational measures for combating money laundering, terrorist financing, and other related threats to the integrity of the international financial system."[27] Pursuant to this objective, FATF has developed the 40+8 "Recommendations,"[28] which establish a framework for combatting money laundering and the financing of terrorism that participating countries are expected to implement. The primary focus of these recommendations is on know-your-customer rules.[29]

E *"Enforcing" the Soft International Financial Regulatory Standards*

Since none of the international standards discussed above are legally binding, states can refuse to incorporate them into their domestic law without incurring

---

24 INTERNATIONAL ASSOCIATION OF INSURANCE SUPERVISORS, http://www.iaisweb.org/home (last visited Aug. 21, 2019).

25 International Association of Insurance Supervisors, *Insurance Core Principles*, INTERNATIONAL ASSOCIATION OF INSURANCE SUPERVISORS, http://www.iaisweb.org/page/supervisory-material/insurance-core-principles/file/58067/insurance-core-principles-updated-november-2015. (last visited Aug. 21, 2019)

26 *About*, FINANCIAL ACTION TASK FORCE, http://www.fatf-gafi.org/about/ (last visited Aug. 21, 2019).

27 *Id.*

28 *FATF Recommendations*, FINANCIAL ACTION TASK FORCE, http://www.fatfgafi.org/media/fatf/documents/recommendations/pdfs/FATF_Recommendations.pdf (last visited Aug. 21, 2019).

29 James T. Gathii, *The Financial Action Task Force and Global Administrative Law*, 2010 J. PROF. LAW. 197.

international legal responsibility. Nevertheless, there are some means for *de facto* enforcing them.

First, the IMF and World Bank have included these standards among the twelve standards that they use in preparing their individual country Reports on Standards and Codes (ROSCs).[30] These reports, which assess how well the country is complying with the provisions of these standards and codes, form part of the IMF's and World Bank's financial sector assessments (FSAP)[31] of their interested member states. This information is made public at the request of the member state. It may influence the technical assistance the IMF and World Bank offer the member state. In principle, the IMF and the World Bank can also use this information in developing the conditions that they attach to any financing that either of them offers to the member state. Furthermore, if the information is publicly available, credit rating agencies and the country's potential investors and creditors, may use it in assessing the risk profile and creditworthiness of the state.[32] Given that the SSBs have limited membership, it is ironic that their standards may, because of the ROSCs and the

30 IMF, *Standards and Codes—Implementing the Fund's Medium-Term Strategy and the Recommendations of the 2005 Review of the Initiative* (June 29, 2006), http://www.imf.org/external/np/pp/eng/2006/062906.pdf (last visited Aug. 21, 2019). The 12 Standards and Codes, include the following: IMF's Special Data Dissemination Standard/General Data Dissemination System (SDDS/GDDS), IMF's Code of Good Practices on Fiscal Transparency, IMF's Code of Good Practices on Transparency in Monetary and Financial Policies, Basel Committee's Core Principles for Effective Banking Supervision (BCP), International Organization of Securities Commissions' (IOSCO) Objectives and Principles for Securities Regulation, International Association of Insurance Supervisors' (IAIS) Insurance Supervisory Principle, Committee on Payments and Settlements Systems (CPSS) Core Principles for Systemically Important Payments Systems and CPSS-IOSCO Joint Task Force's Recommendations for Securities Settlement Systems, Financial Action Task Force's (FATF's) 40+8 Recommendations, OECD's Principles of Corporate Governance, International Accounting Standards Board's International Accounting Standards (IAS), International Federation of Accountants' International Standards on Auditing, Principles and Guidelines for Effective Insolvency and Creditor Rights Systems (this is under review by the staff of IMF and World Bank and UNCITRAL commission); *see also List of Standards, Codes, and Principles Useful for Bank and Fund Operational Work and for Which Reports on the Observance of Standards and Codes are Produced*, IMF, http://www.imf.org/external/standards/scnew.htm.

31 *Factsheet: The Financial Sector Assessment Programme*, IMF (Mar. 8, 2018), https://www.imf.org/external/np/exr/facts/fsap.htm; *Reports on the Observations of Standards and Codes*, WORLD BANK, http://beta.worldbank.org/en/programs/rosc (last visited Aug. 21, 2019).

32 *See generally*, Technical Committee of the International Organization of Securities Commissions, *The Role of Credit Rating Agencies in Structured Finance Markets: Final Report* (May 2008), http://www.iosco.org/library/pubdocs/pdf/IOSCOPD270.pdf (last visited Aug. 21, 2019) (explaining the use of ROSCs by credit rating agencies and investors).

FSAPs, become more enforceable in countries that do not participate in their formulation than in some of those that do.

The Financial Stability Board (FSB)[33] provides another more limited *de facto* means of enforcement. The membership of the FSB consists of the financial supervisory authorities from twenty-four countries and the EU, four international organizations and 6 international SSBs, including those discussed above. It promotes financial stability by, *inter alia*, coordinating the activities of "national financial authorities and international standard-setting bodies as they work toward developing strong regulatory, supervisory, and other financial sector policies."[34] It uses these standards in its peer review process.[35] These peer reviews, or at least the fact that a country's authorities have undergone peer review, may become public.[36]

The BCBS also has a limited *de facto* means of enforcement. Its Regulatory Consistency Assessment Program (RCAPs) is a peer review process that enables the members of the BCBS to assess how well the participating regulatory authorities are complying with the Basel III standards.[37]

A final form of *de facto* enforcement operates through financial markets. A state's failure to comply with these standards can adversely affect its and its public and private sector entities access to financial markets and the interest rates that they pay.

III Financial Responsibility Standards

There are a substantial number of international financial responsibility standards. They fall into two categories. First, there are standards developed by the official sector consisting of representatives of states or their agencies. Second,

---

33 *About the FSB*, FINANCIAL STABILITY BOARD, http://www.fsb.org/about/ (last visited Aug. 21, 2019).

34 *Id.*

35 *Peer Reviews*, FINANCIAL STABILITY BOARD, https://www.fsb.org/work-of-the-fsb/implementation-monitoring/peer_reviews/ (last visited Aug. 21, 2019).

36 *See Basel III—Implementation*, FINANCIAL STABILITY BOARD, http://www.fsb.org/what-we-do/implementation-monitoring/monitoring-of-priority-areas/basel-iii/ (last visited Aug. 21, 2019); *see also* Implementation of Reforms in Priority Areas by FSB Jurisdictions (as of Oct. 31, 2015), FINANCIAL STABILITY BOARD, http://www.fsb.org/wp-content/uploads/2015-Implementation-dashboard.pdf (last visited Aug. 21, 2019) (a table of countries who have undergone the peer review).

37 *Basel III—Implementation*, FINANCIAL STABILITY BOARD, http://www.fsb.org/what-we-do/implementation-monitoring/monitoring-of-priority-areas/basel-iii/ (last visited Aug. 21, 2019); *Implementation of the Basel Standards*, BIS, http://www.bis.org/bcbs/implementation.htm?m=3%7C14%7C587 (last visited Aug. 21, 2019).

there are the standards that civil society and/or the private business sector have developed. Space constraints do not permit a comprehensive discussion of all these standards and so only the most prominent examples in each category are discussed below.

A *Official Sector*

The standards developed by the official sector fall into two categories. The first is standards that aim to encourage more responsible business conduct in general. They are all applicable to the financial sector. The second consists of standards specifically designed for the financial sector.

1 Standards Generally Applicable to Business

The first example of a standard designed to improve the conduct of business is the OECD Guidelines on Multinational Enterprises (Guidelines), the most recent version of which was released in 2011.[38] It covers a broad range of issues, including human rights, employment, environment, competition, corruption, taxation, and transfers of technology.

Government representatives at the OECD developed the Guidelines as recommendations from participating governments to multinational enterprises (MNE s), including financial institutions, regarding the governments' views of what is responsible business conduct around the world.[39] The Guidelines are not binding on either the OECD member states or their MNE s. However, the states agree to encourage the MNE s in their jurisdiction to comply with these Guidelines in their transnational operations.[40]

One mechanism promotes compliance with the Guidelines. The participating states are expected to establish National Contact Points (NCP s),[41] *inter alia,* to receive complaints about compliance with the Guidelines. Consequently, in principle, financial institutions in OECD countries can be held accountable for their conduct through the NCPs in their home countries. In most cases, the NCP process results in a report that may become public but usually has

38 Organization for Economic Co-operation and Development [OECD], *Guidelines for Multinational Enterprises* (May 25, 2011), http://www.oecd.org/daf/inv/mne/48004323.pdf (last visited Aug. 21, 2019). The new section is based on the United Nations Guiding Principles on Business and Human Rights (UNGP s), and it closely tracks those provisions of the UNGP s dealing with the responsibilities of companies.

39 *Id.* at pt. I, art. I ¶ 4.

40 *Id.* at pt. I, art. I.

41 *Id.* at pt. I, art. I, ¶ 11; *see also* Birgitte E. Olsen & Karsten E. Sørensen, *Strengthening the Enforcement of CSR Guidelines: Finding a New Balance between Hard Law and Soft Law*, 41 LEGAL ISSUES ECON. INTEGRATION 9–35 (2014).

no other consequence. However, some countries, such as the Netherlands and Canada, are beginning to impose some sanctions on companies that have not complied with the Guidelines and do not address the issues raised in the NCP report.[42]

A second generally applicable international standard is the UN Guiding Principles on Business and Human Rights (UNGPs).[43] It consists of thirty-one non-binding principles that were unanimously adopted by the state representatives on the UN Human Rights Council in 2011. The UNGPs have three pillars, dealing with the obligations of states,[44] the responsibilities of companies,[45] and the need to offer remedies to affected parties.[46] The responsibility of companies to respect human rights means that they should avoid infringing on human rights and should address the adverse human rights impacts of their own operations and those in which they are directly involved or to which they contribute.[47] The principles also stipulate that businesses should have human rights policies that are approved at a high level in the company and are publicly available. The UNGPs clearly state that companies should follow due diligence procedures to identify, prevent, mitigate, and account for the human rights impacts of their operations. This process should assess actual and potential

42 Rolf H. Weber and Rainer Baisch, *Liability of Parent Companies for Human Rights Violations of Subsidiaries* 27(5) EUR. BUS. L. 669–695 (2016), https://ssrn.com/abstract=2625536 (last visited Aug. 21, 2019); Sander van't Foort & H Palm, *The Functioning of the Dutch National Contact Point During the Specific Instance Procedure*, 2(3) ARACÊ—DIREITOS HUMANOS EM REVISTA 8 (2015), https://arace.emnuvens.com.br/arace/article/download/50/35 (last visited Aug. 21, 2019).

43 U.N. Office of the High Comm'r for Human Rights [OHCHR], Guiding Principles on Business and Human Rights (UNGPs), U.N. Doc. HR/PUB/11/04 (2011), http://www.ohchr.org/Documents/Publications/GuidingPrinciplesBusinessHR_EN.pdf (last visited Aug. 21, 2019). Another norm of general application to companies is the U.N. Global Compact, which was developed by the U.N. secretariat, *The Ten Principles of the U.N. Global Compact*, U.N. GLOBAL COMPACT, https://www.unglobalcompact.org/what-is-gc/mission/principles (last visited Aug. 21, 2019).

44 OHCHR, *supra* note 43, at princs. 1–10.

45 *Id.* at princs. 11–24.

46 *Id.* at princs. 25–31.

47 The UNGPs make clear that for these purposes, "human rights" means the rights expressed in the International Covenant on Civil and Political Rights and on Economic, Social and Cultural Rights and the principles set out in the ILO's Declaration on Fundamental Principles and Rights at Work. *See* U.N. Human Rights Council, Guiding Principles on Business and Human Rights: Implementing the United Nations "Protect, Respect and Remedy" Framework, Princ. II (A) 13, U.N. Doc. A/HRC/17/31 (2011), http://www.ohchr.org/Documents/Issues/Business/A-HRC-17-31_AEV.pdf (last visited Aug. 21, 2019); *see also* Benjamin Thompson, *The Dutch Banking Sector Agreement on Human Rights: An Exercise in Regulation, Experimentation or Advocacy?* 14(2) UTRECHT L. R. 84–107 (2018), http://doi.org/10.18352/ulr.440 (last visited Aug. 21, 2019).

impacts that the company causes, to which it contributes, or which may be directly linked to its operations. The company should communicate how these impacts will be addressed and be monitored.

A small group of banks have formed the Thun Group to encourage the incorporation of the UNGPs into the operations of banks.[48] In fact, a number of significant international financial institutions have adopted human rights policies and/or expressed support for human rights in their public reports.[49]

In order to assist financial institutions to meet their responsibilities under the Guidelines and the UNGPs, the OECD, in 2014 prepared a guidance note for the financial sector on due diligence.[50] It makes clear that the institutions' responsibilities include avoiding causing, contributing to or being directly linked to adverse impacts arising from either their own or their client's business operations. At the time of writing this chapter (June 2019), the OECD is preparing a new note on due diligence for corporate lending and securities underwriting.

2 Standards Specifically Applicable to the Financial Sector

This section highlights two examples of standards specifically applicable to the financial sector.

In 2006, the United Nations Environment Programme and the United Nations Global Compact created the Principles for Responsible Investment

---

48 The Thun Group members includes Barclays; BBVA; Credit Suisse AG; ING Bank N.V.; RBS Group; UBS AG; and UniCredit, *see Get All the Facts, UBS,* https://www.ubs.com/global/en/about_ubs/ubs-and-society/how-we-do-business/sustainability/thun-group.html (last visited Aug. 21, 2019).

49 For example, in 2018 of the thirty-eight financial institutions represented on the Board of Trustees of the IIF, thirty have human rights policies. The thirty financial institutions that have human rights policies are as follows: HSBC, Credit Suisse AG, SEB, Akbank T.A.S, Swiss Re Ltd., Itaú Unibanco Holding S/A, Banco de Crédito del Perú, Erste Group Bank AG, Allianz SE, UBS AG, Commerzbank AG, Standard Chartered Bank, Grupo Santander, The Goldman Sachs Group, Inc., Citigroup, Deutsche Bank AG, Zurich Insurance Group, UniCredit Group, Aberdeen Asset Management, BBVA, Morgan Stanley, DBS Group Holdings and & DBS Bank Ltd, ING Group, BNY Mellon, MetLife, Inc., Standard Bank Group Ltd, BNP Paribas, Société Générale, JPMorgan Chase, and Scotiabank. The eight financial institutions that do not have human rights policies are as follows: Gulf International Bank, Qatar National Bank, Mizuho Bank Ltd., Mitsubishi UFJ Financial Group, ICICI Bank Ltd, Industrial and Commercial Bank of China, Sumitomo Mitsui Financial Group, and Bank of China.

50 OECD Global Forum on Responsible Business Conduct, *Due Diligence in the Financial Sector—Adverse Impacts Directly Linked to Financial Sector Operations, Products or Services by a Business Relationship* (2014), https://mneguidelines.oecd.org/globalforumonresponsiblebusinessconduct/GFRBC-2014-financial-sector-document-1.pdf (last visited Aug. 21, 2019).

(PRI).[51] The PRI's six principles encourage institutional investors and other investment entities to pay greater attention to environmental, social, and governance (ESG) issues in their operations and business relations. At the time of writing this chapter, approximately more than 2300 asset managers, investment managers, and professional service partners have signed onto the PRI, which now functions as an independent entity.[52]

The secretariat of the United Nations Conference on Trade and Development (UNCTAD) has published the Principles on Responsible Sovereign Lending and Borrowing.[53] These principles seek to offer guidance to both sovereign borrowers and their creditors on how they can behave responsibly in their financial transactions with each other. They make clear that the sovereign debtor and its creditors share responsibility for ensuring that the sovereign's debts are sustainable.[54] In the specific case of project finance, sovereign borrowers also have an obligation to undertake *ex ante* social and environmental impact assessments and should make their results public.[55]

There are no *de facto* enforcement mechanisms associated with these standards. They rely on moral suasion and reputational risk ("naming and shaming") to encourage compliance.

B *Private Sector*

The most prominent international standard relevant to social and environmental impacts developed by the private sector is the Equator Principles (EPs).[56] These principles were developed by representatives of financial institutions, working with the International Finance Corporation and some civil society groups. The EPs are based on the International Finance Corporation's (IFC) Sustainability Framework,[57] which provides guidance to the IFC and its

---

51 *About the Principles for Responsible Investment*, U.N. PRINCIPLES FOR RESPONSIBLE INVESTMENT (launched in 2006), http://www.unpri.org/about-pri/the-six-principles/ (last visited Aug. 21, 2019).

52 *See id.*

53 The principles were drafted by a working group comprised of experts and government representatives, *see* U.N. Conference on Trade and Development, *Principles on Promoting Responsible Sovereign Lending and Borrowing* (Jan. 10, 2012), http://unctad.org/en/PublicationsLibrary/gdsddf2012misc1_en.pdf (last visited Aug. 21, 2019).

54 *Id.* at 4.

55 *Id.* at 10–11.

56 EQUATOR PRINCIPLES, http://www.equator-principles.com/about (last visited Aug. 21, 2019); *see also* Sheldon Leader & Luis Felipe Yanes, *infra* ch. 10 in this volume.

57 *Sustainability Overview*, INT'L FIN. CORP., http://www.ifc.org/wps/wcm/connect/Topics_Ext_Content/IFC_External_Corporate_site/Sustainability+and+Disclosure/Environmental-Social-Governance/Sustainability+Framework (last visited Aug. 21, 2019).

clients about assessing and monitoring the environmental and social sustainability of those projects that it funds. There have been three iterations of the EPs since 2003.[58] In each case, the changes have been stimulated by changes in the IFC's Sustainability Framework.[59] Currently the EPs have performance standards dealing with environmental, social, and labor issues.

The EPs are voluntary principles that are intended to guide the conduct of signatory banks engaged in financing projects whose total capital value exceeds $10 million.[60] The EPs have been adopted by ninety-four financial institutions in thirty-seven countries covering the majority of projects being financed around the world.[61] The signatories should prepare annual reports on their implementation of the EPs but there is no meaningful consequence for failure to do so in a particular year.

Reputational risk and moral suasion are the primary mechanisms for promoting compliance with international standards like the EPs. In addition, as discussed in more detail in Chapter 10 in this book, signatory banks could strengthen the EPs by incorporating its requirements into their loan agreements with the project sponsor. This would have the effect of making the borrower bring the project into compliance with the EPs or risk defaulting on their loan agreements.

One possible means of *de facto* enforcement through increasing public awareness about these issues is to require companies to include information on ESG aspects of their operations in their financial statements. This has been a growing area of interest. Some private bodies have sought to develop environmentally and socially responsible accounting standards. One example is the Global Reporting Initiative (GRI). It has developed a set of voluntary standards that seek to promote greater transparency in the reports of companies regarding their ESG practices. There is some evidence that companies that adopt

58 In June 2019, the Equator Principles Association has released for consultations a fourth version of the EPs. The consultation period is expected to end in August 2019. It is unclear when the fourth version will be finalized and adopted by the Association and its members. *See* https://equator-principles.com/ep-association-news/ep4-draft-consultation-begins/ last visited Aug. 21, 2019.

59 Andrew Hardenbrook, *The Equator Principles: The Private Financial Sector's Attempt at Environmental Responsibility*, 40 VAND. J. TRANSNAT'L L. 197 (2007); Suellan Lazarus, *The Equator Principles at 10 Years*, 5 J. TRANSNAT'L L. THEORY 417 (2014); Miki Kamijyo, *The Equator Principles: Improved Social Responsibility in the Private Finance Sector*, 4 SUSTAINABLE DEV. L. & POL'Y 35 (2004); *see also* Leader & Yanes, *infra* ch. 10 in this volume.

60 *See* EQUATOR PRINCIPLES, *supra* note 56 (follow "Download" hyperlink).

61 *See id.*

ESG reporting are rewarded by financial markets with lower costs of capital. However, this evidence is limited and inconclusive.[62] In addition, in some cases—for example companies producing consumer products—there can be reputational risk for companies that fail to adopt such reporting.

IV Lessons on the Use of Soft Law in Promoting Change

This section draws four lessons about the use of soft law to promote change from the examples of the international financial regulatory standards and the financial responsibility standards discussed above.

A *Lesson 1:* Factors Affecting the Efficacy of Soft International Law

The two sets of standards discussed above suggest that the efficacy of a soft international law standard is influenced by five factors. They are as follows:

1) the nature of the problem that the standard's proponents are seeking to address,
2) the nature of the change that they are seeking,
3) the mechanisms that they have for drafting and adopting the standard,
4) the means available for promoting compliance with the standard, and
5) the intended use of the standard.

Each factor is discussed below.

1 The Nature of the Problem

The problem confronting the SSBs was how can they most effectively deal with the impact of the international activity of financial institutions on their existing mandates. All the participants agreed that they had a technical problem: what was the most effective way to incorporate their financial sector's international activity into their existing mandates. Since the technical experts in the financial regulatory authorities had both the responsibility and the requisite expertise to resolve these issues, it was appropriate that they develop the international standards for dealing with them. They also had an interest in both implementing the standards themselves and encouraging other regulators to do so.

By contrast, the problem confronting the participants in formulating the financial responsibility standards raised profound issues about the purpose of

62 Satish Joshi & Yue Li, *What Is Corporate Sustainability and How Do Firms Practice It? A Management Accounting Research Perspective*, 28 J. MGMT. ACCT. RES. 1, 1–11 (2016).

finance. In particular, it raised questions about the social role and responsibilities of financial institutions and the appropriate allocation of the social, human rights, and environmental risks and responsibilities associated with their economic activity. These are essentially political questions that societies and national policymakers are normally reluctant to delegate to unelected officials or international bodies.

These two sets of standards suggest that one factor in determining the efficacy of a soft international law standard is positively correlated with the extent to which the issue is understood as a technical issue, as opposed to a political one.

2 The Nature of the Change

The proponents of the international financial regulatory standards were seeking changes that were limited in scope and were within their power to address. They understood that the industry that they regulated was undergoing change and that they needed to adapt their regulatory frameworks to accommodate these changes. In other words, they were interested in developing international standards that would fill a specific gap in their regulatory practices and that they themselves could implement within the scope of their existing mandates.

In this regard, it should be noted that the financial institutions that operated internationally also had an interest in having their regulators adapt to the changes in their industry. International regulatory standards would help reduce the costs of cross-border financial transactions and thereby facilitate the development of global financial markets.

On the other hand, the promoters of financial responsibility standards were seeking to develop standards that changed the way in which the actors in financial transactions dealt with the social and environmental externalities generated by their transactions. This would necessarily require them to rethink the way financial transactions should be structured and implemented. In particular, financial institutions, investors, and regulators would need to develop a longer-term perspective than they have historically used to assess the environmental, social, and human rights risks associated with their transactions and regulations.

Moreover, the promoters of the financial responsibility standards may not be able to implement the new standards on their own. For example, implementing the EPs could require the cooperation of the project sponsors, project contractors, and the relevant government authorities in addition to the financial institutions who participated in developing the Principles.

These examples suggest that the potential efficacy of the soft international law standard is negatively correlated with the scope of the change being sought. Broad change has more consequences, a greater risk of unintended consequences, and is more likely to generate opposition from some stakeholders in the financial sector than narrow change. It is also negatively correlated with the range of actors with diverse interests required to implement the standards.

3 The Mechanisms for Formulating the Soft Law

The international financial regulatory standards are formulated by bodies specifically established to promote international financial regulatory cooperation. They have dedicated secretariats and formal operating practices and procedures that provide the participants with the support needed to develop the standards.

On the other hand, the standards seeking to promote more responsible financial activity such as the EPs were developed in relatively informal forums of interested parties. Others were developed in international bodies such as the UN Human Rights Council that were not necessarily viewed by all stakeholders as having either a mandate or the expertise to deal with financial responsibility issues.

These differences suggest that soft law instruments are more likely to be effective when they are drafted and adopted in dedicated mechanisms that have the mandate and expertise to work on the particular issues that the standard addresses.

4 Ensuring Compliance

The international financial regulatory standards demonstrate that the efficacy of the standards is positively affected by the strength of the *de facto* compliance arrangements associated with the standards. This can be seen from the role that international bodies like the IMF, the World Bank, the FSB, and the BCBS play in monitoring compliance with the international financial regulatory standards. It is important to note that their efficacy, since they lack legal force, may correlate negatively with the wealth and power of the country that is the object of their compliance efforts.

The financial responsibility standards rely on moral suasion and reputational risk to convince financial institutions and regulators to comply with the relevant standards. Their record suggests that they are more likely to be effective in cases of actors who are suffering from a reputational problem and who think that compliance with the standards can help overcome these problems. They are less effective against actors who believe that they have strong enough reputations to manage the risk or that are impervious to moral suasion. In this regard, it is interesting to note that many transnational banks have found it useful to develop policies in which they express their support for at least some of the international financial regulatory standards.[63] This is the case, even when their operational records are inconsistent with these policies.

5 The Use of the Standard

There are three ways a soft law standard can be used. The first is through practice so that the standard is actually incorporated into national financial regulatory frameworks and into the practices of financial institutions. The second way is through monitoring so that the standard becomes the benchmark for assessing the conduct of those institutions that are the target of the standard. This is the case, for example, with the IMF's and World Bank's ROSCs and FSAPs.

Third, the standard serves as an educational tool.[64] In this case the standard can be used to help its intended targets better understand the issues raised in the standard and how to improve their compliance with its requirements.

The international financial regulatory standards serve all three functions. Regulators in a number of countries have incorporated them into their regulatory frameworks. The IMF, for example, has used them to assess the performance of regulators and the quality of regulatory frameworks in its member states. They perform an educational function both as they are being developed by the SSBs and in the various review processes in which the standards are used.

The financial responsibility standards, although they have had some impacts, have been less effective in terms of implementation and accountability. However, they have been relatively effective as educational tools. For example, the UNGPs or the EPs help shape the thinking of and debate among the relevant stakeholders about how to deal with the social, human rights, and environmental impacts of financial activity. Indeed, many financial institutions had no employees with environmental and social expertise prior to signing on to the EPs. As the standards are implemented and applied, they help generate empirical data on how effective the standards are in dealing with the social, human rights, and environmental impacts of their operations. This information can be used to update the standards. The EPs,[65] for example, have been adapted in response to our growing knowledge about these issues.

---

63 *See supra* note 49.

64 ABRAM CHAYES & ANTONIA HANDLER CHAYES, THE NEW SOVEREIGNTY: COMPLIANCE WITH INTERNATIONAL REGULATORY AGREEMENTS (1995).

65 Since the EPs are based on the IFC's Environmental and Social Framework, the IFC's experience with its framework contributes to the updating of the EPs.

B *Lesson 2:* The Identity of the Actors

It is noteworthy that both state and non-state actors have participated in the development of the soft law standards discussed above. For example, state actors developed the FATF Recommendations and the UNGPs. Non-state actors formulated the Equator Principles. Regulatory authorities are responsible for the core supervisory principles for the financial sector. This suggests that the identity of the formulators of an international standard is not a particularly relevant criterion in determining the efficacy of a particular soft law instrument.

On the other hand, the identity of the parties who must implement the standard is relevant to the issue of its *de facto* enforceability. The financial regulatory standards discussed in this paper indicate that the efficacy of the monitoring and peer reviews associated with these standards is positively correlated with the susceptibility of the implementing party to peer and market pressure and to the persuasive powers of monitoring entities like the IMF. The susceptibility of the target of the standard to market pressure also seems to be a relevant factor in assessing the *de facto* enforceability of the financial responsibility standards.

C *Lesson 3:* The Costs of the Siloed Approach

When standards are developed in exclusive forums, the risk of unintended consequences increases. The international financial regulatory and financial responsibility standards are a good illustration of the challenges that can arise from such exclusivity. The two sets of standards have been developed by different groups of actors with limited interactions between them.[66] This reduces the likelihood that the standard-setters will consider all relevant issues and all potential impacts in their deliberations.

One reason for the lack of coordination is that the different sets of standards have different concerns that are not easily reconciled. The international financial regulatory standards focus on the safety, stability, transparency, and efficiency of financial institutions and systems. The financial responsibility

66 One example of cooperation is that the FATF has worked with the Alliance for Financial Inclusion (AFI) and other international bodies to try and mitigate the adverse impact of the FATF Recommendations on remittances, and correspondent banking relationships. This was needed because the FATF Recommendations incentivize financial institutions to adopt costly know your customer rules that militate against small businesses and poorer customers who either may not be able to provide all the required information or whose accounts generate profit margins that are too low to justify the financial institutions taking on the additional expense associated with these customers and being compliant with the FATF Recommendations.

standards concentrate on the impact of their actions on individuals, communities, and the environment.

One consequence of this lack of coordination is that it increases the risk that the different standards will work at cross-purposes to each other. For example, the Basel III capital adequacy standards use risk weightings that incentivize banks to favor short-term assets over long term ones.[67] While the EPs and UNGPs with their focus on environmental, social, and human rights impacts encourage financial institutions to take a long-term perspective about their operations.[68]

Another example is the FATF Recommendations.[69] They were initially developed without consulting with regulatory authorities in poorer countries who were not members of FATF, or the entities working on financial inclusion or remittances. As a result, they failed to consider the Recommendations' impact on remittances and financial inclusion in poorer countries. The result was that they did not anticipate that many transnational banks would respond to the Recommendations by cutting their correspondent banking lines with banks in some developing countries.[70] Their rationale was that

---

67 Stephany Griffith-Jones & Stephen Spratt, *Will the Proposed New Basel Capital Accord Have a Net Negative Effect on Developing Countries?* INST. DEV. STUD., U. Sussex (2001).

68 It should be noted that some regulators are beginning to acknowledge that the scope of these standards need to broaden. For example, in 2018, a group of central banks and banking supervisors formed the Network for Greening the Financial System. *See* https://www.mainstreamingclimate.org/ngfs/ (last visited Aug. 21, 2019). In addition, the Governor of the Bank of England who at the time was the chair of the FSB, has established a committee to look at the impact of climate change on the financial system. He has also begun to talk about the "tragedy of the horizons," Mark Carney, Bank of England and Financial Stability Board, Breaking the Tragedy of the Horizon—Climate Change and Financial Stability, speech at Lloyd's of London (Sept. 29, 2015), by which he means the possibility that financial institutions may be adopting too short a time perspective to see the risks that they face in the long term. As a result, there is a possibility that these two groups may eventually find that their interests have converged enough to begin articulating a shared vision for an environmentally and socially responsible, efficient and safe financial system. *See* Mark Carney, Bank of England and Financial Stability Board, The Sustainable Development Goal Imperative, speech at U.N. General Assembly, High-Level Thematic Debate on Achieving the Sustainable Development Goals (Apr. 21, 2016); *see also* Task Force on Climate Related Financial Disclosures, *Recommendations of the Task Force on Climate-related Financial Disclosures*, FSB (Dec. 14, 2016), https://www.fsb-tcfd.org/wp-content/uploads/2016/12/16_1221_TCFD_Report_Letter.pdf.

69 FATF, *The FATF Recommendations*, (2012), http://www.fatf-gafi.org/media/fatf/documents/recommendations/pdfs/FATF_Recommendations.pdf (last visited Aug. 21, 2019).

70 *See* Jason C. Sharman & David Chaikin, *Corruption and Anti-Money-Laundering Systems: Putting a Luxury Good to Work*, 22 (1) GOVERNANCE 27, 27–45 (2009) (discussing how the FATF membership and its system is drastically skewed to favor rich countries leaving poorer countries with a lack of "ownership").

these relations had become too risky because they could not be confident that these banks were complying with the Recommendations. The Recommendations also adversely affected the cost of remittance transactions which tend to involve small amounts.[71] Both of these developments reduced financial inclusion. It should be noted that once this impact of the Recommendations became clear, FATF began to consult with other interested bodies and to work to mitigate this impact.[72]

One possible contributing factor to this lack of coordination is the relative informality of soft international law. In the case of hard international law, formal procedures need to be followed relating to the drafting, negotiating, signing, and ratifying of an agreement. There are also formal requirements for establishing the existence of principles of customary international law. While these procedures may be cumbersome and create the risk of reaching agreement at the lowest common denominator, they have the benefit of being predictable and relatively inclusive at least for states.[73] Often overlooked is that the informality of soft law also has the potential to create opaque and exclusionary procedures favoring one set of stakeholders over another. This in turn increases the risk of excluding certain relevant issues from the scope of the negotiations and thus of producing unintended consequences. It also facilitates a relative over-concentration on the aspects of the issues of most interest to the participants in the standard setting exercise.

D *Lesson 4:* Enduring Power of Sovereignty

The final lesson is that despite the powerful forces generated by globalization, sovereignty remains a dominant factor in the global economy and the global financial system. Although the financial system has become global and there have been efforts to develop the institutional arrangements for global financial governance, the international community has not decided to create

---

71 Michael Levi, *How Well Do Anti–Money Laundering Controls Work in Developing Countries? in* DRAINING DEVELOPMENT? CONTROLLING FLOWS OF ILLICIT FUNDS FROM DEVELOPING COUNTRIES 391 (Peter Reuter ed., 2012), http://documents.worldbank.org/curated/en/305601468178737192/pdf/668150PUB0EPI0067848B09780821388693.pdf#page=391 (last visited Aug. 21, 2019).

72 *See* FATF, *Guidance: Anti-Money Laundering and Terrorist Financing Measures and Financial Inclusion—With a Supplement on Customer Due Diligence* (Nov. 2017), http://www.fatf-gafi.org/media/fatf/content/images/Updated-2017-FATF-2013-Guidance.pdf (last visited Aug. 21, 2019).

73 *See, e.g.*, VERA GOWLLAND-DEBBAS, MULTILATERAL TREATY MAKING: THE CURRENT STATUS OF CHALLENGES TO AND REFORMS NEEDED IN THE INTERNATIONAL LEGISLATIVE PROCESS (Springer 2000).

an effective global financial regulatory organization.[74] Instead the focus of financial regulation has remained at the national level. In addition, states have sought to maintain control over international financial regulation by requiring the SSBs and entities like the FSB to report to them in forums such as the G20.[75] They have also ensured that they retain the flexibility to decide for themselves if and how to implement these standards in their own national settings.

These prerogatives do not apply equally to all states. This can be seen from the example of the IMF's and World Bank's FSAPs and the ROSCs. These, in effect, seek to persuade all states, regardless of whether they participated in their drafting, to comply with these standards. As a result, the international standards have become relatively "harder" for the states for whom access to global finance depends on the judgement of international financial institutions like the IMF than for the richest and most powerful states.

A similar concern with sovereignty is evident in the case of the financial responsibility standards. The voluntary nature of the standards, at least in principle, protects state sovereignty. However, this is only the case if the state has an alternate way of funding its proposed projects or activity.

V Conclusion

The examples of the international financial regulatory standards and the financial responsibility standards demonstrate that, under the appropriate conditions, international soft law can be an effective promoter of change. The appropriateness of the conditions is affected by the nature of the issues that the standards address, the nature of the change that its proponents are seeking, the mechanisms that they have for formulating the standard and for *de facto* enforcement and the use they make of the standard. These examples also demonstrate that the fact that soft law is developed in a less formal process than hard law may increase the risks of unintended consequences. Finally, the

---

74 *See* JOHN EATWELL, BARON EATWELL & LANCE TAYLOR, GLOBAL FINANCE AT RISK: THE CASE FOR INTERNATIONAL REGULATION (2000).

75 *See* A Guide to Committees, Groups and Clubs, IMF (Mar. 8, 2019), https://www.imf.org/en/About/Factsheets/A-Guide-to-Committees-Groups-and-Clubs (last visited Aug. 21, 2019); Andrew F. Cooper, *The G20 as an Improvised Crisis Committee and/or a Contested "Steering Committee" for the World*, 86 INT'L AFF. 741, 741–57 (2010).

examples in this chapter highlight that, regardless of the extent of globalization in finance, sovereignty retains its vitality and relevance.

Appendix 1: International Financial Regulatory Standards Discussed in the Paper

Soft law standard	Issuer	Target	"Enforcement"	Intended social change
Basel Capital Adequacy Standards	Basel Committee of Banking Supervisors (BCBS)	1) National Banking Regulatory Authorities	1) Peer Review through BCBS RCAP and FSB	1) Restore national supervisory capacity to perform traditional functions
		2) Banks through the national authorities	2) Review by IMF and WB in ROSC and FSAP	2) Safe and sound banks
			3) Market Pressure	
Core Principles for Effective Banking Supervision	BCBS	1) National Banking Regulatory Authorities	1) Peer Review through BCBS RCAP and FSB	1) Restore national supervisory capacity to perform traditional functions
		2) Banks through the national authorities	2) Review by IMF and WB in ROSC and FSAP	2) Safe and sound banks
			3) Market Pressure	

Soft law standard	Issuer	Target	"Enforcement"	Intended social change
Objectives and Principles of Securities Regulation	International Organization of Securities Commissions (IOSCO)	1) National Securities regulators	1) Peer review through FSB	1) Restore national supervisory capacity to perform traditional functions
		2) Investment Banks, Brokers, and other market actors through the national authorities	2) Review by IMF and WB in ROSC and FSAP	2) More efficient and fair financial markets
			3) Market pressure	
Insurance Core Principles	International Association of Insurance Supervisors (IAIS)	1) National Insurance regulators	1) Peer review through FSB	1) Restore national supervisory capacity to perform traditional functions
		2) Insurance companies through national authorities	2) Review by IMF and WB in ROSC and FSAP	2) More efficient and fair insurance companies
			3) Market pressure	

Soft law standard	Issuer	Target	"Enforcement"	Intended social change
Recommendations	Financial Action Task Force	1) States	1) Naming and shaming through blacklist	1) New capacity to deal with money laundering and counter-terrorist financing
		2) National regulators through states	2) Financial institutions in blacklisted countries can be cut off from financial relations	2) Limit criminal activity
		3) Banks through national regulators		

Appendix 2: Financial Responsibility Standards Discussed in the Paper

Soft law standard	Issuer	Target	"Enforcement"	Intended social change
Principles of Responsible Investing	UN Environmental Program	1) Investment banks	1) Financial institutions	1) Increase attention paid to ESG issues by investors, institutions, issuers, and regulators
		2) Institutional investors	2) Clients	2) Change the ESG conduct of signatories and fund recipients
		3) Financial advisors, brokers, etc.	3) Financial advisors, etc.	
			4) Financial sector regulators	
Principles of Responsible Sovereign Borrowing and Lending	UNCTAD	1) Sovereign borrowers	1) Moral suasion	1) Improved and more sustainable borrowing by sovereigns
		2) Financial institutions		2) Responsible lending by financial institutions
		3) Advisors to sovereigns and financial institutions		

Soft law standard	Issuer	Target	"Enforcement"	Intended social change
OECD Guidelines on Multinational Enterprises	OECD	1) OECD member states	1) National Contact Point	1) Reduce conflict between MNEs in OECD countries and their host states and communities
		2) MNES, including financial institutions, from these states	2) Peer pressure	2) Responsible investor behavior
		3) Host states of these MNES	3) Moral suasion	3) Reduce reputational risk for OECD home states
		4) Other states		
UN Guiding Principles on Business and Human Rights	UN Human Rights Council	1) Businesses, including financial institutions,	1) Moral suasion	1) Educate states, businesses and civil society about human rights responsibilities of business
		2) States	2) Peer pressure	2) Promote more attention to the human rights impacts of business

Soft law standard	Issuer	Target	"Enforcement"	Intended social change
		3) Civil society		3) Promote more human rights responsible conduct by business
Equator Principles	Equator Banks	1) Banks funding large infrastructure, extractive and other projects	1) Peer pressure	1) Promote more ES responsible performance by banks funding large projects
		2) Communities and civil society groups concerned about the ES impact of these projects	2) Moral suasion	2) Reduce conflict generated by these projects
				3) Reduce political risk to banks

CHAPTER 10

Levers for and Obstacles to Social Change: Bank Lending, the Law and the Equator Principles

Sheldon Leader and Luis Felipe Yanes***

I Introduction

A *What Are the EPs?*

"The Equator Principles[1] are a risk management framework, created and adopted by financial institutions, for determining, assessing and managing environmental and social risks in financing projects."[2] This sparse definition already tells us quite a lot. These are principles that have their origin and function under the control of private financial institutions rather than state or international bodies. They are an instrument 'by and for' these financial institutions, which use them as a device of commercial risk management.

The EPs have been adopted by more than 96 financial institutions in 37 countries worldwide,[3] covering over 70 percent of international project finance debt in emerging markets.[4] They were launched in 2003, and revised in 2006 and 2013. A further initiative to update the EPs is currently under way, with a revised version ("EP4") expected to be published by mid-late 2019.

The initiative to draft such commitments was a response to pressure from civil society which had become – and remains – alarmed at the serious social and environmental damage that some of the largest infrastructure projects

* Professor, School of Law, University of Essex. Director of the Essex Business and Human Rights Project.

** Core member of the Essex Business and Human Rights Project. Former Human Rights Specialist of the Inter-American Commission on Human Rights.

1 Equator Principles, *The Equator Principles*, https://equator-principles.com/wp-content/uploads/2017/03/equator_principles_III.pdf (last visited Aug. 21, 2019).

2 *Id.*.

3 *EP Association Members and Reporting,* Equator Principles, https://equator-principles.com/members-reporting/.

4 *See Korean Development Bank: The First Korean Bank to Adopt the Equator Principles,* https://equator-principles.com/adoption-news/kdb-adopts-the-equator-principles/.

 | DOI:10.1163/9789004417021_011

have caused. Significant examples are the Chinese Three Gorges Dam Project, the Turkish Ilisu Dam Project, and the Baku-Tbilisi-Ceyhan pipeline.[5]

The EPs consist of requirements that member lending institutions agree to place on their borrowers, so lenders can be satisfied with the borrower's ability to assess and manage the following areas of concern: labour and working conditions; resource efficiency and pollution prevention; community health, safety and security; land acquisition and involuntary resettlement; biodiversity conservation and sustainable management of living natural resources; indigenous peoples; and cultural heritage.[6] These requirements follow the performance standards set by the International Finance Corporation ("IFC"), part of the World Bank Group.[7]

The lending institutions divide proposed projects into three categories:

Category A: Projects with potentially significant adverse environmental and social risks and/or impacts that are diverse, irreversible or unprecedented;

Category B: Projects with potentially limited adverse environmental and social risks and/or impacts that are few in number, generally site-specific, largely reversible and readily addressed through mitigation measures; and

Category C: Projects with minimal or no adverse environmental and social risks and/or impacts.[8]

For all Category A and Category B Projects, the lender requires the client to conduct an assessment process to address, to the lender's satisfaction, the relevant environmental and social risks and impacts of the proposed project.

B *The Financial Setting and Social Impacts: the Discipline of Project Finance*

It is important to appreciate the particular incentives and social risks associated with the mode of lending the EPs primarily regulate: project finance

---

5 *See* Olaf Weber & Emmanuel Acheta, *The Equator Principles: Ten Teenage Years of Implementation and a Search for Outcome*, https://www.cigionline.org/sites/default/files/no24_0.pdf. For the impact and human rights impact of the Baku-Tbilisi-Ceyhan pipeline, *see also Human Rights on the line: The Baku-Tbilisi-Ceyhan Pipeline*, Amnesty Int'l UK (May, 2003), https://www.amnesty.org.uk/files/baku_line_0.pdf?thEYtrMC3vDnSnj08_X9LpK0UePGyCdh=.

6 *See generally* Equator Principles, *supra* note 1; *EP Association Members and Reporting*, *supra* note 3.

7 *See IFC Performance Standards on Environmental and Social Sustainability*, World Bank Group, https://www.ifc.org/wps/wcm/connect/c8f524004a73daeca09afdf998895a12/IFC_Performance_Standards.pdf?MOD=AJPERES.

8 *See Environmental and Social Categorization*, World Bank Group, https://www.ifc.org/wps/wcm/connect/topics_ext_content/ifc_external_corporate_site/sustainability-at-ifc/policies-standards/es-categorization.

("PF"). As bland and general as this label seems to be, PF actually refers to a special and controversial lending technique. The EPs themselves define project finance as a:

> [M]ethod of financing in which the lender looks primarily to the revenues generated by a single Project, both as the source of repayment and as security for the exposure. ... Project Finance may take the form of financing of the construction of a new capital installation, or refinancing of an existing installation, with or without improvements. The client is usually a Special Purpose Entity that is not permitted to perform any function other than developing, owning, and operating the installation. ... The consequence is that repayment depends primarily on the Project's cash flow and on the collateral value of the Project's assets.[9]

Consider a large oil pipeline which will cost £100 million to build and operate, and for which a loan is sought. Imagine that the project is developed under the auspices of, say, British Petroleum ("BP"). In PF, the loan is not made to BP, but to a specially created project company that owns the pipeline and related assets, and BP in turn owns this company. The pipeline will generate revenue that is estimated to be enough to repay the loan. That revenue is the sole source of funds to repay the bank. What happens if the revenues turn out not to be enough? The lender will have as its only collateral the assets of the project company, not those of BP – the latter known as the project sponsor.[10] BP is itself doubly insulated: under the terms of the loan agreement it is not liable to the lender, and under the governing corporate law it will benefit from the classic separation of its liability from that of the project company.

Many large projects are financed in this way. It may seem to an onlooker as if the project sponsor, often with a worldwide reputation, has borrowed the funds for a particular project when this is not so. The advantage for the sponsor of this arrangement is that if it is a corporate group with several projects under way it can limit its exposure in each one. The failure of one venture will not contaminate the rest. While this might give some comfort to the project sponsor, since its wider assets are not exposed, the risk to the lender is a good

---

9 *See* Equator Principles, *supra* note 1, at 18.

10 In 'project-related' lending the revenue stream is also limited to the single project, but guarantees can also be provided by the project sponsor. *Supra* note 1. On the various forms of partial recourse arrangements that can be used in project finance, *see A Guide To Project Finance*, Dentons (2016) https://www.dentons.com/en/insights/guides-reports-and-whitepapers/2013/april/1/a-guide-to-project-finance.

deal higher than it would be if the latter had access to the sponsor's worldwide holdings as collateral – a concern particularly acute in relatively unstable parts of the world. In response to this higher risk, the lender typically charges a higher interest on the loan. It also will insist on relatively strict amounts of reimbursement with tight schedules, ready to trigger default if this falls behind.[11] In addition to a higher interest rate, the lenders also have an interest in understanding as clearly as possible the risk profile of the project and so, on average, are likely to be more open to doing full economic and social impact assessments. They will also have an incentive to draft contracts which pass these risks onto some other party so that they do not have to assume them.[12]

In this setting, it is not surprising to find corners being cut. The project company can be tempted to compromise local or international social and environmental standards to meet the loan schedule, and the banks are induced to collude with them. Both parties have an interest in steady and prompt repayment. However, this coalition of interests between lenders and borrowers can damage, and has damaged, local communities and the workforce.

Consultations, for example, can take a long time, and a respect for cultural traditions within that process might produce significant delays for a project. In this context, there have been allegations that community leaders have been harassed or threatened to accept the terms of a planned development.[13] Consultations might also be reduced, limited in their scope, or only focused on a small group of people, in order to continue with the agreed schedule.

Furthermore, safety procedures might be loosened to comply with strict deadlines, with potentially catastrophic consequences. Cement, for example, cannot be put in place at very high temperatures, making it difficult in certain countries to continue construction around-the-clock. If cement is set at such high temperatures, there is a risk of it breaking over time. As a consequence, a

---

11 Although no empirical research has been conducted on this point, the work of the Essex Business and Human Rights Project – thanks to many informal conversations with stakeholders – has lead the authors to believe that, while the ability to trigger default is a common feature of all non-recourse lending projects, project finance lenders seen to be more willing to call a default than other creditors. See for example, the work of the EBHR with Amnesty International on the Baku-Tbilisi-Ceyhan pipeline, *supra* note 5.

12 Under this scenario, two categories of risk within PF can be identified: risk that represents significant damage to the progress of a project, which might hinder the expected returns; and risk that damages third parties, such as social and environmental risk. For more on risk allocation and risk mitigation. *See Global Project Finance, Human Rights and Sustainable Development* (Sheldon Leader & David Ong eds., Cambridge Univ. Press 2011).

13 *Accord* Organization of American States, *Inter-American Commission on Human Rights, Resolution 7/2016 on Precautionary Measures* 452–13 (2016), https://www.oas.org/es/cidh/decisiones/pdf/2016/MC452-13-Es.pdf.

dam might collapse, killing hundreds of people and destroying its neighbouring environment.[14]

Banks' reputations have suffered as a result, and in order to counter this, it made sense for them to band together and work out a common set of lending principles. This is, to a certain degree, a consequence of the pressure placed by NGOs from Europe and North America on the headquarters of commercial banks which were, via loans to the parent company, financing projects that were opposed by the local populations. Commercial banks were criticised for supporting projects from which public financial institutions had withdrawn their support given concerns about serious environmental and social harms. Certain investment groups that were interested in promoting environmental and social sustainability used their shareholder rights to demand changes to the policies and practices of these commercial institutions, due to the campaigns carried out by NGOs.[15]

C *The Legal Setting*

The EPs are a set of transnational principles. They are not tied to any national legal system, nor do their origins lie in public international law.[16] They arise from an agreement among private actors and the norms are entirely in the control of those same actors. At the same time, however, to assess the evolution and social impacts of these norms, they must be considered alongside a set of international legal measures that lend them indirect but vital support and could impose potential controls in the name of social change if configured appropriately.

---

14 Although no conclusive information has been published, suspicions have grown that the collapse of the Mariana Dam in Brazil – in which 19 people died and the village of Bento Rodrigues was destroyed – was due to the conditions of the cement and other materials at the base of the dam (with cracks in the base being visible in 2013 and 2014). See Dom Phillips & Davilson Brasileiro, *Brazil dam disaster: firm knew of potential impact months in advance*, The Guardian (Mar. 1, 2018, https://www.theguardian.com/world/2018/feb/28/brazil-dam-collapse-samarco-fundao-mining); Patricia Kowsmann, Samantha Pearson, Scott Patterson & Luciana Magalhaes, *Behind Vale's Deadly Dam Collapse: Multiple Warnings That Went Unheeded*, Wall St. J. (Feb. 24, 2019), https://www.wsj.com/articles/behind-vales-deadly-dam-collapse-multiple-warnings-that-went-unheeded-11551050768.

15 *See* Christopher Wright, *Global Banks, the Environment, and Human Rights: The impact of the Equator Principles on Lending Policies and Practices* 56, GLO. ENVTL. POLITICS (Feb. 2012).

16 *See* Larry Catá Backer, *Principles of Transnational Law: The Foundations of an Emerging Field*, Law at the End of the Day (Mar. 9, 2007), http://lcbackerblog.blogspot.co.uk/2007/03/principles-of-transnational-law.html.

The EPs are a private initiative which draws much of its content from public standards. The Principles were born out of the intention of private financial institutions to self-regulate conduct that had a potential impact on the environment and human rights. They were constructed by using the Safeguards Policy that the International Finance Corporation had adopted in 1998.[17] This is mainly because the initial initiative to create the EPs was led by four banks with the technical support of the IFC, which drafted a set of standards for commercial banks to manage social and environmental risk.[18] After their adoption, the EPs continued to have a close relationship with the IFC social and environmental policies, as they have been updated twice to reflect changes the IFC had made to its own standards.[19]

However, sixteen years after their adoption, the EPs no longer stand alone. In 2011, the United Nations Human Rights Council ("HRC") endorsed the Guiding Principles on Business and Human Rights: Implementing the United Nations "Protect, Respect and Remedy Framework" ("UNGPs"). The UNGPs requires commercial enterprises, including banks, to respect human rights and to exercise appropriate due diligence. They have created an expectation that "banks will conduct their due diligence to identify and address their own impacts, as well as those to which they contribute or to which they are directly linked through business relationships."[20] The process that is currently underway to update the EPs (EP4) has shown that there is a need to align the EPs with the UNGPs, in particular regarding human rights due diligence.[21]

---

17 The 1998 IFC's Safeguard Policies were comprised of several operational policies, in relation to: Environmental Assessment, Natural Habitats, Indigenous Peoples, Involuntary Resettlement, Child and Forced Labour; among others. They were later replaced by the Policy on Social and Environmental Sustainability and the Performance Standards in 30 April 2006. See Int'l Fin. Corp., *Former Environmental and Social Safeguards and Supporting Materials*, https://www.ifc.org/wps/wcm/connect/topics_ext_content/ifc_external_corporate_site/sustainability-at-ifc/policies-standards/safeguards-pre2006, for more on the Safeguards Policy.

18 Wright, *supra* note 15, at 58–59.

19 The EP4, anticipated in 2019, will be the first review of the EPs that is not attached to an update of the IFC's performance standards. The EP4 is expected to consider issues related to human rights and climate change. *See* Press Release, Equator Principles Ass'n, EP Ass'n Annual Meeting 2017 Outcomes (Nov. 2, 2017), https://equator-principles.com/ep-association-news/ep-association-annual-meeting-2017-outcomes/.

20 U.N. Env't Programme Fin. Initiative, *Bank and Human Rights: A Legal Analysis* 19 (2015).

21 In June 2018, the Social Risk Working Group of the Equator Principles Association commissioned a report by Shift on 'Enhancing the Alignment of the Equator Principles with the UN Guiding Principles on Business and Human Rights,' which provided a series of recommendations on how to ensure that the EPs responded to the challenges set by the UNGPs. *See Enhancing the Alignment of the Equator Principles with the UN Guiding Principles on Business and Human Rights: A Public Summary of Shift's Advice to the Equator*

Other international instruments, which existed before the EPs, have been interpreted in a way that links self-regulating initiatives, such as the EPs, with the current state of human rights obligations. In 2017, for example, the UN Committee on Economic, Social and Cultural Rights CESCR published its General Comment 24 in which it affirmed that states had a "duty to adopt a legal framework requiring business entities to exercise human rights due diligence in order to identify, prevent and mitigate the risks of violations of [International Covenant on Economic, Social and Cultural] rights, to avoid such rights being abused, and to account for the negative impacts caused or contributed to by their decisions and operations – and those of entities they control."[22]

D *Soft International Standards*

Given that these lending requirements have been set by, and remain under the control of, private lending institutions it is not surprising that the operative norms are 'soft' in several ways. The EPs explicitly state that they do not create legal rights and duties.[23] They are standards that the borrower is asked to respect.[24] If the EPs' requirements are not met, the EP financial institution (EPFIs) should "work with the client on remedial actions to bring the Project back into compliance to the extent feasible" and "[i]f the client fails to re-establish compliance within an agreed grace period, the EPFI reserves the right to exercise remedies, as considered appropriate."[25] The lender might decide to cancel the loan, as it might consider that this is the most appropriate way to act, but the EPs do not require the lender to do so, even if the borrower has a contractual obligation to comply with the EPs requirements. This means that if the borrower fails to comply with its obligations, other stakeholders are left without means to legally enforce these obligations agreed between the lender and the

---

Principles Association, Equator Principles (Nov. 2018), https://equator-principles.com/wp-content/uploads/2019/01/Shift_Advice_to_SRWG_of_EPA_Public-Version_Final.pdf.

22 UN Committee on Economic, Social and Cultural Right, *State Obligations under the International Covenant on Economic, Social and Cultural Rights in the context of Business Activities*, General Comment No. 24 (Aug. 10, 2017).

23 The Official Disclaimer in the EPs reads " … The Equator Principles do not create any rights in, or liability to, any person, public or private. Financial institutions adopt and implement the Equator Principles voluntarily and independently, without reliance on or recourse to the IFC, the World Bank Group, the Equator Principles Association, or other EPFIs. In a situation where there would be a clear conflict between applicable laws and regulations and requirements set out in the Equator Principles, the local laws and regulations prevail." *Important Notes and Disclaimers*, Equator Principles, https://equator-principles.com/important-notes-disclaimer/.

24 *See* Equator Principles, *supra* note 1, at 5.

25 *See* Equator Principles, *supra* note 1, at 5.

borrower, and any further actions will depend on the sole discretion of the lending institution.

The second dimension of softness concerns discretion in assessing compliance with the EPs. It is entirely up to the lender to decide if the standards have been met in any given case.[26] The lender's decision is not constrained by any higher order standard or procedure from, e.g., the association that Equator banks have formed.

This combination of the absence of legally enforceable rights by communities and other stakeholders when the borrower is not complying with the EPs, together with strong discretion over whether a borrower has or has not satisfied any given Principle, have had consequences for third parties: local populations injured by borrowers' activity. These victims do not have, via the Principles standing alone, any legal recourse. What they do have is the benefit of the requirement that the borrower provide a grievance mechanism designed to receive and facilitate resolution of concerns about the Project's environmental and social performance.[27] This mechanism engages no legal responsibility, but must not impede separate access by claimants to judicial or administrative remedies. In addition, the EPs specify that an independent social and environmental consultant must be appointed to projects in categories A and B to monitor the borrower's risk analyses and propose changes. But there is no formal enforcement mechanism to back up these requirements. As a result, NGOs complain of general inconsistency of application of the EPs.[28]

Such complaints have resulted in further self-regulatory initiatives that go way beyond the EPs. Some financial institutions have developed their own grievance mechanisms,[29] in addition to the requirements of the EPs, the latter

---

26 *See* Equator Principles, *supra* note 1, at 2.

27 *See* Equator Principles, *supra* note 1, at 4.

28 *See* Manuel Wörsdörfer, *10 Years Equator Principles: A Critical Economic-Ethical Analysis*, (Osgoode Hall Law School, York University, Research Paper Series No. 54/2013).

29 *See Respecting People and Communities: ANZ's Approach to Human Rights*, Australia and New Zealand Bank (2016), http://www.anz.com/resources/2/4/246b5001-0820-428b-ac77-e5756b87f52f/humanrightsapp-nov16.pdf?MOD=AJPERES; *Sustainability Report 2018*, National Australia Bank, https://www.nab.com.au/content/dam/nabrwd/documents/reports/corporate/2018-sustainability-report.pdf; *Speaking Up Policy*, Standard Chartered https://www.sc.com/global/av/ng-scb-speaking-up-policy.pdf; *Human Rights Position Statement and 2020 Action Plan*, Westpac Banking Corporation,https://www.westpac.com.au/content/dam/public/wbc/documents/pdf/aw/sustainability/Human_Rights_Position_Statement.pdf; *2016 Human Rights report*, ABN AMRO, https://www.abnamro.com/en/images/Documents/040_Sustainable_banking/080_Reporting/2016/ABN_AMRO_Human_Rights_Report_2016.pdf; and *see Independent Complaints Mechamisms*, Netherlands Development Finance Co., https://www.fmo.nl/independent-complaints-mechanism.

only providing an obligation on the borrower to do so. Despite these individual initiatives, the EPs banks have nevertheless been called on by civil society organizations to provide an effective grievance mechanism given the record of "problematic finance 'under Equator' and of allegations of breaches of these standards."[30]

Some projects have led to more robust measures leading certain lending institutions to rethink and re-evaluate their human rights policies and practices. The Agua Zarca project in Honduras is a prime example.

E *The Agua Zarca Project*

In 2008, a Honduran Company named Desarrollos Energéticos S.A. (DESA) was created with the sole purpose of developing a project to construct and run a hydroelectric plant in the Gualcarque River in the North West of Honduras, designed to provide 21.3MW in power to local communities. The project, since the first studies of the dam took place in 2006, was met with strong opposition from the Lenca Indigenous Peoples. The Lenca people, organized through an NGO called COPIHN (Consejo Cívico de Organizaciones Populares e Indígenas de Honduras) alleged that the river Gualcarque had an important cultural and spiritual value for the surrounding indigenous communities, and that it was an important resource for drinking water, swimming, washing and fishing.

Opposition to the project was met with harassment and violence from the beginning. By June of 2009, the Inter-American Commission on Human Rights (IACHR) issued precautionary measures in favour of Berta Cáceres, the leader of COPIHN, after she had suffered repeated acts of intimidation and harassment by unknown military forces.[31]

In 2012, the EP member, bank Netherlands Development Finance Company (FMO), among other financial institutions, started to finance the Agua Zarca project. During a peaceful demonstration at the dam site in July 2013, 17 year old Tomas García (a member of COPIHN) was shot dead in a close-range shooting by the Honduran Military. Following this event, COPIHN contacted FMO (perceived as the institution with most leverage over DESA) insisting that "they should not fund the Agua Zarca project, as the project sponsor had not obtained, FPIC from the Lenca people, and because land titles had not been properly obtained."[32]

---

30 *See* BankTrack and Oxfam Australia, *Developing Effective Grievance Mechanisms in the Banking Sector,* at 19 (2018).

31 Press Release, The Inter-American Commission on Human Rights, *IACHR Condemns the Killing of Berta Cáceres in Honduras*, 024/2016 (Mar. 4 2016).

32 *See* BankTrack, *Human Rights Briefing Paper: How Banks Contribute to Human Rights Violations*, (2017) at 6. Under the UN Declaration on the Rights of Indigenous People,

Nonetheless the level of violence towards members of COPIHN and other members of the Lenca people continued, with the IACHR persistently calling on the State of Honduras to provide special measures to ensure the life and integrity of Berta Cáceres.[33] In March 2016, Berta Cáceres was murdered. A few days later, Nelson García (another member of COPIHN) was murdered as well. The Inter-American Commission on Human Rights issued new precautionary measures to the other members of COPIHN, as well as the remaining members of Berta Cáceres's family, given the serious risks to their lives.[34]

In July 2017, sixteen months after Berta Cáceres and Nelson García's murders, FMO announced that it was exiting the Agua Zarca project, suspending its operations and seeking a responsible exit.[35] In September 2017, FMO stated that it was taking "further measures to respect human rights," having launched a new policy to identify and respect human rights in investment projects.[36] Some of the measures that it announced were: i) implementing protocols on contextual risks assessment for higher risk projects, with the intention of looking at the possible risks relating to security, conflict and corruption, and the impacts on civil and political rights, workers' rights, as well as land and environmental rights; ii) introduction of an early warning system for risk of oppression towards human rights defenders opposing FMO financed projects; iii) strengthening measures to systematically verify FPIC; and iv) piloting a Human Rights Risk Assessment.[37]

In 2018, FMO indicated in its 2017 -2018 Human Rights Progress Report that among the improvements it had implemented were: i) the inclusion of human

project sponsors should obtain FPIC (free, prior informed consent) of any group of indigenous people that are affected by the project. Furthermore, the Inter-American Court of Human Rights has stated that the right to free, prior and informed consent is an essential component of the right to collective property of indigenous peoples, protected under the American Convention on Human Rights. Inter-American Court of Human Rights, Case of the Mayagna (Sumo) Community of Awas Tingni v. Nicaragua, Judgment of 31 August 2001, para. 153.

33 *See supra* note 31.

34 *See Precautionary Measure MC-112–16*, The Inter-American Commission on Human Rights (2016), http://www.oas.org/es/cidh/decisiones/pdf/2016/MC112-16-Es.pdf.

35 *See* FMO, *Human Rights. An integral part of our investment approach: Human Rights progress report* Oct. 2017 – Sept. 2018, at 10 (2018), https://www.fmo.nl/l/library/download/urn:uuid:3cd20162-8ce3-4d33-ab8c-249811d357ac/fmo+human+rights+progress+report.pdf.

36 *See* FMO, *FMO takes further measures to respect human rights*, (Sep. 27, 2017), https://www.fmo.nl/news-detail/816a6094-74a6-4f21-8cc7-a1383375e144/fmo-takes-further-measures-to-respect-human-rights.

37 *Id.*

rights-related covenants as needed in the legal agreement(s) resulting from the additional focus on human rights; ii) conducting regular ongoing community support checks, including FPIC; iii) discontinuation of projects where the right to water of local communities cannot be ensured; and iv) the human rights risk assessment pilot, which provided a better understanding of the added value of explicit human rights risk assessments by a dedicated human rights specialist.[38]

The unfortunate example of the Agua Zarca project, and in particular the involvement of FMO, reflects the inadequate application of the EPs, as had been alleged by NGOs for years. Given the reputational damage caused, and the inability of the EPs to prevent this, banks, such as FMO, have had to further rethink their policies, implementing new measures to prevent consequences such as those in this project.

F *Hard Law*

If the EPs derive neither from treaty nor any other binding legal instrument, does this exhaust the investigation into the role of hard international law in their formulation and enforcement? No. It is important to reach into other sets of norms, many of them legal, that indirectly affect the shape and impact of the EPs. Bank lending affects companies not simply as borrowers because these borrowers turn around and deploy the funds as investors. In this role, the decisions borrowers take can be affected by international investment law.

Consider another example. When investing in large-scale projects such as dams or oil pipelines, companies will often negotiate legally binding contracts with host governments. Anxious for inward investment, these host governments will often agree to the inclusion of 'stabilisation' clauses. These are enforceable undertakings not to change the law applied to the project – often for its lifetime – which can last for many years.[39] If the undertaking is broken, then the company has a cause of action to recover its extra costs or lost profits arising from the change. Such an undertaking can help allay the fears not only of the project company, but also those of a project finance lender. The borrower's promise to reimburse the project finance loan obtains considerable indirect support from the host government's promise not to add to the borrower's expenses by changing the law governing the project. In some situations, the relevant guarantee of stabilization originates from an investment treaty, and in other situations it is located in the contract between the host government and the investing company. Either way, this mix is a combination of hard and

---

38 FMO, *supra* note 35, at 25–29.

39 *See Human Rights on the Line*, *supra* note 5.

soft standards: the Principles, as soft standards, are agreed via the covenants made between EP lender and borrower as hard contracts, which further interact with investment contracts and treaties between state and borrower, and other states.

As an example, an EP lender might require the borrower to ensure free, prior informed consent (FPIC) of an indigenous community which will be potentially affected by the project. This condition, as part of the EPs, will be contractually guaranteed in the covenant between the lender and the borrower. However, the EPs are not detailed enough on the conditions and procedures of FPIC (acknowledging the there is "no universally accepted definition of FPIC"), and the project company might be operating in a country whose legal regulation of indigenous and tribal peoples is less than ideal, as compared to international standards. In this case, it is possible that the state might be called by a human rights tribunal or other quasi-judicial body to reform its regulatory framework governing the rights of indigenous peoples so that it complies with the relevant standards set forth in international human rights law.[40] If a stabilisation clause is included in the contract between the project company and the host state, fearing a possible investment dispute against it[41] (supported by an investment treaty), the host state will probably not reform its regulatory framework or may exempt the project from reforms. In the end, the indigenous communities are not properly protected, and the risk of their rights being violated increases.

This particular combination of norms standing behind the example of the stabilization promise from a government can and does work to the advantage of the banks and companies. As seen in the example, those who might lose are communities and others such as employees who would benefit from the changed regulations that the host state might have otherwise introduced.

However, other parts of hard international law relevant to the interpretation of EPs point in a different direction. International human rights law, for

40 As an example of a similar situation, *see* Inter-American Court of Human Rights, *Case of the Kichwa Indigenous People of Sarayaku v. Ecuador, Merits and Reparations* (June 27, 2012).

41 On the chilling effects of international investment disputes over the right to regulate of host states, *see* Kyla Tienhaara, *Regulatory Chill and the Threat of Arbitration: A View from Political Science*, Evolution in Investment Treaty Law and Arbitration, Cambridge University Press (C. Brown & K. Miles, eds., 2011); David Gaukrodger, *The balance between investor protection and the right to regulate in investment treaties: A scoping paper*, OECD Working Papers on International Investment (Feb. 2017).

example, can bind a state as it sets its framework for inward investment activity via its domestic measures. Staying with the example of stabilization, if South Africa gives contractual undertakings not to alter the relevant labour law that applies to a project, what happens when the state comes under a fresh obligation to improve basic labour standards, the obligation itself coming from South Africa's commitment to evolving ILO standards?

Acknowledging the impact of those international standards, EP banks might hypothetically be willing to rank compliance with the the international labour standards above stability, perhaps for reputational reasons. In other words, as soft international standards, the EPs are malleable – potentially powerful but open to shifting alliances: in somc cases there can be a convergence of interests between borrowers and those lenders that assign a relatively low priority to social and environmental objectives while formally acknowledging them; but in other cases alignments might exist between lenders, perhaps for reputational reasons, and local communities and other stakeholders that press for higher priority to be given to those same social and environmental objectives. In still other cases, borrowers might align themselves with local communities if the lender wants to push the borrower to lower its construction standards to meet a strict deadline, as seen in the scheduling of the use of cement in the earlier example.

Standing back, we can say that the combination of soft and hard norms that can best guide the deployment of the EPs, will depend – not surprisingly – on whose axe is being ground. Commercial lenders, corporate borrowers, human rights advocates, trade unions etc. will each have a view of the best direction in which the Equator Principles should move – each with its own template for desirable social change. There is a variety of hard international norms which can be drawn on – ranging from those found in investment treaties to those found in human rights treaties. How that combination is best configured can be assessed by looking at what type of social change is sought.

II Matching the EPs against Agendas for Social Change

The EPs are rightly tested against their ambition to make bank lending a progressive force. That ambition can be assessed on two levels. One is aimed at moving societies in a sustained way to enjoy economic growth while preventing well-recognized types of damage, such as various forms of discrimination, labour abuse, and loss of livelihood or civil liberties. The second is to use the EPs to fundamentally transform certain features of the host society. These features could be based on the human rights commitments of the host state, such as that of progressive realisation found in the International Covenant of

Economic, Social and Cultural Rights.[42] It might, for example, aim to nationalise certain key sectors of the economy in order to introduce wide-ranging worker control of enterprises.

In principle the EPs do not impose an obstacle to either type of change.

A *Social Change Aimed at Sustained Prevention of Serious Social Damage*

Based on the authors' experience and that of their colleagues at the Essex Business and Human Rights Project[43] there are several concrete issues that test the robustness and equity of the Principles. These show that what the EPs give with the right hand of commitment to social responsibility is sometimes taken back with the left hand of commercial bank priorities and pressures. Some of these problems could be overcome by hardening in the appropriate way the soft norms applicable to project finance. We can see this in several places.

1 No-Go for a Proposed Project

Implicit in the EPs is the need to draw a boundary line between projects that are viable, but somewhat risky, and those which are not viable because the risk is simply too great. The risk assessment called for by the EPs can orient the investigation in two different directions. One is to treat the social and environmental requirements in the EPs as a means to an end. Thus, the EPs are followed when compliance preserves or enhances commercial return, but they can be ignored if compliance is too expensive and hurts the return. The second approach treats the avoidance of environmental and social damage – such as harm to labour rights, or health and safety in the local community – as a specific project objective. In this case, the application of these social and environmental standards is less influenced by competing commercial concerns. If the environmental and social damage is too severe it should be avoided by, e.g., refusing to go ahead with the project despite an indisputable commercial gain to the borrower of carrying on.

---

42 International Covenant on Economic, Social and Cultural Rights art. 2, *opened for signature* Dec. 16, 1966, 993 U.N.T.S. 3 (entered into force Jan. 3, 1976) (establishing under Article 2 that: "Each State Party to the present Covenant undertakes to take steps, individually and through international assistance and co-operation, especially economic and technical, to the maximum of its available resources, with a view to achieving progressively the full realization of the rights recognized in the present Covenant by all appropriate means, including particularly the adoption of legislative measures.").

43 GLOBAL PROJECT FINANCE, *supra* note 12..

These different directions in the risk assessment reflect two different perspectives: one is a balancing approach and the other is a filter approach. A balancing approach places the risks of social and environmental damage on a scale and balances it against the expected commercial return. This balancing approach values the EPs, but it does not consider their satisfaction as indispensable in the decision-making process. If the commercial return is very high, social and environmental impacts will be given less importance.

A filter approach allows social and environmental risks to have a more prominent role in the decision-making process. The approval of a project will be subject to the satisfaction of the requirements set forth in the EPs. This means that projects promising high return, but also high risks of environmental and social damage, are not approved. A clear example of this filter approach is the recently adopted policy by the FMO where the bank will not approve projects in which the right to water of local communities cannot be assured. Here, social and environmental risks were placed as a filter, necessary for the approval of a project, without considering the potential returns the project might provide.

Given that the weight assigned to the EPs is under the sole control of the relevant financial institutions, with no authoritative input from other stakeholders, there is little prospect that the second approach to risk will be adopted. As a result, certain notoriously high risk projects are allowed to go through despite their heavy potential for damage[44] – the banks hoping that the EP procedures for Category A projects will be enough to avoid the worst. It is only if stakeholder participation is widened that this might change. This would represent a 'hardening' of the EPs in the sense that they would be open to more systematic interpretation, no longer at the sole discretion of each lender, and could serve as the basis for empowering third parties to make the case for avoiding a project that poses too great a threat of social or environmental damage quite independently of the fact that it could otherwise earn a high profit.

2 Avoidance of Damage vs. Compensation for Damage

Once a lender has committed itself to financing a project despite the high risks of social and environmental damage, a further crucial choice opens up: between doing what is necessary to avoid the damage and choosing to allow the damage to happen while standing ready to compensate its victims.[45] It

44 Alicia Henning & Manuel Wörsdörfer, *Challenging Voluntary CSR-Initiatives – A Case Study on the Effectiveness of the Equator Principles*, Working Paper Series (Goethe Univ. Frankfurt, 2015).

45 For development of this point, *see* GLOBAL PROJECT FINANCE, *supra* note 12, at ch. 5.

is usually better to avoid serious damage as compared to the second best – compensation for that damage.[46] The avoidance option might call for slowing or stopping the progress of a project until the problem is put right, whereas the planned compensation option allows the project to carry on, with part of the revenue set aside for eventual victim claims. At what point should one say that the damage is unavoidable and compensation the only recourse? Lending banks will be quicker to draw the line around the more expensive avoidance option and more ready to embrace compensation measures in advance than are other stakeholders. This is despite the fact that some damage done might lie ethically beyond compensation, such as the loss of human life. The reason stems from the discipline of project finance. As discussed above, the lender under this financial strategy counts on only one source of repayment of the loan: the project's revenues. This approach is particularly hostile to surprises: to anything that will upset that flow of funds, such as a call to stop or slow down the operation of an oil pipeline until a problem is put right. The result is what one sees: projects that treat predictable social damage as a business expense, the victims of which are compensated from funds put aside from the project revenues that continue to flow.

Other conditions might come into play when lenders are analysing whether it is preferable to invest in a high risk project and compensate for the damage or to avoid the project altogether. First, both the effectiveness and disposition of a project company's grievance mechanism to respond to the damages made by the project might be a condition to take into account, given that awards by other dispute settlement bodies of adequate compensation for the damages caused by a project might not only prevent the company from having any substantial profit, but could potentially make the company insolvent.

A second and directly linked condition is the effective ability of the host state to hold liable the project company for paying full compensation for the damages caused. A bank might be more tempted to finance a very risky project – rather than avoid the project – if it is developed in a country with a weak judicial system, and a lack of political will to legally hold companies responsible for the damages caused by their projects. However, for some banks, a high risk project in a high risk country would be less likely to be funded given the

46 The Equator Principles Preamble, Equator Principles III, at 2 (June 2013), https://equator-principles.com/wp-content/uploads/2017/03/equator_principles_III.pdf ("We recognise the importance of climate change, biodiversity, and human rights, and believe negative impacts on project-affected ecosystems, communities, and the climate should be avoided where possible. If these impacts are unavoidable, they should be minimised, mitigated, and/or offset.").

fear they may be subject to a damaging international campaign if serious injury occurs.

These two conditions might push lenders and borrowers to prefer to invest in situations of potential high profit rather than avoid potential damages. The lack of transparency, as we will see next, exacerbates the risk of lenders preferring to choose compensation over avoidance.

3 Lack of Transparency

This is a further clear instance in which the left hand of lender practice takes back what the right hand of the EPs promise. The Principles now clearly require reporting on the Environmental and Social Impact Assessment carried out on the project.[47] This is qualified by an exemption for client confidentiality requirements.[48] The latter has led NGOs to complain that certain banks "hide behind excessive interpretations of 'client confidentiality' to withhold information to stakeholders and the public."[49]

Some have argued that there is a "virtual absence of public information about the terms and conditions of individual project finance transactions. As a result, most information about the environmental and social dimensions of project made available to the general public is based on local media stories and field report gathered and disseminated" by NGOs.[50]

This has been made evident in certain cases, such as the Agua Zarca project detailed above, where substantial information on the conditions set by FMO and the social and environmental assessment performed by DESA were not disclosed. A clear disconnect existed between the alleged FPIC process that DESA had allegedly held and on which FMO had presumably based its lending decision, and what was argued by COPIHN on behalf of the Lenca people. The lack of transparency by both FMO and DESA created further tensions between the Lenca people and the Honduran military forces with deadly results. FMO has insisted that it acted in good faith.[51] But the lack of publicly available information on this issue makes such assessment difficult to determine.

---

47 *See A financial industry benchmark for determining, assessing and managing environmental and social risk in projects*, Equator Principles, https://equator-principles.com/wp-content/uploads/2017/03/equator_principles_III.pdf.

48 *Id.*

49 Wörsdörfer, *supra* note 28.

50 *See, e.g.*, Wright, *supra* note 15, at 64–65.

51 FMO, *supra* note 35, at 10.

4 Corporate Liability

The EPs are designed to control the behaviour of the borrower of bank funds. In project finance, this borrower is usually a subsidiary operating with limited funds in a jurisdiction well away from the home state of the parent company. If the borrower runs out of funds, making it unable to compensate victims of a large accident, there is no recourse to the parent. This lending strategy is strongly supported by the orthodox principle of corporate law in most jurisdictions that prevents the liability of a parent company for its subsidiaries' debts from arising on the ground that it and the subsidiary are separate enterprises. This use of a corporate veil is in turn a serious obstacle to certain victims obtaining justice. It goes against the spirit of the EPs, but not against the substance of banks' commercial priorities. The problem of the use of the corporate veil to obstruct justice to victims cannot of course be solved only by the EPs. It needs to be addressed within the different relevant areas of commercial law. However the EPs, with loans being provided under the framework of project finance, help to reinforce the status quo without addressing ways in which to ensure adequate reparations to communities harmed by its borrowers.[52]

5 Competition among Banks Affecting the Categorization Process

Given that it is up to each lender to decide whether the risk of damage produced by a given project is high, medium or low,[53] each lender faces a potential conflict between the pressures generated by competition among lenders to secure business at a lucrative rate and the aim of preventing social and environmental damage. This could lead some banks to rank the risk of damage lower than they otherwise would. Again, given that implementation of the EPs is under the sole control of individual lenders, there is no countervailing voice that would challenge any given risk assessment. However, empirical research

52 Despite the EPs obligating borrowers to create grievance mechanisms, the principles do not provide any obligation in case the borrower becomes insolvent. Therefore, in such cases, victims of injustices carried out by the project borrower will not be able to receive any reparation. Under these circumstances, the parent company – given the protection under the corporate vail – would not accountable for the acts committed by its subsidiary.

53 Further criticism of the EP banks' categorization process has been grounded on the validity of such a classification process – assessing the social and environmental impacts of a project – without conducting an in-depth environmental and social impact analysis. This is exacerbated by the fact that the lenders' reports do not identify specific projects, making it impossible for stakeholders to refute or complain – in due time – the categorization issued by the lending institution. *See* United Nations Environment Programme, *The Equator Principles: Do They Make Banks More Sustainable?*, Inquiry Working Paper 16/05, at 17 (2016).

has shown that when EPs banks collaborate with banks that have not adopted the EPs, peer pressure is placed on the non-adopting bank to implement the principles in the project.[54] This is explained by the fact that in cases of syndication (when more than one bank provides the loan for the project), even if only one of the lenders has adopted the EPs, that lender still has the responsibility to do the due diligence required by the principles. The EP bank will, therefore, pressure the rest of the lenders to adopt the EPs or at least to share the responsibility for such due diligence.

B *Social Change as Fundamental Transformation*

Here we are dealing with changes in society that lead to fundamental alterations of priorities – and in the norms reflecting those priorities. As indicated earlier, these changes can be reflected in new forms of social control over certain types of property, as happens when, for example, a project is nationalized, or changes in government policy lead to a stronger role for employees or local communities in making key decisions.

To what extent can international project finance help to promote such fundamental change? Here we find barriers. The obstacles emerge from a dominant concern that lenders and project companies have: stability.

This is, of course, a feature of all lending. Nonetheless, it is important to stress that limits to transformative or radical social change might not only be in the legal controls set forth in stabilisation clauses. Human rights law, domestically and internationally might also halt – or at least slow – the wishes of a society or its government to implement radical changes. The respect of certain fundamental human rights might limit the way in which certain changes can be implemented. Many have criticised the way in which the protection of property rights, for example, have trumped the advancement of other human rights such as an adequate standard of living.[55] The respect of certain fundamental rights, such as the right to a fair trial and other judicial guarantees, would imply that any process such as nationalisation or expropriation would be carefully reviewed, and could take many years.

In project finance – the type of finance focused on by the EPs – however, the lender's anxiety is heightened, as has been said, by its main reliance on the single stream of revenue from a given project, despite some other ways

54 *See* Jaap W.B. Bos, Gaby Contreras & Stefanie Kleimeier, *Self-Regulation in Collaborative Environments: The Case of the Equator Principles in Banking*, GSBE Research Memoranda (Maastricht University School of Business and Economics 2016).

55 *See* Samuel Moyn, *Not Enough: Human Rights in an Unequal World* (Harvard University Press 2018).

of diluting the risk.[56] This leads, also as indicated earlier, to support by the financial community for stringent stabilization clauses in legally enforceable contracts, whereby a host government will have to make up for lost revenue arising from the changes. For poorer countries, facing stretched resources and committed to bringing about fundamental social change, the impact of the stabilization clause can push the cost of such change too high for the national treasury to bear.[57] This can provoke costly battles, pitting host governments pushing ahead with a plan for change – often with strong public support – against the lending community wanting the bill for such change to be paid along the way. The change might in some cases be abandoned given the impossibility or high cost of providing adequate compensation to the project company. If a government presses ahead, while not paying the compensation due, it might find itself frozen out of future dealings with the international lending community. This might help explain the surprising finding by researchers that interest rates charged by international lenders tend to be higher the greater is a regime's commitment to democracy.[58]

III Overview: the Place of Soft and Hard International Norms in International Lending

EP-based project finance both calls for social progress and stands in its way. It aims to prevent serious social damage coming from the projects it supports, yet weakens at crucial points its ability to prevent that damage. It can also stand in the way of a government's promoting fundamental alterations in its framework of regulation – reflecting a shift in social forces and priorities – by making the cost of such change too high.

In part, these defects are attributable to the structure of the decision-making that goes into lending of this kind. The norms governing this key element in development are under the control of one set of the interested parties – the international lending community. The obligations they enshrine are placed on

56 Despite the main reliance by the lender on the revenue generated by the project itself, in many cases, there will be at least some other level of recourse to the sponsor, and in other cases, the lenders may have passed the risk onto others through use of insurance or derivatives, or through various take and pay contracts for the project outputs.

57 This is a problem that is receiving a large amount of critical attention. See *Human Rights on the Line, supra* note 5.

58 *See* Claudia Girardone & Stuart Snaith, *Global Project Finance Investments and Political Risk* (Cambridge Univ. Press); *Global Project Finance, supra* note 12, at 231.

the project borrower, often without adequate or effective monitoring by the lenders. Communities are left voiceless and blind, as the lack of transparency – in the name of corporate confidentiality – leaves those affected without the proper information to fight back on possible damaging projects.

The EPs origin in the voluntary association of actors in the private sector makes the scheme of social responsibility weak at key points, as indicated in these examples. However, the problem is not necessarily solved by relying on the hard law that arises from international investment law. That depends on what goes into the investment contracts between the project company and the host state. As they are presently formulated, they bear the imprint of the same set of forces that shape the soft norms underpinning project finance lending by the private sector.

Hardening such soft norms is possible however. Host states could require that the EPs are specifically incorporated into the language of the investment contract. Essential conditions, such as free, prior and informed consent to the expropriation of the land of an indigenous community, and allied grievance mechanisms,[59] will then be legally binding and could ultimately be used in domestic litigation or international investment arbitration. Stabilisation clauses can be limited by such conditions, ensuring that host states are able to further regulate on the scope and interpretation of such conditions.

Host states can further harden the EPs by incorporating these fundamental principles into their domestic legislation, before entering into a contract with the project company. The principles enshrined in the EPs can therefore support domestic judicial interpretation when a project company is considered to be in breach of its EPs obligations, but the lender has been unwilling to act upon it. The increasing role of domestic legislation in international investment arbitration,[60] can also allow a tribunal to interpret the obligations of the investor in accordance with the EPs, hardening the justiciability of the EPs at the international level.

A treaty linking business activity and human rights could also help here, but only a treaty of a certain kind. If a treaty was part of an overall strategy to insert human rights standards into business activities, it would strengthen rather than replace the EPs. It could induce the states parties to the treaty to inject a wider range of stakeholders into the process of setting loan conditions – wider

59 As an example of possible investment contracts with mandatory grievance mechanisms by the investor, *see* The IISD Guide to Negotiating Investment Contracts for Farmland and Water, Part 2 Model Contract, 47 (2014).

60 *See* Jarrod Hepburn, *Domestic law in international investment arbitration*, Oxford University Press (2017).

than the group that presently dominates the formulation of those conditions. It could also assign human rights their appropriate weight when brought under the pressure of commercial demands. A Business and Human Rights Treaty, with a substantial number of ratifications (that include both home and host states) and with no incompatible reservations,[61] can provide a significant way of ensuring that human rights are not systematically trumped by commercial return.

It is not enough to 'harden' the soft norms in the Equator Principles. That can, assuming they continue to be used as at present, aggravate the weakness of the Principles as motors for social change. Its inadequate application can also, under extreme circumstances such as in the Agua Zarca Project, provide a negative influence on and damage to the integrity of a society. As was said earlier, this risk of negative effects will exist so long as the background norms in investment treaties, and in national corporate law, are shaped by the same forces that presently control the deployment of the EPs themselves. A Business and Human Rights treaty will help if it clearly indicates that human rights and environmental obligations have priority over other contractual obligations,[62] and that "investors shall not manage or operate an investment in a manner that circumvents international environmental, labour or human rights obligations."[63] Such a treaty is essential if we are to achieve a level of coherence[64] when regulating commercial banks' ability to finance projects that have a potential to damage the enjoyment of fundamental human rights. If not, we are bound to have different self-regulating initiatives across the globe, with a series of diverse domestic legislation, but which do not respond to the real challenges of the complex and globalised economies we face today.

61 *See* Luis Felipe Yanes, *A Business and Human Rights Treaty: The Risks of Human Rights Counter-Diplomacy*, OpinioJuris, (Sep. 8, 2018), http://opiniojuris.org/2018/08/09/a-business-and-human-rights-treaty-the-risks-of-human-rights-counter-diplomacy/.

62 *See* Memorandum from the *Essex Business and Human Rights Project and the Human Rights Centre at the University of Essex to the Office of the High Commissioner for Human Rights* (Feb. 28, 2018) (on file with author).

63 *See* Tara Van Ho, Anil Yilmaz Vastardis, & Luis Felipe Yanes, *Proposed Investment Treaty Provisions on behalf of the Essex Business & Human Rights Project*, submission to the UN Working group on the issue of human rights and transnational corporations and other business enterprises (2018), https://www.ohchr.org/Documents/Issues/Business/Forum2018Submission5.pdf.

64 *See* Sheldon Leader, Coherence, Mutual Assurance and the Rationale for a Treaty, *Building a Treaty on Business and Human Rights: Context and Contours*, (Surya Deva & David Bilchitz, eds., Cambridge U. Press 2017).

CHAPTER 11

Non-Judicial Grievance Mechanisms: Hardening the Soft Law of Corporate Accountability?

*Nikki Reisch**

1 Introduction: the Emergence of "Soft-law" Approaches to Remedying Corporate Human Rights Violations

The activities of corporations have profound implications for human rights around the world. Yet as non-state actors, private companies fall outside the direct reach of most international human rights law.[1] Despite considerable international efforts during the past four decades to regulate transnational corporate conduct,[2] heightened public awareness of the human and environmental harms that businesses may cause,[3] and renewed momentum toward a multilateral treaty,[4] no binding international agreement yet defines the human

* (Formerly) Legal Director of the Center for Human Rights and Global Justice at New York University School of Law.

1 As traditionally understood, international human rights treaties directly bind only the states that are party to them. Private actors can incur liability under international law, however, for gross violations of human rights amounting to international crimes, such as slavery, torture, and genocide. *See, e.g.*, Rome Statute of the International Criminal Court, art. 25, July 17, 1998, 2187 U.N.T.S. 90 (entered into force July 1, 2002); Convention on the Prevention and Punishment of the Crime of Genocide, art. 4, Dec. 9, 1948, 78 U.N.T.S. 277.

2 *See* David Vogel, *The Private Regulation of Global Corporate Conduct, in* THE POLITICS OF GLOBAL REGULATION 16 (Walter Mattli & Ngaire Woods, eds., 2009) (discussing efforts to enact a legally enforceable international code of corporate conduct since the 1970s and the barriers to consensus on its content and sanctions); *see also* Commission on Human Rights, Norms on the Responsibilities of Transnational Corporations and Other Business Enterprises with Regard to Human Rights, U.N. Doc E/CN.4/Sub.2/2003/12/Rev.2 (Aug. 26, 2003).

3 The growth of the Business and Human Rights Resource Centre, www.business-humanrights.org, and the emergence of publications such as the Corporate Human Rights Benchmark, inaugurated in 2017, reflect increased public interest in the human rights performance of businesses. The 2018 Corporate Human Rights Benchmark assesses 101 of the world's largest publicly traded companies against dozens of human rights indicators. *See Corporate Human Rights Benchmark 2018 Key Findings: Apparel, Agricultural Products and Extractives Companies*, [hereinafter "CHRB 2018 Key Findings"], https://www.corporatebenchmark.org/sites/default/files/documents/CHRBKeyFindings2018.pdf.

4 In 2014, Ecuador and South Africa drafted a resolution that established "an open-ended intergovernmental working group with the mandate to elaborate an international legally binding

 | DOI:10.1163/9789004417021_012

rights obligations of corporations, and individuals and communities have no international forum where they may bring claims against private companies.

Host and home state laws govern many aspects of corporate activity, but national regulatory frameworks leave ample legal loopholes, particularly with respect to transnational corporations.[5] Where "hard" conduct-regulating laws exist, procedural impediments, as well as financial and logistical barriers, often make them difficult to enforce against companies, especially for affected communities and other under-resourced actors in the Global South.[6] Moreover, complex global corporate structures obfuscate the locus of control, insulate parent entities from liability for injurious conduct, and make it harder to identify where in the corporate chain jurisdiction lies. Individuals and communities thus have few avenues to pursue legal redress when corporations infringe upon their human rights.

---

instrument on Transnational Corporations and Other Business Enterprises with respect to human rights." Human Rights Council, Elaboration of an International Legally Binding Instrument on Transnational Corporations and Other Business Enterprises with Respect to Human Rights, ¶ 1, U.N. Doc. A/HRC/26/L.22/Rev.1 (Jun. 25, 2014). An initial ("zero") draft of a proposed binding treaty was released for comment in July 2018, *Legally Binding Instrument to Regulate, in International Human Rights Law, the Activities of Transnational Corporations and other Business Enterprises Zero Draft 16.7.2018*, https://www.ohchr.org/Documents/HRBodies/HRCouncil/WGTransCorp/Session3/DraftLBI.pdf, and a revised draft followed in July 2019, *OEIGWG Chairmanship Revised Draft 16.7.2019*, https://www.ohchr.org/Documents/HRBodies/HRCouncil/WGTransCorp/OEIGWG_RevisedDraft_LBI.pdf.

5 "Host state" refers to the country in which a company invests or conducts operations, while "home state" refers to the country in which the parent corporation is registered and/or headquartered.

6 *See, e.g.*, Amnesty Int'l, *Injustice Incorporated: Corporate Abuses and the Human Right to Remedy*, 113–197 (2014), https://www.amnesty.org/download/Documents/8000/pol300012014en.pdf (discussing obstacles related to corporate structure, extraterritorial action, jurisdiction, information and corporate-state relationships); Amnesty Int'l, *Creating a Paradigm Shift: Legal Solutions to Improve Access to Remedy for Corporate Human Rights Abuse* (2017), https://www.amnesty.org/download/Documents/POL3070372017ENGLISH.PDF (presenting legal proposals to eliminate or mitigate barriers to remedy identified in *Injustice Incorporated*); Gwynne Skinner, Robert McCorquodale, & Oliver De Schutter, *The Third Pillar: Access to Judicial Remedies for Human Rights Violations by Transnational Business*, 27–73 (2013) (mapping barriers to judicial remedy in home states for harms caused by TNCs); *see also* Human Rights Council, *Improving Accountability and Access to Remedy for Victims of Business-Related Human Rights Abuse: Report of the United Nations High Commissioner for Human Rights* ¶¶ 4, 21–30, U.N. Doc. A/HRC/32/19 (May 10, 2016) (discussing the structural and managerial complexity of business entities; challenges unique to their cross-border nature; and the need for policy coherence).

In this context, company-created, non-judicial grievance mechanisms (NJGMs)[7] have emerged as an important stop-gap for victims with few means to obtain remedy for corporate-related human rights abuses and an attractive option for companies seeking to mitigate their reputational and financial risks.[8] Their relationship to international law, however—both hard and soft—is tenuous, and potentially antagonistic.

The term "non-judicial grievance mechanism" encompasses a wide and growing category of bodies today, both state-based and non-state-based,[9] including NJGM s established by private companies at the project or operational level to address complaints from affected individuals and communities about the human rights impacts of their activities. Company-created NJGM s—the focus of this chapter—are designed to resolve disputes with businesses, but cannot produce binding adjudications.[10] In this way, they are quintessentially "soft" fora, tasked with addressing breaches of, and ensuring corporate respect for, human rights guaranteed in "hard" international law—international human rights treaties.

First, a word about the terms "hard" and "soft" international law: As discussed in the introduction to this volume, scholars advance alternative definitions of

7 Such mechanisms are also commonly referred to as "operational grievance mechanisms," or, when developed after claims of abuse arise to provide retrospective relief, "company-created human rights remedy mechanisms." *See* Sarah Knuckey & Eleanor Jenkin, *Company-created remedy mechanisms for serious human rights abuses: a promising new frontier for the right to remedy?*, 19 INT'L J. HUM. RTS. 801, 802 (2015).

8 *See, e.g.*, Catherine Coumans, *Mining and Access to Justice: From Sanction and Remedy to Weak Non-Judicial Grievance Mechanisms*, 45 U.B.C. L. REV. 651, 655–56, 688 (2012) (asserting that weak NJGMs are promoted as a voluntary corporate social responsibility (CSR) alternative to binding judicial and regulatory mechanisms, such as "home-state regulation of overseas activities of multinational corporations (MNCs) and access for foreign plaintiffs to home-state courts"); Mining Watch, *Having the Ruggie Pulled Out From Under Us: From 'Sanction and Remedy' to non-judicial grievance mechanisms* (2011) (describing NJGMs as "typical" CSR measures, characterized by problems of uneven application, insufficient independence and transparency, and inability to compel sanction or remedy).

9 SOMO, the Center for Research on Multinational Corporations, has articulated a helpful taxonomy of NJGMs, grouping them into five categories: intergovernmental human rights bodies, national human rights institutions, development finance accountability mechanisms, sectoral industry mechanisms, and company—or project-specific— operational grievance mechanisms. *See* SOMO, *The Patchwork of Non-Judicial Grievance Mechanisms: Addressing the limitations of the current landscape* 1–2 (2014), https://www.somo.nl/wp-content/uploads/2014/12/The-Patchwork-of-Non-Judicial-Grievance-Mechanisms-1.pdf.

10 *See generally* SOMO, *Human Rights and Grievance Mechanisms*, https://www.somo.nl/hrgm/ (last visited Apr. 28, 2019); *see also* May Miller-Dawkins, Kate Macdonald, & Shelley Marshall, *Beyond Effectiveness Criteria: The Possibilities and Limits of Transnational Non-Judicial Redress Mechanisms*, 5 (2016) [hereinafter "Beyond Effectiveness Criteria"].

hard and soft international law and competing views as to whether they represent binary categories, exist on a continuum, or function in a dialectical relationship. In the present chapter, hard international law refers to "legally binding obligations that are precise (or can be made precise through adjudication or the issuance of detailed regulations) and that delegate authority for interpreting and implementing the law."[11] Soft international law refers to norms—principles that purport to guide or regulate conduct—that lack one or more of these characteristics: bindingness, precision, or delegated authority for their interpretation.[12] Most international human rights law exists somewhere on a spectrum between these two.[13] Although codified in conventions binding on state parties, some human rights provisions are actually quite soft in that their content is malleable, their interpretation evolving, and their justiciability contested. By the same token, some international standards not yet enshrined in treaty text bear indicia of hardness, in terms of their detail and influence on behavior. The intent to be binding and the possibility of judicial enforcement remain key features distinguishing hard from soft international law.

Trends in the business and human rights field call into question two frequent assumptions regarding the relationship between hard and soft international law: (1) that soft law is a complement and precursor to hard law; and (2) that the existence of an accountability mechanism hardens soft international law. As Shaffer and Pollack have suggested, soft international law may be antagonistic to hard international law in some contexts, not only by leading to a proliferation of inconsistent and conflictual norms, but also by obfuscating and undermining existing legal obligations.[14] Such antagonism is apparent in the history of efforts to regulate corporate conduct under human rights law.

Attempts to craft international norms governing the human rights impacts of business operations have been ongoing for many years, from early efforts to define binding codes of conduct at the United Nations and within

---

11 Kenneth W. Abbott & Duncan Snidal, *Hard and Soft Law in International Governance*, 54 (3) INT'L ORG. 421, 421 (2000).

12 *Id.*

13 *See* Justine Nolan, *The Corporate Responsibility to Respect Rights: Soft Law or Not Law? in* HUMAN RIGHTS OBLIGATIONS OF BUSINESS: BEYOND THE CORPORATE RESPONSIBILITY TO RESPECT? 138, 142 (Surya Deva & David Bilchitz, eds., 2013) (discussing the difficulty of demarcating hard and soft law in the human rights arena, given that some treaties include "soft" obligations like "undertakings to strive to cooperate or agree to take steps").

14 Gregory C. Shaffer & Mark A. Pollack, *Hard vs, Soft Law: Alternatives, Complements, and Antagonists in International Governance*, 94 MINN. L. REV. 706, 708–09 (2010).

the Organization of Economic Cooperation and Development (OECD), to the voluntary industry-led initiatives that emerged during the corporate social responsibility boom of the early 2000's, such as the United Nations Global Compact,[15] the Voluntary Principles on Security and Human Rights,[16] the Equator Principles,[17] and the Fair Labor Association.[18] Most of these norms remain not only voluntary, but vague; more detailed, substantive rules have failed to gain support.[19] In the face of resistance to international regulation on the part of powerful business interests and some governments, and persistent gaps in the rules and remedies available in host and home states,[20] soft-law

15 *See* U.N. Global Compact, available at www.unglobalcompact.org (last visited June 15, 2019). The first two principles of the Compact commit signatory companies to "support and respect the protection of internationally proclaimed human rights" and "make sure that they are not complicit in human rights abuses." *The Power of Principles*, U.N. Global Compact, available at https://www.unglobalcompact.org/what-is-gc/mission/principles (last visited June 15, 2019).

16 Established in 2000, the Voluntary Principles are "designed to guide companies in maintaining the safety and security of their operations within an operating framework that encourages respect for human rights." Voluntary Principles on Security and Human Rights, available at http://www.voluntaryprinciples.org/ (last visited Jul. 28, 2018).

17 Defined as a "risk management framework" for financial institutions, the Equator Principles are designed to provide businesses with a minimum standard of environmental and social due diligence. The Equator Principles, available at http://equator-principles.com/ (last visited Jul. 28, 2018). *See* Sheldon Leader & Luis Felipe Yanes, *Levers For and Obstacles To Social Change: Bank Lending, the Law and the Equator Principles*, in ch. 10 of this book for more on the Equator Principles.

18 The Fair Labor Association is a multi-stakeholder entity that seeks to ensure company compliance with labor standards based on international law. Fair Labor Association, available at http://www.fairlabor.org (last visited June 15, 2019).

19 *See* SURYA DEVA, REGULATING CORPORATE HUMAN RIGHTS VIOLATIONS: HUMANIZING BUSINESS 64–118 (2012) (concluding that the U.N. Norms on the Responsibilities of Transnational Corporations enunciated the most comprehensive set of human rights obligations, but were never adopted); *see also* Ans Kolk et al., *International Codes of Conduct and Corporate Social Responsibility: Can Corporations Regulate Themselves?*, 8 TRANSNAT'L CORP. 143, 143, 152–53, 167–70 (1999); Michael Blowfield & Jedrzej George Frynas, *Setting New Agendas: Critical Perspectives on Corporate Social Responsibility in the Developing World*, 81 INT'L AFF. 499, 512 (2005); DEBORAH LEIPZIGER, THE CORPORATE RESPONSIBILITY CODE BOOK (3d ed., 2015).

20 A study by the U.N. High Commissioner for Human Rights highlights the weakness of domestic laws governing corporate conduct among the obstacles to judicial remedy for corporate-related human rights violations. *See* Human Rights Council, *supra* note 6. *See also* Radu Mares, *Business and Human Rights After Ruggie: Foundations, the Art of Simplification and the Imperative of Cumulative Progress*, *in* THE UN GUIDING PRINCIPLES ON BUSINESS AND HUMAN RIGHTS—FOUNDATIONS AND IMPLEMENTATION 1, 31 (2012) (discussing the role of home state regulation in preventing and redressing

approaches to policing corporate conduct have largely prevailed over hard(er) law options.[21]

The United Nations Guiding Principles on Business and Human Rights ("UNGP" or "Guiding Principles"),[22] represent the latest soft international regulatory instrument aimed "to encourage, but not to require, a corporation to comply with human rights,"[23] and are the prevailing framework for conceptualizing the relationship between corporations and human rights today.[24] Unlike prior initiatives, many of which were criticized for their inattention to accountability, the Guiding Principles address the need for states and businesses to provide remedies for harms resulting from corporate conduct by, *inter alia*, establishing non-judicial grievance mechanisms as complements and supplements to judicial process.[25]

The development of such "soft," non-judicial mechanisms for redress of business-related human rights harms has outpaced the development of "hard" rules applying substantive international human rights obligations to corporations or defining the content of effective remedy for corporate wrongs. While the UNGP refer to hard human rights law—citing by name core international treaties binding on state parties and describing state duties pursuant to those treaties—they stop short of identifying any legal obligations for corporations. Instead, they set forth the business "responsibility" to respect human rights as a global consensus standard of expected conduct,[26] listing human rights instruments as important "benchmarks against which other social actors assess the human rights impacts of business enterprises."[27] The expectations regarding

---

extraterritorial corporate abuses); Oxford Pro BONO PUBLICO, OBSTACLES TO JUSTICE AND REDRESS FOR VICTIMS OF CORPORATE HUMAN RIGHTS ABUSE (2008).

21 *See* Vogel, *supra* note 2, at 12 n.24 (quoting CHRISTOPH KNILL & DIRK LEHMKUHL, PRIVATE ACTORS AND THE STATE: INTERNATIONALIZATION AND CHANGING PATTERNS OF GOVERNANCE 42, 44 (2002)).

22 Human Rights Council, *Guiding Principles on Business and Human Rights*, U.N. Doc. HR/PUB/11/04 (2011) [hereinafter "UN Guiding Principles" or "UNGP"], http://www.ohchr.org/Documents/Publications/GuidingPrinciplesBusinessHR_EN.pdf.

23 Nolan, *supra* note 13, at 140.

24 While the UNGP are themselves a non-binding, soft law instrument, they are premised on existing, binding obligations of states: Namely, the state duty to protect and to provide effective remedy. *See* U.N. Guiding Principles, *supra* note 22, princs. 1, 25. Some scholars argue that the Guiding Principles "constitute general principles of law recognized by civilized nations," under the Statute of the International Court of Justice. Charis Kamphuis & Leah Gardner, *Effectiveness Framework for Home-State Non-Judicial Grievance Mechanisms*, *in* EXTRACTIVE INDUSTRIES AND HUMAN RIGHTS IN AN ERA OF GLOBAL JUSTICE 76–77 (Amissi Manirabona & Yenny Vega Cárdenas, eds., 2019).

25 UNGP, *supra* note 22, princs. 27, 29 and comment.

26 *Id.*, princ. 11 and comment.

27 *Id.*, princ. 12 and comment.

corporate conduct set forth in the Guiding Principles remain largely focused on the processes and procedures companies should adopt to avoid harm and better ensure their activities are consistent with human rights. The UNGP provide limited substantive guidance as to what corporate conduct is prohibited or required by human rights law or what constitutes adequate, effective remedy for corporate violations of human rights.[28] Nor are detailed answers readily available elsewhere in international law.[29]

Consensus on the creation of corporate human rights remedy mechanisms has thus surpassed consensus on the rules those mechanisms should apply when evaluating the rightness or wrongness of corporate conduct and determining the corrective action needed. This disconnect between the establishment of avenues for redress of human rights complaints against corporations and the absence of hard international law regulating corporate conduct has led some to characterize the current business and human rights regime as one of "remedy without law."[30] In this context, private entities that create human rights remedy mechanisms are poised to play a prominent role not only in policing business practice, but also in making the law in this area through their operational decisions. If, as Pierre Bordieu has observed, capital in the legal field is not the law itself, but the power to say what the law is,[31] then NJGMs are spaces where legal capital may be accumulated by those with economic capital (corporations), or democratized and redistributed to those with moral capital (affected rights-holders)—making the question of who participates in those remedial processes, and on what terms, all the more important.

---

28 Rep. of the Working Grp. on the Issue of Human Rights and Transnational Corps. and Other Business Enterprises, U.N. Doc. A/72/162, ¶ 3 (Jul. 18, 2017) [hereinafter "U.N. Doc. A/72/162"].

29 *See* Benjamin Thompson, *Determining Criteria to Evaluate Outcomes of Businesses' Provision of Remedy: Applying a Human Rights-Based Approach*, 2(1) BUS. & HUMAN RIGHTS J. 55, 67–68 (2017) (collecting sources discussing the difficulty of applying human rights instruments as benchmarks for business conduct).

30 *See* Iona Cismas & Sarah Macrory, *The Business and Human Rights Regime under International Law: Remedy without Law? in* NON-STATE ACTORS AND INTERNATIONAL OBLIGATIONS: CREATION, EVOLUTION AND ENFORCEMENT 222, 223 (James Summers & Alex Gough, eds., 2018) ("[T]he business and human rights regime is premised upon the development of secondary rules on redress and accountability fora, whereas primary rules in respect to businesses appear to be absent . . . [C]an there be effective remedy absent (hard) law?").

31 Pierre Bordieu, *The Force of Law: Toward a Sociology of the Juridical Field*, 38 HASTINGS L. J. 814, 817 (1987) (translated from French) ("The juridical field is the site of a competition for monopoly of the right to determine the law.").

This chapter explores the implications of these trends for efforts to achieve meaningful social change in the field of business and human rights. NJGMs are unquestionably better than nothing; some opportunity for remedy is better than none. But how may righting corporate wrongs through privatized remedial mechanisms affect the development of human rights law, both hard and soft, and its application to corporations? What are corporate NJGMs doing in "remedying" human rights abuses: enforcing mere societal expectations regarding corporate conduct—that is, enforcing soft law—or realizing rights guaranteed to individuals under binding international conventions, domestic constitutions, and statutes—that is, interpreting and applying hard international law?[32]

Much as customary international law is formed through state practice exercised pursuant to a sense of legal obligation, the legal impact of company-created NJGMs may depend on *why* corporations are providing the remedies they do. What does it mean, for example, when corporations articulate their commitment to human rights and establish mechanisms designed to deliver "human rights remedy," yet maintain they are not legally bound by human rights law? Do businesses' general invocations of human rights instruments soften the hard law nature of the international human rights regime, or harden the soft law nature of corporate responsibility?

Whether corporate NJGMs will fulfill the law-hardening function often expected of accountability mechanisms remains to be seen. The creation of bodies to receive and resolve complaints typically gives teeth to applicable standards of conduct. At first blush, the emergence of a growing number of corporate NJGMs suggests that the business and human rights regime is becoming more robust. The robustness of the regime, however, depends not only on the existence of forums for righting wrongs, but also on the content of the norms they enforce and the remedies they provide. Whether diffuse NJGMs function as laboratories of corporate accountability in a loose system of experimentalist, transnational governance,[33] driving the pluralistic development of the law, turns on which standards NJGMs apply in assessing the grievances before

32 David Bilchitz, *A Chasm between 'Is' and 'Ought'? A Critique of the Normative Foundations of the SRSG's Framework and the Guiding Principles*, *in* HUMAN RIGHTS OBLIGATIONS OF BUSINESS: BEYOND THE CORPORATE RESPONSIBILITY TO RESPECT?, *supra* note 13, at 119–23, n.53 (discussing the problems with the position that "human rights only bind corporations as a matter of societal expectation").

33 For a discussion of experimentalism as a form of transnational governance in the human rights field, see Gráinne de Búrca, *Human Rights Experimentalism*, 111(2) AM. J. INT'L L. 277 (2017).

them, and on how the outcomes of company-created remedial processes interact with and influence external processes of norm-creation and enforcement. "Bespoke justice" may provide immediate relief for aggrieved parties. Absent any institutional mechanism for review against objective standards or harmonization of divergent outcomes, however, the operationalization of "human rights remedy" through soft grievance mechanisms delinked from legal liability may be antagonistic rather than complementary to the emergence of hard rules on the human rights obligations of corporations.

Untethered from domestic or international judicial bodies, company-created remedial mechanisms need to generate their own institutional and normative legitimacy. A focus on participatory design and process goes a long way toward bolstering the former. But normative legitimacy requires reasoned engagement with the human rights laws the company creators of NJGMs purport to respect as well as concrete outcomes that measure up against objective external standards setting out the content of human rights and effective remedies. At present, human rights law is treated as an optional consideration for corporate NJGMs that are redressing human rights harms "ex aequo et bono," applying principles of equity interpreted in their own light.

Part II discusses the right to remedy under human rights law. Part III presents the Guiding Principles, a soft-law instrument that has set the prevailing international standard on access to remedy for business-related human rights harm and ushered in an expanding role for NJGMs. Part III addresses the Guiding Principles' emphasis on process over substance, and the failure to grapple with the meaning of "rights-compatible" remedy in the context of NJGMs. Part IV examines corporate commitments to human rights remedies and the challenge and imperative of developing substantive standards of accountability for corporate-related human rights harms. Part V takes a look at one heavily scrutinized corporate-created remedy mechanism, highlighting the interplay of hard and soft international law in its operation and illustrating how uncertainties regarding the content of the right to remedy manifest in practice. Part VI concludes.

II The Right to Remedy

The Latin phrase, "*Ubi jus ibi remedium*," loosely translates to "where there is a right, there must be a remedy." If human rights law bestows meaningful rights on individuals and communities, then rights-holders are entitled to remedy when their rights are breached. It is a longstanding principle of international law that effective remedy for an injury resulting from an unlawful act requires reparation, which aims "as far as possible, [to] wipe out all the consequences of the illegal act and re-establish the situation which would, in all probability, have existed if that act had not been committed." [34] The right to remedy for the violation of human rights encompasses both procedural and substantive dimensions. Together, those components serve multiple purposes for the individual victim(s) and society, including restitution or compensation, retribution or punishment, and deterrence. Given its broad endorsement by states through regional and international treaties, and its reflection in state practice, the right of access to effective remedy is considered customary international law.[35] Drawing on provisions guaranteeing the right to remedy in numerous international[36] and regional human rights instruments,[37] the U.N. Basic Principles and Guidelines on the Right to Remedy for Gross Violations of International Human Rights Law and Serious Violations of International Humanitarian Law (Basic Principles on the Right to Remedy) explain that victims of human rights violations are entitled to "adequate, effective, prompt, and appropriate remedies, including reparations,"[38] in proportion to the gravity of the harms suffered.[39] Such remedies may entail not only restitution and compensation, but also rehabilitation, satisfaction, and guarantees of non-repetition.[40] The

34 Case Concerning the Factory at Chorzów (Germany v. Poland), 1928 P.C.I.J. Series A, No. 17, 47.

35 *See* DINAH SHELTON, REMEDIES IN INTERNATIONAL HUMAN RIGHTS LAW 182 (1999) (stating that "[t]he right to remedy is well-established, even a norm of customary international law").

36 Universal Declaration of Human Rights art. 8, Dec. 12, 1948, G.A. Res. 217A, U.N. GOAR, 3d Sess., 1st plen. mtg., U.N. Doc. A/810; Int'l Covenant on Civil and Political Rights art. 2(3), 1967, 999 U.N.T.S. 171; Int'l Convention on the Elimination of Racial Discrimination Art. 6, 1967, 993 U.N.T.S. 3; Convention on the Rights of the Child Art. 39, Nov. 20, 1989, 1577 U.N.T.S 3; Convention Against Torture and other Cruel, Inhuman or Degrading Treatment or Punishment Art. 14, Dec. 10, 1984, 1465 U.N.T.S. 85.

37 African Convention on Human and Peoples' Rights art. 7, 1982, OUA Doc. CAB/LEG/67/3 rev. 5, 21 I.L.M. 58; American Convention on Human Rights art. 25, 1969, 1144 U.N.T.S. 143; Convention for the Protection of Human Rights and Fundamental Freedoms arts. 6, 13, 41, 1950, 213 U.N.T.S 221.

38 *Basic Principles and Guidelines on the Right to a Remedy and Reparation for Victims of Gross Violations of International Human Rights Law and Serious Violations of International Humanitarian Law*, princs. 2(c), 11, U.N. G.A. Res. 60/147, annex (Dec. 16, 2005) [hereinafter "Basic Principles on the Right to Remedy"].

39 *Id.* ¶¶ 15, 18, 20.

40 *See id.* ¶¶ 11, 18–23; *see also* Human Rights Committee, General Comment No. 31, *The Nature of the General Legal Obligation Imposed on States Parties to the Covenant* ¶ 16, U.N. Doc. CCPR/C/21/Rev.1/Add. 13 (May 26, 2004) [hereinafter "General Comment 31"]. Although the Basic Principles refer to "gross violations" of human rights, that term has no fixed definition. Accordingly, the Basic Principles have been applied to a wide variety

Basic Principles on the Right to Remedy indicate that compensation is owed for "any economically assessable damage," including not just physical injury and material losses but moral damages, among others.[41]

Despite widespread agreement regarding these fundamental elements, the specific form of reparation, or what sources of law and methods should guide the design and content of appropriate remedies in particular cases, remains contested. As Dinah Shelton notes, "[i]nternational instruments do not clarify ... what are considered to be 'effective' remedies."[42] To be sure, the redress to which victims of human rights violations are entitled will necessarily vary from case to case. Various authoritative interpretations of international law, including the General Comments of the Human Rights Committee[43] and the Basic Principles, identify types of measures that may form part of integral reparation for human rights violations. But, based on the facts and circumstance of particular cases, much is left to the discretion of the bodies administering relief to determine which elements among this broad menu of options apply, how to calculate amounts due, and how to deliver reparations. Indeed, constructing a remedy is frequently more difficult than determining liability.[44]

Remedying corporate human rights harms presents additional challenges. International texts acknowledge that non-state actors—such as corporations—can cause or contribute to human rights violations.[45] The Basic Principles on the Right to Remedy recognize the responsibility of non-state actors for righting wrongs. They stipulate that states must provide victims of human rights violations with "equal and effective access to justice ... *irrespective of who may ultimately be the bearer of responsibility* for the violation."[46] They further clarify "[i]n cases where a person, *a legal person*, or other entity is found liable for reparation to a victim, such party should provide reparation to the victim or compensate the State if the State has already provided reparation to the victim."[47] None of the international human rights law instruments codifying the right to reparation, however, specifies whether the nature, form,

of human rights violations. Moreover, the Principles themselves recognize that they are "without prejudice to the right to a remedy and reparation for victims of all violations of international human rights law." Basic Principles on the Right to a Remedy, *supra* note 38, ¶ 26.

41 Basic Principles on the Right to Remedy, *supra* note 38, ¶ 20.

42 SHELTON, *supra* note 35, at 85.

43 General Comment 31, *supra* note 40, ¶ 16.

44 SHELTON, *supra* note 35, 62.

45 *See, e.g.*, UNGP, *supra* note 22, at princs. 17, 22.

46 Basic Principles on the Right to Remedy, *supra* note 38, ¶ 3(c) (emphasis added).

47 *Id.* ¶ 15 (emphasis added).

or quantum of effective remedy should differ when the responsible actor is not a state but a corporation.

Translating state-centered obligations regarding reparation of human rights harm to private sector action is far from straightforward. For example, what consideration, if any, should be given to the financial means of, or benefit gained by, the corporate wrongdoer, particularly if the remedy is intended both to make the victim whole, insofar as possible, and to deter future violations?[48] What source(s) of law and bodies of precedent should guide the valuation of non-pecuniary (moral) damages for human rights harm related to the conduct of transnational corporations—the law and jurisprudence of the home state, host state, and/or international bodies—and what if any weight should be given to local economic conditions?

As discussed in the next section, the UN Guiding Principles have set the prevailing international standard on access to remedy in the corporate context. But they leave these and many other questions about the content of remedies unanswered.

III The UNGP and Access to Remedy: Prioritizing Process over Substance

Despite—or perhaps because of—the continued shortcomings of the international legal framework governing corporations, the focus in the business and human rights realm seems to have shifted in the last decade from defining precise minimum standards of corporate conduct to generating consensus around process-oriented measures and creating fora where individuals can complain when things go wrong.[49] The UN Guiding Principles on Business and Human Rights reflect this elevation of "forum over substance."

48 *See* U.N. Doc. A/72/162, *supra* note 28, ¶ 47, n. 53 (discussing how compensatory remedies can be designed to deter corporate abuses and citing *M.C. Mehta v. Union of India, AIR*, 1987 SC 1086, 1099–1100, for the proposition that compensation should be correlated to business capacity).

49 The "Zero Draft" of the binding treaty, *supra* note 4, emphasizes ensuring "effective access to justice and remedy to victims of human rights violations" among its objectives, but, according to some commentators, neither clearly states that companies have a duty to respect internationally recognized human rights nor attempts to "define exactly which human rights corporations must respect." *See* Charlie Holt, Shira Stanton and Daniel Simons, *The Zero Draft Legally Binding Instrument on Business and Human Rights: Small Steps along the Irresistible Path to Corporate Accountability*, and Surya Deva, *The Zero Draft of the Proposed Business and Human Rights Treaty, Part II: On the Right Track, but Not Ready Yet*, *in* BUSINESS & HUMAN RIGHTS RESOURCE CENTRE, COMPILATION OF

The Guiding Principles are framed around three pillars: (1) the state duty to protect against human rights abuses by third parties, including businesses; (2) the corporate responsibility to respect human rights; and (3) the shared state and corporate obligation to ensure access to remedy. "Pillar Three" articulates the obligations of states, pursuant to their duty to protect, to ensure that individuals affected by business-related human rights abuse have access to remedy, and of corporations to provide for or cooperate in the remediation of abuses that they have caused or to which they have contributed.[50] Referred to as the "forgotten pillar" in the first years after the UNGP's adoption, access to remedy since has garnered increasing attention among policymakers, businesses, advocates and scholars.[51]

One of the means identified in the UNGP for ensuring remedy is the creation of company-level, operational grievance mechanisms. Because corporate-created, operational-level grievance mechanisms are established and administered by companies themselves, they do not possess the independence and impartiality needed to *adjudicate* grievances. Given this posture, the Guiding Principles recommend that operational-level mechanisms "focus[] on dialogue as the means to address and resolve grievances,"[52] and play a crucial early-warning and remediation function[53] to prevent the "escalation" of grievances.[54] Moreover, because international human rights laws are not accepted

---

COMMENTARIES ON THE "ZERO DRAFT" (2018), https://www.business-humanrights.org/sites/default/files/documents/Zero%20Draft%20Blog%20Compilation_Final_0.pdf. *See also* Cismas & Macrory, *supra* note 30 (discussing the emergence of international avenues for redress of complaints against corporations in absence of hard law).

50 UNGP, *supra* note 22, princs. 27–30; *see also id.*, princ. 22 ("Remediation").

51 Pursuant to a resolution of the Human Rights Council, the Office of the High Commissioner on Human Rights is leading a multi-year "Accountability and Remedy Project" focused on access to redress for business-related human rights abuses. *See* OHCHR *Accountability and Remedy Project: Improving Accountability and Access to Remedy in Cases of Business Involvement in Human Rights Abuses* (Sept. 5, 2018), https://www.ohchr.org/EN/Issues/Business/Pages/OHCHRaccountabilityandremedyproject.aspx. The 2017 UN Forum on Business and Human Rights focused explicitly on access to remedy. See OHCHR, *2017 UN Forum: Focus, Aims and Context* (2017), https://www.ohchr.org/Documents/Issues/Business/ForumSession6/ConceptNote.pdf.

52 UNGP, *supra* note 22, princ. 31.

53 *Id.* at princ. 28; *see also* Rep. of the Special Representative of the Secretary General on the Issue of Human Rights and Transnational Corps. and Other Business Enterprises, John Ruggie, Addendum, *Piloting Principles for Effective Company-Stakeholder Grievance Mechanisms: A Report of Lessons Learned*, U.N. Doc. A/HRC/17/31/Add.1, ¶¶ 8–10 (May 24, 2011).

54 UNGP, *supra* note 22, princs. 29, 32 comment. *See also* CAO Advisory Note, *A Guide to Designing and Implementing Grievance Mechanisms for Development Projects* (2008), http://www.cao-ombudsman.org/howwework/advisor/documents/implemgrieveng.pdf;

as a binding legal framework for private companies, corporate human rights remedy mechanisms cannot play a straight-forward compliance role in addressing external grievances, in the way other NJGMs can, such as the accountability bodies at development finance institutions that enforce social and environmental requirements detailed in investment contracts and lending agreements.[55] Consequently, many corporate mechanisms are designed with alternative dispute resolution (ADR) principles in mind, emphasizing mediation and dialogue.[56]

The UN Guiding Principles address the procedures that NJGMs should follow, but say relatively little about the remedies that those mechanisms dispense or the human rights norms on which the *outcomes* of grievance processes should be based.[57] As the UN Working Group on the issue of human rights and transnational corporations and other business enterprises has recognized, the UNGP contain "no explanation of what amounts to an effective remedy."[58]

Virtually all the UNGP say about outcomes of remedial processes is contained in the Commentary to Principle 31, which identifies eight criteria for the effectiveness of NJGMs.[59] These criteria focus almost exclusively on the mechanisms' approach to resolving complaints, not the types of violations addressed or solutions reached. They state that NJGMs should operate in a manner that is legitimate, accessible, predictable, equitable, transparent, *rights-compatible*, a source of continuous learning, and, in the case of operational-level grievance mechanisms, based on engagement and dialogue.[60] "Rights-compatible" is the

---

International Finance Corporation, *Good Practice Note: Addressing Grievances from Project-Affected Communities, Guidance for Projects and Companies on Designing Grievance Mechanisms* (2009), http://www.ifc.org/wps/wcm/connect/cbe7b18048855348ae6cfe6a6515bb18/IFC%2BGrievance%2BMechanisms.pdf?MOD=AJPERES&CACHEID=cbe7b18048855348ae6cfe6a6515bb18/.

55 For a discussion of the effectiveness of independent accountability mechanisms at financial institutions, see SOMO, et al., *Glass Half Full? The State of Accountability in Development Finance* (Jan. 2016) available at https://www.somo.nl/glass-half-full-2/ (last visited June 13, 2019); *see also, e.g.*, DANA CLARK, ET AL., DEMANDING ACCOUNTABILITY: CIVIL-SOCIETY CLAIMS AND THE WORLD BANK INSPECTION PANEL (2003); Daniel Bradlow, *Private Complainants and International Organizations: A Comparative Study of the Independent Inspection Mechanisms in International Financial Institutions*, 36 GEO. J. INT'L L. 403 (2005).

56 Maximilian J. L. Schormair & Lara M. Gerlach, *Corporate Remediation of Human Rights Violations—A Restorative Justice Framework*, J. BUS. ETHICS 1, 3–5 (2019) (discussing the ADR-driven approach shaping the design of most company NJGMs).

57 *See* UNGP, *supra* note 22, princs. 26–31.

58 UN Doc. A/72/162, *supra* note 28, ¶ 3.

59 UNGP, *supra* note 22, princ. 31 comment.

60 *Id.* (emphasis added).

only criterion that concerns the content of remedies provided, but the Principles offer little guidance on its application, stating only: "where [grievance process] outcomes have implications for human rights, care should be taken to ensure that they are in line with internationally recognized human rights."[61] It is unsurprising, therefore, that with few exceptions,[62] the growing literature on the design[63] and efficacy[64] of NJGMs centers largely on the structure of the mechanisms and procedures they follow—not their outcomes.[65]

---

61 *Id.* princ. 31 comment.

62 *See* MARTIJN SCHELTEMA, ASSESSING THE EFFECTIVENESS OF REMEDY OUTCOMES OF NON-JUDICIAL GRIEVANCE MECHANISMS (2013); Thompson, *supra* note 29; *see also* John Ruggie & Jane Nelson, *Rights-compatible Grievance Mechanisms: A Guidance Tool for Companies and Their Stakeholders* 34–35 (2008) (discussing the need to ensure requisite human rights expertise is available to achieve settlements in line with human rights standards).

63 *See, e.g.*, Shift, Global Compact Network Netherlands, and Oxfam, *Doing Business with Respect for Human Rights: A Guidance Tool for Companies*, 102–11 (2016), https://www.businessrespecthumanrights.org/image/2016/10/24/business_respect_human_rights_full.pdf; U.N. Office of High Commissioner for Human Rights, *The Corporate Responsibility to Respect Human Rights: An Interpretive Guide*, UN Doc. HR/PUB/12/02 (2012), http://www.ohchr.org/Documents/Publications/HR.PUB.12.2_En.pdf; Caroline Rees, *Rights-Compatible Grievance Mechanisms: A Guidance Tool for Companies and their Stakeholders* (2008); International Council on Mining and Metals Human Rights in the Mining and Metals Industry, *Handling and Resolving Local Level Concerns and Grievances* (2009); CAO, *supra* note 54; IFC, *supra* note 54.

64 *See, e.g.*, Office of the High Commissioner for Human Rights, *Phase III: Enhancing the Effectiveness of Non-State-Based Grievance Mechanisms: Scope and Programme of Work* (2018), https://www.ohchr.org/Documents/Issues/Business/ARP/ARPIII-PoW.pdf; Beyond Effectiveness Criteria, *supra* note 10; *Glass Half Full? The State of Accountability in Development Finance, supra* note 55; CSR Europe, *Assessing the Effectiveness of Company Grievance Mechanisms* (Dec. 2013); ACCESS Facility, *Expert Meeting Report: Access to Remedy in Context of Business and Human Rights: Improving Effectiveness of Non-Judicial Grievance Mechanisms* (Apr. 3–4, 2014); Barbara Linder, Karin Lukas, & Astrid Steinkellner, *The Right to Remedy: Extrajudicial Complaint Mechanisms for Resolving Conflicts of Interest between Business Actors and Those Affected by their Operations* (2013), http://bim.lbg.ac.at/files/sites/bim/Right%20to%20Remedy_Extrajudicial%20Complaint%20Mechanisms_2013_1.pdf; Caroline Rees, *Grievance Mechanisms for Business and Human Rights: Strengths, Weaknesses and Gaps, Corporate Social Responsibility Initiative*, Working Paper No. 40 (Jan. 2008); Caitlin Daniel et. al., *OECD Watch: Remedy Remains Rare* (Jun. 2015); *see also* Columbia Law School Human Rights Clinic & Harvard Law School International Human Rights Clinic, *Righting Wrongs? Barrick Gold's Remedy Mechanism for Sexual Violence in Papua New Guinea: Key Concerns and Lessons Learned* (Nov. 2015), http://www.rightingwrongsporgera.com; Emma Wilson & Emma Blackmore, eds., *Dispute or Dialogue? Community Perspectives on Company-Led Grievance Mechanisms* (2013), https://pubs.iied.org/pdfs/16529IIED.pdf.

65 *See, e.g.*, *Piloting Principles for Effective Company-Stakeholder Grievance Mechanisms, supra* note 53, at ¶¶ 49–52 (explaining that "it was not possible within the constraints

In some respects, the UNGP's focus on process is justified. Greater consensus exists in the international community on the procedural elements of remedy than on the substance of redress, which is often fact-specific. Moreover, process is vitally important to rights-holders' access to forums for redress of their grievances and to the adequacy of the remedial measures obtained.[66] Experience underscores the need for continued advocacy to ensure that affected communities and would-be users of corporate NJGMs participate in their design and administration, as the UNGP recommends.[67] The 2017 Corporate Human Rights Benchmark (CHRB) study found that "an alarming 91% of companies do not score any points for involving users in the design or performance of their grievance mechanisms."[68]

But an effective process, alone—even a participatory one—does not guarantee just outcomes.[69] Absent clearly defined "minimum standards [that] set the parameters for acceptable outcomes,"[70] the power imbalances inherent in company-created grievance mechanisms risk skewing the results of any dialogue, negotiation, and problem-solving process.[71]

---

of this pilot to assess whether the outcomes of individual grievance-handling processes were compatible with human rights standards"); *see also* CSR Europe, *supra* note 64, at 7 (noting that CSR Europe's work "focuses on the effectiveness of the process of addressing complaints as opposed to the effectiveness of the outcomes. . . . It is beyond the scope of this report to examine the nature of remedy provided"); *see also* Rees, *Grievance Mechanisms for Business and Human Rights*, *supra* note 64, at 32 (discussing the dearth of information on outcomes of grievance processes and underscoring the risk that the proliferation of standards and mechanisms could be confusing both to companies and would-be users).

66 *See* U.N. Doc. A/72/162, *supra* note 28, ¶¶ 18–25 (emphasizing that rights-holders should be central to any remedial process).

67 Principle 31(h) of the UNGP states that creators of operational-level grievance mechanisms should "consult[] the stakeholder groups for whose use they are intended on their design and performance." UNGP, *supra* note 22, princ. 31(h). *See also, e.g.*, *Righting Wrongs?*, *supra* note 64, at 55–64.

68 Corporate Human Rights Benchmark (CHRB), *Key Findings 2017*, at 13, https://www.corporatebenchmark.org/sites/default/files/2017-03/CHRB_Findings_web_pages.pdf.

69 *See* UN Doc. A/72/162, *supra* note 28, ¶ 3; Thompson, *supra* note 29, at 61–66 (discussing the relationship between process and outcome, and noting that "participatory approaches may lead to outcomes that conflict with human rights standards and principles").

70 Corporate Social Responsibility Initiative Working Paper No. 41, *Rights-Compatible Grievance Mechanisms—A Guidance Tool for Companies and Their Stakeholders* 9 (2008), https://www.business-humanrights.org/sites/default/files/reports-and-materials/Grievance-mechanisms-principles-Jan-2008.pdf.

71 *See* Knuckey & Jenkin, *supra* note 7, at 815 (noting the significant risk that corporate NJGM "processes and outcomes may reflect the power differentials between companies and impacted communities, or that companies may be able to exploit power differentials to undermine victims' rights to an effective remedy").

The Guiding Principles do not attempt to identify any substantive minimum human rights standards,[72] nor do they emphasize the importance of ensuring that corporate grievance mechanisms articulate such minimum standards and publicize them to users. Although the Guiding Principles mention several core international human rights instruments by name,[73] they do not delve into the normative content of the range of rights enshrined in those documents, including the right to remedy. For example, the word "reparation" appears nowhere in Pillar Three of the UNGP, despite its centrality to the notion of remedy under international law.[74] The commentary to Principle 25 of the UNGPs indicates that remedy "may include apologies, restitution, rehabilitation, financial or non-financial compensation and punitive sanctions (whether criminal or administrative, such as fines), as well as the prevention of harm through, for example, injunctions or guarantees of non-repetition."[75] Yet, it is silent as to which among this menu of options "victims of corporate human rights abuses can have against companies" under international law.[76] Similarly, the Office of the High Commissioner for Human Rights' own interpretive guide to the UNGP, directed at corporations, fails to cite to the components of adequate remedy under international human rights law or direct corporations to look to the minimum core content of the rights at issue when formulating remedies in a particular case.[77] The UNGP's cursory reference to existing human rights instruments belies the indeterminacy of human rights and the substantial "interpretive work required to relate abstract standards to concrete contexts."[78]

---

72 *See* Comm'n on Human Rights, *Interim Report of the Special Representative of the Secretary General on the Issue of Human Rights and Transnational Corporations and Other Business Enterprises*, UN Doc. E/CN.4/2006/97, ¶¶ 70–81 (Feb. 22, 2006); *see also* Nolan, *supra* note 13, at 138–61.

73 *See* UNGP, *supra* note 22, princ. 12, comment.

74 *See* Jonathan Drimmer & Lisa J. Laplante, *The Third Pillar: Remedies, Reparations, and the Ruggie Principles*, *in* THE BUSINESS AND HUMAN RIGHTS LANDSCAPE—MOVING FORWARD, LOOKING BACK 316–347 (Jena Martin & Karen E. Bravo, eds., 2015).

75 UNGP, *supra* note 22, princ. 25 comment. The text neither references the basis for these elements in international law, however, nor elaborates on the formulation of remedies.

76 Surya Deva, *Treating Human Rights Lightly: A Critique of the Consensus Rhetoric and the Language Employed by the Guiding Principles*, *in* HUMAN RIGHTS OBLIGATIONS OF BUSINESS: BEYOND THE CORPORATE RESPONSIBILITY TO RESPECT?, *supra* note 13, at 78, 102.

77 *See The Corporate Responsibility to Respect Human Rights: An Interpretive Guide*, *supra* note 62, at 63–76 (discussing remediation and Principles 22, 29, 31); *see also* Thompson, *supra* note 29, at 56–57 (discussing the absence of guidance on evaluating the outcomes of NJGM remedial processes).

78 Bilchitz, *supra* note 32, at 121.

The creation of company-level forums for lodging grievances does not dispose of the complex question of which standards (host state, home state, or international laws) apply to transnational corporate conduct or what effective human rights remedy requires of corporate wrongdoers. The uncertainty regarding the content of the norms being enforced by many NJGMs, as well as the parameters for the substantive redress the mechanisms offer, calls into question the meaning of "rights-compatibility"—a deceptively simple term for what is perhaps the most complex of the UNGP "effectiveness" criteria to assess when evaluating NJGM performance.[79]

Part of the problem is that human rights law has not yet developed sufficiently to explain how human rights principles should be applied to the planning and implementation of corporate activity.[80] Human rights law addresses egregious abuses by non-state actors (such as torture, rape, murder, slavery and forced labor) but at present stops far short of providing guidance on how to structure business operations consistent with all human rights principles. The absence of substantive guidance in the UNGP on the applicable minimum human rights standards may not be of concern for NJGMs when the conduct at issue in a given complaint breaches clear and universally recognized norms, as is the case with grave human rights abuses that amount to international crimes. But if, as the UNGP suggests, abuses that constitute breaches of domestic and international criminal laws fall outside of the scope of operational-level NJGMs,[81] corporate remedial mechanisms will focus on complaints concerning areas of human rights where the normative content is less well-defined

79 CSR Europe, *supra* note 64, at 4, 31 (noting that companies tend to report on the existence of grievance mechanisms but not the norms used to assess complaints and determine redress, or concrete outcomes); *see also* CHRB, *Key Findings 2017*, *supra* note 67, at 28 (finding that many companies remain silent about how they actually remediate impacts and lessons learned).

80 *See* Thompson, *supra* note 29 at 67–68 & nn.81–86 (collecting sources on the difficulty of using human rights law as an objective benchmark against which to assess corporate conduct or evaluate outcomes of remedial processes).

81 UNGP, *supra* note 22, princ. 22 comment., princ. 31 comment. Some civil society organizations have criticized the UNGP for not more clearly prohibiting NJGMs from addressing gross human rights violations. *See, e.g.*, Rights and Accountability in Development (RAID) UK, *Principles Without Justice: The Corporate Takeover of Human Rights* vii (2016), http://www.raid-uk.org/sites/default/files/principles_without_justice.pdf ("Governments should make clear that operational-level grievance mechanisms are not an appropriate mechanism for dealing with cases of gross human rights violations, serious crimes such as torture, rape and killings, or for violations of international human rights or humanitarian law, which should be reported to the appropriate national competent authorities and international human rights bodies.").

and often more contested—as is the case, for example, with the rights to water, housing, and a healthy environment, as well as the right to remedy itself. In absence of common rules or an agreed approach to identifying the relevant sources of law in these instances, company-created remedy mechanisms are left to their own devices, to pick and choose those standards that suit their needs. In effect, law becomes an optional element in a system of bespoke justice meted out by private mechanisms.

IV Corporate Provision of Human Rights Remedy

While the UNGPs have prompted more companies to adopt complaint procedures that expressly set out to provide a human rights remedy, the trend should not be overstated. Cross-sector surveys indicate that provision of remedy remains a "consistently weak area of company performance."[82] Many businesses still lack mechanisms to receive complaints from members of the communities that host a company's operations. The 2018 Corporate Human Rights Benchmark study found that nearly half of the 101 leading multinational companies reviewed have no public grievance mechanisms, while 85% have such mechanisms for employees.[83] Similarly, among the ICT, apparel, food, and beverage companies whose efforts to eliminate forced labor in their supply chains were assessed in 2018 by Know The Chain, only a small minority in each category were found to disclose information about their external grievance mechanisms.[84] These figures reflect little progress since December 2013, when the European Business Network for Corporate Social Responsibility reported that only 40% of its members had "started addressing complaints from communities in a systematic way," while 87% had a mechanism for employee complaints.[85] The discrepancy between the availability of employee grievance mechanisms and forums for community complaints may stem from the fact that employees are more likely to have recourse under hard law, be it statutory, common law, or contract, than are community members. This suggests that

---

82 *Corporate Human Rights Benchmark Progress Report: Executive Summary* 6 (2018), https://www.corporatebenchmark.org/sites/default/files/documents/CHRB%202018%20Executive%20Summary-brochure-web.pdf.

83 *CHRB 2018 Key Findings, supra* note 3, at 32. The inaugural 2017 study made similar findings. CHRB, *2017 Key Findings, supra* note 68, at 28.

84 *See* Know the Chain, *Benchmarks* (2018), https://knowthechain.org/benchmarks/; *see also* UN Doc. A/72/162, *supra* note 28, ¶ 59.

85 CSR Europe, *supra* note 64, at 4.

avoidance of hard law remedies (through litigation) may be a chief driver behind company-created grievance mechanisms.

Moreover, the existence of an external grievance mechanism says little about the quality of the remedy it provides. Among those businesses that have public grievance mechanisms, information about their operations and outcomes remains sparse. Few existing mechanisms specify the substantive standards by which they assess the human rights-related grievances they receive or the nature of the remedies they provide.[86] Companies do not typically describe the process of managing grievances, detail the involvement of users in the design, implementation, or performance of mechanisms, or address how their mechanisms avoid interfering with other human rights remedies.[87] As a result, would-be users of the mechanisms often have little way of knowing what they can demand from the company or what types of outcomes to expect when they lodge a grievance.

The uncertainty surrounding the meaning of a rights-compatible remedy and the difficulty of applying international human rights law to corporate conduct has not stopped multinational companies from referencing human rights law and the UN Guiding Principles in their publications regarding their operations and grievance redress.[88] Cursory commitments to human rights principles are more the rule than the exception. Of the 101 companies assessed in the 2018 Corporate Human Rights Benchmark study, "[a] majority (78%) of companies have made a public commitment to respecting human rights."[89] According to another survey conducted in 2016, "84% of corporations with more than $10 billion in asset value have adopted a human rights policy."[90] Much like

86 A July 2017 review of the information publicly available on the websites of the companies included in the Access Facility's now-defunct database of "company grievance mechanisms" revealed that only 1 out of 5 companies names with any specificity the human rights or social and environmental standards that it applies when reviewing its conduct pursuant to a complaint, and fewer than 1 in 10 provides any description of the types of remedies that are available through the complaint body. Analysis on file with author, NYU CHRGJ; The Access Facility, http://accessfacility.org/case-stories (last visited June 15, 2019).

87 *CHRB 2018 Key Findings*, *supra* note 3, at 32–33.

88 The author's review of the 52 "company grievance mechanisms" listed as of July 2017 in a now-defunct, searchable database of non-judicial grievance mechanisms on the Access Facility website, http://accessfacility.org/, found that nearly half had a publicly accessible "human rights policy" and over 10 of them refer to human rights and the UNGP in the descriptions of their respective grievance mechanisms.

89 *CHRB 2018 Key Findings*, *supra* note 3, at 28; *see also* *CHRB 2017 Key Findings*, *supra* note 68, at 24.

90 *See* Cronstedt et al., *International Business and Human Rights Arbitration*, at 13 n.22 (quoting Legal Business, *The New Risk Front for GCs—Nearly Half of Contracts Have*

the UNGP, themselves, such policies often remain at a high level of generality, referencing core human rights instruments by name, but not addressing the contents of those documents.[91] Moreover, companies' public commitments to human rights remedy are weak, with 69% of companies surveyed in the 2018 CHRB "unable to demonstrate a commitment to remedying their adverse impacts on workers, individuals or communities."[92]

A small number of companies have elaborated lengthier human rights policies and more detailed grievance procedures with express reference to the UNGP—but often only after public outcry regarding human rights violations associated with their operations and under pressure from civil society groups. For example, Acacia Mining, a subsidiary of Canadian gold mining company Barrick Gold Corporation, released a series of documents on its grievance procedure for the North Mara Gold Mine in Tanzania, including a "handbook for grievants," a standard operating procedure and reference guides setting forth "security and human rights standards" applicable to grievances and remedies.[93] These materials, which have faced critique,[94] were published only after years of extensive engagement with civil society groups critical of its handling of complaints related to violence by mine security forces.[95] The company's documents are careful to avoid the language of human rights "violations," referring

Human Rights Clauses, LB Research Finds, online: Legal Business (Sept. 8, 2016), http://www.legalbusiness.co.uk/ (search for "human rights")).

91 *See, e.g.*, Gap, Inc., *Human Rights Policy*, http://www.gapincsustainability.com/sites/default/files/Human%20Rights%20Policy.pdf ; Unilever *Responsible Sourcing Policy 2014*, http://www.accessfacility.org/sites/default/files/Unilever%20Responsible%20Sourcing%20Policy%202014.pdf.

92 *CHRB 2018 Key Findings*, *supra* note 3, at 28.

93 Acacia, *North Mara Gold Mine Community Grievance Process: Security and Human Rights Standards Reference Guide* (Apr. 2018), https://www.acaciamining.com/~/media/Files/A/Acacia/documents/grievance/cgp_security_hr_standards_reference_guide_201804.pdf [hereinafter "Acacia, Standards Reference Guide"]; Acacia, Remedies Reference Guide (Apr. 2018), https://www.acaciamining.com/~/media/Files/A/Acacia/documents/grievance/cgp_remedies_security_hr_impacts_reference_guide_201804A.pdf [hereinafter "Acacia, Remedies Reference Guide"]

94 *See* Rights and Accountability in Development (RAID), *Acacia Mining's Revised Operational Grievance Mechanism at North Mara Gold Mine, Tanzania: Assessment and Recommendations* (Apr. 2018), http://www.raid-uk.org/sites/default/files/raid_lhrc_assessment_of_acacia_ogm.pdf; *see also* Catherine Coumans, Mining Watch Canada, *Review of Barrick Gold/Acacia Mining's Draft "Community Grievance Process—Standard Operating Procedure" for the North Mara Gold Mine in Tanzania* (Apr. 2018), https://miningwatch.ca/sites/default/files/review_of_new_north_mara_grievance_mechanism_april_2018_final_0.pdf.

95 For background on human rights violations at the North Mara Gold Mine and problems with the company's handling of grievances, see RAID, *Principles Without Justice: The*

instead to human rights "impacts," and renounce the establishment of any legal rights or liability.[96] A guide detailing "remedies for security-related human rights *impacts*"[97] carefully defines remedy so as to exclude the prospect of punitive measures or measures to address underlying causes, and clarifies that the process is not a legal one. The new Acacia grievance procedures set out a lengthy list of relevant international standards (although the multinational company's home state standards are conspicuously absent).[98] But because these references to hard and soft international law are couched in legalistic disclaimers that suggest none is binding on the company, the standards read like a menu of optional ingredients to an equity-based process of bespoke justice. Such documents underscore both the uncertainty about what law applies to corporate human rights abuses and the discretion exercised by the company fielding the complaint.

Corporate endorsements of international human rights instruments gloss over the considerable debate around the meaning of many of the rights international documents enshrine. Much like the Guiding Principles themselves, these corporate grievance mechanisms treat the "hard" law of human rights as if it does not guarantee individuals any entitlements. If "soft international law" is that which purports to be a rule of behavior, although compliance may be voluntary and subject to auto-interpretation, then company grievance mechanisms treat human rights law, including the right to remedy, as decidedly soft when it comes to their impacts.

Arguably, the language companies employ is not what matters; instead, what is important is whether those who use the corporate grievance mechanisms perceive that their rights have been vindicated and that they have obtained satisfactory redress. Satisfaction of rights-holders should be the touchstone of both grievance mechanism design and evaluation of outcomes. But a singular focus on whether a victim or survivor of corporate-related human rights abuse accepts what is offered through the company's NJGM ignores the

---

corporate takeover of human rights (2016), http://www.raid-uk.org/sites/default/files/principles_without_justice.pdf; Mining Watch Canada and RAID, *In Need of Repair: Acacia Mining's Grievance Mechanism at North Mara Gold Mine, Tanzania* (2016), https://miningwatch.ca/sites/default/files/memorandum_to_acacia_revised.pdf; Mining Watch Canada & RAID, *Privatized Remedy and Human Rights: Rethinking Project-Level Grievance Mechanisms* (2014), http://www.raid-uk.org/sites/default/files/grievance-mechanisms-briefing-bhr.pdf, as well as other resources available on RAID and Mining Watch websites.

96 Acacia, Standards Reference Guide, *supra* note 93, at 2, 4.

97 Acacia, Remedies Reference Guide, *supra* note 93 (emphasis added).

98 Acacia, Standards Reference Guide, *supra* note 93.

power imbalance that typifies company-community disputes over human rights abuses.[99] Moreover, attaching the label of "human rights remedy" to corporate grievance procedures regardless of how the outcomes measure up against the text of human rights instruments or the practice of human rights bodies that interpret and apply those instruments, could soften the notion that human rights law creates both obligations and entitlements.

Moreover, sweeping invocations of hard law instruments may have practical implications for users of the "soft" grievance mechanisms and their administrators. Describing the varied and often vague references to human rights standards provided by different NJGMs, one early study concluded [that] "a mechanism linked to a broad reference to rights may … hamper access due to uncertainty over the basis for complaints"[100] and "make it harder to pin down whether a breach has occurred."[101] Another study that evaluated community views on different corporate-sponsored grievance mechanisms similarly flagged that the absence of clearer hard law standards on users' rights under international law was "a key contributor to power imbalances between the parties to a dispute."[102] Underscoring the importance of external support from persons knowledgeable about human rights law and remedies, the study found that those community members engaged in mediation processes who referred to specific rights language were better able to "clearly articulate interests" and obtained better compensation packages.[103] A study regarding the experience of communities that filed grievances against a foreign logging company operating in the Democratic Republic of Congo reached similar conclusions.[104]

Without clarity regarding the norms subject to enforcement and the components of adequate remedy, grievance redress processes through corporate complaint mechanisms resemble a negotiation more than an assessment of

99 *See* Thompson, *supra* note 29, at 61–62.

100 Rees, *supra* note 64, at 1. *See also id.* at 11–12 (discussing "constraints linked to applicable standards"). The study attempted to identify "the source of the standards for the complaints/grievances," whether they were based on human rights law, whether they focused on particular rights or any human rights, and whether they were mandatory (non-legal) standards or non-binding.

101 *Id.* at 11.

102 Taylor Fulton et al., *What is Remedy for Corporate Human Rights Abuses? Listening to Community Voices: A Field Report* 2 (Dec. 2015), http://accessfacility.org/sites/default/files/Listening%20to%20community%20voices%20on%20effective%20remedy.pdf (last visited June 15, 2019).

103 *Id.* at 25–26.

104 Wilson & Blackmore, *supra* note 64, at 81.

responsibility for harm. The more that the resolution of human rights grievances approximates private settlement, the greater the dependence of the outcome on the relative resources and positions of the parties to the dispute, rather than the integrity of the enforcement mechanism or the strength of the standards it purports to uphold. Of course, power imbalances and differential financial means affect access to justice through courts as well. But if corporate NJGM s are intended to attenuate rather than aggravate those obstacles to judicial remedy, more transparency and specificity are required regarding the rules of conduct applied and the reparations available through company-created remedial mechanisms.

V Case Study: Company-Created Remedy Mechanism at the Porgera Gold Mine

An examination of a company-created grievance mechanism at Barrick Gold Corporation's Porgera mine in Papua New Guinea illustrates the risks of pursuing human rights remedy via corporate NJGM s. It highlights the challenges posed by the absence of clarity and consensus on the sources of law, the methods for formulating remedies, and the relationship between judicial and non-judicial processes. It also exposes the complex interplay of hard and soft international law within corporate NJGM s. Although some have argued that the Porgera case is atypical of other operational-level grievance mechanisms, because the company created a remedial framework *post-hoc*, after abuses came to light,[105] it remains one of very few well-documented examples of remedies provided through a corporate NJGM.

Extensive analyses have already been published about the case.[106] Here, we can focus on two discrete aspects of the remedy framework that have raised

105 *See* Knuckey & Jenkin, *supra* note 7, at 802–04.

106 *See, e.g., Righting Wrongs?*, *supra* note 64; Knuckey & Jenkin, *supra* note 7; Yusuf Aftab, Enodo Rights, *Pillar III on the Ground An Independent Assessment of the Porgera Remedy Framework* (2016), https://www.enodorights.com/assets/pdf/pillar-III-on-the-ground-assessment.pdf; Marco Simons, *Many Valuable Lessons from Barrick's Remedy Framework; It's Cheaper to Rape Poor Women" Should Not Be One of Them,* EarthRights International (Jan. 22, 2016), https://www.earthrights.org/blog/many-valuable-lessons-barricks-remedy-framework-its-cheaper-rape-poor-women-should-not-be-one; Mining Watch Canada and Rights and Accountability in Development (RAID-UK), *Privatized Remedy, supra* note 95; Catherine Coumans, *Barrick Consultant Delivers Biased Report on Inequitable Remedy Mechanism for Rape Victims* (2016), https://miningwatch.ca/sites/default/files/response-to-enodo-report-review-of-porgera-remedy-mechanism-march_2016.pdf; Catherine Coumans, *Brief on Concerns Related to Project-Level Non-Judicial*

particular concern. In October 2011, Barrick Gold announced that it would establish a remedy framework to address numerous individuals' claims of sexual assault by company staff in Papua New Guinea. The announcement followed years of advocacy by community members around the Porgera mine and international allies who raised credible allegations of sexual violence committed by Barrick's former and current employees. The mechanism, the *Olgeta Meri Igat Raits* (All Women Have Rights) Framework ("Framework"), sought to provide both individual reparations and community measures in response to the claims of abuse.[107]

Through a claims assessment board, the Framework awarded settlements to 119 of the more than 130 victims deemed eligible. Rather than provide individualized compensation packages, each settlement included a standardized cash amount. Barrick explained that the compensation amounts were determined with reference to several factors, including the "upper range of awards that have been rendered in the [Papua New Guinea] civil justice system for rape and sexual assault."[108] In exchange for receiving a remedy package, the women were required to sign an agreement relinquishing the right to bring any future civil legal action related to the conduct at issue in the remedy framework.[109] These two dimensions of the settlements—the calculation of the compensation package and the waiver of legal rights—were among the most controversial aspects of the Framework. Both showcase the interplay between hard and soft law in the formulation of redress for corporate-related human rights violations, and how corporate NJGMs may influence evolving areas of the law.[110]

A *Valuing Compensation in the Shadow of Hard Law*

Following the implementation of the Framework, a debate ensued regarding the propriety of the company's approach to awarding monetary damages. An

---

Grievance Mechanisms (2014), https://miningwatch.ca/sites/default/files/briefonnjgmsforcfe2014.pdf; *see also* Schormair & Gerlach, *supra* note 56 (discussing remediation mechanisms at Barrick Gold Corporation's Porgera and North Mara gold mines); Thompson, *supra* note 29, at 81–84 (discussing the Porgera case).

107 *See Righting Wrongs?*, *supra* note 64, at 27; Aftab, *supra* note 106, at 10–12.

108 Barrick Gold, *The Porgera Joint Venture Remedy Framework* 6 (Dec. 1, 2014), http://www.barrick.com/files/porgera/Porgera-Joint-Venture-Remedy-Framework-Dec1-2014.pdf; *see also Righting Wrongs?*, *supra* note 64, at 95–98.

109 Aftab, *supra* note 106, at 14.

110 Other concerns about the Framework's design and implementation, including the lack of consultation with survivor-victims and the overly narrow scope of the harms addressed, have been well documented but are beyond the scope of this chapter. *See generally Righting Wrongs?*, *supra* note 64; *and* Knuckey & Jenkin, *supra* note 7.

independent assessment of the Framework that Barrick commissioned from the consulting firm, Enodo Rights,[111] claimed: "[T]he financial reparations successful claimants received aligned with principles of equity under international human rights law" because when adjusted for "purchasing power parity" in the victims' country, the amounts were more generous than damages awarded by the Inter-American Court of Human Rights for similar abuses.[112] The assessment concludes that the "[c]laimants' remedies were thus rights-compatible and, from the perspective of compensation under international human rights law, complete."[113]

EarthRights International ("ERI"), a human rights and environmental advocacy organization representing some of the survivors, took aim at this assertion. In an online debate with the assessment's author,[114] ERI suggested that GDP-weighting moral damages for human rights violations, such as those at issue in the Porgera case, is not only contrary to international law, but also tantamount to holding that the dignity and bodily integrity of a poor person are worth less than that of a wealthier person. This created perverse incentives for "an economically rational corporation to invest far more resources in preventing abuse in richer economies than poorer ones."[115]

Other evaluations of the reparations Barrick awarded victims of sexual abuse at its Porgera mine similarly found that they do not comport with international standards on remedy, just satisfaction, and compensation.[116] Observers note that the remedial process deviated from the precepts of a human rights-based approach.[117] The Columbia Law School Human Rights Clinic identified many procedural shortcomings in the mechanism, such as the lack of consultation with survivors in the design and implementation phases, the limited scope of claims considered by the Framework, and the inadequate accessibility and

---

111 Aftab, *supra* note 106, at 101.

112 *Id.* at 5.

113 *Id.* at 5, 105–06.

114 *See* Simons, *supra* note 106; *see also* Marco Simons, *International Human Rights Law Does Not Support Giving Less Compensation to Claimants from Poorer Countries,* EarthRights International (Jan. 29, 2016), https://www.earthrights.org/blog/international-human-rights-law-does-not-support-giving-less-compensation-claimants-poorer; Enodo Rights, *The Principle of Remedy: A Discussion with EarthRights International,* http://www.enodorights.com/assets/pdf/a-response-eri.pdf.

115 Simons, *supra* note 114.

116 *See, e.g.,* Knuckey & Jenkin, *supra* note 7, at 810; EarthRights International, Press Release, *Survivors of Rape by Barrick Gold Security Guards Offered "Business Grants" and "Training" in Exchange for Waiving Legal* Rights, https://www.earthrights.org/media/survivors-rape-barrick-gold-security-guards-offered-business-grants-and-training-exchange.

117 *See* Thompson, *supra* note 29, at 81–84.

transparency of the process, on top of deficiencies in the outcomes.[118] With regard to the latter, the report emphasizes that reparation should be proportional to the violation and harms suffered, and thus that available domestic remedies (e.g., in PNG courts) should not be determinative of the amount awarded.[119]

The interaction of judicial and non-judicial mechanisms strongly influenced the compensation packages in the Porgera case, underscoring the interdependence of hard and soft international law mechanisms of human rights accountability. Eleven of the women whose claims were deemed eligible rejected the settlements Barrick offered and instead pursued legal action against the company, represented by ERI. Barrick eventually settled with these individuals, on terms that remain confidential but which reportedly included more generous payments than those received by the other victims.[120] When word of the settlements spread informally, 119 other claimants pressured Barrick to increase their awards. This mounting pressure compelled Barrick to offer "top-up" payments to the women, which the corporation subsequently characterized as "exogenously imposed in the wake of Barrick's settlement with the ERI Claimants."[121] Barrick further asserted that the ERI-led legal action was "the most significant delegitimizing force" for the Framework, "which led to persistent and consistent rumors of relative inequity."[122] Viewed in a different light, however, the private settlements appear to have provided claimants with a vital benchmark against which to evaluate the adequacy of the remedial packages offered under the company's mechanism. In effect, the availability of judicial recourse to enforce hard law norms functioned as an essential guardrail to ensure that the company-created process did not deviate from basic minimum standards of remedy for recognized human rights violations—including those requiring equity and non-arbitrariness.

B *Conditioning Soft Law Remedy on Waiver of Hard Law Rights*

To access the remedy packages, Barrick required eligible victims to sign a broad legal waiver relinquishing their right to pursue "any claim for compensation, or any civil legal action, that relates in any way to the conduct, against the Porgera Joint Venture, PRFA, or Barrick in Papua New Guinea, or in any other jurisdiction."[123] The waiver exempted future criminal actions, but was sweeping in its

118 *See generally Righting Wrongs?*, *supra* note 64, at 1–12.

119 *Id.* at 96.

120 Knuckey & Jenkin, *supra* note 7, at 809–10.

121 Aftab, *supra* note 106, at 15.

122 *Id.* at 118.

123 *Righting Wrongs?*, *supra* note 64, at 110, n.9.

geographic breadth, barring suits not only in the host state, but in Barrick's home state (Canada), and any other forum. From the perspective of human rights law, other authors have raised concerns about, *inter alia*, the inadequacy of the remedy received and the waiver's foreclosure of any opportunity to pursue full reparations, as well as the claimants' lack of informed, free choice in signing the waivers.[124] The waiver provision is raised here to underline how the company brought hard law to bear in this extra-judicial process, when it was in its interest to do so.

The practice of conditioning NJGM remedy on an effective waiver of any legal liability for the corporate actor recognizes that claimants may have enforceable, "hard law" claims against the corporation arising from the conduct in question, potentially under more than one jurisdiction. The waiver also appears to contravene the Guiding Principles: The commentary to Principle 29 provides that operational-level NJGMs "should not be used to … preclude access to judicial or other non-judicial grievance mechanisms."[125] They are meant to complement and supplement judicial mechanisms,[126] not supplant them.[127] Waiver provisions like that used by Barrick, however, ensure that corporate grievance mechanisms truncate the legal rights of claimants if the relief provided by the company is not full and effective remedy.

If there are concerns about the ability of a company-level mechanism to deliver adequate, effective remedy in a case where the norms regarding the conduct at issue—sexual violence—are relatively clear, such concerns should be heightened in cases involving conduct where the norms are less well defined in human rights law, such as cases of environmental degradation, involuntary resettlement, or health impacts. The Porgera case lays bare the need for greater guidance about minimum standards for compensation and reparation of human rights violations by corporations. Otherwise "[t]he significant power imbalance between transnational corporations and many individual

124 *See id.* at 109–16; Knuckey & Jenkin, *supra* note 7, at 811–13; *see also* UN Office of the High Commissioner for Human Rights, *Re: Allegations Regarding the Porgera Joint Venture Remedy Framework* (2013) (stating that there should be a strong presumption against the use of waivers in NJGMs so as not to curtail access to justice, but finding no prohibition on their use); EarthRights International, *FACTSHEET: Abuse by Barrick Gold Corporation*, https://earthrights.org/wp-content/uploads/documents/barrick_fact_sheet_-_earthrights_international_1.pdf.

125 UNGP, *supra* note 22, princ. 29, comment.

126 *Id.* at princ. 27, comment.

127 *See* Knuckey & Jenkin, *supra* note 7, at 813 (discussing the risk of corporate-created remedy mechanisms supplanting local justice systems).

rights-holders and communities risks companies offering inadequate 'take-it-or-leave it' remedy packages that rights-holders feel they have little ability to influence or refuse."[128] Moreover, a lack of clarity regarding what the right to remedy requires of transnational corporate actors under human rights law encourages companies to treat human rights harms as simply another variable cost of doing business. The result: corporations may tolerate harmful conduct in places where it is seemingly cheaper to remedy violations (if remedied at all) than to prevent them.

VI Conclusion

Holding transnational businesses accountable for their impacts on human rights, particularly in countries with weak governance, remains a central challenge for the global community today. This chapter examined the role of corporate non-judicial grievance mechanisms in addressing this challenge. The proliferation of company-created NJGMs following the adoption of the UN Guiding Principles can be understood as a "soft international law" response to dual impulses on the part of private sector actors to: (1) respond to strong civil society pressure to fill glaring accountability gaps where judicial recourse is limited or unavailable to victims of business-related human rights abuses; and (2) exert greater control over the management of disputes concerning the impacts of their operations. NJGMs are both a reaction to the institutional and doctrinal limits of public justice systems and an instance of private encroachment on the public terrain of lawmaking and remediation of wrongs. As forums in which to air grievances, NJGMs represent a potential step toward improved accountability for corporate wrongs. But far from guaranteeing a hardening of the law on business and human rights, grievance mechanisms untethered from substantive human rights law may be unwittingly producing *de facto* human rights norms that are eroding the *de jure* human rights of affected communities and individuals.

The rise in the number and variety of corporate NJGMs multiplies the actors determining what constitutes effective remedy for human rights harms related to corporate activity. If defining the content of effective human rights remedy is an empirical question, more "data" in the form of variance across communities and contexts may mean more clarity. If, however, the answer to that query

128 *Righting Wrongs?*, *supra* note 64, at 104.

rests on a universal normative core, based on human rights law, more data may obscure the answer.[129]

Early experience with problem-solving, dialogue-based corporate NJGMs suggests that untethering grievance redress from set standards allows the institutional culture of the mechanism to set the parameters for remedy. Decoupling legal liability and remedy, by purporting to deliver the latter through "soft" grievance mechanisms that are not designed to identify non-compliance or issue binding judgments, also calls into question the fundamental notion that a remedy rights an acknowledged wrong. A focus on pragmatic, negotiated solutions does not contribute to the development of substantive norms governing corporate conduct as published jurisprudence might. In this way, NJGMs that emphasize problem-solving may not do much to clarify what corporate conduct is prohibited or required, or to what relief victims of human rights violations are entitled.

As Enodo's assessment of Barrick's remedy framework acknowledges, the "rights-compatibility" of a remedy is the most difficult of the UNGP "effectiveness" standards for corporate NJGMs to assess.[130] Its authors state that "'rights-compatibility' provides a measure of substantive equitability, i.e., assurance of *a fair agreement*," and that while UNGP Principle 31 implicates the right to a remedy, that right must be "*adapt[ed] ... to the private-sector context.*"[131] If companies can unilaterally "adapt" the right to the context of their operations, given that international human rights institutions have not done so, it is likely they will do so in their own interest.

The privatization of enforcement can amount to the privatization of law-production.[132] Without continued pressure for public "hard" law developments and judicial engagement in the creation and implementation of remedies for corporate abuses of human rights, private actors involved in the design and

---

129 *See* Larry Cata Backer, *On the Evolution of the United Nations' 'Protect-Respect-Remedy' Project: The State, the Corporation and Human Rights in a Global Governance Context*, 9 SANTA CLARA J. INT'L L. 37, 80 (2011) ("Polycentricity and the necessity of contextually driven flexibility in the form of remedy complicate the ability to produce a coordinated remedial structure. Yet its absence may well make effective access to justice difficult for individuals and economic entities alike.").

130 Aftab, *supra* note 106, at 101.

131 *Id.* at 101 (emphasis added).

132 *See, e.g.*, Paul B. Stephan, *Privatizing International Law*, 97 VA. L. REV. 1573, 1579 (2011); *see also* Shauhin A. Talesh, *How Dispute Resolution System Design Matters: An Organizational Analysis of Dispute Resolution Structures and Consumer Lemon Laws*, 46 L. & SOC'Y REV. 463, 464–66 (2012) (discussing how the structures of grievance mechanisms outside the court system influence the substance and application of law, showing "how the law in action in essence becomes the law on the books").

administration of "soft law" NJGMs may play an outsized role in defining the content of adequate remedy for corporate wrongs. This is even more likely given the still ill-defined content of the right to substantive redress.

Many proposals for reform of NJGMs emphasize the need for more collaborative approaches to the design and implementation of grievance processes, such as "company—community remedy mechanisms" created as partnerships between businesses and primary stakeholders or community-driven operational level grievance mechanisms,[133] and the replacement of the dominant alternative dispute resolution model with a restorative justice approach to remedying corporate human rights harms.[134] Centering rights-holders in the administration of remedial measures is vital to the institutional legitimacy of corporate NJGMs.[135] But it does not obviate the need for objective standards against which to evaluate the outcomes of grievance mechanisms.

To date, the experience of many community complainants—including those in Porgera—suggests that the efficacy of corporate non-judicial grievance mechanisms in fulfilling the right to a remedy for the breach of human rights depends not just on procedural factors, but also on the relationship of the NJGMs to judicial processes and the continued development of the normative content of rights in the public sphere. In other words, the ability of soft law institutions, such as NJGMs, to effect lasting social change depends on their interplay with hard law institutions. Indeed "judicial and non-judicial systems, or hard and soft law, are not dichotomous," but "condition each other's form and performance in a range of ways."[136]

As innovative, soft law fora, corporate grievance mechanisms may not be institutionally tethered to judicial processes, but they should be normatively bound. Most of the emphasis in the UNGP and in the NJGM-related literature to date has focused on removing barriers to access and increasing the involvement of rights-holders in the design, implementation, and evaluation of human rights grievance mechanisms. Those process measures are essential to bolster the institutional legitimacy of corporate-created remedy mechanisms. But greater attention needs to be paid to the *normative* legitimacy of these mechanisms as well—that is, their accountability not just to the people who use them, but, through reasoned engagement, to the human rights law that the

133 *See* Knuckey & Jenkin, *supra* note 7, at 817; EarthRights International, *Community-Driven Operational Level Grievance Mechanisms* (March 2015), https://earthrights.org/wp-content/uploads/final_ogm_report_2015.pdf.

134 *See* Schormair & Gerlach, *supra* note 56.

135 *See* UN Doc. A/72/162, *supra* note 28, ¶¶ 18–54.

136 Beyond Effectiveness Criteria, *supra* note 10, at 46.

businesses purport to respect. Demanding that NJGMs publicly articulate the standards against which they assess grievances, as well as the minimum parameters for any remedies provided, would help ensure that these soft-law institutions enhance rather than erode the existing hard law of human rights.[137]

---

137 *See also* Samantha Balaton-Chrimes & Kate Macdonald, *Wilmar: The Promise and Pitfalls of Problem Solving* 9 (2016) ("More consideration needs to be given to minimum standards for 'solutions' or 'agreements' so they comply with human rights norms. Mechanisms might consider introducing human rights standards as starting points for negotiations . . . .").

CHAPTER 12

Hard and Soft International Law and Their Contribution to Social Change: the Lessons Learned

Daniel D. Bradlow and David B. Hunter***

1 Introduction

The book was born in part from our observations that the globalization in manyof many issues has resulted in the "internationalization" of lawyers representing both state and non-state actors interested in achieving areas associated with globalization, state and non-state actors view international law primarily as a tool to gain some social goal that may have previously been attainable through domestic law—for example, to protect the environment, human rights, or children or to strengthen the regulation of financial institutions or corporate activity. Many lawyers working on these issues became international lawyers because they saw how it could serve the social change objectives of their clients. For example, many environmental lawyers became international environmental lawyers because they saw how their clients environmental concerns had led them to become actively engaged in aor development institutions. This utilitarian approach to international law attracted new advocates to the field of international law. Many international environmental lawyers, for example, who joined the field beginning in the late 1980s were environmental lawyers first and international lawyers second. Not only were they motivated by environmental protection but they also viewed themselves as representatives of a large global environmental movement. Similarly state and non-state lawyers working on issues related to children's rights, public health, abuse of power and business regulation were driven to become experts in international law in order to advance their clients' objectives in these areas.

The emergence of such international law advocates advocates has some significant implications for international law. First, these actors are not focused

* SARCHI Professor of International Development Law and African Economic Relations at the University of Pretoria and Professor Emeritus, American University Washington College of Law.

** Professor of Law and Director of the Program on International and Comparative Environmental Law at the American University's Washington College of Law.

 | DOI:10.1163/9789004417021_013

on the project of international law as an end in itself and with it the notion that we have to go slowly to nurture the growth of international law. These change-motivated advocates, because they see international law as a means to their social objective, would sacrifice the structure and practice of international law for progress in their area of interest.

Thus, even asking the question of how advocates choose between hard and soft international law in pursuing social change reflects a significant change in regard to both who are international lawyers and how they approach the field of international law. This book explores how lawyers and their state and non-state clients use international law to promote social change, with a particular focus on the choice between hard and soft international law approaches. A series of case studies examine this choice between hard and soft international law in a variety of contexts, allowing an assessment of the factors that influence that choice, including the strengths and weaknesses of available legal instruments and the implications of the choice for meeting the underlying social change objectives.

Today, lawyers and their state and non-state clients seeking to promote social change have a wide range of available international legal instruments from which to choose. In addition to treaties, customary international law principles, and general principles of law, these instruments may include any norm, standard, declaration, guidance note, or general comment that is both intended to instruct a particular group of actors about appropriate conduct and, in fact, operates, at least to some extent, to constrain their conduct. Consequently, an important factor in the choice that lawyers and their clients make between these various instruments is their actual impact on the conduct of their intended targets, regardless of their formal international legal status.

Public international lawyers group these various international legal instruments into two categories based primarily on the sources of law identified in Article 38 of the ICJ Statute. Hard international law refers to instruments that fall within the categories of sources of law listed in this Article[1]: treaties,[2]

---

1 Statute of the International Court of Justice art. 38, Apr. 18, 1946, 33 U.N.T.S. 993 [hereinafter ICJ Statute]. Article 38 also lists, as a "subsidiary means for the determination of the rules of law," judicial decisions and the teachings of the "most highly qualified publicists." These judicial decisions, pursuant to Article 59 of the Statute, are only binding on the parties to the dispute. Their value for other international legal subjects is as resources that can assist them in interpreting other sources of hard international law. The teachings of publicists can also only be used to assist in interpreting the harder sources of international law.

2 Treaties are formal documents negotiated between states and are governed by the Vienna Convention on the Law of Treaties. *See* ICJ Statute art. 38(1)(a); Vienna Convention on Law of Treaties, May 23, 1969, 1155 U.N.T.S 331, 8 I.L.M. 679.

customary international law,[3] and general principles.[4] These instruments are binding on states and, in principle, are enforceable in international courts and tribunals. Depending on the relevant domestic law, they may also be enforceable in domestic courts.

Soft international law refers to any international legal instruments that are not binding because they do not comply with the formal requirements of the sources of international law stipulated in Article 38 of the ICJ Statute but still exert some compliance pull and so constrain the conduct of their targets. These instruments may be *de facto* enforceable, although they are unlikely to be directly enforceable in international courts and tribunals. Their enforcement capacity may arise from one or more of the following sources: their use by advocates and courts in interpreting hard law instruments, market forces, reputational risk, technical relevance or the moral or political status of the instrument and its sponsors.

In chapter 1 we posed seven questions about the relationship between hard and soft international law. The case studies that followed this first chapter provide the material for answering these questions. The purpose of this last chapter is to answer the questions and to address some of the additional issues that arise therefrom.

The chapter consists of three parts. The first part is to answer the questions and provide a review of the lessons learned from the case studies about the seven questions. The second part is a discussion of some issues that arise from this review. The third part is a conclusion.

II Insights and Lessons Learned

The seven questions posed in Chapter 1 assume that lawyers and their state and non-state clients select which international law instrument to use in their work, primarily based on their assessment of its efficacy in achieving their objective. This should be the case regardless of whether their social change objective is a positive change in the behavior of the target of their efforts or a

3 Customary international law constitutes generally accepted legal principles, and are established through state practice and *opinio juris*. *See* ICJ Statute art. 38(1)(b). *See also* North Sea Continental Shelf Cases (Germany v. Denmark, Germany v. Netherlands), Judgment, 1969 I.C.J. 3 (Feb. 20, 1969).

4 General principles are legal doctrines that are common among national judicial systems. *See* ICJ Statute art. 38(1)(c); Prosecutor v. Erdemovic ¶ 57, ICTY Case No. IT-96-22-A, Appeal Judgment, Joint Separate Opinion of Judge McDonald and Judge Vohrah (Oct. 7, 1999).

change that is essentially intended to protect the status quo. A corollary of this assumption is that these actors are less interested in the formal international legal status of the instrument than that all relevant actors in fact comply with its terms. Accordingly, those actors motivated by social change objectives they may also be less motivated inconcerned with the progressive development of international law as a goal in itself.

A *Question 1:* Is the Choice between Hard and Soft International Law Binary?

Several of the case studies in this book clearly demonstrate that hard and soft international law instruments in fact complement and support each other in complex ways. The case studies of the Convention on the Rights of the Child (CRC)[5] and the Framework Convention on Trade in Tobacco (Tobacco Convention)[6] described instances of how soft international law instruments influence the drafting, negotiation, operationalization, and interpretation of hard international law instruments. The case study on the Convention on the Rights of the Child,[7] for example, describes how non-binding comments and declarations, along with associated activities of civil society, influenced binding court decisions in specific cases and generally spread what would become generally recognized interpretations of the treaty regime. Another example of the complex interaction of hard and soft international law is the case study on climate change. [8] In this case, by demonstrating the political attractiveness of its "pledge and review" approach, the non-binding Copenhagen Accord was a pivotal instrument in the evolution of the climate regime toward the Paris Agreement, which itself embeds non-binding mitigation commitments in a hard law instrument.

Other case studies suggest that in some situations hard and soft international law instruments function independently of each other. The case study of the International Criminal Court (ICC)[9] is an example of a hard international law regime that was developed relatively independently of soft international

5 *See* Ann Skelton, *Children's Rights: Social Change through the Application of Hard and Soft International Law, supra* ch. 4 in this volume.

6 *See* Patricia Anne Lambert, *A Turning Point in a Slow Revolution: The WHO Framework Convention on Tobacco Control, supra* ch. 8 in this volume

7 *See* Skelton, *Children's Rights: Social Change through the Application of Hard and Soft International Law, supra* ch. 4 in this volume.

8 *See* David B. Hunter, *The Hard Choice for Soft Mitigation Commitments in the Climate Regime, supra* ch. 7 in this volume.

9 *See* Angela Mudukuti, *The Use of Hard and Soft International Law in the Promotion and Protection of Human Rights Through Accountability, supra* ch. 5 in this volume.

law. One reason for this situation could be that the ICC deals with international criminal law and the laws of war. Given this criminal and security focus, states would be reluctant to be bound by any instrument other than a hard international law instrument to which they have chosen to become a party. They would also object to having their citizens prosecuted by any international court that was not established with all the formalities required of a hard international law instrument.

The case study of the International Financial Regulatory Standards (IFRS)[10] is an example of an effective international soft law regime that does not engage with hard international law. This may be attributable to both its technical nature and the fact that it seeks to shape the development of domestic laws and regulations rather than international law. It may also be relevant that the sponsors of IFRS are national financial regulatory authorities who do not have the capacity to conclude hard international law agreements but have the capacity to convert any applicable soft international law standards into binding and enforceable domestic regulations. This suggests that, although in a non-binding instrument, these standards are sufficiently hard for their framers' purpose.

These case studies, therefore, indicate that the answer to this question is that we should view hard and soft international law as being two points on a spectrum rather than as a binary choice. At one end are those instruments that satisfy the formalities of a treaty or other sources of international law listed in Article 38 of the ICJ Statute, and are written with sufficient precision that they establish obligations that are easily understood by signatory states and that delegate to a clearly identified and independent body the authority to make binding decisions regarding the interpretation and implementation of the international legal instrument. The treaty establishing the ICC is an example of such a hard law instrument. At the other end of the spectrum are soft international law instruments that are drafted in general terms that establish norms open to different interpretations and without any formal enforcement mechanism. The consequences for non-compliance with such standards may at most be reputational, although in some circumstances reputational consequences may be sufficiently severe to compel compliance with them. The Equator Principles described in chapter 10 is an example of such an instrument.

In between these ends are a range of different international legal instruments. They include, for example, hard international law instruments that are drafted in imprecise terms that cannot effectively be interpreted and

10 *See* Daniel Bradlow, *Soft International Law and the Promotion of Financial Regulation and Responsibility, supra* ch. 9 in this volume.

implemented without the assistance of subsequent decisions, guidelines, comments or other instruments issued by states and/or non-state actors under the regime. The case studies on the CRC[11], the IAHR regime[12] and the UNFCCC[13] are illustrative of such instruments. They also include soft international law instruments that are drafted with sufficient precision that they, in fact, establish clear responsibilities for their targets represent. The interpretation and enforcement of these responsibilities has been delegated to third party actors, usually non-state entities. The international financial regulatory standards and the way in which they are used by the International Monetary Fund (IMF) and the World Bank are an example of this type of instrument.

B *Question 2:* What Factors Influence an Actor's Choice to Seek Either a Hard or Soft International Law Instrument?

The case studies in this book demonstrate that both state and non-state actors are willing to use both hard and soft international law instruments either in their "pure" form or in combination to promote their objective. The most significant factor guiding their choice of instrument is their assessment of which instrument or instruments, in fact, will be most effective in achieving their intended purpose. For example, in the case of the ICC, both state and non-state actors advocated for a binding and enforceable treaty.[14] By comparison, because commercial banks were self-regulating the Equator Principles, only representatives of commercial banks and the International Finance Corporation were permitted in the negotiation of the first version of the Equator Principles.[15] Other non-state actors had to accept the soft law nature of the Principles and hope the instrument could be strengthened over time as the targeted banks gained experience in its use. Advocates for the accountability of these financial institutions have consistently sought to 'harden' these principles (e.g., through adding a process for enforcement), but they have little leverage to compel the EP banks to create such a mechanism and so it has not been created. A third example is the case study of the

---

11 *See* Skelton, *Children's Rights: Social Change through the Application of Hard and Soft International Law, supra* ch. 4 in this volume.

12 *See* Claudio Grossman, *Promoting Social Change through Treaties and Customary International Law: the Experience of the Inter-American Human Rights System, supra* ch. 3 in this volume.

13 *See* Hunter, *The Hard Choice for Soft Mitigation Commitments in the Climate Regime, supra* ch. 7 in this volume.

14 *See* Mudukuti, *The Use of Hard and Soft International Law in the Promotion and Protection of Human Rights Through Accountability, supra* ch. 5 in this volume.

15 *See* Leader & Yanes, *Levers For and Obstacles To Social Change: Bank Lending, the Law and the Equator Principles, supra* ch. 10 in this volume.

international financial regulatory standards.[16] Both non-state and state actors were willing to utilize soft international law instruments because they thought that soft law would be the most effective option given the technical complexity and dynamic nature of the topic area. The standards derived authority from the fact that they were developed in international bodies in which national regulatory authorities participated and that report to G20 member state governments. In addition, the participating regulatory authorities were willing and able to incorporate the standards into their domestic regulatory frameworks.

The case studies also show that the decision as to which international law instrument to use can change over time as the relevant circumstances change. This can be seen for example in the cases studies of the CRC, the Tobacco Convention, and the treaties for environmental access rights.[17] In each of these cases, advocates moved to promoting a hard international law instrument after gaining experience with the use of soft law instruments. The case studies on the Tobacco Convention and environmental access rights describe how advocates learned from the experiences of actors in other regions working on the same issue with hard and soft international law instruments. They used this experience to assess which international law instrument would be most effective in their particular situation. They could also use these precedents to support their advocacy for their preferred option.

In sum, social change actors make an essentially practical decision to pursue a hard or soft law instrument based on a range of factors whether to pursue a hard or soft law instrument as being more effective for advancing their cause at any point in time. Frequently, this involves athe trade-off may be thatchoice between a treaty with binding and enforceable norms may havebut with relatively fewer participating states participate or may haveand an international legal instrument with to accept significantly weaker norms but with broader participation. We see this trade-off in themost dramatically in regard to the Paris Agreement dealing with climate change. In this case, the parties agreed to non-binding mitigation commitments in order to secure participation by China and the United States in the regime. compromise made to weaken the access to information requirements in order to gain Mexico's and Colombia's

16 *See* Bradlow, *Soft International Law and the Promotion of Financial Regulation and Responsibility, supra* ch. 9 in this volume.

17 *See* Skelton, *Children's Rights: Social Change through the Application of Hard and Soft International Law, supra* ch. 4 in this volume; Lambert, *A Turning Point in a Slow Revolution: The WHO Framework Convention on Tobacco Control, supra* ch. 8 in this volume; Natalia Gomez Peña & David Hunter, *The Hard Choices in Promoting Environmental Access Rights, supra* ch. 6 in this volume.

participation in the Escazú Agreement. The advocates made the choice that broader participation in a formally binding treaty was more important than a treaty with better standards but fewer countries participating. The Paris Agreement's adoption of non-binding mitigation commitments was similarly aimed at securing China and US participation in the regime.

In addition to considering whether achieving a binding instrument will result in less participation or weaker norms, other relevant factors in the choice of instruments include: the objectives of their clients their ability to participate directly or indirectly in the relevant international law-making process, the technical complexity of the issue, the scope and nature of the desired social change, the state or non-state character of the regulatory target and their perceived willingness to change their conduct, the number and identity of the state actors willing to participate in any treaty negotiations, the negotiating and drafting options politically available to them, the balance of forces amongst the stakeholders in the issue, and the urgency with which they wish to act. It is important to note that their decision is ultimately a pragmatic one and so, as some of the case studies show, may evolve as their assessment of these factors and the circumstances in which they are operating change.

C *Question 3:* Is There a Linear Progression from Soft to Hard International Law and What Factors Affect This Progression?

The case studies show that while in some circumstances there may be a progression from soft to hard international law instruments, it is not an inevitable journey. The cases studies on the CRC and the Tobacco Convention are examples of successful progression from soft to hard international law.[18] Some of the other case studies in this volume demonstrate that the relationship can be more dynamic and complex. For example, the case studies of the CRC and IAHR regime show how advocates use soft international law instruments norms and principles to bolster their legal arguments in support of their preferred interpretations of the applicable hard international law instruments when they discover gaps or ambiguities in these instruments and how the decisions of courts can then be used to promote and strengthen soft international law instruments.[19] In this way, advocates use soft international

18 *See* Skelton, *Children's Rights: Social Change through the Application of Hard and Soft International Law, supra* ch. 4 in this volume; Lambert, *A Turning Point in a Slow Revolution: The WHO Framework Convention on Tobacco Control, supra* ch. 8 in this volume.

19 *See* Skelton, *Children's Rights: Social Change through the Application of Hard and Soft International Law, supra* ch. 4 in this volume; Grossman, *Promoting Social Change through*

law to refine and develop a hard international law instrument. They can also use these developments in the hard international law to advocate for new soft international law instruments that can then be used to advocate for particular interpretations of the existing hard international law instrument or even for a new hard international law instrument. The case study on environmental access rights describes how advocates used a hard international law instrument from one region in combination with deliberate efforts to implement capacity building and demonstrate proof of concept at the national level to build their case for a hard law instrument.[20] Finally, as the case study on international financial regulatory standards show, sometimes the proponents of an international soft law instrument may not have any interest in moving beyond a soft international law instrument.[21] In this case, their goal is to establish a clear and precise non-binding standard that exerts a sufficiently strong compliance pull that the relevant stakeholders are likely to substantially comply. In addition, they seek a standard that is flexible enough to be adjusted timeously to changing circumstances.

A noteworthy case study regarding this proposition is the non-judicial grievance mechanisms system.[22] These mechanisms are created under soft international law and only use soft international legal standards to resolve disputes. Their experience suggests that the distinction between primary and secondary soft international law instruments can be significant. At least in some cases, the secondary soft international law instruments urging corporations to create non-judicial forums for resolving disputes was implemented before there was sufficient clarity on the meaning of the primary soft international law instruments establishing the substantive rights and obligations of the different stakeholders. This timing mismatch resulted in corporations—a target of the primary instruments—assuming a decision-making role in the application of the primary standards to themselves.

The problem with this development is that it enables corporations to establish precedents that guide the interpretation of the primary standards. Other stakeholders in these standards cannot easily challenge the decisions corporations make or hold the corporations accountable for their decisions.

Treaties and Customary International Law: the Experience of the Inter-American Human Rights System, *supra* ch. 3 in this volume.

20 Gomez & Hunter, *The Hard Choices in Promoting Environmental Access Rights*, *supra* ch. 6 in this volume.

21 *See* Daniel Bradlow, *Soft International Law and the Promotion of Financial Regulation and Responsibility*, *supra* ch. 9 in this volume.

22 *See* Nikki Reisch, *Non-Judicial Grievance Mechanisms: Hardening the Soft Law of Corporate Accountability?*, *supra* ch. 11 in this volume.

This suggests that the advocates for these standards may either need to pay more attention to the sequencing of these instruments or develop formal and *de facto* mechanisms through which they can challenge the corporate decisions. Examples of such mechanisms include an independent recourse mechanism, court actions, forums in which all stakeholders can meet and discuss the interpretation of the soft international law instrument, and market and reputational pressures.

In sum, the case studies confirm that no necessary relationship exists between hard and soft international law. The two sets of international law instruments can operate on their own or can be used together in almost any combination. The way in which any advocates and their clients choose to use them will depend on the specific facts and circumstances of each case. Moreover, the choice about how to use each instrument is not static and can evolve over time. The factors driving this evolution could include the experience that the parties gain with the use of the instruments and changing circumstances that facilitate further developments in the law in the particular issue area.

D *Question 4:* Are Soft International Law Procedures More Transparent and Participatory than Hard International Law Ones?

The making of hard international law instruments involves a relatively formal process that is intended to protect the interests of sovereign states. The Vienna Convention on the Law of Treaties (VCLT) outlines the requirements for valid treaty formation, entry into force, and interpretation of treaties.[23] Only treaties that comply with the VCLT requirements are treated as establishing binding and enforceable obligations for their signatory states. In the case of bilateral treaties, both states that are party to the treaty must sign and ratify it before the treaty enters into effect. For multilateral treaties, a stipulated number of the signatory states must ratify the treaty before it can enter into force. In principle, no state can be considered bound by a treaty until it has signed and ratified the treaty. The VCLT also has rules on the application of treaties to non-signatory states and signatory states between the time they sign the treaty and when they ratify the treaty.[24]

The making of soft international legal instruments does not have to comply with any procedural requirements relating to the instrument's drafting, negotiation, operationalization, or implementation. The participants in the making of soft international law instruments can therefore follow whatever procedures

23 Vienna Convention on the Law of Treaties, May 23, 1969, 1155 U.N.T.S. 331, 8 I.L.M. 679.

24 *Id.*

suit their particular purposes. The procedures can allow for participation of as many or as few categories of state and non-state actors as deemed appropriate. They can also be as transparent or opaque as the participants think useful.

Given the formality of the treaty making process and the relative informality and flexibility of the soft international law instrument, one would be inclined to think that soft international legal procedures are more inclusive and participatory, particularly in regard to non-state actors, than hard international law procedures. This is certainly true in some situations. For example, the drafters of the UN Guiding Principles on Business and Human Rights and of the World Bank's Environmental and Social Framework incorporated extensive consultations with both state and non-state actors around the world into their drafting procedures. In fact, in both cases, the sponsors of these standards engaged in far broader consultations and allowed for much more active engagement by a range of state and non-state actor stakeholder than would have been the case with a hard international law instrument. It should be noted that in both cases the final decisions were made by state representatives acting in formal decision-making bodies.

In other cases, however, the sponsors of soft international law instruments have used the flexibility of soft international lawmaking to exclude stakeholders and to utilize opaque procedures. The case study of the international financial regulatory standards is an example of such a situation.[25] In this case, the international standard setting bodies have restricted membership. They also engage in only limited consultations with non-member national regulatory authorities and other non-state stakeholders about the standards they are developing. To be sure, they expect that each standard setting body member will engage in consultations with their domestic stakeholders and will follow domestic legal procedures when seeking to incorporate the international standard into their national regulatory frameworks. Despite these limited consultations, the standards can be made *de facto* enforceable against non-member regulatory authorities and states through such mechanisms as the financial sector assessments of the IMF and the World Bank, and through market forces.

This kind of "exclusive" standard setting is also evident in the development of the Equator Principles.[26] The large private commercial banks saw an advantage in having harmonized standards for managing environmental and social risks. A relatively small working group of banks—with the support of the

25 *See* Bradlow, *Soft International Law and the Promotion of Financial Regulation and Responsibility*, *supra* ch. 9 in this volume.

26 *See* Leader & Yanes, *Levers For and Obstacles To Social Change: Bank Lending, the Law and the Equator Principles*, *supra* ch. 10 in this volume.

International Finance Corporation--developed the first set of Equator Principles with little or no input from other state and non-state stakeholders.

On the other hand, some formal treaty regimes have taken significant steps to accommodate the interests and participation of non-state actors. The annual meetings of the UNFCCC Conferences of the Parties (CoPs) regularly have tens of thousands of non-state actors attending the negotiations, organizing informative side events, lobbying negotiators, and ensuring accountability of the government's formal representatives, among other things.[27] Both the case study on the climate regime and the study on the tobacco regime[28] discussed the comprehensive and innovative roles of non-state actors in their respective regimes. In general, a regime's approach to non-state participation may depend on a number of factors, including, for example: (1) whether the subject matter of the negotiations address issues about which non-state actors have technical credibility or expertise; (2) whether the procedures and practice of the regime favor participation of non-state actors; and (3) the posture of the host country towards civil society or private sector participation.

The formal treaty process can also strengthen the participation and voice of small and poor states. In contrast to many soft international law examples, it is not possible to negotiate and adopt a treaty that can be enforced against states without their participation and consent. The case studies on the Tobacco Convention, the CRC, and the ICC illustrate how the formalities of the treaty making process can help ensure that smaller and poorer states are given a voice in the treaty making process.[29]

One lesson learned from the case studies in this volume regarding question 4 is that it is prudent for lawyers and their state and non-state clients to keep an open mind about the relative suitability of the hard and soft international law-making process for their particular purpose. Both offer advantages and disadvantages. The decision about which process to use in a particular case is likely to depend on such factors as the lawyers' and clients' view of how transparent they think the international law making process should be, which state and non-state actors they think should participate in the international law making

27 *See* Hunter, *The Hard Choice for Soft Mitigation Commitments in the Climate Regime, supra* ch. 7 in this volume.

28 *See* Lambert, *A Turning Point in a Slow Revolution: The WHO Framework Convention on Tobacco Control, supra* ch. 8 in this volume.

29 *See* Lambert, *A Turning Point in a Slow Revolution: The WHO Framework Convention on Tobacco Control, supra* ch. 8 in this volume; Skelton, *Children's Rights: Social Change through the Application of Hard and Soft International Law, supra* ch. 4 in this volume; Mudukuti, *The Use of Hard and Soft International Law in the Promotion and Protection of Human Rights Through Accountability, supra* ch. 5 in this volume.

process, and which procedure is most likely to result in the international legal instrument that is most suitable for their purpose. Another relevant factor should be which procedure offers the most effective protection to the most vulnerable stakeholders in their particular issue area.

Another relevant consideration is that the relative informality and flexibility of soft international law can lead to a proliferation of instruments in a particular issue area. Different groups of state or non-state actors can develop their own standards. And they can do so without recognizing or integrating the work of others in the same area, perhaps because they disagree with the standard being developed by other groups or perhaps because they simply want to compete in the same market. The resulting proliferation of standards makes it difficult for small and poor state and non-state actors to fully participate in all relevant standard setting processes. The proliferation of standards can create uncertainty about the applicability of the various standards to particular situations. This in turn may allow the targets of these standards to choose their own standard as the most appropriate and to ignore other standards. If these targets are sufficiently influential, they can do so with relative impunity. On the other hand, if the targets are weak and uninfluential, they may be forced to comply with standards that they did not participate in developing and that may impose higher standards of conduct on them than they deem optimal. The result can be that the weakest and least capable targets are forced to comply with the toughest standards, while the most powerful targets are able to comply with the weakest standards or no standards. This can be seen, for example, in the case studies on the international financial responsibility standards[30] and on the non-judicial grievance mechanisms.[31] It can also be seen in the Equator Principles, which were originally applicable to only projects in developing countries rather than in all countries.[32]

E *Question 5:* Under What Circumstances are Hard International Law Instruments More Effective in Achieving Social Change Goals than Soft International Law Instruments?

The case studies in this volume demonstrate that both hard and soft international law instruments can be effective in changing behavior and that the

30 *See* Bradlow, *Soft International Law and the Promotion of Financial Regulation and Responsibility, supra* ch. 9 in this volume.

31 *See* Reisch, *Non-Judicial Grievance Mechanisms: Hardening the Soft Law of Corporate Accountability?, supra* ch. 11 in this volume.

32 *See* Leader & Yanes, *Levers For and Obstacles To Social Change: Bank Lending, the Law and the Equator Principles, supra* ch. 10 in this volume.

preferred choice of instrument is context specific. As reported in the Tobacco Convention case study, for example, several states have implemented the treaty by passing domestic laws that are designed to reduce smoking in their countries.[33] Under the CRC and the IAHR regimes,[34] advocates have used a combination of hard and soft international law instruments to produce significant changes in conduct at the domestic level. Similarly, the international financial regulatory standards, though soft international law, have resulted in regulatory changes at the national level and have been effective in changing the conduct of the financial institutions that they supervise.[35]

Other case studies in this volume indicate that both sets of instruments can have variable impacts on conduct. For example, even though the ICC has prosecuted and convicted war criminals, it has generated strong opposition and concerns about bias in its operations.[36] Some states, in fact, have threatened to withdraw from the treaty. Moreover, it is unclear what impact the ICC has had on the conduct of regular and irregular armies around the world. Similarly, the case studies of the Equator Principles and non-judicial grievance mechanisms are examples of soft international law instruments that have had limited impacts on the conduct of their intended targets.[37] However, this does not mean they have had no impact. In a few cases, public pressure has forced some banks that are signatories to the Equator Principles to withdraw from funding controversial projects. Overall, though, little evidence exists that the Principles have significantly changed the conduct of major banks.

The case studies offer two lessons regarding when hard international law instruments are more effective in achieving social change goals than soft international law instruments. First, the choice of which instrument advocates utilize in their promotion of social change will ultimately depend more on an assessment of the incentives to which their intended targets will respond than

---

33 *See* Lambert, *A Turning Point in a Slow Revolution: The WHO Framework Convention on Tobacco Control, supra* ch. 8 in this volume.

34 *See* Skelton, *Children's Rights: Social Change through the Application of Hard and Soft International Law, supra* ch. 4 in this volume; Grossman, *Promoting Social Change through Treaties and Customary International Law: the Experience of the Inter-American Human Rights System, supra* ch. 3 in this volume.

35 *See* Bradlow, *Soft International Law and the Promotion of Financial Regulation and Responsibility, supra* ch. 9 in this volume.

36 *See* Mudukuti, *The Use of Hard and Soft International Law in the Promotion and Protection of Human Rights Through Accountability, supra* ch. 5 in this volume.

37 *See* Leader & Yanes, *Levers For and Obstacles To Social Change: Bank Lending, the Law and the Equator Principles, supra* ch. 10 in this volume; Reisch, Non-Judicial Grievance Mechanisms: Hardening the Soft Law of Corporate Accountability?, supra ch. 11 in this volume.

on the legal nature of the instrument they promote. A treaty might be the optimal instrument if, for example, the intended purpose is to encourage greater cooperation among states in regard to a particular issue area. The fact that the treaty is binding on all signatories can give states the confidence to adopt the desired cooperative measures. Some states may also be encouraged by the fact that the signatories to the treaty, in principle, can use the formal international legal enforcement mechanisms, including international courts, to enforce the treaty provisions against a non-compliant state. On the other hand, if the goal is to persuade a commercial entity to behave in a more environmentally and socially responsible way in its development projects, the most effective instrument may be a soft international law instrument. The reason is that the target is likely to be more sensitive to the market and reputational consequences of its actions (a type of "enforcement" that can be brought through non-state actors) than to the risk of a legal enforcement action brought by states under a treaty. The former is likely to be felt more quickly and predictably by the target than the latter.

Second, the nature of the social change being sought will exert a greater influence over the efficacy of the international law instrument being utilized than its legal nature. For example, when the growing cross-border operations of financial institutions created new challenges for domestic financial sector safety and stability, the national financial regulatory authorities recognized that they needed to develop international standards for dealing with the expanded range of activities of their financial institutions.[38] The participating national regulatory authorities could incorporate these standards into their domestic regulatory regimes, thereby improving their ability to comply with their domestic mandates to protect the safety and stability of their financial sectors. Moreover, given the complexity of the issue, the national authorities wanted a standard that could be adjusted as the technical challenge evolved over time. They thus needed technical experts, rather than diplomats, to retain control over the standard. Their response was to meet amongst themselves in forums where they could discuss the issue and develop a relatively flexible international standard that they were willing to implement and to pressure non-compliant authorities to adopt, regardless of its legal form or enforceability.

Another example is the Tobacco Convention, which addresses a clear and well-defined public health challenge.[39] The states that were both the targets of and were willing to become party to the Tobacco Convention were concerned

38 *See* Bradlow, *Soft International Law and the Promotion of Financial Regulation and Responsibility, supra* ch. 9 in this volume.

39 *See* Lambert, *A Turning Point in a Slow Revolution: The WHO Framework Convention on Tobacco Control, supra* ch. 8 in this volume.

with their ability to effectively address this public health challenge in the face of strong opposition from domestic corporate, agricultural, and, in some cases, labor interests. A legally binding treaty strengthened their ability to stand up to these economic interests by enabling the government to point to the risk of the state incurring international legal responsibilities if it failed to comply with the Convention.

The situation is different, however, where the nature of the change being sought is less technical and more political in nature. This applies, for example to the changes being sought through human rights treaties. For example, the case studies of the CRC and the IAHR regime show that they have been effective in winning victories for individuals who have been harmed by specific actions of the state.[40] They have been less effective in changing the general conduct of their state targets since such changes tend to occur slowly. However, these case studies show that advocates can utilize soft international law instruments to fill in gaps in the treaty regimes and facilitate the type of expansive interpretation that can promote changes in behavior over time.

Soft international law instruments that are seeking to promote broad systemic social change also face challenges that make assessing their efficacy difficult. For example, the Equator Principles addresses issues in which there are big gaps in human knowledge.[41] In this case, the benefit of a soft international law instrument is that it is flexible and can relatively easily be adapted in the light of experience and changing mores. They can also be useful in creating a framework to educate all stakeholders about the issue and about what it takes to comply with their standards. In addition, as knowledge develops, they can be adjusted to incorporate the new information and to increase the compliance pull of the standards. In this way, they can help to slowly change conduct.

F *Question 6:* How Does the Existence of a De Jure or De Facto Enforcement Mechanism Change the Strategic Choice between a Hard and Soft International Instrument?

The case studies in this volume suggest that the efficacy of any international legal instrument ultimately depends on it being supported by some form of

40 *See* Skelton, *Children's Rights: Social Change through the Application of Hard and Soft International Law, supra* ch. 4 in this volume; Grossman, *Non-Judicial Grievance Mechanisms: Hardening the Soft Law of Corporate Accountability?, supra* ch. 3 in this volume.

41 *See* Leader & Yanes, *Levers For and Obstacles To Social Change: Bank Lending, the Law and the Equator Principles, supra* ch. 10 in this volume.

enforcement mechanism. The case studies also show that for any international legal instrument to be enforceable it must be drafted with a sufficient degree of precision that it is possible for the regulated target, interested third parties, and those charged with enforcement all to understand what the instrument demands of the target. It is only once this requirement is met that the issue of the type of enforcement mechanism becomes relevant. For example, the case studies on the Equator Principles and on non-judicial grievance mechanisms demonstrate the challenges that arise when the relevant international standard is drafted in language that is open to a wide range of interpretations.[42] In these cases, the instruments' target has great discretion in deciding how to apply the instrument. This, in turn makes it difficult to effectively enforce the standard. This problem is particularly significant at the international level because the mechanisms available to enforce international standards are less effective than those available at the national level, where the independence of the enforcement mechanisms is better established and supported by the coercive powers of the state.

In this regard, a particular interpretation of even soft international law instruments like the Equator Principles, despite their broad language, can become *de facto* enforceable when the reputational costs to the target for failing to comply become sufficiently high that the costs override the target's interest in upholding its own interpretation of the Principles. A similar process applies in cases of broadly drafted hard international law instruments. As shown by the case studies on the CRC and the IAHR regime,[43] the lack of precise language can be overcome using soft international law instruments to interpret the hard international law instrument. This is particularly effective when the interpretation is adopted by a third-party decision maker, such as an international or domestic court. Similarly, in some complex regimes, such as the climate and tobacco regimes, decisions made by the parties at regular meetings can allow for the progressive operationalization of ambiguous treaty terms.[44]

---

42 *See* Leader & Yanes, *Levers For and Obstacles To Social Change: Bank Lending, the Law and the Equator Principles, supra* ch. 10 in this volume; Reisch, *Non-Judicial Grievance Mechanisms: Hardening the Soft Law of Corporate Accountability?, supra* ch. 11 in this volume.

43 *See* Skelton, *Children's Rights: Social Change through the Application of Hard and Soft International Law, supra* ch. 4 in this volume; Grossman, *Non-Judicial Grievance Mechanisms: Hardening the Soft Law of Corporate Accountability, supra* ch. 3 in this volume.

44 *See* Hunter, *The Hard Choice for Soft Mitigation Commitments in the Climate Regime, supra* ch. 7 in this volume; Lambert, *A Turning Point in a Slow Revolution: The WHO Framework Convention on Tobacco Control, supra* ch. 8 in this volume.

Two key conclusions can be drawn from the case studies in this volume regarding the existence of *de jure* or *de facto* enforcement mechanisms as factors to choosing hard or soft international law instruments. First is the importance of precision in drafting the instrument. The more precise the language, the more feasible it is to enforce the standard. This is true regardless of whether the language itself indicates that the standard is mandatory or merely precatory. If the language establishes a clear and unambiguous standard of conduct, it is possible for third parties to determine if the targets of the standard are complying with it. The third parties can then seek to enforce compliance with the standard through such means as naming-and-shaming.

The case study of the non-judicial grievance mechanisms demonstrates the enforcement risks and challenges that can arise from drafting international legal instruments in too broad terms.[45] Since non-judicial grievance mechanisms do not have a means to enforce their decisions, they may, in effect, be forced to defer to the interpretation offered by the more powerful party to the dispute. This risks skewing the definition of broadly drafted norms in favor of those they are intended to regulate.

Second, for the purposes of determining the efficacy of an international instrument in terms of producing social change, the legal nature of the available enforcement mechanism is less relevant than is its ability in context to actually compel the target to comply with the standard. For example, in the case of the international financial regulatory standards, market forces and reputational consequences may be more effective against a non-compliant regulatory authority than a legal enforcement mechanism could be.[46] This would be the case even if the legal enforcement mechanism has the jurisdiction to hear a complaint against the non-compliant authority but it does not have a realistic means to compel compliance with its decisions. Similarly, the high public profile and widespread participation of non-state observers in the climate regime adds to the confidence that states will comply with their non-binding commitments.[47] On the other hand, the ICC case study indicates that the imprudent use of the enforcement mechanism has the potential to undermine the overall efficacy and even legitimacy of a hard

45 *See* Reisch, *Non-Judicial Grievance Mechanisms: Hardening the Soft Law of Corporate Accountability?*, *supra* ch. 11 in this volume.

46 *See* Bradlow, *Soft International Law and the Promotion of Financial Regulation and Responsibility*, *supra* ch. 9 in this volume.

47 *See* Hunter, *The Hard Choice for Soft Mitigation Commitments in the Climate Regime*, *supra* ch. 7 in this volume.

international law instrument.[48] Even if the instrument is effective in individual cases, if it loses widespread support it may not result in the desired broad change in conduct.

G *Question 7:* Should Less Emphasis Be Placed on Article 38's Definition of the Primary Sources of Hard International Law?

The case studies in this book clearly demonstrate that soft international law plays an important role in shaping both international and domestic conduct. This suggests that it may ultimately be unsustainable to limit the sources of international law to those identified in Article 38. The case studies in this book also demonstrate that international law can be created by a broad range of state and non-state actors. While all these actors may not have formal status as subjects or objects of international law, they are all *de facto* able to create international instruments that are able to exert sufficient compliance pressure that their targets feel constrained to conform their conduct to their requirements. In short, regardless of their status and their implications for the stability and predictability of international law, these instruments all should be treated as part of the corpus of international law.

Viewed in this light, the current hard/soft international law discussion is too concentrated on whether an instrument derives from one of the sources of international law identified in Article 38 of the ICJ statute. Describing something as not hard international law in this sense means only that it cannot be considered by states as binding on states, in cases before the ICJ or other formal adjudicatory or diplomatic forums. The hard/soft framework may be less useful in other contexts. Most obviously this is true where the state is not the subject or target of the regulatory effort, say for example in the case of the Equator Principles. But it may also be true where states are the subjects but the applicable standards do not conform to all the formal "hard" international law requirements, such as the UNFCCC mitigation commitments.

In fact, the case studies suggest that the definition of the sources of international law set out in Article 38 is inappropriate for most purposes outside of the traditional public international contexts relating to relations involving only sovereign states. Instead they demonstrate that international lawyers and their clients treat as a relevant source any international legal instrument that exerts a sufficient compliance pull to constrain the conduct of its targets and that as a result promotes the intended change in conduct. The issue of whether

48 *See* Mudukuti, *The Use of Hard and Soft International Law in the Promotion and Protection of Human Rights Through Accountability*, *supra* ch. 5 in this volume.

the compliance pull arises from the *de jure* or *de facto* enforceability of the applicable international instrument may only be relevant to informing how the instrument is used by the international lawyers and their clients in promoting their objectives. This suggests that the most relevant consideration in determining the legal character of an international instrument is the strength of the compliance pressure that it exerts on the regulatory target in the specific context. This approach clearly links the analysis of the legal status of the instrument to both the way in which its terms are drafted and to any associated mechanism for compelling compliance. The case studies suggest that the strength of the instrument's compliance is likely to depend on the following factors:

- The intent of relevant stakeholders on whether the instrument should be binding or not;
- The clarity and precision of the terms in the instrument;
- The availability and strength of a mechanism to persuade or compel compliance; and
- The interest and ability of stakeholders to use the mechanism.

III Some Issues Arising from the Answers and Lessons Learned

The answers to the questions posed in the first chapter and the lessons learned from the case studies raise some more general issues about hard and soft international law and their potential for promoting social change.

First, some state or non-state actors are more authoritative sources of soft international legal standards than others. For example, the international financial regulatory standards were developed by representatives of national regulatory authorities and are *de facto* enforced by international organizations. This probably contributed to these standards being more effective than the international financial responsibility standards discussed in this book, which were developed and are monitored primarily by representatives of interested corporations and civil society.

The significance of the identity of the participants in the formulation, implementation, and enforcement of international law highlights the importance of the relative transparency and inclusiveness of international law making procedures. This issue is of particular relevance in the case of soft international law making. A failure to ensure that the soft international law making process is sufficiently transparent and inclusive to be seen as legitimate and credible by its targets risks undermining its potential to serve as a sustainable source of norms and standards that promote social change.

Determining the appropriate degree of transparency and inclusiveness in any particular soft international law making process will depend on a consideration of all the relevant factors. These factors will include the technical nature of the issue being addressed, the range of issues being addressed in the relevant instrument, the diversity of views and interests being expressed by the range of state and non-state actors interested in the instrument, the range and intensity of the disagreements among these actors and anticipated enforcement mechanisms available to the stakeholders in the instrument.

Second, the optimal form of the instrument will vary depending on whether its primary purpose is norm creation, norm enforcement, or norm interpretation. In principle, both hard and soft international legal instruments can serve any or all three of these purposes. However, the case studies indicate that often norm creation and norm interpretation require instruments that are sufficiently flexible that they can evolve over time in light of new information and changing political, social, economic, environmental, and cultural conditions. Thus, soft international law is generally better suited for these purposes. But this may not always be the case. For example, the IAHR regime and the CRC are both hard international law instruments that are both norm creating. These regimes are made more robust through soft international law instruments that are norm interpreting. The same can be said of the climate regime where norm-interpreting decisions of the annual Conferences of Parties (CoPs) have transformed generalized texts in the UNFCCC or Paris Agreement into complex mechanisms for carbon trading, carbon finance, monitoring, reporting, and verification, among other things.

Third, the range of international law enforcement mechanisms is rather broader than traditional international law would suggest. The standard view is that international law is primarily enforced through state-initiated cases brought to international courts and tribunals, and though state-on-state diplomacy. However, the case studies suggest this is not an adequate description of the universe of enforcement mechanisms. Lawyers and their clients will accept any method of enforcement if it compels the target of the enforcement action to change its conduct and comply with the norms, standards, or legal requirements. Thus, in some circumstances market forces, reputation, actions by international organizations can all be as effective, and in some cases even more effective than courts in enforcing international legal standards.

This broad range of *de facto* enforcement mechanisms raises two concerns. First, the acceptance of non-traditional enforcement mechanisms as being part of international law, albeit soft international law, makes international law messier and less predictable than strict adherence to Article 38 suggests. This makes it harder for states and non-states to know what their obligations are and how to ensure their conduct conforms to international law. It also makes it harder for them to know with certainty what their rights are and how best to protect and enforce them.

Second, these enforcement mechanisms challenge state sovereignty. Not only are states no longer treated as the primary, if not unique, source of international law; it is now possible for non-state actors, including a state's own citizens, to decide on the applicable international law principles. Moreover, these enforcement mechanisms give non-state actors the ability to enforce these standards against the state, including in connection with activities within the state, even when the state disagrees about either the applicable principles or how they should be interpreted. A full exploration of the implications for sovereignty of the growing importance of soft international law is beyond the scope of this book.

IV Conclusion

This book was intended to answer a practical question that confronts any lawyer whose state or non-state client is interested in using international law to promote social change: what are the most effective available international legal instruments for promoting the client's desired social change objectives?

The conclusions this book has identified suggest a multi-part answer. First, the international legal status of the lawyer's client and the other participants in the effort to promote social change is not particularly significant. Both state and non-state actors can create international law instruments capable of producing social change.

Second, the decision on whether to use a hard or soft international law instrument depends on a range of factors that include the nature of the change being sought, the target of the instrument, the negotiating and political dynamics associated with the effort to produce change, the forum and applicable procedures to be used in negotiating and drafting the instrument, the range of actors involved in these negotiations, the language used in the drafting of the instrument, the existence of a *de facto* or judicial enforcement mechanism, and the precedents that the various stakeholders can use to inform their own international law making decisions. It does not depend exclusively on developing an instrument that complies with the formal requirements of the traditional sources of international law.

Third, the case studies demonstrate that the creation of both hard and soft international law instruments is subject to the realities of power. The law making process of both hard and soft international law can be dominated by the most powerful state and non-state actors who can utilize these law making processes to exclude the weakest stakeholders. However, depending on the relevant circumstances, either hard or soft international law making procedures may be able to offer these weaker stakeholders some protections that help them participate in the process. The formality of the hard international law making process offers some opportunity for participation to all states. It restrains efforts to enforce the hard international law against weak states that are not parties to the instrument. On the other hand, the flexibility and informality of soft international law may offer these weaker states and non-state actors a more direct avenue of participation in the international law making process and less formal way in which to hold the stronger parties to account for their conduct.

Fourth, over time Article 38 has dominated our discourse and practice for what is international law in virtually all contexts, well beyond its intended purpose of guiding state versus state adjudications. By restricting the scope of public international law to Article 38, we may also be restricting the evolution of the field to a state-centered view of international law that does not reflect today's multi-stakeholder approach to international affairs. The case studies also in this volume suggest we should recognize the that various forms of international instruments can have legal effects of various instruments in contexts other than international adjudication. This may requiresuggests a need to exploring explore what types of international lawinstruments, including treaties, custom, general principles and a range of soft law instruments, should be considered binding as being part of international law because they are effectively binding and in what contexts.

Fifth, the book suggests that whether a particular international legal instrument is effective depends more on its actual contribution to the desired social change objective than on the legal status of the international law instrument.

In short, therefore, the answer the book provides to its core question is that both soft and hard international law can effectively serve the goal of promoting social change. Which is the better instrument in a particular situation is context specific. International law is slowly adjusting to this reality. It is our hope that this book will contribute to the adjustment.

Index

Access to Information 57, 110–111, 113–115, 119–120, 122–123, 125–126, 128–131, 133, 136, 202
Access to remedy 251, 258, 261–262, 264
Accountability 7, 36, 51, 53, 69, 84–87, 89, 91, 93, 95, 97, 99, 101, 103, 105, 107, 109–110, 117, 122, 178, 184–185, 187, 217, 250–253, 255–259, 261–265, 267, 269–271, 273, 275–281, 285–287, 289, 291–294, 296–298
African Charter on the Rights and Welfare of the Child (ACRWC) 62–63, 69, 72–74, 81–83
Agua Zarca Project 236–238, 244, 249
Al Mahdi 96, 100
Alternative dispute resolution (ADR) 263, 280
Article 38 6, 8
Association of South East Asian Nations (ASEAN) 34
Awas Tingni 38, 46–48, 129, 237

Barrios Altos v. Peru 38, 43
Basel Committee on Banking Supervision (BCBS) 202, 204–205, 208, 216, 222
BAT 182, 193
Beijing Rules 64–65, 67, 74–75, 78, 81, 83
Bilateral Investment Ttreaty (BIT) 197
British American Tobacco (BAT) 182, 193
British Petroleum (BP) 230
Business and Human Rights 200, 209–210, 228, 231, 233, 241, 249–250, 253–257, 261–262, 264–266, 269, 278, 291

Center for Justice and International Law (CEJIL), 37 CERD 66
Charter of the International Court of Justice 6, 8, 144
Children's rights 55, 57–59, 61, 66–70, 75, 77–78, 81–82, 284, 286–288, 292–293, 296–297
Cigarettes 179, 197
Civil society 2, 13, 15, 20–21, 33–34, 52–54, 76–78, 110, 112–115, 117–122, 124–125, 132–137, 140, 158–159, 169, 175, 178–180, 184–186, 188–189, 194, 196, 199, 202–203, 209, 212, 226, 228, 236, 267, 270, 278, 284, 292, 300
Civil society organizations (CSO s) *see* Civil Society
Climate change 14, 18, 22, 27–30, 117, 138–145, 147–151, 153, 155–161, 163–168, 219, 233, 243, 284
Commercial Banks 232–233, 249, 286, 291
Committee on Economic Social and Cultural Rights (CESCR) 66, 234
Committee on Enforced Disappearances (CED) 66
Committee on the Elimination of Discrimination Against Women (CEDAW) 66–67
Committee on the Elimination of Racial Discrimination (CERD) 66
Committee on the Rights of Persons with Disabilities 66
Conference of the Parties (COP) 126, 131, 139, 143, 145, 147–149, 152–154, 166–168, 170, 190, 192, 194–196
Consejo Cívico de Organizaciones Populares e Indígenas de Honduras (COPIHN) 236–237, 244
Convention on the Rights of the Child (CRC) 14, 55–56, 58–70, 72–76, 78–83, 259, 284, 287–288, 292–293, 296–297, 301
Copenhagen Accord 139, 147–150, 159, 161, 163, 204
Corporate Human Rights Benchmark (CHRB) 250, 265, 268–270
CRIN 61, 66, 76–78

Democratic Republic of Congo (DRC) 92–93, 95–97, 100, 105, 108, 272
DESA 236, 244
Desarrollos Energéticos S.A 236
DRC 92–93, 95–96, 100
DRC 92–93, 95–96, 100

ECHR 67
ECLAC 125–126, 128, 131, 133

ECtHR 67
Environmental access rights 14, 110–112, 115, 117–118, 122, 135, 287–289
Environmental and Social Risk 244
Equator Principles (EPs) 15, 154, 212–213, 217–219, 228–230, 232–236, 238–246, 248–249, 286, 291, 293–294, 296–297, 299
European Convention of Human Rights 157
European Court of Human Rights 67
European Union (EU) 2, 67, 70, 104, 118, 146, 149, 163, 169, 188, 193, 195, 197, 208

Financial Action Task Force (FATF) 206–207, 218–220
Financial institutions 15, 200–203, 205, 209, 211–219, 221, 225, 228, 232–236, 242, 254, 263, 287, 294–295
Financial regulators 201–203
Financial sector 12, 15, 201, 203, 207–209, 211, 213–214, 216, 218, 225, 291, 295
Financial sector assessments 207, 291
Financial Stability Board 205, 208, 216, 219, 221–223
Food and Agriculture Organization (FAO) 178
Forced Disappearances 36, 38–43, 45, 51
Framework Convention Alliance (FCA) 169, 185–186
Framework Convention on Tobacco Control (FCTC) 14, 169–171, 173–199, 284, 287–288, 292–293, 295, 297
Free, prior informed consent (FPIC) 236–239, 244
Freedom of Expression 13, 36–38, 49–52, 111, 196
FSAP 207–208, 217, 221–223

G20 221, 287
GATT 198, 200
General Comment (GC) 5, 55, 63, 70, 72–78, 83, 210, 234, 254, 259–260, 282
Global Reporting Initiative (GRI) 213
Global warming 28–30, 138–139
Globalization 1–2, 13, 21, 30, 136, 172, 174
Greenhouse Gases (GHGs) 138, 142–147, 152–153, 155–156, 160–161, 163, 165–166

Hard international law 4–6, 8–11, 13–14, 52, 55, 58, 68–69, 81, 83–86, 93, 100, 104, 108–110, 135–136, 142, 144–145, 152, 159, 165–166, 168, 176–177, 190, 196, 198–199, 220, 238–239, 253, 256, 282–288, 290–291, 293–294, 297–299, 301–303
Human Rights Council (HRC) 58, 65–67, 71, 102–103, 210, 216, 233, 251, 254–255, 262
Humanitarian Law 12, 33, 37, 101, 259, 267

InterAmerican Court of Human Rights (IACHR) 33, 37, 48, 53, 236–237
Intergovernmental Negotiating Body (INB) 180–181, 183–184, 187, 191
Intergovernmental organization (IGOs) 178, 189
Intergovernmental Panel on Climate Change (IPCC) 138, 142, 157
International Association of Airport Duty Free Stores (IAADFS) 182
International Association of Insurance Supervisors (IAIS) 206–207, 223
International Bank for Reconstruction and Development 200 *see also* World Bank
International Centre for the Settlement of Investment Disputes (ICSID) 190, 193–194, 196–197, 199
International Court of Justice (ICJ) 4, 8–9, 85, 144, 167–168, 201, 255, 282–283, 285, 299
International Criminal Court 14, 42, 84–109, 250, 285–286, 292, 294, 298
International finance 212, 229, 233, 263, 286, 291
International Finance Corporation (IFC) 212–213, 217, 229, 233–234, 263–264, 286, 291
International Financial Regulatory Standards 15, 202–203, 206, 214–218, 221–222, 285–287, 289, 291, 294, 298, 300
International financial responsibility standards 15, 203, 208, 300
International Human Rights 15, 27, 34, 45, 52, 67, 102, 188, 239, 250–251, 253, 255, 257, 259–260, 262, 264, 266–267, 269, 271, 275, 279
International Labor Organization (ILO) 62, 210, 240
International Law Commission (ILC) 33, 87–88

International Monetary Fund (IMF) 200, 207, 216–218, 221–223, 286, 291
International Organization of Securities Commissions (IOSCO) 205, 207, 223
International Tobacco Growers' Association (ITGA) 182
International Standardization Organization (ISO) 3

Joseph Nye 18

Katanga 93, 95–96, 99–100
Kyoto Protocol 139, 143, 145–148, 155, 158–159, 163–164, 168

Latin America and Caribbean (LAC) Declaration 123–127, 129, 132, 135
Lubanga 92–94, 96, 99, 108

Maderas y Derivados de Nicaragua S.A. (MADENSA) 46
Mayagna (Sumo) Awas Tingni Community v. Nicaragua 38, 46–47, 129
Minimum age of criminal responsibility (MACR) 55, 65–66, 74–78, 83
Mitigation Commitments 14, 138–139, 141–142, 146, 148, 150, 152–153, 155, 157–158, 162–164, 168, 284, 286, 292, 297–299
Multinational Enterprise (MNE) 209

National Contact Points (NCPs) 209–210
NATT 185–186
NCP 209–210
Network for Accountability of Tobacco Transnationals 185
NGO 2, 23, 31, 33, 37, 51–53, 59–60, 65, 71, 78, 82, 88–89, 114–115, 159, 162, 184–185, 232, 235–236, 238, 244
Nicaragua 38, 41, 46–48, 129, 237
NJGM 252, 256–258, 263–267, 271–274, 277–281

Organization of American States (OAS) 33, 35–36, 41, 48, 50, 54, 122, 129, 136, 231, 237
Organization of Economic Cooperation and Development (OECD) 160, 207, 209, 211, 225–226, 239, 254, 264

Office of the Prosecutor (OTP) 90, 92, 94–97, 105, 107

Paris Agreement 14, 138–139, 143, 146–148, 151–158, 162–163, 165–166, 168, 284, 301
PMI 197
Project Finance (PF) 212, 228–231, 238, 241–248

QUNO 69–71, 73, 82–83

Regulatory Consistency Assessment Program (RCAP) 208, 222
Reports on Standards and Codes 207
Right to remedy 251–252, 258–260, 264, 266, 268, 271, 278
Rio Declaration on Environment and Development 111–113, 117–118, 121, 123, 125, 127, 135, 142
Rio+20 121
ROSC 207, 217, 221–223
Ruggie Principles 266

Soft international law 1, 3, 5–15, 55, 58, 64, 66–67, 73–74, 82–83, 102, 116, 121, 132, 136–137, 139, 142, 158, 167–168, 174–176, 198–201, 203, 205, 207, 209, 211, 213–215, 217, 219–221, 223, 225, 227, 253, 258, 271, 273, 276, 278, 282–303
SOLCARSA 46
Sources of international law 4–5, 12, 144, 167, 283, 285, 299
Sovereignty 10, 19, 21, 43, 52, 117, 164, 182, 217, 220–222, 301–302
Standard Setting Body (SSB) 203–208, 214, 217, 221, 291
State actors 2–4, 6–7, 9, 12–15, 19, 24, 33, 37–38, 65, 116, 140–143, 165, 167, 199, 218, 260, 267, 286–288, 290–293, 295, 300–303

The Access Initiative (TAI) 118–120, 123–124, 132–133, 136
TFI 178–181, 184, 191
Trust Fund for Victims (TFV) 85, 98–101
The Hague 62, 157
Tobacco Industry Research Committee 171
Trade-Related Intellectual Property Rights (TRIPS) 189, 198

UNDESA 123
UNESCO 55, 96
UNICEF 59–60, 65, 178
United Kingdom (UK) 30, 91, 93, 103, 107, 119, 171–173, 193, 197, 229, 232, 267, 270, 273
United Nations 6, 14, 18, 23–24, 29–30, 33, 41, 48, 52, 55–61, 63–67, 69–74, 77–80, 87–88, 91, 102, 104, 106–107, 111–115, 119–121, 123, 125, 139, 141, 143, 147–149, 151–152, 154–155, 174–178, 180, 188, 201, 209–212, 216, 224, 226, 233–234, 236, 245, 249, 251, 253–255, 261–266, 268–269, 277–280, 291
United Nations Conference on Environment and Development (UNCED) 112
United Nations Conference on Trade and Development (UNCCTAD) 212, 225
United Nations Convention on the Rights of the Child (UNCRC) 60, 66, 79
United Nations Economic Commission for Europe (UNECE) 114–115
United Nations Environment Programme (UNEP) 120–121, 123, 136, 155, 211, 245
United Nations Framework Convention on Climate Change (UNFCCC) 14, 24, 139, 142–145, 147–153, 157–158, 160, 163, 168, 291, 299, 301
United Nations Guiding Principles on Business and Human Rights (UNGP) 209–211, 217–219, 233, 254–256, 260–263, 265–270, 277, 279–280, 291
United Nations Security Council (UNSC) 101–103, 104, 106

Vienna Convention on the Law of Treaties (VCLT) 5, 144, 148, 188, 190, 192, 283, 290

Washington College of Law 33, 37
World Bank 119, 157, 178–179, 196, 200, 207, 216–217, 221, 229, 234, 263, 286, 291
World Conference on Tobacco or Health (WCTOH) 172, 175, 178
World Health Assembly (WHA) 173–177, 180–184, 187–188, 198–199
World Health Organization (WHO) 4–5, 14, 17, 20–21, 25, 28, 30, 32, 34, 42, 44, 51, 53–58, 68, 74, 77, 79–81, 86–88, 91–94, 96, 98, 101, 106, 108, 124, 134–136, 140, 160, 162–163, 169–171, 173–185, 187–197, 199, 208, 215–216, 218–219, 239, 256, 260, 271–272, 274, 280, 284–285, 287–288, 292–293, 295–297, 301
World Resources Institute (WRI) 118–119, 148, 159